The contents of education

The contents
of education

A worldwide view of
their development from the present
to the year 2000

S. Rassekh
G. Vaideanu

Unesco

The designations employed and the presentation of material throughout this publication do not imply the expression of any opinion whatsoever on the part of Unesco concerning the legal status of any country, territory, city or area or of its authorities, or concerning the delimitation of its frontiers or boundaries.

Published in 1987 by the United Nations Educational,
Scientific and Cultural Organization,
7 place de Fontenoy, 75700 Paris
Printed by Richard Clay Ltd
Bungay, Suffolk

ISBN 92-3-102421-3
French edition: 92-3-202421-7

© Unesco 1987
Printed in the United Kingdom

Preface

Study of the changing contents of education forms part of general thinking on the future of education, which is one of the many permanent tasks entrusted to Unesco by the international community.

For this reason, the General Conference decided at its twenty-first session that, as a follow-up to the symposium on desirable trends in educational content over the next two decades (Paris, 1980), Unesco would publish a study on 'the evolution of educational content as a whole to meet the requirements of the world of work and scientific, technological and cultural progress'. The present work is the result of that decision.

In order to prepare this publication the Organization commissioned five case-studies to be carried out on the content of general education courses in the twenty years to come in five countries: China (prepared by the National Commission of the People's Republic of China for Unesco), Hungary (prepared by Peter Szebenyi), the Netherlands (prepared by Johan C. van Bruggen), the Philippines (prepared by Minda C. Sutaria) and the United States (prepared by Dr Christopher Dede). Two specialists, Shapour Rassekh and George Vaideanu, both highly experienced in this field, were subsequently requested to make a study summarizing the information collected and thereby outlining the main trends to be seen in curricula.

Shapour Rassekh (Iran) holds a degree in economics and a doctorate in sociology; he was a teacher at the University of Tehran and was Secretary of State for Planning for more than ten years. He has written several studies on social planning. From 1980 to 1982 he was a consultant with the International Institute for Educational Planning (IIEP).

George Vaideanu (Romania), Doctor in Educational Sciences and a teacher at the University of Jassy, was Director of the Bucharest Institute of Educational Research (1967–73) and subsequently Chief of the Structures and Content of Education Section of Unesco (1973–80). He is the author of a large number of works on the content of education, particularly the content of aesthetic education, the aims and methods of intellectual education, interdisciplinarity and educational content in the context of lifelong education.

Both men have not only gone through a considerable number of studies and a mass of information on education; they have tried to incorporate specifically educational issues in the even wider context of the major economic, social, cultural and moral changes that are taking place throughout the world and to discern their inevitable consequences for education.

One can appreciate the value of this project, which should interest those responsible for drawing up curricula, teacher trainers and educators in general, in both industrialized and developing societies. While bearing in mind the diversity of the situations covered, the authors have, however, always emphasized the meeting points and possibilities for the exchange of experience. They have tried to place each country's curriculum specialists, teacher trainers and educators in a position to situate their own education system's present and future in the context of world problems so as to enable them to draw the conclusions they deem appropriate in each particular case.

The authors undertook their work at Unesco's request, but they are responsible for the choice and the presentation of the facts contained in this book and for the opinions expressed therein, which are not necessarily those of Unesco and do not commit the Organization.

Contents

Foreword 11

PART ONE: THE SOURCES OF EDUCATIONAL CONTENTS
AND THEIR DEVELOPMENT FROM THE PRESENT
UNTIL THE YEAR 2000

Introduction 19

Chapter 1. Population growth 23

Effects on education systems 26
Stable population levels or continuing population explosion? 28
Significant developments 31
Notes 33

Chapter 2. Economic changes 35

Danger of exhaustion of natural resources 41
Crisis or renewed economic growth? 44
Promises of the future 48
Technological development and the structure of the labour force 50
Impact of economic development on education systems 53
The changing costs of education 57
Notes 59

Chapter 3. Socio-political changes 61

What type of society for tomorrow? 67
Effects of social and political changes on education 73
The development of education as an independent variable 76
Notes 79

Chapter 4. Cultural changes and scientific progress   81

Science and culture, tomorrow   84
The impact of scientific progress and cultural changes on the methods and contents of education   90
Educational technologies   92
Notes   94

Chapter 5. World problems   97

Supporters of a new world order   100
Decline and renewal of values   101
Education and world problems   103
Notes   104

Chapter 6. The internal dynamics of education systems   105

The position of teachers   105
The teacher–learner relationship in the school of tomorrow   107
Relations between school and the outside world   108
The future of educational management and administration   109
Notes   112

PART TWO: TOWARDS NEW CONTENTS

Introduction   115

Impact of the new sources of educational contents   115
Schools: decline or transformation?   116
Wishes and plans   117
Description of a few projects: similarities and differences   119
Work in progress   121
Preliminary definitions   123
Notes   127

Chapter 7. Current developments   129

Concepts in full expansion: systems approach, curriculum theory and practice, taxonomy of educational goals, educational technology   130
Lifelong education   135
The new triad of educational objectives   143
The critical reception of scientific and technological achievements   149

Renewal of interest in moral values and moral education 155
The integration of technology and productive work in general education 162
New ways of organizing contents 166
The emergence of new contents in curricula 173
Summing up 177
Notes 181

Chapter 8. Future prospects 185

Education under growing pressures: conservatism or change? 185
Remarkable achievements and forward-looking solutions 188
General indicators of the relevance of contents 199
Interdisciplinarity 208
The shape of a possible syllabus 218
Notes 233

Chapter 9. The path of innovation 237

Towards relevant methodologies 237
Educational research: structure and essential activities 242
Initial and in-service training of teachers 254
Notes 261

Conclusions 263

Annex: *The study of the future: an outline* 271

Basic concepts 271
Major trends in the study of the future 272
Theories of the future 276
Studies on the future of education 278
Notes 282

References 283

Foreword

The sources used for renewal of the contents of education have increased considerably in number and are receiving serious attention. Case-studies and recommendations made by conferences of ministers of education provide proof of the great importance education authorities and curriculum planners attach to the relevance of that content. Analysis of a wide range of literature (case-studies, comparative studies, final reports, resolutions passed by conferences of ministers, etc.) and a large number of meetings with Unesco specialists, researchers and education authorities in many countries have enabled us to evaluate desired changes and likely changes, projects that reflect a determination to improve and innovate and the difficulties that need to be overcome. Reflection on the education of the future has emerged as an integral part of the global projects for socio-economic and cultural development devised or launched in many countries in recent years.

Not so long ago curricula were planned on the strength of single-subject studies carried out by specialized and relatively independent bodies. Such studies were piecemeal and concentrated on the hard facts to be introduced into the teaching–learning process for assimilation by the students. Nowadays attempts are increasingly made at global analysis of all sources likely to ensure the relevance of educational contents, thereby endowing learning with a broader base and greater substance. We may therefore say that a new philosophy is emerging in the way contents are selected and organized.

That is why we considered it essential to examine the socio-economic and cultural context that will necessarily be the backdrop for any educational project in the years to come. Humankind's needs and aspirations and developments in science and technology are all factors that will influence education and on which education will, in its turn, be called upon to act. Admittedly, the situation differs so much from one part of the world to another that only case-studies would appear to be meaningful. And as far as the future is concerned the diversity is intensified because of the different perceptions of world problems and of the solutions to them and the lack of correspondence between different countries or regions. While the Federal Republic of Germany, for instance, in which the school population will very probably be shrinking, will be obliged to reduce the number of pupils per class and increase its educational facilities for adults, countries such as Brazil, India, Mexico and Nigeria will still be committed to the struggle against illiteracy and battling to provide schooling for all school-age children. However, even though the disparities between countries are and will continue to be considerable, the contents of education cannot in future fail to reflect certain developments, which we shall try to describe in broad outline.

The first part of this work is therefore devoted to analysing major economic, social, scientific and cultural developments, with a view to determining their impact on the contents of education over the next two decades. It claims to be, however, not the fruit of original research but rather a distillation of the lessons drawn from some thirty years of worldwide experience in exploring the future, particularly the future of education. A summary of studies on this subject has been appended to the work, showing the variety of approaches adopted (imaginative forecasting, forecasting by extrapolation, constructive forecasting using models and scenarios, etc.) as well as the many different kinds of people who pursue this type of study (science-fiction authors, technocrats, humanists and so on). It suggests to us that we should adopt a fairly cautious approach in our future-oriented study, beginning with a realistic analysis of the present and recent situation in the world and in various regions of the world and going on, not to present a hard-and-fast picture of human society in the year 2000—which would be presumptuous on our part—but to discern the dynamics, the factors at work and the powerful constraints that will in all probability act on the future and to which the future itself cannot fail to react.

While we have carried out this investigation of the forces and facts that are seminal to the future with concern for objectivity, we have not done so with the purely speculative intention of discovering what the world of tomorrow is bound to be like as a result of some kind of ineluctable developments beyond the control of humankind, in the way in which the historian strives to know the facts of a now unchangeable past. By highlighting both the promises and threats underlying the factors studied we have explicitly or implicitly indicated the direction that human effort should take. In our view, futurology is not mere forecasting; according to J. de Bourbon-Busset, a member of the 'Groupe Prospective' of Gaston Berger, the aim of futurology is not to foretell the probable future but to prepare for a desirable future and to attempt to go even further: to make the desirable future probable. Despite the fact that the future is unpredictable and uncertain up to a point, it must be acknowledged that the unprecedented development of science and technology has endowed human freedom of action with very powerful means humankind can use to mould its own future. Education obviously has a major role to play in this active construction of the future. It is even held by some that the erstwhile role of the economy as the dominant sector in industrial societies will increasingly be assumed by education as a result of the third industrial revolution. We have therefore included in our review of the determining factors for the coming two decades an examination of the institution of education both as a dependent variable and as an independent variable likely to exert a not negligible influence on the ingredients that will go into the education of tomorrow.

Starting from the premiss that man can influence his own future, we have, in the second part of the work, after attempting to describe the phenomena that are used as factors of renewal in current education, traced the broad outlines of what the *desirable* contents of education should be. But, again, this work is not a presentation of the authors' research and personal opinions: it is based on analysis of a large number of case-studies, the conclusions of educational researchers, recommendations made by ministerial conferences and an examination of international and national projects and experiments that are interesting even though of narrower scope. Nevertheless, we have not ignored our own experience in arriving at a particular conclusion, adopting a position, underlining facts that hold a key to the future or determining priorities.

Analysis of the studies published and of recommendations made by conferences of ministers has shown that, with the third millennium in sight, many countries have set about preparing projects to bring the characteristics of their education systems more into line with social requirements and young people's aspirations. The measures taken and the schemes contemplated may differ, but, whatever the differences in situation, education will not be able to disregard certain events that will compel it to reconsider its responsibilities and add to its objectives. The progress of science, in particular, and the existence of contemporary world problems are beginning to act as common denominators in determining the contents of education. In presenting current trends we have attempted to highlight interesting experiments, provisional conclusions, original and effective approaches and lines of action that are indirect but have proved useful. For instance, in analysing trends such as rejection of the three classic objectives of education or attempts to link the learning of science and technology with the inculcation of a critical attitude to their values and applications we have tried not only to forestall possible errors but also to indicate ways and means that are sometimes ignored because they are indirect or apparently less effective.

Because of the magnitude of the field under consideration we have had to define our approach. Our study, then, centres on the contents of general education (formal education). But in adopting this main theme we found that it is becoming increasingly difficult for both those responsible for curricula and teachers to isolate the contents of education and treat them separately.

Forty or fifty years ago the school could still be considered the chief, independent domain of education and the unique preserve of the teaching of science. Nowadays basic facts are learned outside the school, and a large proportion of new information concerning space or modern physics, technology and the arts is transmitted through the media. What role should now be attributed to the school, and how best can we link the 'curriculum' with the 'co-curriculum' or knowledge with the information acquired outside school? This question, which has doubtless been asked with greater or lesser insistence in other times, now needs to be answered.

In some books and usually in official documents the word 'content' is used in the singular, doubtless to show that what is meant is *a set or connected system of objectives and knowledge* specific to a certain level or a certain school in a given country. We have used a plural word (contents of education) to emphasize that what is being dealt with are the contents not only of formal education but also of non-formal and informal education and, at the same time, to discard from the outset the idea of a single content, of a model that might progressively come to be regarded as suitable for all situations. It should be mentioned also that what is called 'the content of education' is in practice composed of a set of types of content (social sciences, natural sciences, etc.) that should be interdependent and balanced.

This study is therefore devoted to the contents of school and out-of-school education, but a forward-looking analysis cannot ignore the context—difficult to verify or evaluate—in which people do and will learn; that is, the parallel education or sum of information received by the learner in the family environment, in the community setting (rural or urban) or through the media. Even if the dividing lines between the contents of education meaning formal education and the contents of education in the broad sense of the term are not clearly defined, the two notions are certainly situated on different levels; the distinction is a useful one for curriculum planners, for teachers and for non-teaching educators.

On the delicate issue of possible curricula, we have taken the liberty (out of a desire to encourage the inclusion of relevant and well-integrated contents without overloading syllabuses—a real danger that could well jeopardize any attempt at improving the effectiveness of education) of suggesting a methodological framework for curriculum planning. The difficulty lay not in identifying new types of education or content but in sifting and ordering. At this stage of our work it was important to have criteria for selection, which made it necessary to begin by devising a new philosophy of education. To make our selection we combined two sorts of screening: *the aims* of education conceived in relation to society and to the individual, and general *indicators* of the relevance of its contents as a set of principles and criteria produced by educational theory and confirmed by educational praxis. We developed a framework comprising ten types of content, which must be considered not as a model but as a methodological guide towards *multidimensional, integrated and open-ended content*, an *aide-mémoire* for curriculum planners at all levels.

The preparation of young people for an unpredictable future that is different from the present prompted us to accord an important place to familiarization with world problems, forward-looking exercises and the new educational purposes to be introduced within the various types of content: education for peace and co-operation, education for participation and solidarity and so on. In order to avoid any divisions between the various types of content and educational activities (formal, non-formal and informal) particular care should be taken in connecting them (horizontally) and integrating them (vertically). In this way the school will be able more effectively to fulfil its role as the main structure for educating young people, a role that has been challenged by some writers precisely because it sometimes tends to concentrate on actual teaching and to avoid specific moral, political or civic problems or situations. While it is quite evident that in most countries the school will in the next two decades still be the essential structure for training young people, it is just as evident that it should evolve along with society.

There is already a widespread feeling that the promotion of new contents (skills, values, attitudes, outlooks on the world) and their integration in curricula implies an extensive and searching re-examination of the education system, since it affects structures, teacher training, attitudes and mentalities. We therefore included in our study an examination of the instruments essential for implementing transformation of the system, particularly the subsystems of educational research and the training of teachers and educators.

Lastly, we would remind the reader that there are regional or international structures capable of organizing the collaboration needed for an approach to all the issues involved. It is the quality of national approaches and the willingness of nations to engage in international co-operation that will eventually determine the success of the renewal of content desired by all Unesco's Member States.

Part One

The sources of educational contents and their development from the present until the year 2000

Introduction

Every system of education is a living reality whose goals, structures, processes, contents and methods are influenced by two types of factors: external factors, or socio-economic and cultural sources, and internal factors, or the system's inherent dynamics.

There is constant interaction between these two types of factors, the external factors being incorporated by the internal dynamic, which, in its turn, influences the receptivity of the system to external influences.

In this first part, we shall deal with the external sources of educational contents which, in the coming years, may well exercise greater influence than internal sources.

Charles Hummel (1977) was right to say that the future of education depended more on external factors than on the endogenous elements of education systems. A number of arguments can be put forward to support such a statement. They include the decisive effect of economic growth or stagnation on the future development of education, the growing influence of political aims on the objectives of education systems, and the impact of scientific and technological progress on school curricula. It must also be admitted that in most cases the endogenous elements of education systems act more as obstacles than as factors conducive to necessary change in the systems in question. These internal sources are analysed in Chapter 6 of this study, which will deal with the inherent dynamics of education systems and, in particular, their capacity to resist change brought in from outside.

What we are going to put forward in the chapters which follow should not be seen as the fruit of original and independent research. It is a synthesis which tries to take into account the lessons of over thirty years' world experience of prospective studies. The following are some of the lessons on which our synthesis will be based:

* *One of the first lessons is that greater importance must be attached to analysing the present 'if we are to improve our understanding' of the future. There is agreement on this point between authors as different*

Introduction

as the American Daniel Bell (1973) and the Frenchman Pierre Chaunu (1975), and many others.
● *In detailed study of the present, particular emphasis must be put not only on the analysis of clear-cut trends (i.e. those which already exist and which are most likely to exercise some influence in the future) but also on identifying significant developments, those whose importance will soon become apparent. A dynamic approach is to be recommended here. Attention will be paid to the problems to be solved, challenges to be met, constraints to be submitted to or bypassed and also to aspirations which may determine the course of the future.*
● *Nowadays, enlightened minds subscribe to the idea of a common destiny for the whole world. The global dimensions of the major problems confronting mankind on all sides are increasingly acknowledged. For the next twenty years, however, realism requires that account be taken of the different levels reached by the different countries in their economic and scientific development, as well as of increased tension in the social and political contexts. Broadly speaking, the immediate future of the different societies can be divided into three categories: pre-industrial, industrial and post-industrial. The prospects for education cannot be identical in these three types of human societies.*
● *Many prospective studies begin their analysis with a picture of the future society as far as it can be predicted. While refraining from putting forward a model which would be identical for all human societies, we shall analyse certain common tendencies, certain forces which can be seen at work in homogeneous groups of societies.*
● *Despite the partly uncertain character of the future, it must be agreed that the unprecedented development of science and technology has placed very powerful tools at the disposal of human freedom, and that they can be used to shape the future of mankind. Education has a major role to play in this conscious construction of the future. It has even been suggested that while the economic sector has been dominant in industrial societies, the third industrial revolution might well usher in education as the dominant sector.*
●*Rejecting Utopian or idealistic conclusions and conservative views regarding the future, we would favour a realistic view, as has already been seen in the foregoing paragraphs. What we mean by realism is not a defeatist vision of history, for we still believe in human wisdom even if this wisdom can only be acquired through hardship and suffering.*

This realism helps us to avoid the pitfalls of preconceived ideas and ideological orientations, and to rise above a Utopian or apocalyptic vision of the world and its history in the near future. The same realism leads us to take into account the rather conservative nature of education systems, which often take a long time to adapt to contemporary requirements. The period of twenty years does not seem sufficient to us for such an adaptation

Introduction

to take place, especially if we bear in mind that education should from now on meet not only the needs of the individual and of society but also the challenges posed by the world's present problems, which are so acute and widespread that they cannot escape the notice of any impartial observer.

In order to ensure a realistic approach, a set of hypotheses has at times been proposed for the future of the world, and the consequences of each hypothesis in regard to education and its contents are then inferred. Other people have used the term 'conditional future'. It implies determining the type of adaptation in the world of education which should accompany a given change in the political, economic, scientific or technological contexts. These approaches seem to us to be of the greatest interest. On the other hand, we have doubts as to the usefulness, for prospective studies, of a classification of societies which is exclusively based on their political orientation (inter alia collectivist or liberal societies), for such orientations are obviously likely to undergo many changes. Moreover, it is open to discussion whether certain tendencies (such as the desire to ensure equal opportunities for access to and success in education) are not now to be seen in both collectivist and liberal countries which have reached similar levels of industrial development.

At the present time, everybody, or almost everybody, agrees that the world has been living in a state of crisis for the past decade or so. There have been all kinds of clashes and conflicts, distortions and upheavals. This crisis has affected almost all aspects of mankind's life and activities, and few countries have so far been spared misfortunes that do not seem to be the prerogative of any particular system.

In the developed countries, the crisis is most clearly seen in material aspects of life: the pace of economic development is slowing, poverty is spreading and unemployment now affects millions of families. Economists admit that they are at a loss to understand the real causes of this disastrous situation. The usual explanations no longer fit. Could it be the difficulties of transition from what are known as the 'second generation' manufacturing industries to the advanced industries of the 'third generation'? Are we witnessing the collapse of the capitalist economic system? Could the repercussions of the successive oil price increases, especially those of 1973 and 1979, the overheating of the world economy in the 1950s and 1960s, and lastly the excessive liquidity of this economy be regarded as the principal causes of the crisis? The answers are uncertain. (see Centre d'Études Prospectives . . ., 1983; Institut Français de Relations Internationales, 1984 (annual); United Nations, Department of International Economic and Social Affairs, 1985 (annual); World Bank, 1985 (annual since 1977). It is all the more difficult to explain the present crisis as it makes a variety of other forms, for example political, social, cultural and moral.

Introduction

The countries of the Third World, with the exception of a privileged few, find themselves in a critical situation because of a decline in revenue and an increase in expenditure: unfavourable terms of trade for agricultural produce, customs barriers resulting from the protectionism of market economies for their industrial products, the decrease in official development aid and increase in defence and security spending. To these economic difficulties must be added the cultural, demographic and political problems which most of them have to face.

A complex situation necessarily requires 'complex thinking', taking into account not only the multiplicity of problems but also the plurality of their causes and of the complex interactions between them. As the etiology of the crisis does not fall within our scope, we shall simply outline its four main aspects, which are demographic, economic and technological, sociopolitical and cultural, while at the same time stressing the interdependence of these different aspects. In fact it is not certain that all the different crises really started at the beginning of the 1970s. Some are of earlier origin and, to take the example of the population explosion, began a few decades previously. For the sake of consistency, however, our analysis generally starts with world events about ten or perhaps fifteen years ago, when necessary pointing out that a particular clear-cut trend had an earlier origin.

I
Population growth

Recent history has witnessed unprecedented population growth in different areas of the world. While it took thousands of years for the world's population to reach the impressive figure of one thousand million in about 1830, less than a century was needed for another one thousand million to be added to this figure (1925). Since then, this growth rate has been constantly increasing, with a result that only 37 years later the world had three thousand million inhabitants, and 13 years after that in 1975 it reached the figure of four thousand million. In 1980, the figure of 4.5 thousand million inhabitants had already been reached (Peccei, 1981).

The years after the Second World War were marked by a number of demographic changes of capital importance.

One was a population explosion in the developing countries which was caused by both a considerable decline in mortality (especially of infants) and the maintenance of a high fertility and birth rate. The population of the developing regions as a percentage of overall world population sharply increased (see Table 1), leading some people to predict that it might reach at least 80 per cent by the end of this century.

Another resulted several countries beginning to operate birth control and family planning policies made possible by scientific progress in the genetic field. Only a small number of the developing countries succeeded in substantially reducing their population growth rate (e.g. the Republic of Korea). In other countries there was a slight decline in the average birth rate, as is shown in the Table 2.

TABLE 1   World population divided into regions, from 1950 to 1985 (in millions of people)

Regions	1950	1960	1970	1980	1985
World total	2 504	3 014	3 684	4 453	4 842
Developed regions	832	945	1 047	1 136	1 173
Developing regions	1 672	2 069	2 636	3 317	3 669

Source: United Nations, *The World Population Situation in 1983*, New York, United Nations, 1984.

TABLE 2   Average birth rate for all the less developed regions of the world

1960–65	1975–80
40 per 1 000	33.6 per 1 000

Source: United Nations, *The World Population Situation in 1979*, New York, United Nations, 1980.

It should be borne in mind that this last figure is more than twice the average for the developed countries.

Third, in the developed countries the decline in both the birth and death rate sometimes resulted in a situation in which the rate needed to keep the population at existing levels was not reached. To cite only a few examples, the natural growth rate in 1980 was of the order of 1.7 per thousand in the United Kingdom, 2.3 per thousand in Switzerland, 4.7 per thousand in France and 0.7 per thousand in Sweden (United Nations, 1981, p. 74).

The result was that between 1950 and 1975 the annual population growth rate was only 1.1 per cent in the developed regions, whereas the less developed regions witnessed an annual increase of the order of 2.2 per cent.

One result of this difference in growth rates was a considerable rejuvenation of the population in the Third World in contrast to an ageing of the population in the developed countries of the world. Table 3 clearly shows what distinguishes developing countries from developed countries in regard to the age structure of their populations and the percentage of 'dependants'.

We know that more than half the population of the countries of the Third World consists of people under 20 years old. This and the percentages given in Table 2 make clear the burden borne by adults in such countries, where young people are continuing their studies, and consequently remaining outside the world of work, for longer and longer periods of time.

Finally, a new wave of international migrations occurred. There were four important developments in this area in the 1970s.

First, there was significant migration of qualified labour to the oil-producing countries which form part of the developing world. According to a United Nations report on the social situation in the the world (1982), between 3 and 4 million foreign workers went to the countries of the Middle East during the 1970s.

Second, restrictions were imposed by the developed countries on the immigration of workers from the less developed countries. According to the same United Nations report, from the beginning of

TABLE 3   Age structure of the population in the world and its different regions in 1950 and 1980 (in %) and dependants expressed as a percentage of the population aged between 15 and 64

Regions	1950			1980			% of dependants	
	0–14	15–64	65+	0–14	15–64	65+	1950	1980
World	35.1	59.6	5.3	35.6	58.6	5.7	67.9	70.6
Developed regions	27.8	64.6	7.6	23.0	65.6	11.4	54.8	52.6
Developing regions	38.8	57.1	4.1	40.0	56.2	3.8	75.2	77.8

Source: United Nations, *The World Population Situation in 1983*, New York, United Nations, 1984.

the 1950s to the beginning of the 1970s more than 30 million foreign workers immigrated to Western Europe.[1] Since the mid-1970s, net immigration to Western Europe has only slightly increased, partly as a result of a marked slowing down in economic growth and increases in unemployment which have made it necessary to apply restrictions on immigrant labour.

Third, another wave of migrations was the result of political pressure, religious persecution and similar situations. The dramatic case of the 'boat people' is an eloquent example of this kind of migration. In 1983, the United Nations High Commissioner for Refugees (UNHCR) gave the figure of 10 million political refugees throughout the world, adding that thirty years ago, the number of people obliged to leave their countries for political reasons was only 1.5 million.[2]

Finally, extreme poverty or hunger as a result of drought or other natural calamities, such as those which have occurred recently on the African continent, gave rise to another type of mass population movement during this period.

There can be little doubt that this more or less enforced mobility has important psychological and moral repercussions for the people concerned: all kinds of mental disturbances, home-sickness, the loss of traditional values without assimilating another code of ethics or another mode of life. These impose on education a responsibility which is both very delicate and very difficult, that of enabling the immigrants to adapt to a new environment without cutting them off from their cultural roots.

Following the Second World War urbanization was also instrumental in bringing about a major population redistribution, especially in the developing countries. The United Nations report on the world population situation in 1977 shows that the annual urban growth rate in the less developed regions of the world between 1950 and 1975 was more than double that of the more developed regions (4.4 compared

TABLE 4   Urban population as a percentage of total population, from 1950 to 1985

Regions	1950	1960	1970	1975	1980	1985
World	29.4	33.6	37.0	38.3	39.9	41.6
Developed regions	53.6	60.3	66.4	68.7	70.6	73.4
Developing regions	17.4	21.4	25.3	27.1	29.4	31.8

Source: United Nations, *The World Population Situation in 1983*, New York, United Nations, 1984.

to 2.2 per cent). Everywhere in the Third World, urbanization is continuing at a pace which far outstrips the real capacity of existing towns. Megalopolises are fast being constructed whose management costs have become prohibitive.[3]

This rapid urbanization has weakened the rural and agricultural sector as people leave the rural areas for the towns and urban employment and towns in turn encroach on arable land within their jurisdiction, and make it necessary to increase imports of food. This process of urban expansion, like other processes which are almost impossible to reverse, such as deforestation, desertification, soil erosion and other factors in the loss or degradation of arable land, is one of the causes of the food crisis and in some cases famine which has now begun to affect a part of the Third World.[4]

EFFECTS ON EDUCATION SYSTEMS

The effects of these population movements, which affect both the structure and the dynamics of the populations concerned, on the different education systems have been numerous. We shall now deal with some of the most important.

First, the school enrolment explosion started in the 1950s and continued in the 1970s and the beginning of the 1980s, although at a slower pace than during the previous decade. This growth was particularly marked in secondary and higher education, as can be seen in Table 5.

This quantitative explosion was bound to affect the quality of education, especially in the countries of the Third World. Despite this quantitative explosion at all levels of education in the developing countries, there are still large numbers of children of school-going age who are not enrolled; a problem to which must be added the long-standing problem of millions of illiterate adults.

Table 5 also sheds light on another interesting point, which is that

Population growth

TABLE 5　　　　　　　Average annual enrolment rate at the three levels of education

Regions	Primary education			Secondary education			Higher education		
	1965–70	1971–77	1970–82	1965–70	1971–77	1970–82	1965–70	1971–77	1970–82
Developed countries	0.7	−1.2	−0.58	2.3	2.3	−0.58	7.2	4.3	+3.75
Developing countries	4.2	4.0	4.9	8.1	6.2	8	11.6	8.1	13.1

Source: Unesco, *Unesco Statistical Yearbook, 1980*, Paris, Unesco, 1980; *Unesco Statistical Yearbook 1984*, Paris, Unesco, 1984.

the declining birth rate in the developed countries has led, during the past few years, to the closure of a considerable number of primary-school classes and, consequently, to a decline in the demand for teachers in these countries.

Next, in the developed countries, where the percentage of the adult population is much higher in proportion to that of the youthful population (see Table 3), there was a growing awareness of the importance of adult education within the framework of lifelong education.

Third, we have already noted the fairly rapid growth rate of the urban population both in the developed and developing regions. This accelerated urbanization often resulted in less interest being taken in the rural world and in a strengthening of the urban orientation of school curricula, which are not always suited to the living conditions and the needs of children from rural areas.

Fourth, urbanization makes education increasingly expensive, primarily because of the higher cost of urban infrastructures and, in some cases, the higher qualifications of teachers working in towns. Developing countries have had to devote a considerable part of their slender resources to financing the now inevitable expansion of their education systems. Some of these countries have even devoted as much as 5 to 7 per cent of their Gross National Product (GNP) to this sector. It is obvious that they will find it very difficult to exceed this level of expenditure on education, although the need to improve the quality of education might often require further investments. Although average expenditure on education in 1977, expressed as a percentage of GNP, did not exceed 4.3 per cent for the developing countries overall, Africa spent 5.2 per cent, a proportion which is comparable to that spent overall by Europe and which is almost exorbitant. Table 6 clearly shows the constant increase in *per capita* expenditure on education during the period 1965–80.

Fifth, these population movements also made the host countries realize the need for their education systems to cater to the requirements of the new arrivals. Authorization has sometimes been given

TABLE 6   Public expenditure on education per head (in United States dollars) during the period 1965–80

Regions	1965	1970	1975	1980
World total	38	57	109	183
Developed countries	87	137	264	456
Developing countries	5	7	19	38

Source: Unesco, *Unesco Statistical Yearbook 1980*, Paris, Unesco, 1980; Unesco, *Unesco Statistical Yearbook 1984*, Paris, Unesco, 1984.

for the language of origin of the immigrants to be used in the basic education of their children. Sometimes, the geography, history and other aspects of the society and culture of origin have also been included in the curriculum (for example in the Scandinavian countries). This situation has led to renewed interest in scientific study of the question of bilingualism (see, for example, Fitouri, 1983).

Lastly, population growth in the last few decades has led to the introduction in many countries, especially in Asia, of population and birth-control education (see Unesco, 1978*b*). In the same way, problems of under-nourishment and malnutrition have led to the organization in some places of nutrition education courses, but these are still at an experimental stage.

STABLE POPULATION LEVELS OR CONTINUING POPULATION EXPLOSION?

According to certain estimates, the world population will continue to increase until the end of the century at an average annual rate of 1.8 per cent. The population growth rate of the developed regions will decline still further, while the present growth rate will be roughly maintained in the developing countries, as can be seen in Table 7.

According to the United Nations, the annual population growth rate for the developed countries will drop from 1.1 per cent between 1950 and 1975 to 0.7 per cent between 1975 and the year 2000, while the parallel rate for the Third World will be the same in the two successive 25 year periods. The year 2000 will thus see a geographic distribution of the world population of 21 per cent in the developed regions and 79 per cent in the developing regions.

With regard to the forecasting of school enrolment at the different levels, Unesco made a projection (Table 8) which clearly demonstrates the immensity of the task to be accomplished from 1980 to 2000,

TABLE 7   Total population (millions) and population growth at the world and regional levels

	Population forecast for the year 2000		Annual growth rate	
	United Nations	*Global Report*	United Nations	*Global Report*
World	6 254	6 351	1.8	1.8
Developed regions	1 360	1 323	0.7	0.6
Developing regions	4 894	5 028	2.2	2.1

Source: based on United Nations forecasts and *The Global 2000 Report* ... (United States, 1980–81)[5]

especially in the developing countries, where school enrolment must increase by 163.6 million at the primary-school level, 120.2 million at the secondary-school level and 23.1 million in higher education.

The urbanization process is another aspect of demographic trends. According to a United Nations forecast (United Nations, Department of International ..., 1980), the urban population expressed as a percentage of the global population will increase, between 1975 and 2000, from 69.8 per cent to 81.8 per cent in the developed countries, and from 27.2 per cent to 40.4 per cent in the developing countries. The urban growth rate for the developed regions during the same 25-year period will be of the order of 40 per cent, whereas the corresponding rate in the developing regions will be more than 157 per cent.[6] According to *The Global 2000 Report* (United States, 1980–81, p. 12), in these latter regions about 400 towns will pass the one million inhabitants mark.

This rapid urbanization, primarily caused by the continuing exodus from the land, will clearly have important implications for the education systems in these regions. An increase in the average unit cost of education is to be expected and, as a result, greater pressure on education budgets; there will also be an increase in the size of urban schools and, perhaps, a greater number of pupils in each class, and possibly a decrease in the staff-pupil ratio. The quality of education is bound to suffer as a result. Can the mass media be used to solve the problem? This is a proposition which invites scepticism for a variety of reasons.

As far as international migration is concerned (whether in search of employment or political asylum), the selective and protectionist policies applied by the rich countries have helped to slow it down or stop it altogether (this, however, is not true of illegal immigration) in these countries, but the influx of migrants has continued unabated into the developing countries.[7] The widening gap in standards of living between the developed and developing countries, and the

TABLE 8 Projection of enrolment at the different levels (in millions)

	Level of education		Enrolment at different levels in millions		Annual average growth rate			
			1980	2000	1960–70	1970–80	1980–90	1990–2000
World	Primary		417.4	589.2	3.3	2.0	1.9	1.5
	Secondary		177.2	303.6	6.0	3.7	2.9	2.5
	Higher		46.5	74.9	8.7	5.1	2.4	2.4
	Total		641.1	967.7	4.2	2.7	2.2	1.9
Developed countries	Primary		125.5	133.7	1.1	−0.9	0.4	0.2
	Secondary		80.6	86.7	4.3	1.3	0.1	0.3
	Higher		29.7	34.9	8.2	3.4	0.5	1.1
	Total		235.7	255.4	2.5	0.3	0.3	0.5
Developing countries	Primary		291.9	455.5	5.3	3.6	2.5	1.9
	Secondary		96.6	216.8	9.1	6.4	4.8	3.4
	Higher		16.8	39.9	10.4	9.1	5.2	3.6
	Total		405.3	712.3	6.0	4.4	3.2	2.5

Source: Unesco, Trends and Projections of Enrolment by Level of Education and Age, 1960–2000 (estimates made in 1982), February 1984.

threats posed by the unstable political climate in the contemporary world certainly do not help to reduce migratory movements of workers or refugees.[8]

The demographic changes that have just been predicted for the coming years will also affect educational content. Population education might be given more space in curricula, and the need to adapt education systems to the specific needs of migrant workers or refugees will perhaps be even more keenly felt. The balance between rural- and urban-oriented content may be abandoned in favour of the latter. Instead of constantly increasing the duration of compulsory schooling as is now done, attention will perhaps be given to the possibility of creating several cycles of education, each lasting for a shorter period than the previous one, which will succeed one another throughout the lives of the students. Educational content will then have to be revised in the light of this new concept of lifelong education.

SIGNIFICANT DEVELOPMENTS

The study of statistics on population does not only reveal clear trends, but also elements indicative of great changes which will have consequences we cannot yet foresee. Among the most significant of these is the tendency of average life expectancy to lengthen, this trend being particularly noticeable in the Third World where life expectancy is still far less than that of highly developed societies.

Table 9 shows not only changes in life expectancy in the recent past but also future prospects in this area.

In many countries, increased life expectancy has recently coincided with a tendency to retire workers, employees and civil servants early as a way of reducing unemployment. As a result, elderly people face a long period of retirement which cannot be adequately occupied with day-to-day activities. Futurologists are of the opinion that the future will bring 'a reduction of the debilitating effects of ageing which result in, for example, senility, heart disease and arthritis' thanks to progress

TABLE 9   Changing life expectancy at birth

	1950–55	1975–80	1995–2000
World total	47.0	57.5	63.9
More developed regions	65.2	71.9	73.7
Less developed regions	42.4	55.1	62.5

Source: United Nations, *World Population Prospects as Assessed in 1980*, New York, United Nations, 1981.

now being made in medicine and public health. There will thus be a need in the coming years to devise new forms of activity for this significant section of the population, in addition to the activities with which it is already familiar: for example, studies (*inter alia* in free or open universities, or in universities of the 'Third Age'), cultural activities, domestic employment and hobbies. There is already talk of a self-help economy and of the possibility of elderly people actively participating in the work of the social or humanitarian voluntary organizations.

Lowering of the retirement age has its drawbacks. It is a costly policy, and some countries therefore tend to push back retirement age (the United States Congress, for example, has decided to increase retirement age to 66 for workers born after 1943, and to 67 for workers born after 1960 (IFRI, 1984, p. 61). It also encourages many retired people to seek employment on the black market. It is thus open to question whether early retirement is an entirely positive factor in the creation of jobs for young people.

The increasing ability to apply both quantitative and qualitative methods of birth control must be seen as another promising development. Increasingly effective means of birth control are being devised which are less and less hazardous to health. There is also a prospect of using scientific methods not only to determine the biological state and health of the foetus but also to correct abnormalities and apply eugenic remedies, if necessary, before the birth of the baby.

Biotechnology offers astounding possibilities of character selection and emphasizing specific human capacities. It also has important social and moral implications which will soon have to be given serious attention (see Felden, 1981; Kahn and Wiener, 1967; Sasson, 1984).

The large-scale migrations of workers and refugees will not only have considerable effects on the economic structures and achievements of the host countries, they may also create political and social tensions in these same countries (OECD, 1983*b*, p. 48). It can also be predicted that these migrations will lead to more frequent inter-ethnic marriages. Such developments may result in the enhancement of the sense of individual identity and may also encourage greater knowledge of other peoples and other cultures.

NOTES

1. For the points of departure and destinations of these international migrations see United Nations, Department of International Economic and Social Affairs, (1980, Ch. 6). For the percentage of immigrants in the total population of individual countries (from 6, 7, and 8 per cent respectively in the United Kingdom, the Federal Republic of Germany and France, to 25 per cent in the region comprising the Persian Gulf and North Africa), see United Nations (1983, pp. 65-6) and the following table:

Estimated number of migrant workers in a number of regions

Regions	Year	Number in thousands
Western Europe	1981	6 279
South American region	1974	2 870
Arab region	1980	2 822
West African region	1975	1 280

Source: ILO, *World Labour Report*, Vol. I, Geneva, ILO, 1984

2. The study by the International Labour Organisation (ILO, 1984b), gives the following details as to the number of refugees:
 • The United Nations High Commissioner for Refugees (UNHCR) had been officially informed in 1981 of more than 8 million such cases.
 • This same commissioner protects about 5 million people in Africa, 2.5 million in Asia, 0.6 million in Western Europe and 0.3 million in South America.
 • A commission for refugees in the United States of America, applying the less restrictive criteria of the Organization of African Unity (OAU), concluded that in 1981 there were 12.6 million refugees in the world, of which more than 8 million were political refugees and nearly 4.6 million displaced persons, without taking into account 'resettled' persons. Half of these 12.6 million people had found refuge in African countries.
3. The United Nations *Concise Report on the World Population Situation in 1983* gives a list of the world's twenty largest cities for each of the years 1950, 1970 and 1980. Here is the list of the world's most populous cities for 1980 and their respective populations expressed in millions: Tokyo-Yokohama—17; New York and north-east New Jersey—15.6; Mexico City—15; São Paulo—12.8; Shanghai—11.8; Buenos Aires (greater)—10; London—10; Calcutta—9.5; Los Angeles and Long Beach—9.5; Rhine-Ruhr—9.3; Rio de Janeiro—9.2; Bei-jing—9.1; Paris—8.8; Bombay—8.5; Seoul—8.5; Moscow—8.2; Osaka-Kobé—8; Tien-Tsin—7.7; Cairo-Gizeh-Embabeh—7.3; Chicago and north-west Indiana—6.8.
4. The International Conference on Population and the Urban Future (Rome, 1-4 September 1980) foresaw the possibilty of 25 megalopolises with more than 10 million inhabitants by the year 2000. Only 5 of these megalopolises will be in the developed regions, the rest being situated in developing countries.
5. The most recent projections by the United Nations (1982, quoted in *The World Population Situation in 1983*, give the following figures for the world's population in the year 2000: 6,123 million will be the world total, with 1,272 million in the developed regions and 4,851 million in the developing regions).

6. According to a more recent projection by the United Nations (1982, p. 148), published in 1982, the annual growth rates of the urban population from 1980–1985 and from 1985–2000 are given as follows:

Regions	1980–85	1985	2000
World total	2.8	2.8	2.8
More developed regions	1.4	1.3	1.1
Less developed regions	4.0	4.0	3.7

7. It is thus not surprising to see that in the world population projections the highest annual growth rate is predicted for Africa (2.9 per cent), followed by Latin America (2.7 per cent), and Asia and Oceania (1.9 per cent). See United States, 1980–81, p. 9.
8. According to the Director-General of Unesco, (M'Bow, 1982), 20 million workers now live outside their countries of origin, and 10 million refugees have also been forced to leave their countries. For the extent and development of international migrations, see *Concise Report on Monitoring of Population Trends and Policies*, submitted by the Secretary-General of the United Nations to the Population Commission, 18–20 January 1984.

2
Economic changes

After thirty years of unprecedented economic growth, the world entered a crisis in the mid-1970s from which it is still struggling to emerge. Several factors have been held responsible for the new state of affairs, such as the rise in the price of oil, the industrial world's main energy source; inflation due to the excessive liquidity of the Western economic system and the consequent introduction of price control policies or other anti-inflationary measures; the two monetary crises of 1971–72 and 1979, which led initially to widespread currency fluctuations and subsequently, because of rising interest rates in the United States, to a marked appreciation in the US dollar, the main currency used in international trade; and, lastly, the heavy indebtedness of the Third World and the sharp decline in productive investment in that part of the world.

Some writers take the view that technological change and the restructuring of industry are at the root of the present crisis (CEPII, 1983).

'The present period of crisis and instability, after decades of relative stability in growth rates and in world economic structures,[1] can be interpreted as a transitional phase between two industrial revolutions' (CEPII, 1983, p. 4). It is a time of progression from 'traditional' manufacturing industries such as textiles, steel, motor vehicles, machine tools, shipbuilding, etc., which are already in decline,[2] to new, high-technology industries such as electronics, computer technology, robotics, nuclear power and biotechnology, which are booming. Quite clearly, the transition is not easy. A great number of problems, including unemployment and social tensions, are being generated in the process.

In our view, however, technological change and the start of the third industrial revolution cannot fully account for the current economic crisis. The policies of growth at all costs, pursued after the end of the Second World War, are certainly responsible in some measure for triggering off the crisis. They generated unprecedented inflation which inevitably led to recession when countered with sudden austerity measures. The situation was exacerbated by an inordinate increase in public spending and real wage rises in excess of the rate of increase in productivity. The allocation of a substantial volume of resources to the military sector ($120 to $130 in the 1980s for every man, woman and child on earth) was bound to make matters worse. The rise in oil prices in 1973 therefore merely added its weight to a number of other factors that had already made the situation extremely critical.

There is one point to be made before embarking on a systematic study of the prominent features of economic development over the past ten years. In economics, the cause and effect relationship is not one-way or one-to-one; the effect reacts in turn on the cause. The events in question must therefore be viewed in terms of interaction.

The first development to be noted is a sharp decline in the rate of growth of production in all the major economic regions between 1973 and 1983 and a concurrent reduction in the rate of expansion of international trade (see Table 11).

Since the second oil shock (1979), the world economy has become entrenched in a deep and prolonged recession. What distin-

TABLE 11 Medium-term growth trends in the world economy (average annual rate of growth over a five-year period)[1]

Period	World economy	Developed market economies	Centrally planned economies	Developing countries	World exports	Non-oil exports
	Gross domestic product				International trade	
1960–64	5.7	5.4	6.2	6.7	6.6	6.6
1962–66	5.7	5.6	6.4	5.3	7.0	6.6
1964–68	5.8	5.5	7.7	5.5	8.3	8.0
1966–70	5.6	5.2	7.4	6.2	9.0	8.8
1968–72	5.6	5.1	6.4	7.2	9.5	9.8
1970–74	4.9	4.2	6.9	6.8	8.7	9.6
1972–76	4.1	3.4	6.3	6.0	6.7	7.6
1974–78	3.4	2.6	5.5	4.9	4.3	5.5
1976–80	3.9	3.6	4.1	4.8	5.4	6.3
1977–81	3.0	2.8	3.3	3.8	3.2	4.4
1978–82	2.6	2.3	2.9	3.2	2.9	4.0

Source: United Nations, *World Economic Survey, 1981–82, Current Trends and Policies in the World Economy*, p. 10, New York, United Nations, 1982.

1. According to the United Nations *World Economic Survey* for 1985, growth rates increased in 1984 as a result of a brief recovery. This trend does not seem to have continued in 1985: GDP growth rates were around 4.6 per cent for the world as a whole and the developed market economies, 5.5 per cent for the centrally planned economies and 2.9 per cent for the developing countries, while the volume of world imports increased by 9 per cent.

guishes the recent recession from those occurring before the Second World War is the accompanying inflation. On the one hand, there has been excessive liquidity for a variety of reasons and, on the other, the increase in productivity and hence output has been inadequate. Efforts to counter this inflation through restrictions on credit or consumption or by means of other austerity measures have failed to remedy the situation. Indeed, economic stagnation has become more severe, resulting in large-scale unemployment which rapidly exceeded the ominous rates of 6, 7 and 8 per cent, even in the developed countries (where there were 32 million unemployed in 1983) and in 1983 reached peaks of 12 to 13 and even 14 per cent, as shown in Table 12.

It should be added that this general unemployment was by no means confined to the developed market economies. The situation was and still remains more serious in the Third World, where there was imported unemployment in addition to the chronic problem of underemployment (see Tables 13 and 14).

It should be noted that many present-day economists consider that the world economy entered a new long-term cycle of economic stagnation and depression some years ago.

Next, the decline in output in all regions, the recession, and the steep rise in oil prices were some of the factors leading to a worsening of the indebtedness of states, especially in the less developed regions of the world. The external debt of those countries[3] is currently put at

TABLE 12   Selected developed market economies: unemployment rates, 1976–1983, as a percentage of the civilian labour force

Country or country group	1976–80	1980	1981	1982	1983
Major developed market economies	5.3	5.6	6.5	8.0	9.0
Canada	7.7	7.5	7.6	11.0	13.0
France	5.3	6.3	7.3	8.3	9.5
Germany, Federal Republic of	3.4	3.1	4.8	7.6	9.0
Italy	7.1	7.4	8.5	9.0	9.5
Japan	2.1	2.0	2.2	2.2	2.5
United Kingdom	6.4	7.3	10.6	12.0	12.5
United States	5.2	7.0	7.5	9.7	10.5
Other economies					
Belgium	8.2	9.4	11.7	13.9	14.5
Denmark	5.7	6.1	8.1	9.1	9.0
Ireland	8.5	8.3	10.3	12.1	14.0
Netherlands	4.3	4.7	7.5	10.4	13.0

Source: United Nations, *World Economic Survey, 1983, Current Trends and Policies in the World Economy*, p. 103, New York, United Nations, 1983.

TABLE 13   Open unemployment: developing regions, percentage of labour force (1980)

All developing countries	6.0
Latin America and Caribbean (low-income countries)	8.1
Latin America and Caribbean (middle-income countries)	5.6
Africa and Middle East (low-income countries)	14.8
Asia (middle-income countries)	3.4

Source: ILO, World Labour Report, Vol. I, Geneva, ILO, 1984.

TABLE 14   Preliminary estimates of unemployment and underemployment in developing countries, 1975 (in millions)

Region	Total unemployment	Total underemployment
Asia	18	168
Africa	10	53
Latin America	5	28

Source: ILO, Employment, Growth and Basic Needs, Geneva, ILO, 1976.

over $700,000 million, which according to World Bank estimates represents 33.8 per cent of their GNP and 135.4 per cent of their exports. The deterioration in the balance of payments, especially in the Third World, is another aspect of this new and complex situation (see Table 15).

Many Western societies are living beyond their means. It is not surprising, therefore, that external or internal state borrowing in most developed countries is on the increase.

Fourth, one of the basic trends in recent years has been the increasing interdependence of all national economies. It was awareness of this trend that prompted the United Nations in 1974 to adopt a Declaration and a Programme of Action on the Establishment of a New International Economic Order. The declaration called for the abolition of the present international economic system with its inequality, domination, dependence, narrowly selfish interests and fragmentation,
and its replacement by an order 'based on equity, sovereign equality, interdependence, common interest and co-operation among all states, irrespective of their economic and social systems'.

The object of the New International Economic Order is to bring

TABLE 15   Balance of payments on current account, by country groups, 1978–84 (billions of dollars)

Region	1978	1979	1980	1981	1982	1983	1984[1]
Developed market economies	31.3	−5.7	−41.7	−5.5	−5.5	−0.3	−35.5
Developing countries	−34.0	10.6	35.9	−41.1	−102.8	−76.2	−53.5
Centrally planned economies	−6.2	−0.3	1.6	3.5	16.8	19.9	19.0

1. Preliminary estimates.

Source: United Nations, *World Economic Survey, 1981–82*, New York, United Nations, 1982, and the same survey for 1985.

about a radical change in the structure of the international economic system so that the developing countries are in a much stronger position for self-reliant rather than dependent development.

It is still too soon to assess the practical consequences of the Declaration and the Programme of Action. Countless articles have been written on the subject over the last ten years (United Nations, 1980) and it has given rise to numerous conferences, agreements, resolutions and decisions. Decision-makers in Third World countries have become deeply aware of the need for endogenous, self-reliant development and it is now common practice to question imported models of development.

Although little progress has been made towards establishing the New International Economic Order, steps have been taken in the United Nations Conference on Trade and Development (UNCTAD) and the General Agreement on Tariffs and Trade (GATT) and other international bodies to assist in stabilizing basic commodity prices, increasing the export value of such commodities, diversifying industries in developing countries, establishing a system of compensatory financing to support basic commodities, etc. The New International Economic Order will also certainly have repercussions in sectors other than the economy, and attempts have been made to examine its implications for the reform of education systems, especially in the developing countries (see Oxenham, 1982; Sanyal, 1982).

Another development is the increased economic dependence of the developing countries. Although they account for over two-thirds of the world population and 91 per cent of agricultural employment, these countries produce only 44 per cent of the world's food. This kind of dependence, aggravated by the natural disasters and social upheavals afflicting many developing countries, has placed those countries at a considerable disadvantage compared with certain large-scale producers and exporters of agricultural produce. Whereas in the past the developing countries were net exporters of foodstuffs, they now import nearly 50 million tons of wheat, while international food aid does not even amount to one-tenth of the quantity imported. The world community has not yet succeeded in building up sufficient stocks of cereals to protect itself both against price fluctuations and against the possibility of widespread famine. However, the persistence of the old international economic order has created an acute problem of agricultural surpluses in some regions such as Europe; in other areas, millions are suffering from hunger. It must be recognized, however, that certain developing countries have made praiseworthy attempts to diversify their agriculture and increase the output of basic foodstuffs so as to keep the spectre of famine at bay. These countries are thus creating a more solid basis for their industrialization efforts and provide an encouraging example for the rest.

The decline in international development aid (the international development strategy recommended that the rich countries should devote at least 0.7 per cent of GDP to development aid, but in practice a rate of only barely 0.34 per cent has been recorded) and the use of a large proportion of the funds of certain less developed countries for the purchase of arms (one of the world's most flourishing businesses) have obviously made it more difficult for those countries to achieve economic self-sufficiency. As far as industrial production is concerned, the share of Third World countries is still less than 10 per cent of overall world output.

Finally, where international trade is concerned, it is estimated that the North possesses over 90 per cent of world industrial production capacity and controls over 90 per cent of world trade; 90 per cent of research is carried out in the developed countries. The imbalance in trade relations between different countries and the unfavourable situation of raw material producers (except in the case of oil) are prominent features of the present world economy. In 1980, the five dominant economies (United States, France, Federal Republic of Germany, United Kingdom and Japan) accounted for 39 per cent of world trade (i.e. exports plus imports) and held a 49 per cent share of world income (in terms of current prices and exchange rates) (CEPII, 1983, p. 141). Growth in trade among developing countries, a major objective of their economic co-operation since the 1960s, has not yet made sufficient headway (trade within the Third World at present represents only 22 per cent of the total exports of those countries (United Nations, 1980, p. 47). A study of the share of each developing region in overall world trade (in 1980) shows that these regions as a whole do not even account for one-quarter of the total (Latin America, 6 per cent; Africa, 4.5 per cent; Middle East, 7.2 per cent; rest of Asia excluding Japan and China, 7.2 per cent; total, 24.9 per cent).

Taking only the figures for exports, the world total came to $1,964,000 million at current prices in 1980. The respective shares of the rapidly developing countries and the rest of the Third World come to only 5.3 and 6.8 per cent of this total (CEPII, 1983, pp. 92–3). These figures show clearly that in this as in other branches of the world economy, the developed countries are really in control and can easily impose their own 'law' unless the developing countries achieve an awareness through appropriate means of their potential for collective self-reliance and their ability to negotiate on an equitable basis with the developed countries.

DANGER OF EXHAUSTION OF NATURAL RESOURCES

Industrialization has led to an increased rate of exploitation of non-renewable natural resources, which generated fears in the 1960s that these resources might ultimately be exhausted. There were resources that seemed to be available in great abundance, but we now have to consider some of them, in particular, land, water, air, energy and forests, which, because their supply is not unlimited, will create major problems for the future development of the world economy.

Land: The *Global 2000 Report* (United States, 1980/81) notes that most good quality land has already been cultivated and that an increase of more than 4 per cent in such cultivated land between now and the end of the century cannot therefore be expected. In the early 1970s, a hectare of arable land supplied the needs of 2.6 persons. In the year 2000 the same surface will have to support 4 persons. These projections are borne out by forecasts of the Food and Agriculture

TABLE 16   Projected arable area in various regions—in millions of hectares

	1971–75	1985	2000
Industrialized countries	400.3	392.2	399.1
Centrally planned countries	414.5	417.5	420.0
Less developed countries	662.0	706.0	723.5
World	1 476.8	1 513.7	1 538.6

Source: United States, 1980/81, Vol. II, p. 97.

Organization of the United Nations (FAO). The ratio of cultivated arable land to the number of inhabitants, which was 0.37 hectares in 1975, will probably drop to 0.25 hectares by the end of the century (FAO, 1981, p. 66).

Water: The world consumption of water is expected to increase by 200 to 300 per cent by the end of the century (see, *inter alia*, the Doxiadis projection referred to in *The Global 2000 Report*). Although there would appear to be sufficient water in the world to meet the enormous demand that will exist in the year 2000, regional shortages and a deterioration in the quality of water in many regions of the world are foreseen. It should be noted that the demand for water is growing in the less developed regions of the world, the very regions where the supply of fresh water for human consumption or for irrigation is already inadequate. Even in the industrialized countries there is likely to be keen competition between various uses for water (to increase food production, to supply new energy systems, to meet growing industrial needs, etc.) and in some regions an aggravation of the shortage of water. Furthermore, water pollution by hydrocarbons and other chemical substances exacerbates the situation we have just described.

Air: The United Nations Environment Programme (UNEP), established in 1973, draws attention in its 1980 report to a very high concentration of carbon dioxide in the atmosphere which, aside from its harmful direct effects, could bring about a considerable increase in world temperatures, thus upsetting the whole ecological balance. Urban expansion, the increase in the number of modern means of transport (aeroplanes, cars, etc.), waste gas from factories, etc., will not improve this state of affairs in the years ahead. Switzerland's forests are already jeopardized by air pollution of this kind.

Energy: For a number of years, and especially since the publication of the famous Club of Rome report, *The Limits to Growth*, people have been predicting what Harold Shane calls the twilight of the petroleum era in the relatively near future. While *The Global 2000 Report* is optimistic on the availability of non-combustible mineral resources, it predicts a persistent shortage of energy and persistently high prices, uncertainty regarding the substitution of new energy sources for oil (oil will still be the main source of energy in 1990, providing 46 to 47 per cent of the world's total energy supply), and an inability of the capacities for the exploration and production of new oil reserves to keep pace with rapidly growing demand.[4]

A great deal is being expected at present from the continual improvement in conservation and energy-saving measures. Recent experience, in the wake of the first energy crisis, has shown how effective such measures can be. Other promising indicators are: the development and technical improvement of the mining, transport and use of coal; the increasing contribution of the petrochemical industry to improving basic coal technology; the wider use of non-conventional geothermal, solar, wind and other sources of energy; the search for alternatives to current nuclear reactor projects (Kahn et al., 1978), expresses the hope that nuclear fusion will soon begin to replace nuclear fission, since the risks of radioactivity in the case of fission are still relatively high); and the development of hydraulic energy.

Forests: Norman Myers (see Peccei, 1981), has estimated that the world's forests are being destroyed at a rate of 50 hectares a minute. According to some specialists, one-third of the trees that existed in 1882 had been cut down by 1982. *The Global 2000 Report* notes that if present trends continue, the forests in South Asia, Amazonia and Central Africa will have been halved by the year 2000. The decline in the developing regions as a whole will be about 40 per cent, and in the industrial countries only 0.5 per cent.

The serious problems of deforestation, desertification, soil erosion, etc., that the developing countries will still have to contend with over the next two decades will severely impede their efforts to achieve self-sufficiency in food (see Lenoir, 1984). The European countries are at present exposed to rain that has been polluted by various chemical agents emitted by factories or cars, and this has already done considerable damage to forests in certain technologically advanced countries, including Switzerland and the Federal Republic of Germany.

Since the alarm was raised regarding the exhaustion of natural resources and the pollution of the environment, many scientists and research institutions have endeavoured to find adequate solutions to the depletion of non-renewable resources and their recycling and the deterioration of the environment, with a view to helping to restore ecological balance. Quite substantial progress has been made in practical terms, for example the launching of major projects to combat pollution of the marine environment and air pollution in cities, to recycle waste water, etc. Internationally, the setting up of UNEP is a further sign of the growing awareness of the vital importance of the ecological issue.

Futurist studies based on a realistic approach (see Freeman and Jahoda, 1978) mention a number of promises that might be fulfilled by advances in science and technology in the near future. Although the more advanced part of the world, the northern hemisphere, will continue to be the main producer of surplus food during the next few decades, there is a strong chance that improved irrigation together with the use of organic fertilizers and appropriate methods and techniques will lead to a marked increase in agricultural production in the semi-arid regions around the tropics.

The forecasts for non-combustible mineral resources are not really disquieting, but the need to use them sparingly and to increase the amount of recycling is generally recognized. There will therefore probably be an upsurge in research with these two ends in view (Freeman and Jahoda, 1978, note by way of example that 40 per cent of the world supply of copper already comes from recycling). On the basis of current technological progress, it should soon be possible to exploit minerals deep under the sea, and there is no reason why mankind should not later find a means of exploiting extraterrestrial resources.

Ideas and practical proposals concerning the consumption of the world's living resources are quite plentiful. For example, there is the World Conservation Strategy worked out jointly by the International Union for the Conservation of Nature and Natural Resources (IUCN), UNEP and the World Wildlife Fund (WWF) (Geneva, 1980) which, if implemented, would at least halt the losses that the world has been incurring since the beginning of the industrial age.

CRISIS OR RENEWED ECONOMIC GROWTH?

Optimists are few and far between when it comes to discussing the immediate future of the world economy. Most economists think that the world economy has entered either a long period of stagnation or one of growth at too slow a pace to remedy unemployment and other serious disequilibria such as balance of payments deficits, state indebtedness, the impoverishment of most of the Third World, etc. Even Herman Kahn, who almost always sees the future through rose-coloured glasses, has no hope that the poor majority who constitute three-quarters of mankind can reach before the year 2200 the level of prosperity characteristic of post-industrial economies (Kahn et al., 1979, p. 19).

Given these prospects, many economists have suggested major changes in both the structure and the functioning of the international economy. New models of various kinds have been proposed and books and articles have been written examining and evaluating them. Each model depends on a basic assumption. For example, the Barriloch model starts with the idea of a more equitable distribution of wealth throughout the world so as to meet the basic needs of the poor countries (see Herrera, 1976). The United Nations model (*The Future of the World Economy*), proposed by Wassily Leontief et al. (1977), aims at narrowing the wide gap between the rich and poor countries by the year 2000 by speeding up the development of the poor countries as compared with the rich, while preserving the environment and the world's natural balances. J. Forrester and D. Meadows (Meadows et al., 1972) based their model on the assumption that there are physical limits to economic growth, while their Club of Rome successors (Mesarovic and Pestel, 1974) lay greater stress on the limitations within each major region and the need to switch from the pursuit of undifferentiated, exclusively quantitative, exponential and cancerous growth, as in the past, to a policy of 'organic', harmonious and balanced development, backed up by the real interdependence of all parts of the world (see Cole, in Freeman and Jahoda, 1978; Richardson, 1981).

Although these models are interesting and contain a great deal of useful information on possible future trends, we cannot confine ourselves to them because of their prescriptive character. We shall consider, instead, what seems to be a realistic rather than an ideal vision of the future, as contained in a number of studies based more on an examination of the trends of economic development in different regions of the world. We shall focus in particular on studies such as the OECD's *Interfutures* study (OECD, 1979), France (1980), the annual World Bank *World Development Reports* and International Monetary Fund (IMF) studies.

We shall begin with development prospects in both developed and developing countries. They seem at present to offer little reassurance. Many factors have combined to turn into something structural the relative or total stagnation that initially seemed to be a temporary setback. These factors include: restrictive and deflationary monetary policies, insufficient productive investment, productivity more or less stationary, the protectionist trade policies of so many developed countries, the marked decline in international co-operation to finance development programmes in the Third World, state indebtedness, especially in the Third World, which in present circumstances is impeding the expansion of trade between the developed and developing countries and is thus preventing economic recovery on both sides, and the lack of willingness to make any change in the present international division of labour on the part of the countries best placed to do so.

We have already noted that the annual rate of growth of the world economy dropped from 5.7 per cent in 1960–64 to only 2.6 per cent in 1978–82. There is no sign for the time being of any reversal in this downward trend, in spite of the slow improvement in the situation in the United States and Japan. Table 17 gives a clear picture of recent trends in GDP growth.

To give an idea of the gap between these two major regions, it should be noted that the developing countries account for only

Economic changes

TABLE 17 GDP growth, 1960–82 (percentages)

Region	1960–73	1973–79	1980	1981	1982
Developing countries	6.0	5.1	3.0	2.0	1.9
Industrial countries	5.0	2.8	1.3	1.0	0.2

Source: World Bank, *World Developmnt Report 1983*.

$2,231,000 million (23 per cent) of the total world GDP of $9,626,000 million.

The projection made by the American team working on *The Global 2000 Report* (United States, 1980–81) concerning annual average GNP growth rates in various regions of the world, calculated by means of complex simulation techniques, shows that while this growth rate can be estimated at 2.3 per cent per year for the world as a whole during the period 1975–85, it will drop to 1.5 per cent per year in the period 1985–2000.

OECD (1979) researchers also rule out the possibility of strong growth for OECD countries during the period in question because of a number of social curbs on rapid growth, e.g. institutional ossification, a weakening of the ability of governments to co-ordinate their policies, social fragmentation, a change in values that is tending to undermine the productivity ethic, etc.

One of the consequences of this state of the world economy is unemployment, which does not look as though it can diminish in the next few years for various reasons which include technological change, the increasing use of robots, the sharp expansion of capital-intensive industries that lend themselves to automation (for example, the military industries) and the relative saturation of demand for basic commodities in the advanced countries (for example foodstuffs or even certain industrial goods such as textiles, some kinds of tools, etc.). The International Labour Organisation (ILO) has made the projection shown in Table 18 for the available labour force in the period 1950–2000, in millions of individuals:

TABLE 18

Region	1975	1980	1985	1990	2000
Developed countries	520	550	576	596	639
Developing countries	1 125	1 245	1 381	1 534	1 907

Source: ILO, *World Summary*, Vol. V, Geneva, ILO, 1977.

In other words, on the basis of present trends, the number of jobs to be created between 1980 and the end of the century works out at 89 million for the developed countries and 662 million for the less developed countries. In the Third World, concealed underemployment and unemployment and the fact that independent and self-reliant development at a sufficiently fast pace seems improbable in the near future make this task all the more Herculean.

International trade expanded considerably in the 1950s and 1960s and at a faster pace than the rise in world output, but during the 1970s the rate of increase in exports, especially those from developing countries, showed a marked decline (see Table 19).

In addition, the terms of trade (except in the case of energy) have deteriorated since 1979 for countries exporting raw materials. Since 1979, the recession has hit world trade as a whole. World exports grew by only 1.5 per cent in 1981 and actually declined (by about 2 per cent) in 1982 (World Bank, 1982, p. 26; 1983, p.9).

The share of the developing countries in world exports of merchandise decreased considerably between 1955 and 1980 (27.3 per cent in 1955; 21.4 per cent in 1980) (World Bank, 1982, p. 26). This contraction of Third World exports has led to a worsening of the burden of debt which they have been contending with for several years. It is estimated that this debt and the interest it has accrued now exceed the very high threshold of $700,000 million ($686,000 million in 1984 (World Bank, 1985)). We know from experience that the customary expedients such as 'rescheduling', i.e. spreading out debt repayments over a longer period, do not provide an effective remedy. On the other hand, non-repayment of debts, with the ensuing chain reaction, could result in a collapse of all market economies. The entire world financial system must therefore be reorganized. Various proposals have already been made, for example higher prices for the raw materials exported by developing countries (Leontief et al., 1977), a new approach to development financing in the Third World (the Independent Commission on International Development Issues/Brandt Commission), a lowering of interest rates (appeal by

TABLE 19 Annual average rate of increase in the value of Third World exports (at constant prices)

Years	Growth rate
1965–73	7.9%
1973–80	3.4%
1980–82	−0.5%

Source: World Bank.

the IMF), an agreement by creditors to forgo repayment of debts by the poorest countries, etc. The matter of the variable interest rates on half the medium-term external debt of the developing countries is another problem to which solutions are being sought.

The insufficient solvency of the developing countries is obviously a major obstacle to the development of world trade and hence to the expansion of output in the developed countries.

PROMISES OF THE FUTURE

The trends discernible in the world economy are not all adverse. Some favourable long-term trends are:

(a) the substantial industrialization efforts in most Third World countries;

(b) the fairly successful efforts of some of them to find more outlets for their manufactured goods on the world export market;

(c) some measure of growth in trade among the countries of the South;

(d) the introduction of the first arrangements to enable the world to move towards the New International Economic Order;

(e) the gradual realization in both developed countries and the Third World of the need for some co-ordination of economic policies to promote a recovery and to end or alleviate the world economic crisis.

These various points deserve to be considered in somewhat greater detail.

The Brandt Commission's *North–South* report (Independent Commission..., 1980, p. 172) states that the share of the developing countries in world manufacturing remained stable at around 7 per cent in the 1960s. It subsequently rose to 9 per cent in 1977. In the period 1970–76, their manufacturing output grew at 7.5 per cent per year—more than twice as fast as in the industrialized countries of the OECD. All the same, industrialization in the Third World has been and still is very uneven. In addition, the increase in industrial output was much slower between 1976 and 1980: 4.4 per cent in the developed market economies, 4.8 per cent in the developing countries and 5.35 per cent in the centrally planned economies, figures that obviously do not warrant undue optimism about the future.

Some countries, both large and small, such as Taiwan, Singapore, the Republic of Korea and Hong Kong, have succeeded in breaking into the international manufactured goods market. As noted also in the Brandt Commission's report (p. 174), manufactured goods are looming larger in the total exports of developing countries (10 per cent of non-fuel exports in 1955, 20 per cent in 1965 and over 40 per cent in 1975). However, most of these exports come from only a few countries, eight of them accounting for 78 per cent of the total exports of manufactured goods from the Third World to the OECD countries between 1970 and 1976.

In the first half of the 1970s, the South's exports to the South grew faster than exports to the North, which was a reversal of the trend in the 1960s (Independent Commission . . ., 1980, p. 175). They reached 22 per cent of the South's total exports and 32 per cent of their exports of manufactured goods. A recent OECD study (1983*b*) indicates that in 1981, 60 per cent of the exports of the non-oil-producing developing countries went to the industrial countries, 8 per cent to oil-producing countries, 25 per cent to the non-oil-producing developing countries and 7 per cent to the Council for Mutual Economic Assistance (CMEA) countries, which is further proof of the increase in South–South exports. This augurs very well for the future.

In the present world climate, it will obviously take a long time to establish the New International Economic Order. However, we must mention certain arrangements that have already been made and that hold promise of progress in that direction. For example, new donors of aid have appeared on the world scene. In 1981/82, the countries adhering to the Organization of Petroleum Exporting Countries (OPEC) allocated the equivalent of $8,180 million to PDA (public development assistance), that is to say 21.9 per cent of total world PDA (OECD, 1983*b*, Table 12).[5] Positive steps were taken by certain developed countries on behalf of the poorest countries under the 'generalized system of preferences', for example, a system that accords preferential treatment to some countries without demanding reciprocity. We should also note the rapid development and relative strengthening of the system of multilateral institutions for the financing of development, the gradual development of international codes of conduct, regarding technology and transnational corporations, for instance, and the initiation of procedures to stabilize raw material prices by various means such as the application of different kinds of international agreements or the creation of joint funds to finance the buffer storage of such products. Within the developing countries, efforts have been made to diversify production in the primary sector, to take over some of the processing of raw materials, to reduce imports and to expand exports. This has led the IMF experts to forecast a further decline in the annual current-account deficits of those countries: from $109,000 million in 1981 to $56,000 million in 1983 and finally to $50,000 million in 1984 and 1985.

TECHNOLOGICAL DEVELOPMENT AND THE STRUCTURE OF THE LABOUR FORCE

As far as production is concerned, one of the basic trends is related to the composition of the world's labour force. According to ILO figures, the percentage of the labour force in the major economic sectors changed in the period 1950-81 in the world as a whole and in the developed and developing regions as shown in Table 20.

These figures show clearly that between 1950 and 1981, the agricultural labour force declined in percentage terms everywhere, especially in the developed countries. The expansion of the industrial sector was much more pronounced in the Third World, while the services sector grew rapidly in the advanced countries. Table 21 gives a more detailed picture of the distribution of the labour force among the different sectors of economic activity in eight countries at different levels of development.

In the centrally planned economies, however, it should be noted that there was a particularly rapid increase in the labour force in the secondary sector owing to an all-out industrialization effort, while employment in the services sector was neglected by comparison (ILO, 1984, p. 90).[6]

Some data from the United States shed light on the situation in highly industrialized countries. Of the 17 million jobs created in the United States between 1970 and 1980, 90 per cent did not involve the manufacture of material objects but the provision of information, the transmission of knowledge and services in general. In addition to computers, some other new technologies that can generate a considerable amount of employment are: biotechnology, the development of new sources of energy, the exploitation of the resources of outer space and the seas and oceans, etc. (see Naisbitt, 1982). In the next few decades, we may therefore expect a transition in the advanced countries from an industrial economy to a tertiary society, while in the developing countries industrialization and the concentra-

TABLE 20 Percentage breakdown of the world labour force, by sector

	Agriculture			Industry			Services		
	1950	1970	1981	1950	1970	1981	1950	1970	1981
World	64	51	—	16	23	—	19	26	—
Developed regions	38	19	10[1]	30	38	34[1]	32	44	56[1]
Developing regions	79	67	59	8	16	20	12	18	21

1 These figures refer to developed market economies.

TABLE 21 Structure of the economically active population in eight countries at different levels of development (in percentages)

Level	Country	Primary sector (agriculture and mining)	Secondary sector (manufacturing industries)	Tertiary sector (trade, transport, insurance, services)
Underdeveloped	Bangladesh (1974)	77.1	4.6	15.6
	Afghanistan (1979)	61.6	10.7	24.1
Moderately developed	Algeria (1977)	22.3	7.8	23.6
	Malaysia (1979)	35.4	17.1	36.9
Developed	Italy (1980)	12.8	24.1	42.5
	France (1981)	8.5	22.8	51.3
Highly developed	Japan (1981)	9.9	24.3	53.3
	USA (1981)	4.5	21.4	70.0

Source: ILO, *Year Book of Labour Statistics*, Geneva, ILO, 1982.

Note: The following branches of economic activity have not been included in the above percentages: electricity, gas and water, building (poorly defined activities).

tion of labour in the secondary sector should continue for some time to come.

Another trend discernible in the advanced countries is the emergence and development of a self-service economy (see Gershung, 1979). Following Schumacher (1976), some writers such as Toffler and Naisbitt have predicted the decline of large-scale enterprises and a tendency towards the decentralization of activities. This could also prove to be one of the major trends of post-industrial society. In the last ten years, two-thirds of all new jobs in the United States were created by companies with fewer than twenty employees (see Naisbitt, 1982, Preface). Nevertheless, a comparable development seems unlikely in countries now in the process of industrialization, where factors conducive to concentration will persist for another few decades.

Naisbitt's book on 'megatrends' or major world trends also stresses that the uncontested authority of the ruling 'technostructure' cannot survive in a society in which information is no longer a monopoly of the rulers. Other writers have put forward other arguments to show that the company of the future will be based on the real participation of the workers in the life of the enterprise, a development closely linked to the democratic nature of the political environment.

The development of technology is clearly not the only factor influencing the structure of employment. Social change is a further vital factor. For example, the increase in leisure time and leisure activities, the general introduction of social security provisions and different kinds of insurance, the increasing attention given to physical health in present-day societies and growing public sensitivity to the quality of the environment have led to an expansion in the tertiary sector that could not have been predicted solely on the basis of technological progess.

In the years ahead, we are certain to witness an expansion, at least in the developed countries, of the 'quaternary' sector, which includes the knowledge industry, research and development, and scientific and artistic creation. Table 22 gives some indications of the extremely rapid development of the R&D sector in recent years.

In the two most powerful countries, the United States and the Soviet Union, the number of scientists and engineers engaged in research came to 673,000 and 1,411,200 persons respectively in 1981. In a work dealing mainly with the United States but applicable in general to the technologically most advanced countries (Sheppard and Carroll, 1980), it was predicted that the service sector would account for about 70 per cent of all employment by the year 2000.

TABLE 22   Personnel engaged in research and development activities in the period 1969–81 in some developed countries (index 1969 = 100)

	1969	1975	1979	1981
Belgium	100	138	—	—
United States	100	—	111	120
France	100	—	127	—
Federal Republic of Germany	100	138	163	171
Sweden	100	175	196	—
Switzerland	100	—	186	—
USSR	100	—	152	160
Japan	100	—	152	168

Source: Unesco, *Unesco Statistical Yearbook 1983*, Paris, Unesco, 1983.

In this connection, Isaac Asimov, the well-known science fiction writer, says that the twenty-first century may prove the great age of creativity, with machines finally replacing human beings for the execution of all monotonous tasks. Computers will take care of the running of the world and humans will finally be free to devote their time to what they alone are capable of doing, that is to say creating (Sheppard and Carroll, 1980, p. 10).

To sum up, the following is a list of the social consequences of technological progress and specifically of automation and information: replacement of manual tasks by observation activities, with a concomitant change in the work environment; elimination of dangerous and unhealthy tasks; increase in the efficiency, quality and homogeneity of production; decrease in the number of jobs calling for unskilled workers, an increase in skilled employment and a widening of the gap between these two types of employment; decline in the importance of intermediate control (and hence a change in the hierarchical structure of business); possibility of decentralization of production into small units; need for the systematic retraining of all staff; impact on the number of jobs (it has been argued that there will be unemployment in the short term, new jobs in the medium term and finally leisure time in the long term); transfer of new jobs from the secondary to the tertiary sector.

IMPACT OF ECONOMIC DEVELOPMENT ON EDUCATION SYSTEMS

While educational expenditure grew at a very fast pace in the 1950s and 1960s, it stabilized thereafter or continued to grow at a rather sluggish pace and even showed a downward trend in some cases, owing to the economic recession.

Table 23 confirms this observation, in spite of a slight improvement between 1980 and 1982.

This new situation has obliged education systems to make savings and keep their unit costs as low as possible. In some cases alternatives have been sought, such as new sources of educational funding like parents, communities, companies, trade unions, etc.

These financial difficulties have arisen in a new international climate, in which the Third World is receiving less development aid than in the past. Although the Third Development Decade strategy called for aid equivalent to 0.7 per cent of the total GNP of the rich nations, in practice the rich nations have allocated only 0.34 per cent of their GNP for that purpose. We have no precise information as to the significance of such public development aid for education systems in the beneficiary countries. For 1975, the World Bank (1980, p. 73) gives the following information: external aid to education in the developing countries covered only 9 per cent of the total education budget of those countries, a percentage that is unlikely to have changed much in the meantime.[7] It may further be mentioned that the relatively high standard of buildings and materials supplied to developing countries under this kind of aid frequently leads to greater pressures on the current education budget in those countries.

One of the consequences of the current recession has been a worsening of youth unemployment in both developed countries and the Third World. In addition to economic stagnation, this widespread unemployment stems from two aspects of technological progress—increasing automation and the need for different kinds of qualifications. Youth unemployment has created serious doubts among both

TABLE 23   Public expenditure on education as a percentage of GNP

Continents, major regions and groups of countries	1965	1970	1975	1979	1980	1982
World total	4.8	5.4	5.7	5.6	5.7	5.8
Africa	3.5	4.2	4.6	4.6	4.5	4.9
America	5.1	6.3	6.1	6.0	6.3	6.4
Asia	3.5	3.5	4.8	5.0	5.0	5.1
Oceania	3.7	4.4	6.2	5.8	5.9	5.8
Europe (including USSR)	5.1	5.2	5.8	5.5	5.6	5.6
Developed countries	5.1	5.7	6.0	5.9	6.1	6.2
Developing countries	2.9	3.3	3.9	4.0	4.0	4.3

Souce: Unesco, *Unesco Statistical Yearbook 1982*, Paris Unesco, 1982 (data for 1965–79); *Unesco Statistical Yearbook 1984*, Paris, Unesco, 1984 (data for 1980 and 1982).

the young themselves and their parents concerning the relevance and external applicability of formal education. The school as an institution has been called into question. Indeed, some people have recommended replacing the school system by non-formal and even informal types of education and training. Other measures that it has been possible to implement have included the introduction into schools of productive or socially useful work, the gearing of education to employment, particularly at the secondary-school level, the involvement of various institutions in the retraining of young people, the introduction of vocational training programmes after compulsory schooling, etc.

It may be said that, on the whole, education has had great difficulty in keeping pace with changes in the structure of the labour market. Apart from a few exceptions (including India for the training of engineers and doctors), the training of technical and scientific personnel in the developing countries is lagging far behind the growing needs of the secondary sector, while in the highly advanced countries the training requirements of the tertiary and quaternary sectors are still not being met.

Unesco statistics for 1981 show that 21 per cent of secondary-school-level students are engaged in technical studies in the developed regions of the world and only 10.2 per cent in the developing countries.

It should be added that the unduly rapid expansion of the student population in general secondary education in the developing countries, which is comparable to the growth rate in higher education (especially in the non-technical branches) and is mainly due to the lure of a certificate,[8] has obviously failed to provide an adequate solution to the new employment situation, which has led to unemployment among the educated and to its attendant disappointments and psychosocial problems.

The economic crisis has had a beneficial effect, at least in some education systems, since it has increased the interest that began to emerge in the 1950s in a form of education based on the development objective (see Adams, 1977). However, this objective is now defined in new terms and instead of identifying development with growth, people have become aware of the qualitative aspect of development (improvement of the quality of life). Human beings are now placed at the centre of development, and their participation in the process and in its fruits is assigned vital importance. Emphasis is being laid on the holistic and integral character of development and on the notions of independence and participation. Development education has been defined by Pierre Pradervand (1982) as 'a process which, through active participation in all decisions influencing their lives, enables individuals and groups to attain greater, more meaningful autonomy and solidarity'.

In the near future, some of the effects of the economic developments already referred to may be expected to persist, e.g. financial difficulties in education systems, the need for continuing economy of resources, the mobilization of new resources for education (see International Seminar on Financing Educational Development..., 1982, pp. 69–84), the need to promote self-reliance in the developing countries, to adapt the subject-matter and different types of education to changes in the labour market and advances in the secondary and tertiary sectors, to link education more closely to productive work and development, etc.

We may also expect in the years ahead:

- More frequent alternation of study periods and work, in an education process henceforth considered as spanning a whole lifetime (lifelong education).
- More emphasis on the quality and the internal efficiency of education, with the help of modern educational technology and the most advanced learning methods (economies in learning time are necessary in the same way as economies in spending).
- Greater emphasis on self-instruction and on independence and creativity, particularly important qualities for those living and acting in tomorrow's society and economy.
- A tendency in many countries to abandon attaching undue importance to certificates and to use criteria other than educational qualifications in selecting candidates for employment.
- A change in educational priorities in developing countries, with the state assuming responsibility primarily for basic compulsory education and literacy education and delegating at least part of the responsibility for financing secondary and higher education to parents, companies, trade unions, local communities, etc.
- A de-institutionalization of education: in the developed market economies we may also expect in the coming years a renewal of individual or private initiative replacing institutional assistance in the educational field as elsewhere (Naisbitt, 1982). The new communication media (for example the video cassette) will make it possible to teach children in their own homes, as advocated by Toffler.
- A review of school size: there was a tendency in previous decades to increase school size to achieve economies of scale, but this enlargement and the resulting bureaucratization created an impersonal atmosphere (see Husén, 1982) ill-suited to the demands of tomorrow's society. The new media and distance education (by radio, television, correspondence, etc.) make this geographical concentration unnecessary and open up new vistas of individualized education, with curricula adapted to the abilities and aspirations of each individual. For the

THE CHANGING COSTS OF EDUCATION

Unit costs depend on a variety of factors. Changes in unit costs when compared with the efficiency of education systems tell us a great deal about whether the quality of education is improving or deteriorating.

We know that in the last few decades, there has been a steady increase, for several reasons, in the unit costs of education in almost all countries. The increase in costs in the developed countries is due to an improvement in the quality of education, the provision of new facilities,[9] and rises in teachers' salaries (in relation to changes in the index of consumer prices). In the case of the developing countries, apart from the increase in teachers' salaries, mention may be made of the ageing of educational personnel (more people at higher salary levels) and the more rapid increase in the numbers enrolled in secondary and higher education, which are considerably more costly than primary education (the ratio between average unit costs in higher education and primary education is 2 to 1 in the industrialized countries and 9 to 1 in Asia) (see Coombs and Chaudhury, 1981, p. 50).

Table 24, concerning the movement of unit costs at constant prices (1977 dollars) in the developed countries, gives a clear picture of this increase, which necessarily slowed down in the 1980s for the reasons we have already mentioned.

Table 25 sheds a great deal of light on the evolution of public per capita spending on education during the period 1965–82 in different regions of the world.

It will be seen that, except in North America, educational expenditure slowed down sharply or even declined from the beginning of the 1980s.

In the next two decades, we expect serious efforts to be made in the developed countries to reduce or rationalize unit costs in education. In the past, most educational innovations have tended to increase unit costs. The time may have come, as Coombs said, to design and introduce further innovations to improve the internal efficiency of education systems while at the same time reducing per capita student costs.

In the developing countries, where there is obviously more to be done, improving the quality of education implies investing still more for each student. One solution, according to Coombs and Choudhury, would consist in diverting some of the funds for higher education into primary education, where per capita spending is too low. In higher education, on the other hand, considerable economies can still

TABLE 24 Public expenditure on education per capita in Europe and North America (US dollars, 1977 prices)

Country	1965	1971	1977
Austria	86	158	350
Belgium	138	210	530
Bulgaria	33	44	85
Canada	282	529	675
Czechoslovakia	73	89	116
Denmark	226	385	605
France	158	226	415
German Democratic Republic	112	228	231
Federal Republic of Germany	106	203	316
Hungary	59	58	102
Ireland	75	115	183
Italy	105	131	166
Netherlands	180	324	587
Norway	183	305	660
Poland	66	63	86
Portugal	11	22	67
Spain	17	38	67
Sweden	303	512	797
Switzerland	180	247	520
Turkey	18	19	62
USSR	125	146	157
United Kingdom	174	203	266
USA	348	499	557
Yugoslavia	70	54	110

Source: Unesco and United Nations Economic Commission for Europe, *Development of Education in Europe: A Statistical Review*, Paris, April 1980.

TABLE 25 Evolution of per capita spending on education, 1965–82 (US dollars)

	1965	1970	1975	1977	1980	1982
World total	38	57	109	126	183	181
Africa	5	7	18	24	42	39
America	94	151	228	226	381	424
Asia	7	11	33	44	64	67
Europe	61	92	226	261	338	298
Oceania	63	104	331	338	460	490
USSR	67	90	146	155	—[1]	—[1]
Latin America	14	19	44	51	90	96
North America	187	317	480	511	808	918

1. The figures for the USSR for 1980–82 are included in the figures for Europe.
Source: Unesco, *Unesco Statistcal Yearbook 1980*, Paris, Unesco, 1980; *Unesco Statistical Yearbook 1984*, Paris, Unesco, 1984.

be made in the use of facilities, space, the time of teaching staff, etc., to make education at that level more efficient.

Given the economic and financial circumstances in those countries that we described above, greater international co-operation in a spirit of generous fellow-feeling would seem to be essential. In 1977, the world as a whole spent $398,000 million on education (compared with $51,000 million in 1960); the share of the developing countries in total public spending on education was only 8.7 per cent in 1960 and 12.5 per cent in 1977.

Of course, one cannot expect everything to come from outside. The countries in question therefore have three possibilities open to them, according to Eicher (1982):

(a) increasing the funds available for education (a difficult objective, as we have already noted);[10]

(b) mobilizing new human and material resources (in local communities, companies and among those actually involved);

(c) improving the efficiency of the resources used in education (a possibility on which we wish to lay considerable stress).

These countries can also think up viable alternatives to the formal education system, such as the organization of efficient and low-cost non-formal or even informal types of education.

NOTES

1. World output grew by 5 per cent per year on average between 1948 and 1973. During the same period, international trade increased sixfold (*Interfutures*, OECD, 1979).
2. To give an idea of this decline in figures, the world output of raw steel dropped from 709 million tons in 1974 to 644 million in 1982. According to OECD estimates, job losses in the iron and steel industry between 1974 and 1982 came to 29 per cent in the developed countries as a whole, 38 per cent in the United States, 17 per cent in Japan (IFRI, 1984, pp. 128–30).
3. According to preliminary estimates, the ratio of debt servicing to export revenue in Latin America increased from 33 per cent in 1980 to 53 per cent in 1982, while GDP declined by 3.6 per cent in the same period. See the World Bank's *World Development Report Summary* for 1983, p. 3. Debt servicing for the developing countries as a whole amounted to $108,000 million in 1982.
4. According to the *The Global 2000 Report* (United States, 1980–81), there will be a 58 per cent increase in the use of oil between 1975 and 1990. For the same period, the report predicts an average annual increase in total energy consumed of 3.3 per cent for the low-income countries and 4.4 per cent for the high-income countries.
5. Official development assistance from the member countries of OECD's Development Assistance Committee (DAC) has been growing at an average annual rate in real terms of 4 per cent in the last 5 to 10 years, slightly exceeding GNP growth in those countries (OECD, 1983*b*, p. 26).

6. The percentage of the labour force employed in the tertiary sector ranges from 24 per cent in Romania (1977) to 40 and 41 per cent in the USSR and the German Democratic Republic respectively (1979–80).
7. Some figures on the scale of multilateral aid, which is, of course, supplementary to bilateral aid: in 1975, Unesco, the United Nations Development Programme (UNDP) and the World Bank devoted some $2,900 million to improving and developing education systems throughout the world, especially in the less developed countries. Average annual World Bank lending for education and training developed as follows in the period 1970 to 1983 (in millions of dollars) (Phillips, 1977): 1970–74, 169.5; 1975–78, 412; 1979–83 (estimate), 905.
8. See Table 5 and the following more recent table on the periods 1965–70 and 1970–81. Annual average percentage increase in enrolment at different levels of education for the periods 1965–70 and 1970–81:

Region		1st level	2nd level	3rd level
World total (excluding China)	1965–70	3.3	2.6	4.4
	1970–81	2.9	2.6	3.1
Developed countries	1965–70	0.4	2.3	7.2
	1970–81	−0.4	0.6	3.3
Developing countries	1965–70	4.0	8.0	8.9
	1970–81	4.0	6.0	8.4

Source: Unesco, *Unesco Statistical Yearbook 1983*, Paris, Unesco, 1983.

9. On the impact of the use of new educational technologies on costs, researchers find that costs per student are not reduced by these new technologies, apart from very exceptional cases (Eicher et al., 1984).
10. According to Coombs and his assistants, who have made estimates of future needs in respect of the expansion of education systems, a sizeable increase in financial, human and material resources will be essential in the 1980s and 1990s. This increase can only be achieved by reducing military spending, which is less necessary for human survival than any other form of expenditure.

3
Socio-political changes

The maintenance of the relative strengths of the two superpowers and the gradual emergence of a multipolar political world, with the rise of new economic or political powers such as Japan and China, are two major transformations of the last quarter of a century. The Third World, particularly the Group of 77, and the Movement of Non-Aligned Countries now represent new forces to be reckoned with in the international arena.

The world powers are constantly building up their military forces. 'Armaments absorb fabulous sums. In 1968 they took $154 billion and in 1975 $300 billion, or 6 to 7 per cent of world GNP, ten times as much as aid to the underdeveloped countries.' (Trotignon, 1978, p. 192.) Present-day military spending has topped the $800 billion mark and for 1985, expenditure of the order of $1,000 billion was anticipated. Increasing quantities of arms are being sold abroad and this has become a particularly thriving business[1] grossing $300 million in 1952, $18 billion in 1974 and $20 billion in 1981. The poor countries spent over $28 billion on arms in 1970, as against $25 billion for health and education (Trotignon, 1978, p. 192). The growing militarization of the world, instead of guaranteeing permanent security, makes war a constant threat.

The 1960s and 1970s saw another major political development, namely the continuity of the nationalist and independence movements in much of the Third World. Once countries had achieved their political independence, they strove hard to free themselves from the economic and cultural domination of the West as well. There was talk everywhere of a return to sources and of the rehabilitation of cultural identity. Everywhere, too, there was a questioning of imported development models, and the search went ahead for more suitable models meeting the specific needs of each society (process of endogenous, self-directed and self-reliant development in which the resources of the country itself are mobilized for the particular objectives of the society in question). It has to be acknowledged, however, that the achievement of economic and cultural independence has not always lived up to hopes and plans.

Another noteworthy political movement gathering strength has been the constitution of regional political and economic formations bringing together countries having shared interests and wishing to co-operate more effectively. Two eloquent examples in Europe are the European Parliament and the European Economic Community (EEC). Regional or subregional systems or institutions of major importance can be found in every continent, however. To take just the African continent, we may mention the East African Community (EAC), the Central African Customs and Economic Union (CACEU), the West African Economic Community (WAEC), the African Development Bank (ADB) and the OAU.

Within societies during that period, on the other hand, a trend was observable towards fragmentation. Societies split up into ethnic, religious, linguistic and other groupings, each of which demanded greater freedom of action. States have adopted two radically different attitudes to such fragmentation. Some have made political structures more flexible and have decentralized decision-making power, giving ample scope to local and regional initiative. Other governments with centralist tendencies, however, have tightened their grip and made structures even more rigid.

Three major social movements in the last quarter of a century should be recalled: (a) the youth movements in the years 1968-70, calling for more freedom, equality and participation; (b) the women's liberation movements and speeding up of the access of women to equal rights in all areas, landmarks being the 1975 World Conference of the International Women's Year, held in Mexico City, and the proclamation of the United Nations Decade for Women (1975-85);[2] (c) the movements of political origin launched first in the United States and then in other Western countries for the defence of fundamental human rights and freedoms. Many associations were formed to uncover and condemn flagrant violations of these rights and freedoms in various countries.

The financial and social difficulties of the recession affected nearly all countries and dealt a considerable blow at the notion of the Welfare State in the industrialized countries. Its theory was also savaged by the 'neo-liberals and new economists', as shown in particular by Ignacy Sachs (1982). A state management crisis has become apparent in many countries. As Bell (1978) said, governments have become too big to deal with small problems and too small to tackle big problems. The growing complexity of societies and of social and economic problems is accentuating the relative weakness of central governments in this situation. It should nevertheless be noted that this inadequacy has not prevented the state, in more than one democratic country, from further extending its areas of intervention. In the Third World countries, the idea of a state making all social services available to the individual has always exerted an undeniable attraction. They have very often found it difficult, however, financially and administratively, to afford all citizens such protection. The judgement of Ignacy Sachs applies to some cases:

A mechanical imitation of welfare state institutions in Third World countries can only lead, at best, to the establishment of a second privileged group, since such protection would be utterly unable to provide for the majority of inhabitants of rural areas and many city-dwellers who are locked into the informal sector [Sachs, 1982, p. 144].

On foreseeable social and political developments in the world in the years ahead, official material does not abound. In France, however, an interesting paper produced by the Commissariat Général au Plan (France, 1980) mentions a number of trends most likely to continue in the near future. We reproduce this forecast below and shall add our own comments. Here are what are thought to be some probable developments:

(a) Internal and international threats will hang over the Western democracies, whose vulnerability will be heightened by foreseeable social and economic tensions.

(b) These tensions will mean that persisting centralization of power and even militarization of regimes in other regions cannot be ruled out.

(c) There will be major risks of conflict between various states and within those states. A prime factor in tension between states could be competition for resources, particularly energy (oil). Industrial and technological rivalry and the scramble for markets will be another possible source of conflict.

(d) The two superpowers will gradually lose their hold on the international environment. Nationalistic reactions to the globalization process and a growing desire, in the non-Western part of the world, to develop a distinctive cultural identity to counter the still considerable lure of Western society and civilization, coupled with a vastly increased volume of conventional and nuclear weapons and a consequently broader spread of power throughout the world, will sorely test international organizations which exist precisely to promote concerted action and co-operation between states (they will continue to be instruments of dialogue rather than means of action (p. 57)).

(e) The growing number of conflicts and tensions will not prevent new political coalitions from emerging and gaining ground in the future.

(f) The Third World has for a century had a shared past, but a vigorous process of differentiation is already under way that offers different prospects to different nations (countries with energy resources or other raw materials will be clearly marked off from countries lacking in this respect). Part of the Third World (e.g. Africa) will undergo a great deal of social and political instability induced both by domestic tensions and by external influences. The present political cohesion of the Third World will be placed under great strain by these tensions and by growing divergences of interests resulting from this differentiation.

(g) Europe, where community solidarity offered the prospect of major world power status, will probably suffer from a great deal of internal dissension.

Many of these forecasts are shared by other researchers. One book already mentioned, *Europe 2000* (Hall, 1977), foresees three socio-political movements in the next two decades: (a) a trend towards the polarization of Western societies; (b) intensified nationalist movements in the Third World; and (c) heightened competition and conflict worldwide over raw materials, particularly energy. The forecasts of Heilborner (1974) are somewhat grim, pointing to the likelihood of countries moving towards totalitarianism or anarchy: 'As the history of old and modern democracies shows, political pressure in time of war, civil unrest or general anxiety tends towards authority and never in the opposite direction.' Unlike Heilborner, Toffler remains optimistic. He sees a trend, in the years ahead, towards semi-direct democracy, towards a delegating of decision-making power and towards power for minorities.

The reality of tomorrow may, in our view, lie between these two extremes. The threats hanging over liberal democracy are real and powerful, but demands for personal autonomy and for the autonomy of hitherto underprivileged groups are no less real and powerful.

In addition to the ominous trends described above, mention must be made of the possibility of some promising developments whose consequences it will only be possible to gauge at some time in the future. These include:

(a) efforts to reform government institutions, whose powers grew considerably during the predominance of the Welfare State and which, nowadays, are being widely challenged;

(b) new opportunities for extending democratic models of the organization of public affairs throughout the world;

(c) continued interest in international organizations despite often unexpected returns to bilateral arrangements, and the quest, through successive approximations, for a new world order no longer confined to the economic field or technology (primarily communication) but also extending to political, cultural and human considerations.

A word of explanation on each of these promising developments is essential.

In the first case, government reform is prompted in part by the fear that an omnipresent, omniscient and all-powerful state may emerge and take root which, like a 'Big Brother' or a 'Godfather', would use the modern resources at its disposal to control the slightest act, word or thought of the population. There has accordingly been no lack of moves to set limits on government intervention in people's personal lives and, in particular, on the computer storage of details about citizens, which would jeopardize individual freedom.

Among the steps proposed to reduce the presence and intervention of the state are many projects such as the privatization of specific social services, decentralization, promotion of participation and of direct democracy, reduced spending power for the state, the restriction of state monopolies, the revival of local communities and of voluntary associations, the formation of committees for the defence of human rights, environmental protection, demilitarization and the like, an increased role for independent associations in the life of communities (independent trade unions, churches, brotherhoods, etc.).

Second, democracy is not a flawless form of government. It is less imperfect, however, than the other known forms of government. According to Kahn and his colleagues (Kahn et al., 1978), if mankind experiences a century of relative peace without major economic crisis or inflation, the number of democratic governments will probably increase, although there can be no certainty about this. One may hope, along with some authors like Toffler, that more countries will adopt this form of government as people become more keenly aware of their rights.

Third, where reorganization of the international order is concerned, it is enough to glance at the impressive quantity of material devoted to the New International Economic Order, the New World Information Order and reform of the United Nations to realize the growing importance of this area of debate and action. The process of globalization, which is well under way in the material and economic fields, is now extending to new areas, including politics. We shall just mention, among all the studies on ordering the affairs of the world, those published by the Institute for World Order (Falk, 1975; Kothari, 1975; Mendlovitz, 1975).

In terms of regional-level political and economic union, Europe is now displaying greater vitality than in the past and may quite well resume its prominent place in the concert of nations *vis-à-vis* the two superpowers of the Pacific shores, namely the United States and Japan. Globalism might be attained after a preliminary phase of regionalism, as demonstrated on a smaller scale by the experience of countries with a federal system (United States, Switzerland, etc.).

The weakening of the national state,[3] now incapable of overcoming many problems (ensuring peace, security, prosperity, etc., and meeting many other needs of its citizens), undoubtedly makes a necessity of close collaboration between such states.

Some authors, in realistic vein, propose reforms and improvements of greater or lesser substance to the international organizations as they exist today. A good many believe in the need for greater integration of the United Nations system as a whole (Lester Pearson said in his day that the effectiveness of the United Nations was dangerously impaired by dissipation of effort due to the proliferation and specialization of its agencies). Many have assigned new roles to the United Nations so that it can cope with the new problems confronting the world, e.g. shortage of food, energy and natural resources management, environment and ecology, disarmament, and so on. Many proposals have been put forward to make the system more effective and adapt it to rapidly changing needs (see *inter alia* the 1982 report of the United Nations Secretary-General on the work of the organization.

Reports drawn up outside the United Nations system, like the Brandt Commission's *North–South* report (Independent Commission . . ., 1980, particularly Chapter 16) also contain proposals for reform intended to promote and strengthen international co-operation in economic and social development. The Brandt Commission proposed the establishment of a new financial institution to facilitate large-scale transfers of resources. It also proposed other reforms in this same area of international funding.

With regard to the probable development of political systems in the Third World, few forecasts have so far been advanced other than a move towards greater autonomy *vis-à-vis* the outside world and greater democracy at home. The prominence and role of the Third World in the New International Economic Order will undoubtedly increase in the future (see Lesourne, 1981, Ch. II).

The development of interdependence with the Third World has been an essential feature of international policies since the end of the colonial period to the present day. The Third World is becoming aware of its own existence. Whether they are oil-producing countries acquiring the political capacity to constitute a cartel, countries in the course of industrialization wishing to secure access to the markets of the developed countries, or poor countries pressing their claims on the grounds of poverty, all are demanding a new international economic order (Lesourne, 1981, p. 58).

Solidarity within the Third World is undoubtedly one of the keys to its future power in regard to the other four components of the new multipolar world: the United States, the USSR, Japan and the EEC. However, there are a great many signs pointing to a similarity of problems and yet to a growing divergence of interests and positions between Third World countries. Much will therefore depend on how the countries of the South see the merits of their economic and political ties.

WHAT TYPE OF SOCIETY FOR TOMORROW?

The answer to this question obviously cannot be the same for the developed and the developing countries. Answers will also differ according to whether 'liberal' or 'collectivist' political systems are involved.

The society of tomorrow has been described, in the case of the developed countries, as a technological society, an affluent society, a service society (i.e. one with a predominant tertiary sector), a computerized or telematic or cybernetic society, and so on. Each of these tags is part of the picture but only a part, for we have every reason to suppose the following:

- Non-egalitarian societies will have a great deal of difficulty between now and the end of the century, for all the good intentions of their leaders, in ridding themselves of the pockets of poverty which still exist within affluent communities.
- Affluence and high consumption for everyone are certainly not for tomorrow, particularly with the present recession and the gradually shorter supply of non-renewable resources like oil. Hence we can see why recent authors have, since the early 1970s, been more insistent on the notion of a society of shortage (Ophuls, 1976) and of recycling (Seaborg and Corliss, 1971) than on the prospects of mass consumption or indeed wastage.
- The progress and spread of scientific knowledge have not prevented other types of knowledge from also laying claim to recognition (see Gurvitch, 1958, pp. 103–36). Apart from the growing prominence of political and social knowledge in everyone's lives, there has been a noteworthy revival of religious thinking and a keen interest in esoteric knowledge. The final stage of society will probably not be the positivist era for which Auguste Comte hoped. An author such as Charles Davy (1961) even thinks that present-day society, with its pronounced scientific bias, will move towards a new culture that is both religious and artistic in tendency but which would neverthe-

less incorporate the best of scientific civilization (i.e. logical thought, respect for fact, the test of experience, etc.).

● If we take the terms 'post-industrial' and 'neo-industrial' used by some authors to describe future society, we can see that they, too, lay themselves open to some criticism. The prefix 'post' could be misleading in suggesting that the industries of the Second Industrial Revolution will have no place in the society of tomorrow, which is obviously not so. It is by no means unlikely that various considerations, such as ecological requirements, will prompt researchers and policy-makers in the developed countries to think at times in terms not of high technology but of 'appropriate technology', at least for particular sectors. Furthermore, many relatively advanced societies will continue their industrialization effort in the next few decades, which will mean that relatively few societies will really find the new age within their reach.

To sum up, it seems to us to be unrealistic to speak of future society in such general terms. We therefore prefer to throw light on the forces at work rather than on their consequences. Hence we shall lay greater emphasis on the broad trends, factors with clear future implications, conflicts between the forces of change and the forces of stability, and so forth.

When one speaks about 'broad trends', one usually has in mind the foreseeable development of specific aspects of society, and primarily demography and ecology (in sociological terms: social morphology). These aspects are in fact the most 'apparent' and lend themselves more readily to measurement and quantification. Other aspects, however, can only be assessed qualitatively (e.g. the social psyche and collective attitudes) and any conjecture about how they will develop is particularly difficult. With regard to life and relations in society, forecasting is less hazardous in the case of a quantifiable process like urban development. On the other hand, the forecasting of probable changes in social behaviour patterns gives rise to a great deal of controversy.

For the purposes of this study, we shall briefly examine the relationship between the individual and society, the social structures or relations between various groups or classes of society, institutions and, finally, social services, among which health and social protection usually predominate, and we shall endeavour to summarize the major trends which futurologists see as most likely to persist.

First, with regard to the relationship between the individual and society, two trends have been observed in recent years, particularly in the developed countries, viz. a demand for freedom and a need for roots. David Riesman (1973), speaking of the changing American character, which may be paralleled elsewhere, observes a freeing of the individual from the restrictions placed on him by tradition and his fellow citizens, and the achievement of what he calls 'inner-direction', namely the submission of the individual to his own conscience. The developing countries, too, are increasingly aspiring to democratization, equal opportunities and genuine participation in the taking of important decisions (see United Nations, 1983, Ch. II). This quest for personal autonomy will, according to many authors, be counterbalanced by another trend, namely a return to small groups, to local communities and to those direct and amicable relations that sociologists call 'face-to-face', which contrast sharply with the impersonal relations of life in the big cities.

Next, as regards relations between groups and the social structure, Peter Hall (Hall, 1977) foresees a move towards 'polarization' in Western societies as a result of the marginalization of particular groups such as immigrant workers and young unemployed graduates. According to that study, there will also be the possibility of revolt by marginal groups against the established majority. According to Toffler (1981), the happy outcome of such social fragmentation is beyond doubt, with an irresistible rise of minorities and their accession to power (which could happen in the Western democracies to a greater extent than elsewhere). The same author speaks of a general trend towards the delegation of power at the appropriate level and towards decentralization in the same Western societies. The complexity of societies and social situations is increasing and it has to be acknowledged that governments will find it increasingly hard to control them. Delegation of power and decentralization will therefore become a necessity, even if in the short term some socio-political systems tend to rigidify.[4]

Finally, where social institutions, and the family in particular, are concerned, studies on recent and possible future developments are quite plentiful.

Regarding the family, the following main trends have been recorded in recent decades: drop in family size, calculated according to the number of persons per household;[5] transfer of a considerable part of the traditional functions of the family to other institutions (this is particularly so in the industrialized countries); profound change in relations within the family (they are now based more on mutual respect and co-operation than on domination); growing instability of the family in the developed countries, reflected by the increased number of divorces (see United Nations, 1983, Table 4, p. 31); challenge to marriage as the basis of the conjugal family by the extension of cohabitation and concubinage (United Nations, 1982);[6] frequency of illegitimate births.

Opinions differ widely about the future of the family in Western societies and range from the idea of an end to the nuclear conjugal family to that of the start of an era of family consolidation in which the ample free time of parents and the use of very advanced technologies such as minicomputers would enable the family to retrieve some of its functions, such as that of educating (Toffler foresees a period in which children would learn at home and play at school, which is more or less the reverse of the present situation).

What is beyond doubt and can be regarded as a broad trend affecting the family of today and tomorrow is the attraction that the labour market exerts on women, particularly those with a certain standard of education. The United Nations *Concise Report on the World Population Situation in 1977* testifies to such a trend since the worldwide proportion of women in the working population rose from 31.3 per cent in 1950 to 34.9 per cent in 1975.[7] Increased pressure by women on the job market will have far-reaching effects both on unemployment, also expected to rise in the years ahead, and on families. Women who work outside the home accelerate and intensify their emancipation, and this modifies both roles and relations within the family. These changes cannot fail to influence the socialization of the children, adding thereby to the responsibilities of the education system faced with a task not completed by the family (the education system should therefore prepare both boys and girls for a redistribution of tasks between the sexes in the family and in future society). On the other hand, the impact of these changes is lessened by the high proportion of part-time jobs in women's work and the trend towards more such jobs, particularly in the developed countries (see ILO, 1984, Table 2.7, p. 55).

Where social services are concerned, the post-war period saw the gradual introduction of social security systems in the developed countries and an assertion of the crucial role of the Welfare State in this area. Table 26 clearly shows that the economic crisis of 1973 did not halt increased spending on social security, which continued at least until the early 1980s even though the growth rate dipped after 1975. A development of this kind was bound to bring more state involvement in people's daily lives, an involvement to which there has been, since the early 1980s, particularly in the United States, a great deal of reaction and opposition (see Marien, 1976, Ch. 12).

The example of the Welfare State has certainly exerted a powerful influence on people and leaders in the Third World. It would even be fair to say that one of the best contributions of Western civilization to the Third World countries has been the introduction of modern medicine and of various forms of social security. The gap between developed and developing countries nevertheless remains large, despite progress by the developing countries in the last twenty years or so.

TABLE 26 Social security spending in the EEC (as a percentage of GDP)

	1970	1975	1980
Netherlands	20.8	28.1	30.7
Federal Republic of Germany	21.4	27.8	28.3
Belgium	18.5	24.5	27.7
Denmark	19.6	24.5	27.7
Luxembourg	16.4	22.4	26.5
France	19.2	22.9	25.8
Italy	18.4	22.6	22.8
Ireland	13.2	19.4	22.0
United Kingdom	15.9	19.5	21.4

Source: IFRI, Ramses 83/84..., p. 165, Paris Economica/La Documentation Française 1984.

According to the *United Nations Report on the World Social Situation in 1983*, there were, at the end of the 1970s, some 3 million doctors in the world—2 million in the developed countries, with 190 per 100,000 inhabitants, and 1 million in the developing countries, making 33 per 100,000 inhabitants. For all categories of medical personnel, the approximate density per 100,000 inhabitants was 1,000 in the developed countries and 200 in the developing countries (United Nations, 1983, p. 89).

The number of hospital beds also differs widely between the two types of country. The developed countries had 87 and 95 beds per 10,000 inhabitants in 1960 and 1975 respectively whereas the corresponding figures for the developing countries were only 11 and 14 (United Nations, 1983, p. 91).

The differences in terms of expenditure on health (both capital and operating expenditure) among various regions are even greater. Expenditure per inhabitant is 80 times higher in the developed countries than in the least developed countries, and 25 times greater than in the middle-income developing countries (United Nations, 1983, p. 92).

What is likely to happen in the years ahead? It is a fact that in many developed countries the number of doctors trained and undergoing training exceeds society's needs and that medical schools are often starting to limit their intakes. The situation is obviously quite different in most developing countries, where new solutions are applied, more suited to local conditions. Such solutions, which stand a good chance of being adopted in the future, include:

1. Promotion of the training of 'health workers', who cost less than doctors and are sometimes more effective where raising the standard of public health is concerned.

2. The development of hygiene and disease prevention, particularly with a view to making the physical environment more healthy, providing drinking water, improving nutrition and increasing resistance to disease by vaccination or other means. Prominent among these measures is health education in schools.[8]

3. Increasing recourse to technical assistance for the training of doctors abroad.

4. The provision of crash courses for men and women who, while not academically qualified, in practice engage in a medical-type occupation (healers, medicine-men, midwives or others patronized by part of the population, particularly in rural areas).

5. Optimum use of hospital beds by various means, such as more effective and consequently shorter treatment; the establishment of dispensaries in rural centres and regular visits to neighbouring villages by mobile teams from such centres; and, finally, improved conditions for medical care in patients' homes.

6. Intensified international food aid for children in the Third World (malnutrition and undernutrition, singly or jointly, are responsible for between a third and a half of deaths of sick children under 5 years old, according to a United Nations estimate).

In short, it seems that the years 1980–2000, both in the developed countries and in the Third World, will be marked by better rather than more medical and health services. An effort will be made to ensure better use of existing medical and health resources and to distribute them more equitably within each country rather than to bring about a rapid increase in spending on this sector. It should not be forgotten that, as reflected in the *United Nations Report on the World Social Situation in 1983* (pp. 91–3), public and private spending in this area is already substantial.

With regard to social security, Table 72 shows the considerable progress made.

TABLE 27 Number of countries with some type of social security (cumulative totals)

Year	Old age, invalidity, death	Sickness, maternity	Work injury	Unemployment	Family allowance
1940	38	34	87	22	8
1950	54	52	111	27	34
1960	82	86	120	35	63
1970	110	104	127	38	65
1979	124	114	131	43	69

Source: United Nations, *United Nations Report on the World Social Situation in 1983*, pp. 40–1, New York, United Nations, 1983.

TABLE 28 Expenditure on social security benefits as a percentage of GDP

Economy	1970	1975	1977
Developed market	11.9	15.6	16.6
Centrally planned	12.8	14.4	14.9
Developing	3.5	3.5	3.8

Source: ILO, *The Cost of Social Security*, Geneva, ILO, 1981.

Without going into the intricacies of the present situation, it is relevant to recall the difficulty experienced, even in the developed countries, in extending and funding insurance schemes. Figures for spending on social benefits as a percentage of GDP make it clear that the increase between 1970 and 1975 was much faster than thereafter in the developed world.

We can safely say that in the period 1980–2000, if the recession continues for a number of years yet as many economists predict, governments will tend to reconsider their social spending. New funding sources will be sought at the same time as efforts are made to economize on resources already allocated.

In addition, social security systems will, in the years ahead, be contending with a number of problems such as that of the equitable distribution of services, which is still a long way from being achieved (distribution between men and women, between rural and urban populations, between public sector wage-earners and self-employed workers, etc.) and the share to be borne by individuals in welfare spending by states.

EFFECTS OF SOCIAL AND POLITICAL CHANGES ON EDUCATION

Education has been one of the areas where equal opportunities have been fought for. While the objective has as yet only been attained in part, as many critics have shown, progress has nevertheless not been insignificant.[9] A Unesco survey (Kluchnikov, 1980) points out that at the end of the 1970s, equality of access to education was regarded as an integral part of the policy for social equality and constituted one of the major objectives of Member States, which is confirmed by the documents of the regional conferences of ministers of education and those responsible for economic planning.[10] For example, one of the consequences of the gradual admission of women to equal rights has been the widespread access of girls to education and their increased share in total enrolment, as shown in Table 29.

Socio-political changes

TABLE 29   Female enrolment at the various levels of education as a percentage of total enrolment

Region	Year	1st level	2nd level	3rd level
Developed countries	1965	49	50	38
	1981	49	51	48
Developing countries	1965	41	32	27
	1981	43	39	35

Source: Unesco, *Unesco Statistical Yearbook 1983*, Paris, Unesco, 1983.

As we can see, there is virtually no longer any discrimination in this respect in the developed countries at any level of education, while in the developing countries, despite undeniable progress, much remains to be done.

Table 30 compares the growth rate of overall enrolment in education and that of female enrolment at each level in the developing countries.

In other words, the pace of increase in female enrolment has in all cases exceeded the overall growth rate, and this may be regarded as auguring well for the future.

Furthermore, the entry of women into all branches of activity—including those previously kept for men—has made it necessary to overhaul the curricula in girls' schools; and the proportion of girls and women attending technical and vocational schools will certainly continue to rise.[11]

Changes affecting the family as an institution, owing in particular to the access of women to education and the job market, have prompted the recent expansion of pre-school education.

The annual increase in enrolment at the pre-school level was therefore of the order of 6.3 per cent for the developed regions between 1965 and 1970 and 3 per cent between 1970 and 1980, while the growth in enrolment in the Third World during those periods was 7.4 and 11.7 per cent respectively. (More recent figures indicate a growth rate for this type of education in the period 1975–82 of 4.6 per cent in the developing countries—see *Unesco Statistical Yearbook*

TABLE 30   Enrolment in education: overall growth rates and female enrolment growth rates in the developing countries

| | Rate of growth of male and female enrolment |||| Rate of growth of female enrolment ||||
Period	Total	1st level	2nd level	3rd level	Total	1st level	2nd level	3rd level
1965–70	4.9	4.0	8.0	8.9	5.5	4.6	9.8	10.4
1970–81	4.6	4.0	6.0	8.4	5.1	4.4	7.1	10.3

TABLE 31. Enrolment figures (in thousands) at the level of education preceding the first level (excluding China)

Region	Year			
	1965	1975	1980	1982
World	20 543	36 086	44 219	48 183
Developed countries	17 827	29 998	32 554	33 388
Developing countries	2 716	6 088	11 665	14 795

Source: Unesco, *Unesco Statistical Yearbook, 1982*, Paris, Unesco, 1982 (data for 1965, 1975 and 1980); *Unesco Statistical Yearbook 1984*, Paris, Unesco, 1984 (data for 1982).

1984.) Immense scope still exists for expanding this education in the Third World.

More generally speaking, changes in the family as an institution suggest that the education system is going to have to play a more important part in the socialization of children and the transmission of cultural norms and values to the young. Conversely, however, the education system will itself be influenced by the profound change in relations within the family, which will bring about a comparable change in relations within the system between teachers and those taught. The relationship based on authority and compliance seems to be giving way to new links of reciprocity in which the teacher acts as an adviser rather than as an authoritarian superior.

Before turning to other effects of social and political change on education, we should nevertheless note that the democratization process and equality of opportunity are liable to be hampered in the same way as the development of other social services such as health and social security. We have already spoken of the reduction in the rate of increase in enrolment during the 1970s and early 1980s in relation to the two previous decades. On this point, too, the change in education has been practically the same as the change in the other two social services in question. The recession and its adverse effects, such as unemployment, cuts in national budgets and so on, have led education systems and the other social services towards new policies involving a quest for the optimum use of resources, a qualitative improvement of the services offered, more equitable distribution of services and, where necessary, more stringent selection of beneficiaries.

Some of these policies may conflict with others, however. For example, the requirement of equality (equality of access and chances of success) often runs counter to the quality consideration, as shown by Husén (1982). Furthermore, an egalitarian policy is not always in keeping with the trend towards 'meritocracy' which, according to the same author, is very likely to intensify in the future.

The education system has for some time been subjected to strong pressures to be more in touch with the real world. In the real world, one finds conflicts and the stockpiling of weapons, all the problems caused by the widening gap between industrialized and developing countries, persistent political and economic domination despite the liberation of former colonies, the still frequent violation of fundamental human rights, and the scramble for world markets.

Faced with such a situation, many educators and sociologists have, like Paulo Freire and Ivan Illich, recommended an education that liberates in every respect. Others, less radically, have advocated an overhaul of curricula with more emphasis on the notion of interdependence and co-operation between all nations.

Many countries have modified or expanded their civics syllabus to include an introduction to the major social, economic and political issues of the day, presented from a new angle, and there can be no doubt that the idea of education for peace, international understanding and disarmament has made headway, as reflected in the *Final Report* of the Intergovernmental Conference held by Unesco in 1983 on this topic (see Haavelsrud, 1976; Rana, 1981; Thee, 1981; Unesco Institute of Education, 1983). While globalization may now be regarded 'as the pivot around which a changing world is moving' (France, 1980, p. 59), it has to be recognized that education must prepare people for it, involving as it does the interdependence of peoples and nations. However, while the education system must be more in touch with actual social, political, economic and community situations, society must be more sympathetic to young people and adapt itself more to their wishes and their need for autonomy, authenticity, participation, and justice (Coleman et al., 1974). Kincaid is right in thinking that the young should be offered new goals and new 'myths' that are quite at variance with those underlying present behaviour patterns and practices. This would involve giving people precedence over objects, opting for quality rather than quantity, preferring co-operation to competition, setting greater store by wholeness than by specialization, and so on (Kierstead et al., 1979). In other words, we need a society that is more humane, more co-operative and more considerate of individual creativity and self-fulfilment so that the young feel at ease in it and work with a will to consolidate it.

THE DEVELOPMENT OF EDUCATION AS AN INDEPENDENT VARIABLE

We have so far taken education to be a dependent variable. Since education is a social service and since we are dealing with foreseeable changes in social services, some thought could also appropriately go to the foreseeable development of education as an independent variable. Here are the forecasts offered by Harman concerning the developed countries, which, it is true, are often taken as an example for the rest of the world. In studying many of the prospects for education, Harman identified thirteen trends which in his view will materialize in practice with varying degrees of fullness, or will be subject to variation, according to whether we move towards a society centred on the human person, or towards a post-industrial society (third-phase industries) or towards a chaotic period (period of violence followed by a military-type regime).

Here are the thirteen trends enumerated by Harman (OECD/CERI, 1972):

1. Growing proportion of the population concerned by education and increasing share of national income devoted to it (this of course does not concern public funds alone or just expenditure on formal education).

2. New awareness of the role of education as a contribution to the achievement of social goals and to the easing of manifest social problems.

3. Growing integration of education and the other social institutions with which it has functional relations.

4. Extension of the period of education both in early childhood and in adulthood, in the form of post-secondary education, refresher training, lifelong education, schooling for parents, family education, and so on.

5. Tendency of education to move into industry, the place of residence and the home.

6. Tendency of education and work to cease to be sequential and become simultaneous as we enter the learning society.

7. Discarding of traditional teaching methods.

8. Reduction of competition through tailor-made curricula.

9. Broader distribution of educational costs on a national basis.

10. Extension of participatory and supervisory powers to new groups such as teachers, pupils and minorities.

11. Obliteration of the distinction between general and vocational education to the point perhaps of eliminating from primary and secondary schools any narrowly utilitarian training.[12]

12. Increased differentiation in the roles of those responsible for facilitating learning: educational assistants, instructors, teachers and the like.

13. Abandoning of authoritarian attitudes and a move towards an atmosphere of shared learning, mutual respect between teachers and those taught, and de-professionalization.

Most of these prophecies have been confirmed by other forecasters in the field of education. They nevertheless call for a few comments. On item 1, when it comes to foreseeing the proportion of income devoted to education, views have been less optimistic since 1973 (see Coombs, 1981).

With regard to item 4, it needs pointing out that the raising of the school-leaving age is no bar to alternation between school and work for lifelong education purposes.

As regards items 7 and 13, less optimistic forecasts have also been made. For example, Hummel (1977) fears the possibility of a return to more authoritarian teaching and a more rigid educational framework in response to the general instability and insecurity of the years ahead.

On item 8, it must be observed that modern technological progress (video cassettes, microcomputers, etc.) could help us to draw closer to the goal of individualized teaching and learning and self-learning or self-training (see Schwartz, 1973, Ch. 7).

All these trends are as yet insufficiently reflected in practical achievement. Some are more in the nature of promises for the future, particularly where the individualization of education is concerned. In this connection, mention should be made of the work carried out in a number of Japanese laboratory schools to organize early learning for particularly gifted children and stimulate the raising of their IQs by the most suitable means. It is to be hoped that the merits of making full use of intellectual ability will be seen more clearly in the decades ahead.

The outlook for the developing countries for the year 2000 is reflected to some extent in the hopes expressed by their educational leaders at many regional and international conferences. Shiva Lingappa (1979) picks out five objectives for the development of education systems in those countries:

1. Democratization of education.
2. Promotion of national cultural identity and socio-economic modernization.
3. Integration of schooling into the life of the community.
4. Establishment of close links between education and employment.
5. Establishment of close relations between education and development.

The achievement of these aims of education (regarded as an independent variable) requires a favourable social and societal climate that the countries in question would be well advised to foster, aiming for political democracy, a serious development effort and the promotion and renewal of culture.

Socio-political changes

NOTES

1. The major arms exporters are the United States, the Soviet Union, France and the United Kingdom. They alone account for over four-fifths of the international arms supply. In 1974, the individual share of those countries in international arms dealing was 41 per cent for the United States, 25 per cent for the USSR, 19 per cent for France and 10 per cent for the United Kingdom. On arms sales, from 1960 to 1980 the value of weapons sold to the Third World nations increased fivefold. By the early 1980s it had attained the figure of $100,000 million a year, more than ten times the aid granted by the industrial nations to the developing countries (Kastler, 1983). Since 1977 some countries have been spending six times more on arms than they invest in public health and twice what they spend on education (Bonnefous, 1982).
2. Noteworthy also of course were the two subsequent world conferences on the Decade for Women, held in Copenhagen in 1980 and Nairobi in 1985.
3. Robert Nisbet seems to be right when he says that nowadays the West is on the threshold of a new Reformation. While in the sixteenth-century Reformation the established Church bore the criticisms and protests that were levelled, it is now the turn of the state. We may accordingly be inclined to think that there is a need for a Copernican revolution making the interests of humanity as a whole the prime consideration.
4. Although George Orwell described the individual of 1984 as totally crushed by mammoth omnipresent institutions regulating every detail of his life, one should not forget that other thinkers like John Naisbitt see the future as the field of action and revenge of the individual: 'Individual initiative and intelligence are preparing to take over the business bungled by the large organizations, which after some decades of domination are beginning to show cracks.'
5. The average number of persons per household in developed and developing countries were, respectively, 3.5 and 5.2 in 1965 and 3.1 and 5.0 in 1980.
6. It has been observed that in a country like Sweden, the proportion of lawfully married women aged 20 to 24 years is about 21.5 per cent while, also in Sweden, unmarried women cohabiting represent 28.6 per cent in that age-group.
7. The following table shows that between 1950 and 1975, the proportion of women in the working population increased nearly twice as fast in the developing countries as in the developed countries.

	1950	1975
More developed countries	36.7	39.7
Less developed countries	28.2	32.7

Source: ILO, *Labour Force Estimates and Projections 1950–2000*, Geneva, ILO, 1977. ILO's unpublished figures for 1980 for these two broad regions are respectively 41.8 and 34.9 per cent.

8. The International Development Strategy for the Third United Nations Development Decade, adopted for the 1980s, contains a whole paragraph on health objectives during the decade. Here is the text, which bears out our forecast of major trends:

> The attainment by the year 2000 of a level of health that will permit all peoples of the world to lead a socially and economically productive life is an important objective of the international community. Primary health care is a key measure for the attainment of this

objective. All countries will broaden the access of the poorest groups in their populations to health facilities and, with the assistance of the international community, will ensure immunization against major infectious diseases for all children as early as possible during the Decade. Safe water and adequate sanitary facilities should also be made available to all in rural and urban areas by 1990. The reduction of mortality rates will be a major objective. In the poorest countries, infant mortality should be reduced to less than 120 per 1,000 live births. Life expectancy in all countries should reach 60 years as a minimum, and infant mortality rates should reach 50 per 1,000 live births, as a maximum, by the year 2000. Particular efforts should be made to integrate the disabled in the development process. Effective measures of prevention and rehabilitation are therefore essential [United Nations, General Assembly 1981, p. 110].

It should also be recalled that in 1979, the World Health Organization launched its *Global Strategy for Health for All by the Year 2000*, which outlines a desirable worldwide health policy for the next two decades (WHO, 1981).

9. For criticism by the radical school, see the writings of Gentis, Bowls, Carnoy, Levin and others. For a global examination of the world situation in this respect, see Carron and Ta Ngoc Châu (1980, 1981) and Unesco (1981c).

10. Unesco statistics show that in the years 1960–80, the developing countries achieved a substantial expansion of enrolment at all levels of education, democratization of which has thus been attained in part.

Level of education	Enrolment ratio by age-group in 1960 and 1980	
	1960	1980
Primary	46.9%	68.1%
Secondary	21.1%	39.9%
Higher	3.7%	11.2%

Source: Unesco, *Unesco Statistical Yearbook 1984*, Table 2.11, Paris, Unesco, 1984.

11. The annual expansion of technical education during the decade in question averaged approximately 4.5 per cent (as against 3.9 per cent for general education); the proportion of girls and women in the total enrolment figures rose from 40 to 44 per cent (the annual growth rate of female enrolment averaged about 5.4 per cent). It must be pointed out, however, that girls are still to be found chiefly in certain traditionally 'female' branches such as home economics, health-related programmes and, to some extent, commercial education (Unesco, 1983d).

12. There are many who think that work will be integrated into education but at the same time that the teaching of technology and a trade will be entrusted to the company.

4
Cultural changes and scientific progress

Scientific and technological thinking has profoundly influenced the culture of modern societies, particularly in the developed countries. In the name of rationalism and scientific positivism, growing numbers of people have challenged the value of religion as a response to human questioning and problems. Unbelief and secularism have developed in Western countries with a Christian tradition as well as in the socialist countries. The decline in religion has not been entirely offset by the renewal of interest in spiritual matters by some young people or by the great effort made by religious institutions to project a better image of themselves. The ecumenical movements which sought to bring the various churches closer together in order to eliminate misunderstanding and increase their power of persuasion have not yet achieved success.

It is worth noting, however, that religious belief is not the only form of belief on the decline. Positivism and scientism also seem less credible to the majority of people today. In recent years, science and technology have also come in for their share of doubt and protests in spite of their authority and strong roots. Even in developed societies, criticism has been directed against the subjection of science to political power, the use of technology for the destruction of man and nature and the fact that science is not concerned with or is unable to respond to the basic and most urgent needs and problems of mankind (see Jaubert, 1975; Peccei, 1981).

Another important change which began in the 1950s and has become more marked in the past ten years is the appearance of what is generally known as *mass culture*, which is transmitted and sometimes even produced by the mass media (radio, television, the press, the cinema). Some people criticize the lowering or levelling of culture brought about by this process of adaptation for the masses, while others see in it an opportunity for the general improvement of aesthetic taste and the promise of new higher cultural values.[1]

Large cultural organizations such as Unesco have contributed to a greater knowledge and a better mutual appreciation of different cultures. All the same, the growth of cultural exchanges between different peoples and nations has been accompanied by radical questioning, and even by the outright rejection by many countries in the Third World, of 'cultural imperialism' (the industrial culture of the West and the revolutionary culture of the East have often been equally censured). There are increasingly insistent calls for regard to be shown for the cultural identity of each people or ethnic group. In this connection, it is also worth mentioning that national languages and even regional dialects are being reassessed as vehicles of culture in many countries. Several formerly colonized countries where a foreign language is spoken have introduced their national language into their education systems, at least in basic education. A number of countries have accepted and given official status to the many dialects or languages spoken in different regions within their boundaries, and India is one example of this.

In the years following the Second World War, states and public authorities made considerable efforts to preserve and to make the most of the cultural heritage (monuments, museums, libraries etc.). International co-operation has played a valuable part, benefiting the poorer countries in particular.[2] Further progress has been made in recent years in the organization of cultural activities and the framing of suitable policies in this field, as can be seen from the documents and recommendations of the World Conference on Cultural Policies in Mexico City (July–August 1982).

When certain parts of a culture penetrate other cultures, this need not always be interpreted in terms of cultural imperialism. There are many examples of mutual influences which have been well received without being thought of as imposed from outside. One just has to think of certain products of contemporary culture (jazz), certain fashions in clothes (jeans), and certain kinds of hairstyle (African plaits), which show that tastes are becoming similar and that preferences are converging across frontiers. Ecological movements, pacifist movements and the popularity of civil instead of military service are other examples of the emergence of certain common ideas in spite of cultural differences. The mass media, and particularly the press and the cinema, play a key role in the worldwide spread of these cultural fashions or models. The transmission of television programmes by satellite, now being developed, will offer unprecedented prospects for this type of convergence.

If we turn now to the progress of science and technology over the past thirty years, it is clear that it has profoundly altered not only man's view of the world but also his position in the universe. The spectacular achievements of modern technology include the conquest of space, the peaceful use of nuclear energy, progress in electronics, the increasingly frequent use of computers in all sectors of human activity and the unprecedented discoveries and achievements of biotechnology (artificial insemination, organ transplants, etc.). Science itself has undergone great changes. One need only mention some of the recent and less recent discoveries in different sciences. Among the exact sciences, for example, physics has been turned upside down since the beginning of the century by the theory of relativity, the quantum theory, the discovery of the equivalence of mass and energy, the concept of a four-dimensional universe, wave mechanics etc.; in chemistry, the fields of synthesis and biochemistry have developed considerably. Biology has made immense progress thanks to the discoveries of biochemistry[3] and the revelations of endocrinology and genetics are evidence of this. Satellites and space flights have provided a better knowledge of our earth and its internal structure and have opened vast horizons to human perception, providing a major stimulus for several disciplines including meteorology. Modern mathematics, with the theory of sets and statistics and with the laws of probability, has profoundly affected scientific thinking and method. Finally, the social and human sciences (see Havet, 1970, 1978) have developed considerably in recent decades and new disciplines have appeared, such as cybernetics, robotics and sociobiology.

One of the features of the present day which adds to and greatly reinforces other types of inequality is the increasingly unequal access of the developed and the developing countries to science and technology. Some figures from a Unesco document on the analysis of world problems (the approved text of this, to be found at the beginning of Unesco's *Second Medium-Term Plan* (1984–89) (Unesco, 1983c) are revealing in this connection. Where the production of knowledge is concerned, 90 per cent of research and development in the world is carried out in thirty industrialized countries representing less than 30 per cent of the world's population. As regards the spread of knowledge, of the 600,000 book titles published in 1978, only 16 per cent belonged to the developing countries. In addition, the per capita consumption of printing paper is almost fifteen times higher in the developed countries than in the Third World. The industrialized countries possess 80 per cent of the computers, 90 per cent of the radio frequencies and over 87 per cent of all television sets.

In other words, the fantastic development of modern science is not motivated by the most vital problems of mankind. Instead, it serves the interests of the developed countries and, more particularly, of their already privileged sectors, which end up deriving very substantial profits from it [Peccei, 1981.]

Of these privileged sectors mention should be made of the military industries which acquire the lion's share—60 per cent—of research staff.

One of the particularly important happenings of the last ten years has been the explosive growth of information and the spread of knowledge. People today are bombarded from every side by all types of knowledge and information, often ill-matched or contradictory, among which they occasionally have difficulty in finding their way. This explains their bewilderment and the resultant tendency towards scepticism. This kind of situation imposes new responsibilities on education systems, as we shall see below.

We have already referred to the movements involving young people around 1968. Where culture is concerned, these movements encouraged new values which some have described as a counterculture and some as third-generation culture or 'Consciousness III' while others consider them to be post-materialist values or the 'ascendant' values of the open society. A questioning of the dominant values of industrial societies, such as commercialism, the urge to produce more and more and the search for profit at any price, is now common in advanced societies.[4]

SCIENCE AND CULTURE, TOMORROW

In the years ahead, science, which has become the dominant sector of developed societies to an even greater extent than the economy itself, will undoubtedly experience unparalleled growth. We have already mentioned the areas where the progress of science and technology has been particularly great in recent years, and these will obviously continue to develop during the next two decades, e.g. space science, the extension and the applications of chemistry and biochemistry, biotechnology and particularly biological operations on human beings, the search for new sources of energy, computer science, electronics, lasers, communication, automation and robotics, the technologies connected with the conservation and recycling of resources, the processing of waste and the control or elimination of pollution.

Future-oriented studies provide an idea of the astonishing things that science and technology can be expected to achieve. Thus, Stephen Rosen (1976) in his book *Future Facts*, describes over 300 products or processes which may be developed in the next few decades. These include artificial hearts powered by nuclear energy, the electric aspirin, solar energy from satellites, the storage of foodstuffs on the seabed, proteins produced from waste, flying trains, the chemical transfer of knowledge, the portable telephone, etc. More recently, Albert Ducrocq (1984) put forward the view that mankind will experience more changes by the year 2000 than it has known to date. He considers that the most spectacular scientific and technological achievements in the next fifteen years could include the following.

Everyone will be able to have a computer in his pocket. The large-capacity pocket-size microcomputer will simultaneously act as a calculator, memorandum, notebook, clock, diary, address book, file and library. The equipment of the individual in the electronic age will include the alarm chronometer, 'smart cards', mini tape-recorders, translation machines, printers, paging devices, etc.

Tomorrow, fibre optics will connect the individual to the rest of the world, bringing to his home the resources of a whole city. He will be able to make purchases, buy a newspaper or request an audio-visual programme from his house, and the house will henceforth be 'operated' like a modern industrial firm.

Energy and raw materials will no longer dominate the economy. Tomorrow will see the victory of 'substitution'. It will also be possible to recycle any material including oil. Grey matter will replace raw materials, i.e. the non-material will replace the material.

Robots will come into use everywhere, including private homes. 'The total for 1984 was about 570,000 robots, including 230,000 in Japan alone. It is expected that their numbers will increase to 1,300,000 in 1990' (Ducrocq, 1984, p. 24).

People will be encouraged to use plastic money, i.e. to carry a card incorporating a chip, which will be like a portable bank terminal.

People will travel for pleasure rather than for business since 'teleconferencing' will easily take the place of business travel. In 1983, 813 million passengers were carried on the 10,000 aircraft of 122 major airline companies in the five continents. Air travel has a great opportunity for rapid development and this number of passengers could have doubled by the beginning of the twenty-first century. All travel formalities will be simplified thanks to information technology.

The construction of the fifth-generation computer will usher in a new era, the reign of artificial intelligence, which will assist and add to the intelligence of the human being.

Living matter will be annexed by industry (biotechnology). Bacteria will be used in the food industry and even in metallurgy. Live substances such as plants will have a more important role to play in the production of materials than 'dead substances' such as coal and oil.

As man is the only source of wealth and the only driving force in industry and material progress in general, the most important form of investment in the year 2001 will be training, which is education directed towards skills and creativity. Particular emphasis will be placed on general culture, the ability to learn independently, a computer for every pupil, distance education via fibre optics, the use of educational radio and television in the countries of the Third World, the use of a proportion of free time for training or self-training, etc.

Health, which is the most important possession, will make great progress (transplants of all sorts, manufacture of artificial organs, slowing down of the ageing process, production of many biological substances, use of the potential of space for the same purpose, etc.).

Although these developments are fantastic, man must be able to remain master of science and technology through an appropriate education, and to harness them to serve his noble ideas. This is the point where the role of culture becomes vital.

Since the time of Sir Edward Burnett Tylor's *Primitive Culture* (1974) culture has been defined as all the customs, skills and forms of behaviour acquired by man as a member of society. It designates the complex aggregate of sciences, beliefs, arts, ethics, laws, customs, and so on which takes the form of an overall system in which all of the parts simultaneously reflect a certain view of the world and of reality (religious culture, rationalist culture, sensate culture as seen by Pitirim Sorokin; culture of accomplishment, culture of the present, transworld culture, culture of participation in a form of construction, and culture of choice, following the distinction of Bolle de Bal and some participants at the World Congress of Sociology in 1966).

As culture forms a whole, we can ask questions about its general direction rather than the development of each of its component parts.

In general, it could be said that there are three schools of thought about forecasting the future of culture:

(a) the idea of the continuity of past trends;
(b) the idea of a break;
(c) the idea of change within continuity.

Herman Kahn and his co-workers mention several basic long-term trends such as the strengthening of the empirical, hedonistic and secular nature of modern culture, and they may be said to represent the first school (see Kahn and Wiener, 1967, Ch. I, part E). Some changes may also be anticipated but these will not threaten the actual basis of the dominant Western culture. For example, several thinkers (such as Ferkiss (1969)) mention new values connected with the advancement of post-industrial societies.

A number of thinkers have, however, followed Oswald Spengler in predicting the imminent decline of Western civilization, and believe that the very foundations of this civilization will be replaced by others, better adapted to the needs of the age (Sorokin, 1957, 1970). Some protagonists of radical change consider that the sources of inspiration for such change are already present. One just has to look at the features specific to non-Western cultures to discover the models required for the regeneration and refertilization of Western civilization (see Garaudy, 1977). Others again predict the emergence of a totally different civilization (e.g. Sorokin who expects the development of a new civilization which will achieve a harmonious integration of the intuitive, rational and 'sensate' bases of the 'cultural super-systems' of the past).

We have adopted a realistic approach and will confine ourselves to the major trends already in evidence without prejudging their long-term effects on specific civilizations. These major trends may, for all that, give rise to counter-trends, just as placing emphasis on science can give rise to frustration and a questioning of the value of science.

Where the developed countries are concerned, we find in the field of culture several basic long-term trends which have been outlined by Willis Harman among others (OECD, 1972): accumulation of scientific and technological knowledge; appearance of a society based on knowledge; growing gap between technological solutions and problems created by technology; development of a 'learned élite', that is to say a meritocratic ruling élite whose dominance is based on knowledge; increase in the proportion of people motivated by their own development (their 'self-fulfilment'); trend towards the elimination of boundaries between work, leisure and education.

Other researchers have listed different major trends in the same countries: greater importance of the new mass media in people's lives and leisure and a trend towards mass culture; trend towards the international standardization of young people's life-styles; reassertion of cultural identity by minority and underprivileged groups.

These trends have also given rise to counter-trends. For example, there are at least three reactions to mass culture: *educators* stress the need to immunize the individual against the assault of the media by building up his capacity for critical judgement; *technologists* recommend the use of new technologies (such as computers, cable television, etc.) in order to tailor the choice of programmes to individual wishes (Toffler, 1981, pp. 155 et seq.); the *directors of the media* promise more media space for educational content and a more watchful eye on commercial and recreational content.

Signs of interest in universal values and in the appreciation of other cultures can be observed alongside efforts to 'return to one's roots'. As we know, television broadcasts by satellite will soon make it possible for foreign cultures to be appreciated throughout the world. This will also encourage peoples to think more about their own cultural identity and define themselves more objectively in relation to others.

The external and superficial aspects of culture will undoubtedly tend to become standardized but there is no proof that a stronger trend will not develop towards the assertion of the most authentic and profound aspects of cultural identity, that is to say, the beliefs and values which form the base of a culture.

The consumer boom of the 1950s and 1960s met with financial, material and, sometimes, institutional limitations from the beginning of the 1970s. It was then necessary to appeal everywhere for a reduction in excess consumption and waste, the adoption of conservation measures and the recycling of scarce resources (Gabor and Colombo, 1981; Meadows et al., 1974).

A new awareness of the environment has been brought about as a result of the harm done by industrialization when solely in pursuit of profitability, harm which includes the waste of natural resources, mentioned above, and pollution, which threatens to upset the balance of ecological systems. There has been progress in environmental protection thanks to the efforts of scientific researchers, certain specialized institutes and public and private initiatives, and mention should be made here of the United Nations Environmental Programme (UNEP). In addition, there has been a more general development among the public in industrialized countries, where a kind of environmental ethic has emerged, sometimes assuming the form of political militancy, with the idea that a new relationship must be established between man and nature. One sees here the role that could be played by environmental education which must develop an attitude and provide a scientific basis for what is still nothing more than a vague longing for better things, now seen in qualitative terms.

The new demands for a better way of life will very probably counter-balance or replace the demand for more possessions and will have a profound influence on people's lives tomorrow. They will most certainly include a wish for cultural activities and pleasures, which will in future be considered as essential to the development of the individual, since, to quote the striking phrase of Jacques Rigaud (1975): 'The pursuit of the quality of life necessarily leads to culture which constitutes the dignity of life.'[5]

A genuine culture is one in which education, work and life are integrated and, fortunately, a trend can in fact be observed towards the elimination of strict boundaries between work, education and leisure. We shall see in the second part of this book that the integration of work in schools and that of education in the world of work, the rotation of study and work, have become common practice in many developed and developing countries. The use of leisure time for education and culture is also a long-established practice.

The concept of work as a form of punishment for man, a sort of eternal damnation, is giving way to another view in which work becomes an opportunity for self-realization and personal development, just like leisure. Many industrial experiments have made use of good design to eliminate the distinction between the world of work and the world of culture. Modern teaching methods turn learning into pleasure, a sort of entertainment rather than a painful necessity. Learning through play now has a place of honour in education. All of these developments must necessarily influence intellectual life in the coming decades.

In the developing countries, the movement to achieve modernization was frequently confused with Westernization and was rejected with many violent demonstrations, revealing the desire of non-Western societies to return to their own cultural identity. However, we have the feeling that this movement is beginning to follow a new tack and is making a deliberate effort to integrate imported elements into the country's culture, while preserving its cohesion and integrity (see Unesco, 1981*a*).

According to Jean-Michel Lecercq (1984):

Education [in Japan] no longer stresses to the same degree as before the need for a constant watch on Western civilizations in order to extract their scientific and technical secrets, but it still continues to place emphasis on familiarity with foreign traditions and experience. Thus, in spite of their remoteness and obvious individual traits, the Japanese learn very early to seek out foreign contributions without the least fear of losing their individuality and forgetting their heritage, which no longer needs to demonstrate its capacity to hold its own.

A similar situation could develop in Third World countries which are anxious to develop while conserving their cultural heritage.

Modernization would thus involve assimilating foreign contributions and creating new forms by drawing on old forms which retain their vitality and significance. Of the aspects of Western culture which developing countries long to acquire, science and technology come at the top of the list. Sooner or later, however, these countries will realize that progress in science and technology also involves dangers and that a balance must be found between the development of science and the moral and spiritual values of society. This search for a balance will definitely be one of the major trends of the next few decades. The former Director-General of Unesco, René Maheu (1973, p. 10), wrote that, where the domain of the spirit does not exist, the spirit cannot live and man is no longer master of his destiny.

THE IMPACT OF SCIENTIFIC PROGRESS AND CULTURAL CHANGES ON THE METHODS AND CONTENTS OF EDUCATION

In a world where the daily life of the individual and of society is increasingly permeated by science and technology, education has a great part to play not only in the transmission of scientific and technical knowledge but also in the development of attitudes which will enable man to control that knowledge and its application. Education must also establish a balance between science and technology, considered as instruments, and the values which constitute the foundation of human life and action.

With regard to education's first function, the final twenty years of our century will see the rapid development of new branches of science and their applications, such as electronics, telecommunications, information technology, nuclear energy, lasers, automation, cybernetics and biotechnology. Education will therefore have constantly to add to and adapt its contents in the light of progress in these fields and to adopt new holistic, interdisciplinary and transdisciplinary approaches to cope with the enormous volume, diversification and constant growth of knowledge.

Education will in future deal more directly with real problems, making use of various types of analysis and explanation supplied by different scientific disciplines. The reductionist and simplifying tendency which used to prevail in science and education will be replaced by a new approach which takes account of the complexity and diversity of the facts under study. The laws of probability will be taught to everyone and a relativistic approach will replace a categorical one.

As scientific progress is unfaltering, there will have to be permanent provision for retraining within the existing or future educational framework for those whose education has been made obsolete by scientific and technological progress. Scientific and technological change also means that schools must teach their students how to learn. Present teaching methods must be altered accordingly and greater emphasis must be placed on a capacity for self-instruction, on instruction in the use of documentation sources and on the organization of educational credits, facilitating the development of lifelong education.

In addition to transmitting knowledge, education is also required to instil the appropriate attitudes towards that knowledge. It must foster a critical spirit in the individual, teach him to have regard for the diversity of things and ideas and, above all, encourage him to develop his unique potential. In other words, education must above all else be a means for developing awareness instead of just a means of training and indoctrination.

By awareness we mean specifically awareness of the moral, spiritual and aesthetic values which are the foundation of human existence and which science and technology must serve. These values include the dignity of man, love of one's neighbour and harmony with nature, which, although age-old values, can be renewed and regenerated in every age. The old values must also be harnessed in order to create new ones which will help the individual to adapt to changed times. To quote Rabelais, it is a well-known fact that 'science without conscience is the ruin of the soul', and indeed many countries are making a fresh effort to spread moral and civic values (see Mehlinger, 1984).

In an effort to counter the over-emphasis on science in school curricula and to return to the sources of their culture, some countries have laid greater stress on the arts and humanities in education. Even in a country like Japan, which is in the forefront of scientific progress, music has come to figure prominently in primary- and secondary-school curricula in recent years. Greater emphasis in the revised curricula has also been accorded to other aspects of general culture such as history and geography. In the developing countries, this return to cultural origins clearly also stems from a wish to escape from imported cultural values and patterns of education. The most important expressions of this are the adoption of local, regional or national languages as the medium of communication, the teaching of the traditions and history of the country in its schools, the revival of old patterns of education in which the school was still linked with community life, culture and work, and the integration of the teaching of African art into secondary-school and university curricula (Unesco, 1981a, pp. 42–52).

The new emphasis on the cultural heritage is obviously not limited to the developing countries. In the developed countries too, every means is being used, including museums, theatres, cinemas, libraries, art collections, visits to historical monuments and sites, in order to promote this type of education. These same countries are also attempting with greater or lesser success to encourage cultural and artistic creativity among the younger generation. Education, tomorrow, will further develop this learning of culture and will aim to foster creative abilities such as film-making, the production of new plays, musical composition, and so on. In the developing countries, providing a good introduction to the culture of the country within the education system is an effective way of consolidating national independence. Education can thus become an instrument of liberation and can bring an end to alienation.

Regional conferences of those in charge of education in the Third

World have frequently emphasized the role of education in liberating and in ending alienation. For example, the preparatory meeting of Arab ministers in Tunis in March 1982 recommended that education should be made an effective instrument for the training of Arab citizens who can contribute to the development of their environment and society, cope with the problems of their country and tackle the challenges of their time. The Conference on 'Africa and the problems of the future' (Dakar, July 1977) stated that the old style of education contributed powerfully to cultural alienation but that the new style of education must, on the contrary, help to strengthen African cultural identity. The basic medium of a people's culture is its language and this is why top priority must be given to the use of African languages as instruments of education. The Conference of Ministers of Education and Those Responsible for Economic Planning in Member States in Latin America and the Caribbean (Mexico City, December 1979) stressed the need to review the content of education so that it corresponded more closely to the cultural values, wishes and development aims of the countries in the region.

EDUCATIONAL TECHNOLOGIES

Where the impact of scientific and technological progress on education is concerned, special attention must be paid to the development of educational technology although education remains a labour-intensive activity and the applications of technology are still much more limited than in other sectors like industry or administration.

We find two main types of technology in education: (a) audio-visual technology such as radio, television, cinema, video, etc.; and (b) information technology, particularly computers and microcomputers.

The developed countries and a very small number of developing countries demonstrated their interest in applying the new communication technologies to education at the end of the 1950s and the beginning of the 1960s. Administrators gave a particularly enthusiastic welcome to them. There were great hopes that the new media and the new technologies would solve most of the problems confronting education systems, e.g. the quality of education, equality of access to education, the shortage of qualified teachers, etc. The expectation was that the use of these new technologies would make it possible to lower the unit costs of education considerably while appreciably improving its effectiveness. As Oliveira (1982) pointed out, this period was also one of enthusiasm for planning, economic development and technology in general. It soon gave way to a period of disappointment and a questioning of growth, planning and technology itself. Several years ago, experts began to draw conclusions from the experience of the past twenty years and a more realistic assessment has begun to emerge. It is now known that the new technologies solve some but not all problems and that they also create other problems which are just as big. Radio and television were the most widespread of the first type of new technology and it is recognized that they have added considerably to the number of learners and have sometimes made a useful contribution to education, but they have not managed to reduce unit costs significantly except in very special cases (Hawkridge, 1982). They have also come up against certain limits (including those set by the opposition of teachers who fear that their role may be diminished by the new media) and have even created problems (for example, in the developing countries whose technical and even financial dependence has increased because these media are mostly produced in the industrial countries).

There are apparently much brighter prospects for the use of information technology such as computers, microcomputers, etc., in education.[6] These consume little energy and could revolutionize teaching methods when combined with communication technologies. They can stock and display enormous amounts of information within a limited space and can be an excellent aid for self-instruction. The success of these technologies obviously also depends on a large number of factors which include:

(a) the initial investment needed to develop not only the necessary hardware but also, and most importantly, the software;

(b) qualified staff to operate and service them;

(c) introduction and training for teachers so that the administration can rely on their co-operation;

(d) the quality of the information stored and the capacity for updating it at regular intervals;

(e) a favourable social and intellectual climate (large volume of research, easy access to documentation, etc.).

Opinions differ on the future of the new technologies and on their impact on schools. Some hold that education will be completely 'de-institutionalized', that is to say the school will be phased out and replaced by other forms of education such as distance education while others think that the school will survive (Hawkridge, 1982). In our view, the survival of the school will not prevent the simultaneous development during the next twenty years of other forms of experience (such as open learning), linked to school or not, which will make the school less 'monopolistic' and less rigid than in the past. Tomorrow's learners will be able to learn in a classroom, read on their own, view video and television programmes at home, listen to cassettes or the radio, learn by computer, etc., and all this within the framework of self-education. The school may even act as a centre which will provide co-ordination and integrated planning for this type of all-embracing educational activity. Thus schools in the industrialized countries are now being equipped with microcomputers to improve classroom instruction but not to replace it.

Two conclusions can be drawn from past experience: first, more advantage may be derived from combining these technologies than from relying on any one of them and, second, the new technologies have been used much more frequently in higher education, adult education, teacher training, non-formal education and even technical and vocational education than in primary and general secondary education.

In concluding this chapter, we may say that educational technologies are part of a general scheme and must be judged in relation to all the components of this scheme; much care is required if they are to bear fruit. The extensive literature on the use of the new educational technology merits attention (see Dieuzeide, 1974; Megarry et al., 1983; Whiston et al., 1980).

NOTES

1. It is said that radio has played a major part in introducing the public to serious music and that television has helped the general public to discover opera. Critics, on the other hand, accuse the media of encouraging passivity in the public. It is claimed that radio and television are often responsible for cultural impoverishment and alienation. However, no one denies that the electric and electronic revolution which, as McLuhan has shown, is comparable in importance to the invention of writing and the revolution brought about by Gutenberg, has become a major feature of our age and that it is increasingly absorbing and occupying our contemporaries, particularly in the developed regions of the world. Some relevant statistics:

    Estimate of the number of television receivers per thousand inhabitants by continent in 1970, 1976 and 1981

Continent	1970	1976	1981
Africa	3.4	6.8	17
North America	302	412	618
South America	68	89	111
Asia	22	28	38
Europe	178	237	309
Oceania	200	259	291

    Source: Unesco, *Statistics on Radio and Television 1960–1976*, Paris, Unesco, 1978; *Unesco Statistical Yearbook 1983*, Paris, Unesco, 1983 (for the year 1981).

Estimate of the number of radio receivers per thousand inhabitants by continent in 1970, 1976 and 1981

Continent	1970	1976	1981
Africa	45	72	89
North America	1 027	1 310	2 020
South America	164	259	315
Asia	48	81	102
Europe	332	387	479
Oceania	428	632	870

Source: as table above.

There were 293 radio receivers and 121 television receivers per thousand inhabitants worldwide in 1981.
2. Important examples of this: the rescue of the monuments of Nubia and the temples of Abu Simbel (1960), the rescue of the temples of Philae in Egypt (1979) and of Borobudur in Indonesia (1982).
3. Such as the discovery of molecular structure which is based on deoxyribonucleic acid or DNA.
4. Below is the list of 'ascendant' values as opposed to declining values according to R. Jungk (1973, p. 195):

Declining values
(a) lack of concern for others
(b) chauvinism
(c) domestic virtues
(d) egotism and self-satisfaction
(e) careerism
(f) individual economic security
(g) private property
(h) confidence in 'progress' and smug optimism

Ascendant values
(a) group awareness
(b) positive attitude towards mankind
(c) creativity and intellectual mobility
(d) search for group membership
(e) vocational mobility, search for new forms of experience
(f) feeling of responsibility for the prosperity of society as a whole
(g) social justice and public service
(h) search for aesthetic values

According to the authors of the OECD's Interfutures study group's report (OECD, 1979), an outburst of 'post-materialist' values may already be observed in the young generations. These values are: town improvements; nature conservancy; a society in which ideas count for more than money; protection of freedom of speech; a less impersonal society; increased participation in the living and working environment and at the political level.

Charles A. Reich (1970), considers that the ascendant values are those of the present young generation (which the author calls 'Consciousness III'). These are:

(a) the freeing of the individual from the automatic acceptance of the imperatives of society;
(b) the absolute worth of every human being—every self;
(c) a feeling of universal brotherhood in place of competition and antagonism;

(d) replacement of functional and impersonal relationships with family and community relationships;

(e) critique of present society, which is considered to be hypocritical, unjust and untrustworthy;

(f) personal commitment to the welfare of the community;

(g) demand for genuine and responsible participation in the decision-making process;

(h) constant openness to change and all experience;

(i) enthusiasm and hope;

(j) anti-careerism;

(k) importance of music as a medium of expression;

(l) a constant search for new ways to be together;

(m) acute awareness, similar to that of an artist, of what is happening round about.

5. On the way in which the new generation could change the commercial and 'artificial' nature of contemporary culture, see Reich (1970).

6. In the view of Hall (1977), education in Europe must be reshaped along the following four lines in the last quarter of the century (1975–2000):

(a) equalization of opportunity;

(b) lifelong education, i.e. education throughout the life of the individual;

(c) participation and independent learning;

(d) transformation of the teacher into a counsellor.

The new information technology can play a major role in these four areas (p. 168). Hall considers that the new technology can achieve these aims without going over the financial limits. A major drive is also under way at present in the industrial world to reduce the various costs associated with the transmission of information by telecommunications (pp. 157 et seq.).

5
World problems

Ever since mankind has existed, it has, of course, been confronted with problems which have varied in extent from one age to another. Nevertheless, it would be fair to say that it has never been faced with a series of problems as great as the ones that it is experiencing today. World problems today seem to present the following five characteristics: universality, globality, complexity, deep-seatedness and gravity:

Universality: no part or region of the world is free from these problems, and there is no longer any hope of solving a major problem like the depletion of natural resources or pollution at the level of one country or even of one region.

Globality: the crisis covers all aspects and all sectors of life.

Complexity: the different aspects of world problems (demographic, geopolitical, ecological, social, economic, cultural, technological, etc.) are closely linked and each merges into the other. No single problem can be thoroughly examined without taking into account its relationships with others.

Deep-seatedness: experience shows that ordinary measures are no longer adequate to solve present world problems; treating the symptoms does not make it possible to root out the evil.

Gravity: the major problems of mankind are such that they endanger the very survival of the human race.

Though it is true that certain features of present-day world problems have existed for decades, the problems as a whole have come into being and compelled recognition as a new global reality over the past twenty years, when changes have occurred at an unforeseeable rate. One might even say that these problems emerged almost suddenly, catching the different collective systems of thought and action off their guard.

The complexity of world problems no doubt accounts for the different ways of looking at them and the different explanations of them that have been put forward.

Some people see them as problems with varying dimensions and many different causes, whereas others see the problems as all stemming from one major cause, which may be political, economic, moral or religious. Nevertheless, although opinions differ about their origin and outcome, there is quite broad agreement on their description. Here we shall follow the description proposed by Unesco in the first part of the Organization's *Second Medium-Term Plan (1984–1989)* (Unesco, 1983c, pp. 11–54), which gives an accurate assessment of the many aspects of the present situation.

Problems are becoming global, but the solutions envisaged are not always equal to this new situation, despite efforts made to achieve greater solidarity.

Asymmetries and inequalities still exist among peoples in every respect.

Although the United Nations General Assembly adopted the Declaration and Programme of Action on the Establishment of a New International Economic Order as long ago as 1974, the terms of trade between the industrial and the developing countries remain imperfect, the process of industrialization in most of the developing countries and the transfer of technology to these countries for the same purpose still fall far short of expectations and the Third World still plays only a small role in the regulation of international trade and in the management of the international monetary system.

The arms race is being stepped up and political negotiations on the most dangerous strategic arms have not yet reached any satisfactory conclusion.

Human rights are violated in many countries of the world today, more than thirty-three years after the adoption of the Universal Declaration of Human Rights.

The deterioration of the environment and the gradual depletion of natural resources are two of the problems for which many solutions have been proposed and adopted at international conferences, but these have not really had satisfactory effects so far.

Communication and information are starting to create upheavals in the lives of societies. They also pose problems with regard to culture, education, social control and individual freedom, etc. The inequality of countries in this field and, *inter alia*, in the production and flow of information, is one of the imbalances of the present-day world that call for a solution.

The phenomenal progress of science and technology figures prominently in current world problems. Everyone knows that these two pillars of contemporary civilization have immense potential for solving the basic problems of mankind such as hunger, disease and ignorance. However, one might well ask whether achievements match expectations in this respect since science is concentrated above all in a limited number of countries. In both developing and developed countries, there is a large area of incomprehension between the mass of the population and the world of technology, resulting in feelings of uneasiness and mistrust.

Another important feature of our times is the challenging in the Third World of Western development models in which development is equated with economic growth. One idea coming to the fore implies 'a redefinition of the objectives of growth in terms of the enhancement of human and cultural values'. After a period of 'free-for-all', awareness of the need for co-development based on the interdependence of all is coming to be reflected in actual facts.

For years, emphasis has been laid on the specific social and cultural characteristics of each nation, especially in the Third World, where the refusal to take account of this identity during the colonial period is still well remembered. It can be seen everywhere that the more pressure is brought to bear on individuals and communities in order to achieve uniformity, the stronger this awareness of a specific identity grows.

Despite their unprecedented development in the 1950s and 1960s, education systems form a part of the world's problems as they are still not adapted to the priority needs of societies, such as the need for equal opportunities while at school and on entry into society, the need to keep up with scientific and technological progress, the need for integration in a constantly changing labour market, and so on. In recent years, the view has been voiced that education is in a state of crisis, and there have even been calls for the de-schooling of society and other forms and ways of learning have been advised.

One final problem, and by no means the most insignificant, concerns the uncertainty of values. In addition to the growing diversification of systems of standards and of values in societies throughout the world, mankind is battling with the relativization and even a radical questioning of the standards and values on which human societies have always been based. New patterns of behaviour are spreading among young people and among adults, e.g. violence, the quest for money and power through unconventional means, eroticism and love without commitments, etc., some of which are transmitted from developed countries to economically less developed societies and are shaking all the social structures of those societies.

Nevertheless, one must not despair. 'In the past few years, however, there have in a number of countries been attempts to rebuild society on the basis of a revival of its most deeply rooted cultural values' (para. 161). Of course it is those values that will enable the society to make room for progress without self-betrayal.

However searching Unesco's assessment of world problems may be, it could not take all their aspects and dimensions into consideration, partly on account of the Organization's intergovernmental character and partly because its attention is primarily focused, as it should be, on the four fields which fall particularly within its purview, viz. education, science, communication and culture. It will thus be seen that the list of world problems drawn up by international non-governmental organizations such as the Club of Rome is more extensive. Aurelio Peccei (1981), President of this Club, was thus able to draw up a list which, while including many of the problems indicated by Unesco (population explosion, devastation and deterioration of the biosphere, the world economic crisis, the arms race, disordered technical and scientific development, East–West confrontation and the North–South divide), includes others such as institutional ossification, political corruption, bureaucratization, the general feeling of instability and insecurity, loss of faith, the revolt of youth, and lastly, the lack of moral and political leadership, especially at the world level.

SUPPORTERS OF A NEW WORLD ORDER

A second view of the world's problems comes from those who support a new world order, who feel that all the major problems in the world are attributable to the fact that such an order does not exist. This explains the plans for reform proposed by different authors, ranging from ecological humanism to the establishment of a world government (see Brown, 1972; Falk, 1972; Wagar, 1971; Ward and Dubos, 1972), from a more equitable distribution of wealth among nations to the reorganization of the United Nations in the direction of a fairer sharing of power. E. Reves, author of *Anatomy of Peace*, proposed after the Second World War a Copernican revolution in the political world, which would in future give man a central role and make the nations gravitate around that centre. There are many thinkers who, with their globalist approach, are driven by concern about a worldwide nuclear war which could be fatal to mankind. W. Wagar thus proposes the establishment of an international force to safeguard peace, replacing national armies.

Other writers put forward the idea of a universal government, noting that morphological, economic, political and even cultural problems of the contemporary world have taken on a universal dimension. Georg Picht (1974) considers that the sovereign territorial state of the past is no longer equal to the political and economic tasks of the technological world. Saint Marc (1971, 1978) is led by the universal character of environmental problems to hope for the establishment of a world government. Demonstrating the accelerated deterioration of man's physical and social environment, he considers that the solution to this alarming state of affairs lies neither in Marxism nor in capitalism but in a new civilization based on what he calls ecological humanism. In his opinion

the defence of the air and of the seas and of their living resources must now be the responsibility of *the entire world united for this action* in an international community for the protection of nature, a blueprint for a *world government*. Only a universal policy can put an end to universal tragedy.

Lastly, man's fundamental wish for unity is sometimes mentioned as prefiguring the advent of a world state. According to Teilhard de Chardin, the future will see mankind united on a worldwide scale. This unity will be the result of the coming together of both minds and hearts and, in this latter case, the decisive role will be played by man's eternal aspiration to union with God.

DECLINE AND RENEWAL OF VALUES

The third view of the state of the world is put forward by those who consider that civilization as it now stands, with its basic values, is about to die a natural death and that we are living in a period of transition which will end with these values being replaced by others that are more adapted to the new times.

On the death of the present civilization, one can read the works of several great minds of our time such as Sorokin,[1] Toynbee and Teilhard de Chardin, all of whom place their hope in the imminent emergence of spiritual values. Wagar (1971) foresees the emergence of a new 'post-economic' civilization. Marcel de Corte (1949) also thinks that the present crisis of civilization is metaphysical in nature. Though man still dominates the world, the world is also always ready to crush him. We must at all costs restore the balance if a nascent civilization is to replace a dead civilization. In Marcel de Corte's opinion, two things are essential if civilization, currently dominated by abstract, unnatural and mechanistic ideas, is to be regenerated: religion (its vital thrust and not a mechanical form based on outmoded rites and practices) and spiritual élites. Many authors with ethical or spiritual concerns believe that since the Renaissance, Western civilization 'has leapt from the spirit towards matter in a disproportionate and immoderate manner', leading to the need to restore balance and harmony between the different dimensions of civilization, between mind and matter, between faith and science, between the divine and the human.

Many sociologists, since about 1970, have indicated the gradual emergence, especially among the young, of a range of new values in clear contrast with the values that are dominant in Western societies. Some authors, looking to the future (e.g. Dore, 1984), are rather of the view that Western culture has every likelihood of dominating the world and that even Third World countries will be induced to infuse their foreign relations with 'modernity', meaning conformity with the Western model. Other authors, however, more aware of the effects of increasingly frequent and increasingly close contacts between the different civilizations and cultures, hope that a wide-ranging dialogue between Western civilization and all the other cultures, such as those of Asia, the Amerindians, Africa and Islam, will lead to a new civilization that is better adapted to the needs of modern man and more capable of surviving current crises. In the opinion of Roger Garaudy, one of the promoters of such a dialogue, a new conception of relations between man and nature, between man and man, and between man and the divine would have to emerge from it. Here is how Garaudy (1978) describes the conception of these relations specific to Western civilization, which he thinks has taken the world up a blind alley: 'the Western conception of relations between man and nature stems from the promise held out by the Renaissance and Descartes to make man the lord and master of nature'. By considering nature to be a mere reservoir of raw materials, however, and a dump for our waste, it has led to an inhuman type of growth.

The Western conception of relations between man and man, with the same 'conquistador' ethics, based on competition and domination, has made our Western societies hesitate for centuries between the individualism of the jungle and the totalitarianism of the ants' nest, and has established between the West and the rest of the world, master–slave relationships which started with the genocide of the Indians and the revival of ancient slavery and its attendant deportations.

The Western conception of relationships between man and God has led to growing disregard of the transcendent dimension of man and his history and to the 'death of God', which necessarily leads to the death of man. In economics, it has reduced man to the mere dimensions of worker and consumer, and in politics it has exposed him to all sorts of disorders due to the fact that all truly human goals are disregarded and the ultimate aim of action is made the quantitative growth of production and of consumption (Garaudy, 1978, pp. 341–2).

Garaudy (1978, p. 35) states that other civilizations have devised and have experienced other relationships with nature, with man and with the divine, and he says that dialogue between all the cultures of the world is necessary in order to get out of the blind alley; and to establish a true dialogue, everyone must be convinced from the outset that they have something to learn from the other person. 'Through the dialogue of civilizations', he says, 'man can survive and live.' (See also Garaudy, 1977.)

It is relevant to recall that this idea of the 'cross-fertilization' of different cultures, intended to save the world from the chaos in which it finds itself, was launched for the very first time around 1870 by a great Eastern thinker, Bahá'u'lláh, then condemned to exile by two empires of the Asian continent. He had a vision of the disorders of our time caused, among other things, by what he called 'the excesses of Western civilization', and he recommended the establishment of a new world order based on the three values of justice, peace and unity. In this new order, the best of Western civilization (including science serving the well-being and happiness of mankind) would be integrated into a system of values, the most important of which would basically be the revival and regeneration of those ethical and spiritual values which constituted the essence of all the great earlier religions. Divine unity, the unity of religions and the unity of mankind are the three principles on which a new conception of relations between man and man and between man and the divine could be built. In the new civilization, it would be necessary to reconcile the material and the spiritual, faith and reason, science and religion, East and West (see Esslemant, 1980; *Gleanings* . . ., 1976; Hofman, 1972).

EDUCATION AND WORLD PROBLEMS

Though not everyone agrees on the causes of the ills, it is clear that ideas tend to coincide on the need for a fundamental change in all aspects of human life. Education certainly cannot remain on the sidelines of these new schools of thought and action and it has a major role to play in the renewal of values. It is expected to meet not only the basic needs of man and of society (the need for harmonious personal fulfilment, the need for social justice, etc.), but is also expected to be in touch with major world problems and to prepare young people for tomorrow's world and its demands. In addition, it can and must take into account the new things that people are wishing for, such as a better quality of life and of the environment, their desire for autonomy and participation, the wish to have roots in small communities, etc. If it is true that the spatial dimension of human life has become global, education must also impart a universal outlook. If inequalities in economic development are such that a quarter of the world's population lives in near absolute poverty, education must help to break the vicious cycle of underdevelopment in different ways, such as preparation for productive work, inclusion in the curriculum of education on population, nutrition, functional literacy, etc. Respect for the rights of others, awareness of human solidarity, an attitude of non-violence and of peace can all be learnt and strengthened at school. Environmental education can prepare the way for more harmonious and more reasonable relations with the natural environment. Control of technology and of the communication and news media can be acquired through a good education. Education plays an important role not only in the transmission but also in the renewal of cultural values. Lastly, education can and must assume its responsibilities in ethical development and in the formation of character and of the qualities that are essential for life in the future society, viz. open-mindedness, the capacity for personal judgement, and an ability to adapt to changes and to assimilate them positively and creatively (Busshoff et al., 1981, Ch. 17).

We will see in the second part of this work that various educational systems are already opening up to the problems of the contemporary world. More than ten years ago, many establishments of higher education, especially in the United States, started to provide courses in futurology. An examination of major world problems is necessarily included in these courses. Unesco, for its part, has for several years encouraged Member States to provide courses to prepare young people for peace, respect for human rights and appreciation of the cultures of other countries and nations. The distinction between traditional learning and innovative learning (Botkin et al., 1979) is particularly relevant to what we are saying. Innovative learning is aware of world problems and prepares the individual to cope with them creatively and constructively. Charles Hummel was right when he said that education must in the very near future achieve an acceptable balance between the industrialized countries and the developed countries and create solidarity among all mankind, necessary for the survival of the human race. This, as he points out, is, in the broadest sense of the term, an educational task. It is a race between education and catastrophe (Hummel, 1977).

NOTE

1. In Pitirim Sorokin's opinion, the present crisis is expressive of the difficult transition from one system of culture (which he describes as sensate, that is to say empirical, utilitarian, material and hedonistic) to another (which he calls integral, that is to say harmoniously integrating at one and the same time the senses, reason and intuition). (See Sorokin, 1948, 1957, 1970.)

6
The internal dynamics of education systems

So far we have looked into the social, economic, political and cultural sources of educational changes likely to occur in the next twenty years. The time has now come to examine the inner workings of education systems in order to see which factors may have an influence on their future—not forgetting the constant interaction between external factors and the specific dynamics of the world of education.

Authors such as Huberman (1973) have enumerated the obstacles and factors of resistance or inducement to change and innovation on the basis of a number of experimental research studies. Their findings enable us to review the positive or negative factors inherent in the world of education which, in all probability, will influence education in the next two decades. The internal dynamics of education systems can be analysed with reference to the following four features: (a) position of teachers; (b) teacher–learner relationships; (c) relations between school and the outside world, particularly the family, the media, the local community and business firms; and (d) school management and administration.

THE POSITION OF TEACHERS

The beliefs that were prevalent when new technologies were introduced into schools (programmed learning, use of radio, television and, later, computers for educational purposes, etc.)—fears, or hopes, that they would be a substitute for teachers—were not subsequently borne out. In some cases, the role of teachers using these aids has changed slightly in the process. But other factors have been instrumental in increasing the responsibilities and workload of those same teachers. For instance, they have had to give the child an appropriate moral and social education for want of adequate parental teaching in this sphere, organize self-learning activities for each pupil, act not only as examples and guides but also as advisers to their pupils, and hence forgo the role of stern judgement conferred upon them by traditional society. The growing complexity of teachers' duties and responsibilities gives us reason to believe that in the future closer attention will be paid to their recruitment, training and selection and that the process of retraining and further and continuing education will have greater prominence in the forthcoming management of education systems (see Goble and Porter, 1977; Laderrière, 1974).

It is also to be expected that, in addition to teachers themselves, there will be a larger number of personnel to assist in the learning process (such as auxiliary teaching staff, instructors, audio-visual specialists, etc.) or in individual learner counselling (e.g. specialists in educational and vocational guidance, programmers and others). It is not to be ruled out that the use of personnel whose role is to relieve teachers of their extra-curricular duties (such as supervising children in the vicinity of the school or practical and administrative duties) may ultimately reduce the unit cost of teaching—the bulk of which is at present accounted for by teachers' salaries.[1]

Another trend to be anticipated in the coming years is broader participation by teachers in all decisions affecting school life. Unless they are actively involved, it will be difficult to overcome the natural resistance to change and innovation found in so many teachers. To ensure the success of teacher participation, teachers must be better informed about what is happening outside the school. Ervin Laszlo has even gone so far as to propose that teachers alternate between academic work and political responsibilities (Kierstead et al., 1979). Of course, other ways of ensuring that teachers are better informed may be contemplated. Elsewhere we spoke of the need to prepare future generations for coping with the major problems of the world and the challenges of tomorrow's society. To organize future-oriented education of this kind we need a new kind of teacher who will be well informed about present problems and future studies. Participation thus takes on a broader meaning and can no longer be confined to decisions concerning life inside the school. An obvious point springs to mind, summed up eloquently by Jean Thomas (1975, p. 127) when he says: 'The attitude of the teaching profession is what ultimately determines the success or failure of an innovation.' Finally, it may be added that participation should restore the prestige of the teaching profession, which has suffered greatly in recent years.

THE TEACHER–LEARNER RELATIONSHIP IN THE SCHOOL OF TOMORROW

In the developed countries, the relationship between teachers and learners will undoubtedly undergo major changes in the coming decades. With learners' active participation in the process of learning on their own initiative and with the enhancement of creativity in all learners, it will be difficult to sustain the one-sided, authoritarian teacher–pupil relationship. The teacher's authority will no longer be based on the pupil's passiveness and ignorance, but on the teacher's ability to contribute to the full development of his or her pupil, relying on the latter's active participation (Fragnière, 1976). The teacher's role will no longer be synonymous with that of an encyclopedia or a data bank at the pupil's disposal. Creative teachers are those who help their pupils to make rapid strides towards learning on their own initiative, who teach their pupils how to deal with the mass of information with which they are faced; they are guides and advisers, far more than merely agents for the mechanical transmission of knowledge.

What we have just said concerns the future of education as heralded by the progress in technology and ideas already made in the world of education. But external factors such as the widespread instability and insecurity of today's and probably tomorrow's world may well cause some political systems to become more rigid and education systems to revert to more authoritarian methods of teaching and more inflexible structures, as Charles Hummel feared. Although there is already evidence of such a trend in some countries with a centralized power structure, this by no means invalidates our claim as regards the long term.

Furthermore, it must be borne in mind that schools will no longer have a monopoly on teaching, and that even if society is not deschooled in the sense understood by Ivan Illich, the introduction of lifelong education is bound to bring about greater flexibility in school systems, in particular in regard to the age of school entrance and leaving, the number of days of school attendance (part-time attendance combined with direct work experience outside the school might be considered) (Husén, 1982), the place of learning, and the examination, assessment and reward system (Husén, 1979, p. 190).

Teacher–learner relationships cannot remain unaffected by these more flexible arrangements. They are bound to be remodelled along the lines of what Georges Gurvitch described as a reciprocity of viewpoints.

RELATIONS BETWEEN SCHOOL AND THE OUTSIDE WORLD

The institutional isolation of the school, which, according to Husén, has become more acute in recent decades, has increasingly elicited reactions in favour of harmonizing and integrating the school as an institution with other social institutions. At all regional or international conferences, those responsible for education throughout the world have made recommendations and put forward projects for opening up the school to the world around it and especially to the world of work and the local community. There is also more and more talk of the need to narrow the gap between education and the media and between educational policy and cultural policy.

It is not our intention here to reopen the debate on the need for greater harmonization between education and other institutions or between educational action and development efforts, since there is already an abundant literature on these subjects. We shall merely ask the following question: if in theory everyone agrees that school must be made more receptive to the world around it, what are the features of education systems that prevent them from responding to this need in practice? There are several possible answers to this question. First, far too much is expected of the school, which already has so many functions to perform. Second, neither teachers nor educational administrators have been adequately prepared to take on these new responsibilities. Third, there are no material or psychological incentives or motivations for school and educational personnel to adopt more receptive attitudes to the world outside and to take up the resultant challenges. Fourth, traditional school structures and curricula are too rigid to be harmonized with other institutions and other development actions without a major effort. Fifth, there is sometimes, if not a conflict of interests and motivations, then at least a marked difference in approach between the various educational agents and between the latter and external agents (learners, teachers, parents, administrators, political decision-makers, employers, etc.) as was revealed by case-studies of innovation carried out by the OECD's Centre for Educational Research and Innovation (CERI) (OECD/CERI, 1973a). Finally, there is little initiative for promoting such harmonization in the outside world: for instance, radio and television are often bent on pursuing their own commercial or political interests; conventional development projects often overlook the important contribution that could be made by education systems that are closely interlinked with the development process; and the family expects far too much of the formal system without always giving it the support it needs.

These obstacles to harmonization are obviously not insurmountable. They existed as long as the school was able to confine itself to its own four walls. Since the inception of the movement to 'deformalize' school in so many developed countries, however, the various positions have begun to converge. The connection between school and the world of work is gradually becoming established and is gaining strength. Several procedures and forms of linkage have already been tried out and developed in various countries, and it was to a study of these that the 1981 session of the International Conference on Education was devoted. Rapid progress has been made in giving teachers a grounding in the new technologies (educational television, computers, teaching machines, etc.). There is a growing awareness of the need to develop young people's critical faculties in dealing with the media, so as to replace their previous passive fascination by an approach based on discernment and an ability to handle the media. As regards the relations between education and development, it is readily acknowledged in international development funding agencies that education is an essential component of any development project and that, as such, it must be combined with the other components in any such project.

New structures have been set up to encourage and facilitate dialogue and consensus-building among those responsible for educational and other institutions. Numerous examples could be cited of business representatives and educators getting together around a table to discuss and decide on the co-ordination of their respective fields of action. Structures of this kind are likely to reduce the clashes of interest observed in most societies. It is common knowledge, for example, that in the medium and higher social strata of developed societies, parents invariably press for an extension of their children's schooling, just as it is known that modern industry, which is tending towards greater automation, is now looking for a small number of highly qualified personnel and a large number of workers with rather limited qualifications. This is what leads to the well-known phenomenon of over-qualification in these societies; it can be a source of considerable frustration and social tension among young people. Arrangements for concerted discussion and co-ordination should be able to provide sound answers to this kind of problem.

THE FUTURE OF EDUCATIONAL MANAGEMENT AND ADMINISTRATION

Max Weber was right when he foresaw the spread of bureaucracy to all sectors of social life. Where there is bureaucracy there is a rational approach to management, a tendency towards uniformity of procedures and a rank-ordered distribution of power. The tendency towards bureaucracy has been one of the major trends in education systems since the 1950s. In many countries, the overall number of teachers and educational administrators comes a close second to numbers in the armed forces. Educational administration has become a major undertaking. Even at the level of each establishment, mass school enrolment has brought with it highly complex administrative problems requiring the use of new management methods and techniques.

The question now is whether education systems are heading towards more bureaucratization or less. It is obviously very difficult to answer this question and to anticipate what will become of educational administration between now and the end of the century in the three types of society which concern us. It can be said with some certainty, however, that in countries with a centralized structure educational administration has become so complex, being so vast in scope, that it has often been necessary, if not formally to decentralize it, then at least to make it less concentrated by devolving some of the responsibility for decision-making and action to regional or local authorities. If, as we have seen, the trend towards the personalization of education is one of the major trends to be expected in the next few years, a far more flexible administrative structure will be needed to cater for the wide variety of individual requirements (Third Conference of Ministers of Education . . ., 1980*b*). Identical formulae can no longer be prescribed for the multitude of cases which may arise.

It could be argued that the use of new technologies such as informatics might satisfy the need for flexibility without there being any concomitant need to deconcentrate the educational administration. On the other hand, one might well ask whether informatics is not, rather, a means of making information available to all concerned, thus making genuine decentralization and participation a distinct possibility.

In the Third World, it is becoming increasingly obvious that, beyond a certain threshold of expansion, educational administration is very expensive, and that it must consequently be pared down to some extent or at least deconcentrated. In a context of budgetary restrictions, efforts must be made to guarantee a better utilization of available resources, some of which are indeed wasted as a result of excessive expenditure on administration and administrative staff or underemployment of teaching staff.

The difficulty with deconcentration in developing countries lies in the fact that in many of these countries local and regional facilities are still very weak and unable to cope with the new tasks required of them; hence the need for major in-service training or retraining programmes at all levels within the countries themselves.

Two other measures emerge as essential for these countries if one recalls the obstacles to change and innovation as defined by Havelock and Huberman (1978): improved planning systems and improved selection of persons responsible for implementing innovative projects, and adjustments to their remuneration.

Another concern in developing countries, as in some developed countries, has to do with the problems of linking school education and out-of-school education (Regional Conference of Ministers of Education . . ., 1980). A prerequisite for such a linkage is for the central administration to be relieved of a substantial part of its routine responsibilities so that it can attend to this matter of vital importance for the future. The answer to such problems is obviously not to rely wholly on the control of a single administration, but to seek ways of co-ordinating the work of various educational institutions, while respecting the autonomy of each (for example, co-ordination of school education with the various forms of out-of-school adult education, in-service refresher courses, etc.).

On the subject of the inertia or, alternatively, responsiveness to change of education systems in the future, opinions are divided. Charles Hummel (1977, p. 185) takes a rather pessimistic view, at least as far as the market economy countries are concerned:

The expansion of education systems will make them still more inert and more resistant to change than they already are. Far-reaching reforms will have to be backed up by particularly powerful forces if they are to succeed. There is a danger that the 'old democracies', where unstable political situations seem to be gradually arising, may lose the necessary strength to launch important reforms.[2]

It is interesting to note that this author places his hope in the 'young developing countries' which is where 'the remarkable educational innovations in the future will appear'. In fact, the danger of inertia is not peculiar to any particular political system. Education systems will thus have a special effort to make in the years to come in order to avoid sclerosis. Several attitudes and measures may be adopted to that effect: responsiveness to innovative educational experiments in other societies and utilization of relevant information exchange networks; strengthening of research systems for the development and renewal of education; considerable scope for personal and local initiative; and continuing evaluation of the experimental applications of initiatives taken, as a basis for decisions as to their widespread implementation.[3]

NOTES

1. See Table 4.2 in the *Unesco Statistical Yearbook 1983*.
2. We are more optimistic than this author as regards the mobility of education systems in the developed countries. These countries have always proved particularly energetic in undertaking reforms in response to urgent problems. The case of France, which, despite its tendency towards administrative expansion and inflexibility, has produced novel ideas to combat youth unemployment, such as the youth employment convenant, the sandwich course system, etc., affords an instructive example.
3. Apart from this kind of empirico-rational approach, it is also to be expected that there may be other approaches in other socio-political systems: a coercive approach, for example, in regimes with a centralized power structure.

Part Two

Towards new contents

Introduction

IMPACT OF THE NEW SOURCES OF EDUCATIONAL CONTENTS

Part I of this work has shown that both curriculum designers and educators are faced with a new and extremely complex set of problems. The quality of the reactions and responses to these problems will determine the capacity of education to play an active role in the decades to come.

In the first place, the sources of a relevant 'curriculum' have grown more numerous. It should be borne in mind that for centuries the contents of general education were derived from just a few sources—science, religion or ethics, the mother tongue and foreign languages, and sometimes physical exercise. In recent decades, that is to say, within a very short space of time, the sources potentially giving rise to changes in the traditional structure and substance of educational contents have grown considerably in number; moreover, to the sources mentioned above must be added a specific, endogenous source, namely, the findings of educational research into the organization of contents and learning.

Secondly, as a result of the world scale of certain problems and of the role played by scientific and technological discoveries in the life of every human community, these sources are exerting a real pressure on content; this pressure is felt all the more strongly since every individual and every family is faced in everyday life by complex problems of a global character that they are not always in a position to tackle or solve. These difficulties then become grounds for criticizing school, and particularly the subject-matter taught there. Apprehending the messages and needs deriving from these sources and meeting the expectations of pupils and users (in the various sectors of social life) becomes a formidable task that directly concerns not only educational authorities and administrators but also the devisers of syllabuses (timetables and curricula), teachers and evaluators, learners, non-teaching educators, parents and other users.

Introduction

SCHOOLS: DECLINE OR TRANSFORMATION?

Some specialists believe that, because of their conservative character, their fragmentation and their inertia, education systems will have no role to play in building a new society and that, on the contrary, they will be on the receiving end of the changes in social life brought about by science, technology and socio-political activities. Others go further and speak, like Ivan Illich, of the 'de-schooling of society'. Such theses have fuelled a great deal of debate and have very probably helped the defenders of school to define their tasks, to act more effectively or, at least, to overcome a certain amount of indifference or isolation.

We know that McLuhan went as far as to say that when the child left the television screen to go to school he could only regress. Many educators will reject this with indignation and a matching riposte, claiming that television is incapable of disciplining the minds of the young (when it does not actually corrupt them with models of violence, weakness and stupidity) [Schaeffer, 1980].

We also know that Christopher Jencks (1973), a research worker at Harvard University, discusses and rejects a thesis cherished by Americans, namely that education helps to create equality of opportunity between individuals and that their success after school depends on the quality of that education. Jencks considers that: (1) the influence of family environment, television, etc., is beginning to outweigh that of school; (2) the monitoring of schools is not successful in evaluating what is essential for the development of pupils, namely the behaviour of teachers and the quality of school life; and (3) even where school exerts a greater influence than usual over children, that influence is unlikely to persist into adult life.

In the sphere of educational thought and research, Jencks's thesis has elicited a number of responses.[1]

Continuous learning and self-evaluation are today spoken of as ways of coping with the growing complexity of social and occupational life, fostering attitudes and skills vital to all those leaving school on completion of compulsory or basic education. For decision-makers, administrators and planners, the problem is not the role or legitimacy of school education, but rather its development, relevance and capacity for innovation. This emerges even more clearly in Unesco's programmes adopted by its Member States, in which the reform of education is seen in the light of contemporary world needs and future requirements. However, many educational researchers and authorities are concerned about the efficiency and genuine democratization of school and about the resistance of education systems to innovation. Education is at a crossroads: it needs to abandon once and for all the rigidity, élitism, compartmentalization and artificial barriers

Introduction

with which learners are confronted; it needs to open itself up courageously to new content, principles and methods. In taking stock of the situation of education, we should not overlook the role of systematic education over the centuries—including its role in the establishment of our industrialized society, based essentially on science and technology—or the resistance to innovation within education systems. Can we, for example, disregard the role that both economists and educationists attribute to the Japanese education system in the attainment of levels of economic performance that have been the focus of so many studies? Let it be said from the outset that we share the view of many specialists: education systems have, by nature, a twofold role to play—receptive and active; they are capable of evolving, and of preparing for or fostering desirable socio-economic changes. Within education systems we find forces of resistance, outlooks and structures that need to be modified; but we also find resources and the potential to produce a number of solutions to the major problems of our time. For example, with regard to peace education, which might seem to have limited prospects of success, Magnus Haavelsrud and Johan Galtung[2] *express, in a special issue of the* International Review of Education, *a point of view that seems to us both optimistic and realistic:*

There are few who argue that education has no role to play in the creation of future society. . . . There are . . . however, those who see education as a factor in the creation of a better society for the future. It is on this premiss that the contributions to this Special Issue on peace education are founded. . . . This interest in education's role in improving present-day society . . . means that conceptualizations—as well as the implementation of these in practical programmes— need to be seen in the light of values embedded in the vision of future society [Haavelsrud, 1983].

WISHES AND PLANS

Reactions to all the pressures that the sources of contents exert on education systems are of two kinds—those that take the form of wishes or recommendations and those that take the form of plans. If it is agreed that wishes are the expression of a recognition of problems, and that plans are the expression of the will to change and improve, the two reactions may be regarded as successive and interlinked stages: recommendations and wishes are often to be found at the origin of plans. However, there is a considerable gap between what is required in the way of a solution or necessary improvement and the measures that will translate what is desirable into a research or operational project; and on occasion, as some authors have pointed out, there is a conscious divorce between rhetoric and action, that is to say, between the need at the political level to advocate and undertake ambitious changes in education and training systems and the near certainty that the administrative and technical infrastructure as well as local customs will reduce the margin of effective change to the point where it will affect only a few schools, teachers or administrators [Havelock and Huberman, 1978, p. 104].

This remark is not meant to minimize the role of recommendations and of a certain philosophy of education that can foster aspirations and faith in humanity and values, and thereby mobilize the latent resources of learners and teachers. We should not forget the beneficial role played by the philosophy of the Renaissance and of the Enlightenment in the transformation of education. We should not forget, above all, the unique example of Ancient Greece where, as Karl Marx observed, an ideal that called forth strong and stable aspirations was able to shape human beings both physiologically and spiritually. In any event, education is justified as an activity and an institution only to the extent that it is directed towards some ultimate goal.

We have tried to avoid using the term 'desirable', which might have suggested that our approach was normative. However, perusal of the relevant literature, of Unesco's programmes approved by the Member States, and of the recommendations adopted by ministerial conferences or meetings of specialists reveals a number of changes—desired, necessary, or desired because necessary—to which current research or projects in some instances correspond. What is desired is not imposed from the outside, or invented by some international body or by futurologists: it is sought, by education authorities and researchers, in response to the requirements of the contemporary world, to emerging sources of educational content and to national needs. And these changes, desired or in progress, frequently receive special attention in Unesco's programmes, since the Organization is very well placed to perceive future requirements and the impact of world problems on education.

So it is that the growing interest in the social and human sciences and in the axiological quality of content is beginning to express itself in the form of changes in the syllabus, in curricula and in teacher-training courses. This concern should be seen as reflecting not only the desire to ensure that contents are balanced, but also the outcome of a particular experience and conviction, namely, that the harnessing of science and technology in the cause of progress increasingly demands a sound ethical and humanistic training; it may be said that what concerns us here is not only a choice but also a reaction against a former error.

Here, in the same vein, are some examples or statements of position derived from various sources but pointing in the same direction. In his introduction to the general policy debate at the twenty-second session of

Introduction

the General Conference of Unesco, the Director-General highlighted a trend that has established itself in the Organization's structure and programme:

At Belgrade, three years ago, in the light of the experience of the first years of implementation of the programme and of the discussions of the relevant commission of the General Conference, I proposed that greater importance should be attached, in addition to the social sciences in the strict sense, to human sciences such as anthropology, linguistics, geography and history, and that the name of the Social Sciences Sector should be changed accordingly [*Unesco General Conference, 1983, p. 12*].

Again, a comparative study on compulsory schooling (primary and lower secondary) in a changing world, published by OECD in 1983, observes that in some countries the 'back-to-basics movement' has led to the introduction of a core curriculum; it reports that in the United Kingdom an effort has been made to identify eight broad areas of experience as the foundation of a core curriculum—'aesthetic/creative, ethical, linguistic, mathematical, physical, scientific, social/political and spiritual' (OECD, 1983a, p. 57). Here we have a case of standard-setting and a syllabus structure that highlights the importance of spiritual education. From such examples it is clearly possible to draw arguments and conclusions for the improvement of educational content over the next two decades.

DESCRIPTION OF A FEW PROJECTS: SIMILARITIES AND DIFFERENCES

Research into future trends in education has become widespread, and such projects or such research invariably pay special attention to the contents of education. The studies commissioned by Unesco in connection with the first International Symposium on the Evolution of the Content of General Education over the Next Two Decades (Paris, 1980) and the discussions that took place at the symposium—attended by participants representing many specialities and countries—showed this to have become a topic of experimental research and deliberation for research workers and likewise for decision-makers and planners.

Comprehensive schemes cover all the main aspects of education systems and usually place the education of the future in a broader context. Research by specialists operating in an individual capacity tends to reveal bolder and more original approaches; this is true in the case of Alvin Toffler's 'The Third Wave' (1981) and of Don Glines's fairly closely worked out scheme entitled 'Minnesota Experimental City MXC'. In this educational city, there would be no schools, teachers or boards of

Introduction

school governors. The city would be a system of lifelong learning extending from the womb to the grave. More significant where our study is concerned, however, are the national or regional projects and research implemented or approved by the relevant authorities.

The project published in 1978 by the Central Council of Education of Denmark—the result of painstaking research and lengthy debate—links the school with socio-economic development and sets it in the context of parallel forms of education. It contains special chapters on analysis of the present education system, the relationship between student expectations and labour market conditions, teachers and recent educational currents. An important chapter deals with 'Reforms concerning the content, methods and structure of the education system' (Denmark, 1978, pp. 125–64). In the light of prevailing trends (Chapter IV), the reform proposal lays down objectives for each level (pre-school education, primary education, etc.) and each problem. It envisages the provision for all of twelve years—and, in the long term, thirteen years—of schooling, at the end of which school-leavers should possess a 'general vocational qualification' or the necessary training to pursue a course of higher education. We shall return to this project later in order to outline its ideas on the selection and organization of content; we would observe for the time being that it pays particular attention to making structures more flexible so as to accommodate those who wish to change courses in mid-stream.[3]

The Major Project in the Field of Education in Latin America and the Caribbean[4] *is the outcome of a joint effort by the states of the region, by Unesco and by the Economic Commission for Latin America (ECLA). Devised on the basis of the Mexico City Declaration adopted in 1979 by the Regional Conference of Ministers of Education and Those Responsible for Economic Planning of Member States in Latin America and the Caribbean, the project was adopted by the same authorities in Quito in 1981, and also benefited from the research by J. Blat Gimeno (1983), published in 1981. The cultural and linguistic unity of the region makes it possible for an overall approach to be adopted, particularly since the countries share a number of demographic, economic and political problems (see Lema and Marquez, 1978; Rama, 1978). The human and natural resources are outstanding, but development has by no means reached the point of satisfying the expectations of the peoples. The Major Project pays special attention to the real democratization of education and to the 'renewal of the content, methods and structures of the different forms of school and out-of-school education and their adjustment to the actual needs of day-to-day life and the foreseeable requirements of society' (Intergovernmental Regional Meeting . . . . 1981a, p. 48).*

Other, ad hoc projects focus on the improvement of school curricula and textbooks, on educational technology or simply on the promotion of modern teaching methods. A good example of a specific project centred on

Introduction

the aims and content of pre-university general education was described in a Japanese curriculum council programme document in 1983. Contents at this level have been reviewed four times since the Second World War and at upper secondary school level five times—in 1947, 1951, 1958 and 1968, and again recently (1980–84), when a new review was undertaken which defined a set of priorities and a new stage in the development of Japanese education. The Japanese authorities have been fairly cautious in carrying out these changes, choosing their moment and always acting on the basis of proposals by specialists. As we approach the third millennium, Japanese educationists seem particularly concerned to relate science and technology more closely to other values and to human aspirations; to this end, they pay special attention to the shaping of attitudes and the development of creativity and feeling, and, to achieve this end, they are concerned to lighten curricula and improve the quality of school life.

The Conference of Ministers of Education and Those Responsible for Economic Planning in African Member States, held in Harare in 1982, paid special attention to the strengthening of cultural identity, the use of African languages in teaching, the introduction of productive work into schools and the teaching of science and technology, thereby expressing the particular concerns of a region faced with special difficulties and striving for endogenous development. Let us finally mention an example of a specific approach dealing with 'hidden contents' or the containers of the things contained: a booklet produced by the Ministry of Education of Quebec includes a case-study on the Montreal Integration Project, concerning the use of audio-visual media to unify learning and make it part of pupils' personal lives.

This involves introducing, at the elementary level, tried and tested educational experiments, active methods in which the child is at the centre of and participates in his or her education and in which maximum use is made of play and creativity. The approach is thus one based on individualized teaching, automatic evaluation, the integration of disciplines, teamwork by teachers, the use of audio-visual resources and the introduction of multi-media techniques (Canada, 1974).

WORK IN PROGRESS

Many countries have set about formulating projects with their sights on the year 2000. In the USSR, for example, the Academy of Pedagogical Sciences, which has a strong technical potential, has tested a number of innovations (hypotheses) experimentally (see 'Research, Theory and Practice in the USSR', 1983).

The Educational Development Forecasting Laboratory of the USSR Academy of Pedagogical Sciences has developed a model of the general education school for the last decade of the twentieth century.... A considerable part of the model school's organizational and educational tenets—the overall regime, the system of pupil activity and the basic forms of educational direction—have proved successful in initial experiments, in which the teaching staff of schools in Moscow, Leningrad, Kiev, Simferopol and many smaller towns and villages took part.... The regime of the projected school differs radically from the 'extended-day' regime, under which groups or classes work under the supervision of teachers, staying at school until 6 p.m. and following a uniform pattern of activities, tutoring system, daily routine, and so on.

The greatest advantages of this new regime are: (a) an alternation of work and rest periods which is more conducive to good health; (b) more time spent in movement and in the open air and a general improvement in the ordering of periods for meals, sleep, productive work, physical exercise and sport; (c) its conformity with the requirements of the psycho-physical development and activities of all age-groups; (d) its adaptability, the time spent on (and choice of) optional studies can be extended according to the inclinations and attitudes of the individual pupil; (e) the greater opportunities offered for developing the pupils' social activity.

Provision is made for optional attendance until 6 p.m. The school day is divided into two halves, one for compulsory and one for optional activities [Kostyashkin, 1980, pp. 489–90].

The case-study on Hungary reports the launching of a long-term forward-planning exercise:

Even before the full introduction of the new curricula, begun in 1977–78, work started on the long-term development of education up to the year 2000. This work is taking place simultaneously in a number of institutions, such as the Pedagogy Committee of the Hungarian Academy of Sciences, the Ministry of Education, the Ministry of Labour and the Central Planning Office. Some researchers are producing their own analyses and proposals. In 1980, a commission set up for this purpose prepared a synoptic report which was submitted to a group of experts. Guidelines for the framing of more detailed plans have gradually taken shape and were adopted in 1982.

We shall return to these guidelines, which provide for a basic curriculum set out in terms of objectives rather than disciplines, the gradual introduction of 12 years of schooling for all, and so forth. In Bulgaria, 1979 saw the adoption of 'Theses' on the development of education up to the end of the twentieth century. These provide, among other things, for the introduction of 12 years of compulsory schooling, the maintenance of a balance between general and vocational education and an appropriate relationship between compulsory and optional subjects.

Other criteria, apart from how advanced they are in relative terms, may be applied to educational forward-planning exercises. For example, the initiators of projects or publications are sometimes education authori-

Introduction

ties or centres for curriculum development; in other instances, business leaders, industrial firms or non-governmental organizations are instrumental in launching and financing studies on the future development of education. It is also possible to distinguish authorities from organizations and authors involved in a personal capacity, such as H. Shane and D. Tabler. As regards the scale of changes involved, projects fluctuate or hesitate between bold visions and schemes, which sometimes run the risk of remaining no more than good intentions, and modest innovations, which arouse the objections of all who expect the future to bring a marked improvement in social life and education systems. The Danish project refers to the difficulties confronting project designers:

Attempts at remodelling the entire educational system on the basis of some theoretical model prepared in advance which has not been developed and tested in practice are not only at variance with the principles of co-determination, but would to all appearances create uncertainty and disapproval, and could easily lead to a blocking of further progress. The dilemma of all reform policies is that the targets can be set so high that they will not meet with general approval, and as a result of this the reform work will come to a standstill. The second risk is that the targets are set so low that they will in fact meet with general approval—but they will not lead anywhere [Denmark, 1978, p. 196].

The variety of approaches and attitudes to the future may also be noted: certain projects speak of the contents of education after 1990 in terms of a future that is possible or probable, whereas others see the future as something to be predicted or planned. Some projects include alternatives and provide for multiple and combinable options; in other cases, a single model, the product of lengthy discussions, has finally been adopted as appropriate to a probable and plannable future. The nature of the approach adopted would seem to be directly related to the degree of centralization to be found in the education system, to the latitude accorded to teachers and, finally, to the management of culture, research and education and the quality of the philosophy of education promoted by the education authorities.

PRELIMINARY DEFINITIONS

Before proceeding with a more detailed analysis of current trends and prospects with regard to the contents of general education, it will probably be useful to define more precisely certain terms and expressions—on occasion similar, at least in appearance—which we shall be employing frequently and sometimes in an allusive fashion in the pages that follow.

Educational contents constitute a body of knowledge, know-how, values

Introduction

and attitudes, taking the concrete form of syllabuses (timetables and curricula) and devised in accordance with goals and objectives assigned to the school by each society; those contents, organized by level or type of educations institution and by class and discipline, are worked out with an educational goal in mind and are the object of a specific process—learning. By 'contents', then, we mean explicit contents, expressed in the form of teachers' guides, curricula or school textbooks.

The devising of contents is an epistemological, axiological and pedagogical activity which consists of selecting and organizing information relevant to the academic levels and specific goals of each education level or class. The operation of selecting and organizing the knowledge to be taught, initially the task of the curriculum developer, is completed by the teacher who organizes the learning process in a specific setting. It is at this point that the latent or 'hidden' contents come into play.

In defining the notion of 'instructional programme',[5] *the* Unesco Glossary of Educational Technology Terms *makes reference to various terms in current use:*

Subject-matter to be taught along with establishment of the teaching time for each subject-matter, as well as the list of contents to be acquired—in other words, the required knowledge. The programme generally takes the form of administrative texts. A 'curriculum' is the organization of learning, in a particular discipline or at a given level. The purpose of the curriculum is to define the objectives of the learning, educational content and the methods and the materials to be employed. In the past, the term 'syllabus' was used to designate an instrument which served as a means for the educational institution to define the content of instruction (the programme) and its practical organization from the standpoint of learning activities [Unesco, 1984b, p. 213].

'Instructional programmes', or curricula, are the foundations of school textbooks (the pupil's learning tool) and methodological manuals (the teacher's teaching tool) (see Foulquié and Saint Jean, 1961, p. 383; Good, 1973, pp. 132, 567, 568). According to the characteristics of the particular education system, curricula are developed or assume their final form at the central government level, or at the state level (United States, Federal Republic of Germany, etc.), or at the level of educational establishments. In the broad sense of the term, educational contents include both information described and organized in the form of curricula, and the 'latent'—or implicit—contents, in other words what is communicated through the quality of school life, teachers' attitudes, the psychological context of teaching activities, and so on. The notion is frequently encountered in recent studies in this broad sense. 'The curriculum', a comparative survey states, 'includes the whole experience that a child undergoes during schooling and covers the educational aims and goals, courses, classroom activities, staff–student relationships, resources and many other

Introduction

factors which impinge on the teaching–learning situation in schools' (OECD, 1983a, p. 59).

This extension of the concept has important practical consequences. An increasing number of studies highlight the importance of these 'hidden contents', i.e. non-verbal inputs in lessons, and of the classroom atmosphere for the effectiveness of the learning process. In the course of demonstrating that a positive attitude by teachers could bring about a considerable improvement in the results achieved by learners, some researchers have highlighted the difficulty of distinguishing between explicit and implicit contents, between the container and the things contained, and between the various components of the curriculum. Finally, we shall see that, in the light of the principle of lifelong education, this definition of the contents of education is growing steadily wider and increasingly includes information acquired by pupils outside school.

The contents of out-of-school activities—participation in groups concerned with technology, literature, future studies, etc., in musical or sporting competitions, visits to industrial firms or cultural institutions, and so on—rest, in almost all countries, in the hands of teachers and/or pupils. Such activities are made optional and enable pupils to choose according to their interests or skills.

In some cases, these activities are incorporated wholly or in part in syllabuses and included in timetables; dovetailing of school and out-of-school activities is ensured by the fact that pupils, teachers and, on occasion, youth organizations (this is particularly true of the socialist countries) play a major role in the choice of topics, methods and forms of activity. This is a field in which educational innovation is more marked and finds freer expression, which is perhaps why out-of-school activities often constitute the point of entry ('infusional approach') for new contents, such as education relating to the quality of life and the environment, peace education, human rights teaching, etc. Budgetary or other constraints can curb the scale of these out-of-school activities considerably.

Educational contents in the broad sense of the term include both the contents of school (formal) and out-of-school (non-formal) education and those of informal education (so-called parallel schooling). The information acquired outside school is a rapidly growing source of knowledge; the volume of information gathered through films and television, newspapers, entertainment and so forth varies greatly from one individual to another; the mass of data, images and impressions is built up independently of the school in accordance with the preferences or interests of young people, depending on the cultural level of the family, the local community, etc. It is seldom analysed or made the subject of decision-making; in some cases, this information fills gaps, particularly in astronomy, space exploration, modern technology, etc. Curriculum developers and teachers are not able to master the whole range of educational content, nor can they be expected *to do so; on the other hand, it is increasingly incumbent on them to take steps, within the organized educational process (in and out of school), to ensure that the various types of content are better integrated and that use—if only partial—is made of the aforementioned mass of data and impressions, so large in quantitative terms. The extent to which pupils are trained to seek out, select and interpret such information is both a criterion of educational success and a factor in academic success. Rather than opposing two types of education—formal and informal—we have thought it more constructive to reconsider the role of the school which, by preparing pupils to deal with and integrate the culture and ideas present in the media and daily life, could help to give unity to the spiritual lives of young people and to avoid 'spiritual alienation'. It is increasingly important in this realm to draw a distinction between diversity and disorder, between individualization of culture and a loss of a sense of values, between the new and potentially significant and the merely eccentric, and between innovation and deviation or anomaly. It is equally important to distinguish information from knowledge, in the sense of a synthesis or educational element organized in relation to ultimate goals and objectives and with a view to the harmonious development of pupils.*

Information is not knowledge. In view of the growing volume of information of all kinds and from all parts of the world, and its atomization, education should place emphasis on the development of conceptual codes of reference and codes of interpretation designed to facilitate the mastery and assimilation of information [International Symposium . . ., 1980d, p. 4].

The term 'general education' will be employed in its restricted sense of non-vocational pre-university education, that is, primary schooling and lower and upper secondary education. As already stated, account will be taken of both school and out-of-school education, relating curricula to informal education. In many countries, primary and lower secondary schooling jointly constitute compulsory education. One could also include here basic education conceived as a cultural, moral, political and practical (e.g. technology, agriculture, etc.) training necessary for all members of a community so that they may participate actively in development and in the cultural and political life of society. It is assumed that the content of general pre-university education includes, or can include, technology and productive (socially useful) work, which are now acknowledged as forming part of general culture.

Introduction

NOTES

1. Because of its conclusions, this study has provoked a lively debate in the United States and elsewhere. On the strength of statistics, the team of eight headed by C. Jencks arrives at the conclusion that the quality of education received by an individual has little effect on his or her success in life. Success in a career depends on many factors other than those traditionally taken into account, such as family environment, intellectual performance observed and measured in school, etc. The study attributes an important role to IQ. Some specialists point out that Jencks's definition of success is based on questionable criteria, for example salary and the relative status of various professions. Others have countered this thesis with research suggesting that learning is essential for success in life (see the whole body of literature on lifelong education) and that the academic success of all children depends essentially on the quality of learning.
2. One finds the same idea expressed in Unesco's Second Medium-Term Plan:

   Education alone will not solve all problems, and the hopes placed in it can sometimes be excessive, especially where the solution of certain great social problems and world problems is concerned. But its role is not less important on that account: it can provide a better grasp of problems and their interrelations, supply the knowledge needed in order to understand and solve them, and arouse the attitudes that will lead to action and results [Unesco, 1983c, paragraph 5006, p. 116].

3. With regard to this project, it may be recalled that in Denmark, the country of Nikolai Grundtvig (1783–1872) and of people's universities, the education budget increased from 2.8 per cent of the GNP in 1957 to 7.5 per cent in 1974, and the number of pupils rose from 481,000 in 1946 to 806,000 in 1975.
4. This project was made possible by a series of studies carried out by Unesco and by specialists in the region. Concerning the Mexico City Declaration adopted in 1979, the Quito meeting stated:

   after acknowledging the sustained effort that had been made by the countries of the region in the past decade to develop education, and recognizing that serious shortcomings still persisted in the field of economic and social development ... the conference indicated the principal educational goals to be attained in the region by the year 2000 [Intergovernmental Regional Meeting..., 1981a, p. 7].

   For the Quito meeting, held in 1981, Unesco prepared a document (Intergovernmental Regional Meeting..., 1981b) which we shall make use of, particularly the section entitled 'Improvement of the Efficiency and Quality of Education Systems'; the document includes statistical tables by country on the decennial increase in population (1980–2000), on enrolment and enrolment ratios (1970–2000), on illiteracy and the population aged 15 and over, and on public spending on education as a percentage of the GNP (1970–78).
   At the meeting of the Interim Intergovernmental Regional Committee for the Major Project in the Field of Education in Latin America and the Caribbean in Saint Lucia in July 1982, almost all countries presented national plans of action which concentrated on two objectives: extension of school education and literacy training and education for adults.
5. The *Glossary* cited renders '*programme d'études*' by 'instructional programme', rather than the more usual 'curriculum', which it defines in a special sense. (Translator's note.)

7
Current developments

As we come to analyse the trends now emerging in the definition of educational contents, a few preliminary remarks should be made regarding the inherent difficulties of such an undertaking and the caution that is called for. The term 'trend' is itself quite patently a highly complex one, since it can be applied to different levels of education, to different factors involved in the learning process—educators, students, researchers, decision-makers—as well as to the various aspects of the curriculum: content, methods, evaluation. Moreover, there are undoubtedly variations from one region or group of countries to another; while there are general trends, there are also some that are more limited in their extension, and others whose intensity fluctuates in time. A case in point is foreign language courses, interest in which has declined in some countries while increasing in others. This 'play' in a given trend is due to factors that are sometimes difficult to identify. It varies in degree according to whether it stems from a decision based on an appropriate analysis or simply from a concern to 'fall into line'. As J. Bousquet has pointed out, the developing countries have sometimes borrowed attractive and original modern approaches without analysing their relevance to national traditions and requirements. At times this results in the 'rejection' of the foreign body. The observer also runs the risk of failing to appreciate the importance of certain new departures which, although unobtrusive, ultimately exert a profound influence upon educational practice, as for example certain innovations that have been introduced in the past ten or fifteen years in the industrialized countries; on the other hand, the observer may be inclined to overestimate the importance of an innovation which turns out to be short-lived. As Brian Rose (1972, pp. viii–ix) has so cogently observed: 'we may often be tempted to wonder whether our times are as revolutionary as we sometimes assert ... will our contemporary teaching machines be relegated to history as a passing fad, of no greater importance to the teachers of A.D. 2000 than Froebel's first building box?'[1] The question is worth asking, even if it is considered that the promotion of computer science in the school syllabus and computer-assisted instruction in the learning process have every likelihood of being pursued, even outside the industrialized countries.

CONCEPTS IN FULL EXPANSION: SYSTEMS APPROACH, CURRICULUM THEORY AND PRACTICE, TAXONOMY OF EDUCATIONAL GOALS, EDUCATIONAL TECHNOLOGY

The concern to give the teaching/learning process greater precision and coherence has been prompted as much by certain theories or findings of research as by the desire of those in charge of education to improve its efficiency and quality.

This endeavour has received decisive, and beneficial, impetus and support from general systems theory and its applications to the design, organization, operation and evaluation of the learning process. Berger and Brunswic have clearly stated the scope and usefulness of the systems approach:

The systems approach is a method; it is not a science.... Its purpose is to enable all those working within a complex situation ... to analyse this complexity, describe it, recognize dysfunctions when they occur and allow for the various levels of social or institutional realities. But it also helps the person taking action to keep maximum control over the chain-reaction he sets in motion and to assess its impact [Unesco, 1981d, p. 10].

As regards curriculum theory and practice in English-speaking countries, these have quite properly attracted interest on the part of educators and researchers in many countries. It is in our view significant that the term 'curriculum' has gained acceptance in German—even in 'the homeland of didactics', where, without becoming assimilated to the term '*Didaktik*', it features in the titles of works on the design, organization, methodology and technology of the teaching/learning process (see Frey et al., 1975; Haft and Hameyer, 1975). After a certain amount of hesitation, French-speaking countries have had to recognize that neither *programme scolaire* nor *plan d'études* really covers the full meaning of the concept of 'curriculum'. Without attempting to go into every aspect of this meaning, we propose to set out here a number of the concept's features and merits.

The theory of curriculum planning, which is clearly geared to practice, takes account of the educational process, of what actually happens in the classroom. Unlike didactics, it attaches particular importance to study of the interactions between the components of this process—objectives, content, learning methods, teaching resources, forms of organization of instruction, evaluation methods and techniques—and to turning such interactions to account. Curriculum specialists stress equally that one 'cannot put the cart before the horse' (for example, content cannot be determined prior to or independently of the definition of objectives) and that each component interrelates with all the other components. Designed and organized along these lines, the learning process becomes more coherent and, hence, more efficient (see Fig. 1).

Evaluation plays an important part, providing the teacher with useful feedback and enabling pupils to know how well they have performed and to situate themselves in relation to the targets set. Logically, it is the objectives which determine how the learning process is prepared and organized, and which serve ultimately as evaluation criteria, evaluation becoming itself a method of learning and of making a searching assessment of results.

Preparing the learning process in the spirit of curriculum planning calls for a greater input than is required in order to draw up an annual programme of activities (listing themes to be covered and dates). It entails systematic co-operation among the teachers of a given class, and between these and the teachers of the class preceding it. This thorough preparation, which takes up the teachers' time before the beginning of the academic year, simplifies their work subsequently and obviates the risk of any breaks occurring between the different sequences involved. This more disciplined and coherent approach in educational practice has also proved its worth in the work of drawing up curricula and syllabuses and of preparing teachers' handbooks, etc., a task which is undertaken by curriculum development centres in many countries.

The taxonomies of educational objectives (Bloom, 1956; Krathwohl et al., 1964) have been geared to the same goals—strict precision, coherence, relevance of the learning and evaluation methods—their influence being exerted at the levels of curriculum design, teacher education and educational practice. The publication of that work was rightly regarded as an event in the world of education. In the preface to the French-language Canadian edition of Volume II, Dr F. Robaye writes:

When I discovered Volume I of Bloom's *Taxonomy of Educational Objectives* in its French translation by Marcel Lavallée, I had the feeling that something important had just occurred in the educational field. For the publication of that work filled a gap of which any teacher worth his salt was aware. By this I mean that teachers who were truly worthy of their noble profession were

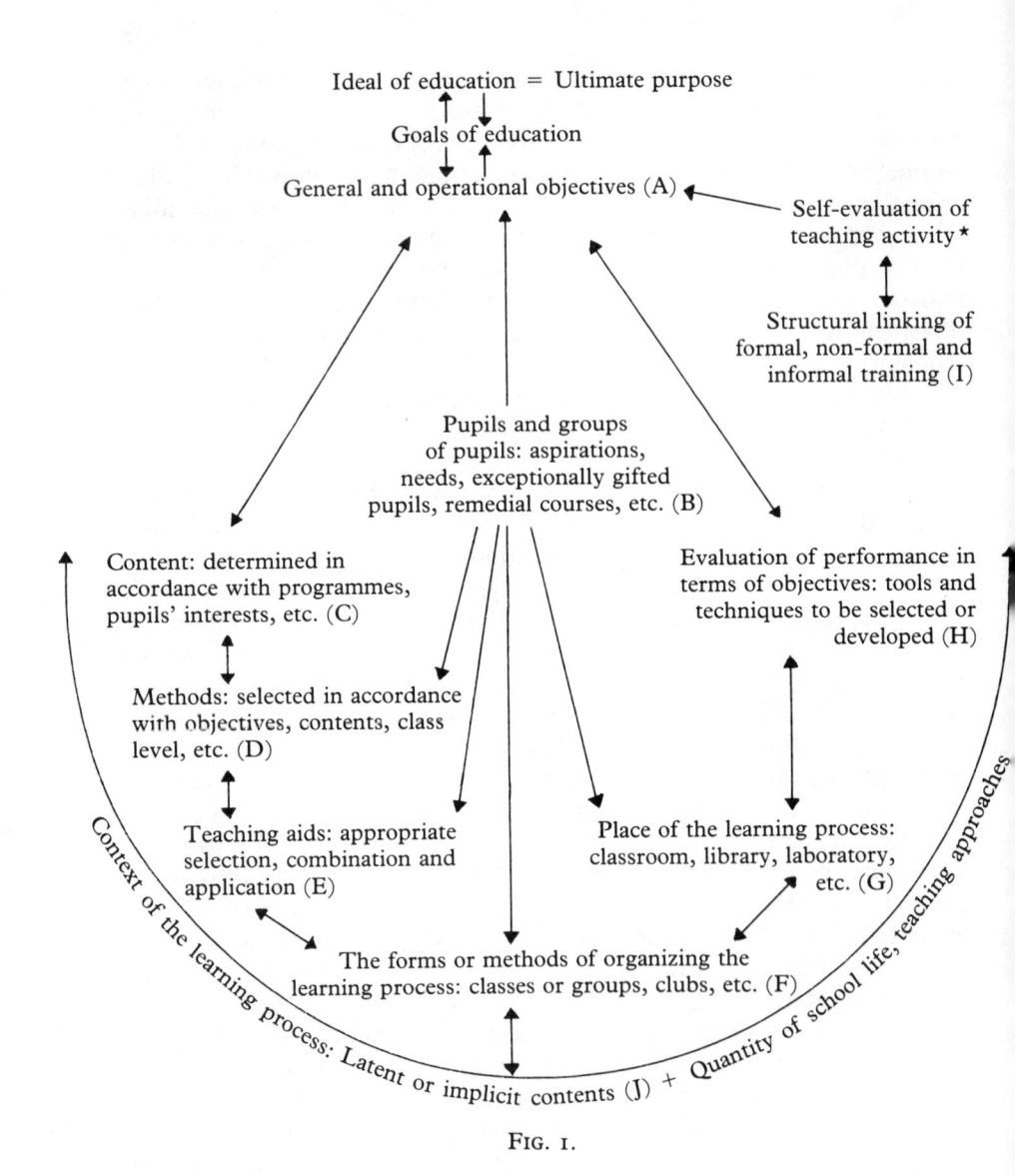

Ideal of education = Ultimate purpose
Goals of education
General and operational objectives (A)

Self-evaluation of teaching activity *

Structural linking of formal, non-formal and informal training (I)

Pupils and groups of pupils: aspirations, needs, exceptionally gifted pupils, remedial courses, etc. (B)

Content: determined in accordance with programmes, pupils' interests, etc. (C)

Evaluation of performance in terms of objectives: tools and techniques to be selected or developed (H)

Methods: selected in accordance with objectives, contents, class level, etc. (D)

Teaching aids: appropriate selection, combination and application (E)

Place of the learning process: classroom, library, laboratory, etc. (G)

The forms or methods of organizing the learning process: classes or groups, clubs, etc. (F)

Context of the learning process: Latent or implicit contents (J) + Quantity of school life, teaching approaches

FIG. 1.

Notes:
(1) All the components are linked with all the others.
(2) Clearly, the likelihood of breaks occurring in a single training activity is very considerable; the transition from ultimate goals to general and operational objectives presents numerous problems.
(3) For latent or implicit contents, and the 'quality of school life', see the introduction to Part II.

* A distinction is to be drawn between ad hoc self-evaluation and systematic self-evaluation.

Source: This diagram of the curriculum, in the broad sense of the term, is modelled upon a simpler diagram by D. Wheeler published in *Curriculum Process*, London, University of London Press, 1974.

painfully alive to the difficulty of evaluating, of monitoring the effectiveness of their work ... Indeed, any taxonomy of educational objectives implies an ideal adult model. A certain courage is needed today in order to acknowledge that we choose one or other of the many models with which we are presented [Krathwohl et al., 1964].

As the authors of a more recent taxonomy put it, 'the etymology of the term clearly expresses its meaning: to educate is to lead (out), hence to guide towards a goal. "Leading" and "nowhere" are mutually exclusive terms' (de Landsheere and de Landsheere, 1975). It has been pointed out that, being closely bound up with the ultimate ends and goals of education, which are directly determined by the educational policy and philosophy of each country, taxonomies of educational objectives have little chance of being successfully borrowed or transferred elsewhere. It has also been noted that many teachers, engrossed in the precise definition of operational objectives, are beginning to overlook the end purposes and values by which these objectives are justified, and that a gap is thus opening up between efforts geared to achieving certain performance targets and the higher level of attitudes and capacities; that for example by focusing at lower secondary school level on the need to establish the appropriate distinction between 'foodstuffs' and 'nutritive substances', the teacher loses sight of the reason for this effort and of the link between this observable and measurable objective and the sphere of ultimate goals. However, such observations have not prevented progress being made in the taxonomy of objectives which, appropriately adapted, are used for curriculum design and the defining of educational practice in many countries. When he presented Bloom and Krathwohl's taxonomy for the first time in Romania, in 1971, Vaideanu (1971) was greeted with more expressions of interest than reservations. It is fair to claim that, today, the principle of taxonomy of objectives is firmly established and in widespread use.

The concept of educational technology also exerts an increasingly marked influence on the design and operation of the teaching/learning process. The application of this concept—deriving from industry—to the development of the pupil's personality has not failed to give rise to certain misgivings and objections. Nevertheless, the concept recurs both in the technical activities and in the operational projects conducted by Unesco, which moreover has produced a glossary of educational technology terms in various language versions (Unesco, 1984b). Educational technology is understood in principle to refer to a coherent set of methods, means and techniques of learning and evaluation, designed and used in accordance with the objectives being pursued and in relation to educational contents and the pupils' own interests. For the teachers, using an appropriate technology means knowing how to organize the learning process and to ensure its success. Mastering these theories and concepts, which not only converge but intermesh, has yielded indisputable improvements, the most obvious being undoubtedly a greater coherence in curriculum design and planning, in the operation of the learning process and in the organization of evaluation activities and competitive and other examinations. And greater coherence means improved efficiency in the learning process. Bertrand Schwartz (1973, p. 127) rightly stresses the importance of such coherence:

If the objective is formulated in terms of abilities, the evaluation procedure is then quite naturally integrated into the method itself. It is designed to enable pupils to measure at any time the distance between the stage they have reached and the final objective. It may be noted that we are hereby taking a clear stand against a type of education which uses certain methods for purposes of instruction but employs for examinations—for the sole purpose of making a selection—procedures which bear no relation to these methods.

This is also why these theories and concepts recur in the seminars which Unesco organizes for curriculum planners and teacher trainers, and in the case-studies and educational reform projects already referred to.

However, the technological nature of these research advances has sometimes prompted misgivings at the level of educational practice, and triggered off reactions at the theoretical level, in particular on the part of those for whom the educational process remains first and foremost an art. For example, the American educationist John Goodlad (Goodlad, 1979; Goodlad et al., 1979) has expressed fears that a technological approach to education may jeopardize its ultimate humanist purpose, limiting the scope and importance of formal education, at a time when man is more than ever in need of a sound humane and social training, rooted in the individual's freely expressed aspirations, one which cannot be confined to a technological straitjacket.

However, such objections, which are indeed largely justified, have led rather to an improvement in these new approaches than to their abandonment. The conclusion has been reached that a course in the philosophy of education is becoming all the more essential in that the common training core of student teachers now includes such components as 'the systems approach to education', 'educational technology', 'the devising of knowledge tests', etc. The dangers and losses resulting from an excessively systemic approach, from the 'technologization' of so complex and subtle a process, have been measured. We are now more conscious of the fact that technology is a teaching tool or aid, and that it must not be allowed to become the refuge of mediocre teachers or those tied to routine. After so many experiments, successes and mistakes, we now know full well that, where the learning process is concerned, there is no method, means or teaching machine that can serve as a panacea.

LIFELONG EDUCATION

As a guiding concept, lifelong education has roots in the thinking of Graeco-Roman antiquity and that of Islam, as well as in ancient Chinese and Indian philosophy. It recurs in the writings of J. A. Comenius (1592–1670), that of Galileo on the world of education, and of Jean-Jacques Rousseau (1712–78), as well as among the representatives of the educational movements which arose between 1880 and 1920: 'child-centred education', 'activity-method teaching', etc. However, as an active principle in educational reform projects, exerting an influence on the realignment of education systems at every level and in all their components, lifelong education constitutes an achievement of our own era, and more specifically of the past two decades. The stages through which this fundamental concept has evolved, the debates which have enriched and clarified it and the practical measures taken to apply it in the different countries are highly characteristic of the way in which progress is achieved both at the theoretical level and in the realm of decision-making. It is fair to say that the gearing of all the education subsystems of a given country to the lifelong education approach represents an original and appropriate response to the challenges of our time, and the sole means of preparing the individual to become an actively involved and articulate member of a democratic society, to defend his rights and the essential values of such a society, and to educate himself and develop successfully in a world undergoing both foreseeable and unforeseeable changes. A whole range of different approaches may today be noted (see, for example, Busshoff et al., 1981; CERI, 1973*b*; Cropley, 1979; Dave, 1973; Faure et al., 1973; Goad, 1984; Hameyer, 1979; Hawes, 1975; Heidt, 1979; Hely, 1962; Hummel, 1977; Ingram, 1979; Pineau, 1977; Suchodolski and Kuczynski, 1982); no country can claim to have already instituted a comprehensive, fully co-ordinated system of lifelong education, but all are endeavouring to organize their education systems more closely in accordance with this principle.[2] It has been agreed that the fundamental step where lifelong education is concerned is that of the relationship between, and/or confrontation of, social forces and movements and educational structures, and this step has not often been made by the latter (Gelpi, 1984).

It is clear that the evolution of the concept of lifelong education has been determined primarily by the demands of a society whose development has continued to accelerate, confronting the individual with problems of growing complexity. This evolution constitutes an example both of the force of the external pressures exerted upon educational systems and of the capacity of these systems, and of the subsystem responsible for reflection on education, to analyse society's messages and to find solutions. In particular, the debates on the organization of adult education and its components have played a major role in promoting the principle of lifelong education, which tied in with arguments and experiments pursued in the past. Hummel (1977) mentions the report of the Ministry of Reconstruction of the United Kingdom produced in 1919, which described adult education as a permanent national necessity, and an inalienable prerogative of citizenship. Mention might also be made of Denmark's 'people's universities', the founder of which, Nicolai Grundtvig (1783–1872) is sometimes, wrongfully, overlooked by historians of education.

Closer to us in time, certain debates concerning adult education have also been responsible for the decisive headway made by the principle of lifelong education. Mention may be made in particular of the congresses on the theme of adult education held in Denmark (Elsinore, 1949), in Canada (Montreal, 1960), in Japan (Tokyo, 1972) and in Paris (Unesco House, 1985). However, while it is true that the debate on lifelong education was launched in the context of adult education, the specialists who clarified and enriched the concept during the 1960s represent the whole range of educational levels and subsystems, and a great number of disciplines.

Mention should also be made of the work done during the past two decades by Unesco, which has on the one hand initiated or provided the guidelines for such debates and, on the other, explored or encouraged the application of the principle by Member States with a view to improving their own education systems. In *Learning To Be* the concept was already present:

Whether they do so consciously or not, human beings keep on learning and training themselves throughout their lives, above all through the influence of the surrounding environment and through the experiences which mould their behaviour, their conceptions of life and the content of their knowledge. However, until the present day, there were few structures in which this natural dynamic could find support, so as to transcend chance and become a deliberate project. Especially, preconceived ideas about instruction—it was for the young and took place in schools—prevented people generally from conceiving of lifelong education in normal educational terms. Yet it is true that in the space of only a few years the same obvious fact has come home to people from one end of the world to the other: most men are not sufficiently equipped to face the conditions and vicissitudes of life as lived in the second half of the twentieth century. Hundreds of millions of adults need education, not only for the pleasure of perfecting their capacities or contributing to their own development, as before, but because the demands for overall social, economic and cultural development of twentieth-century societies require the maximum potential of an educated citizenry.

As has been noted, the educational enterprise will only become efficient, just and human by undergoing radical changes affecting the essence of educational action, as well as the time and place for education, in short, by adopting the concept of lifelong education [Faure et al., 1972, p. 142].

Lifelong education became one of the pivots of Unesco's programmes during the 1970s, and a series of studies, meetings[3] and operational projects were devoted to the subject. Efforts were focused both on methodological aspects and on identification of the impact of lifelong education on the objectives, structures, contents and methods of learning and evaluation, as well as on the initial and continuing training of teachers. Particular attention was given to the linking of the different structures and to ensuring greater flexibility in moving from one level to another and the smoother integration of the curriculum components; means were defined for training pupils in self-instruction and self-evaluation techniques. It thus became possible to measure the scale of the transformations to be carried out and to assess the comprehensive, innovatory and integrating role of this new approach.

For its part, the Unesco Institute for Education (UIE, Hamburg) has given considerable prominence in its activities to lifelong education, publishing monographs and organizing meetings on the question. It is from one of these monographs (Dave, 1973) that we have taken the 'theoretical and operational framework for lifelong education' which in our view gives a truly comprehensive view of the concept. Moreover, a seminar organized in 1974 by the UIE on the development of criteria and procedures for evaluating curricula in the context of lifelong education represented a sort of stock-taking exercise. The participants, from a wide range of countries, were given certain working tools: basic concepts (definitions), evaluation criteria (projects), evaluation guides. They in turn contributed reports on the progress achieved in applying the principle of lifelong education: N. Adiseshiah: 'A Learning System in Tamil Nâdu'; Filipovic Dragomir: 'Permanent Education and Reform of the Education System in Yugoslavia'; C. Kupisievicz: 'On Some Principles of Modernizing the School System as a Base for Adult Education'; Japan Council of Economic Research: 'Human Development in a New Industrial Society'; Sigeo Masui: 'A Brief Note on the Conceptualization of

A THEORETICAL AND OPERATIONAL FRAMEWORK FOR LIFELONG EDUCATION

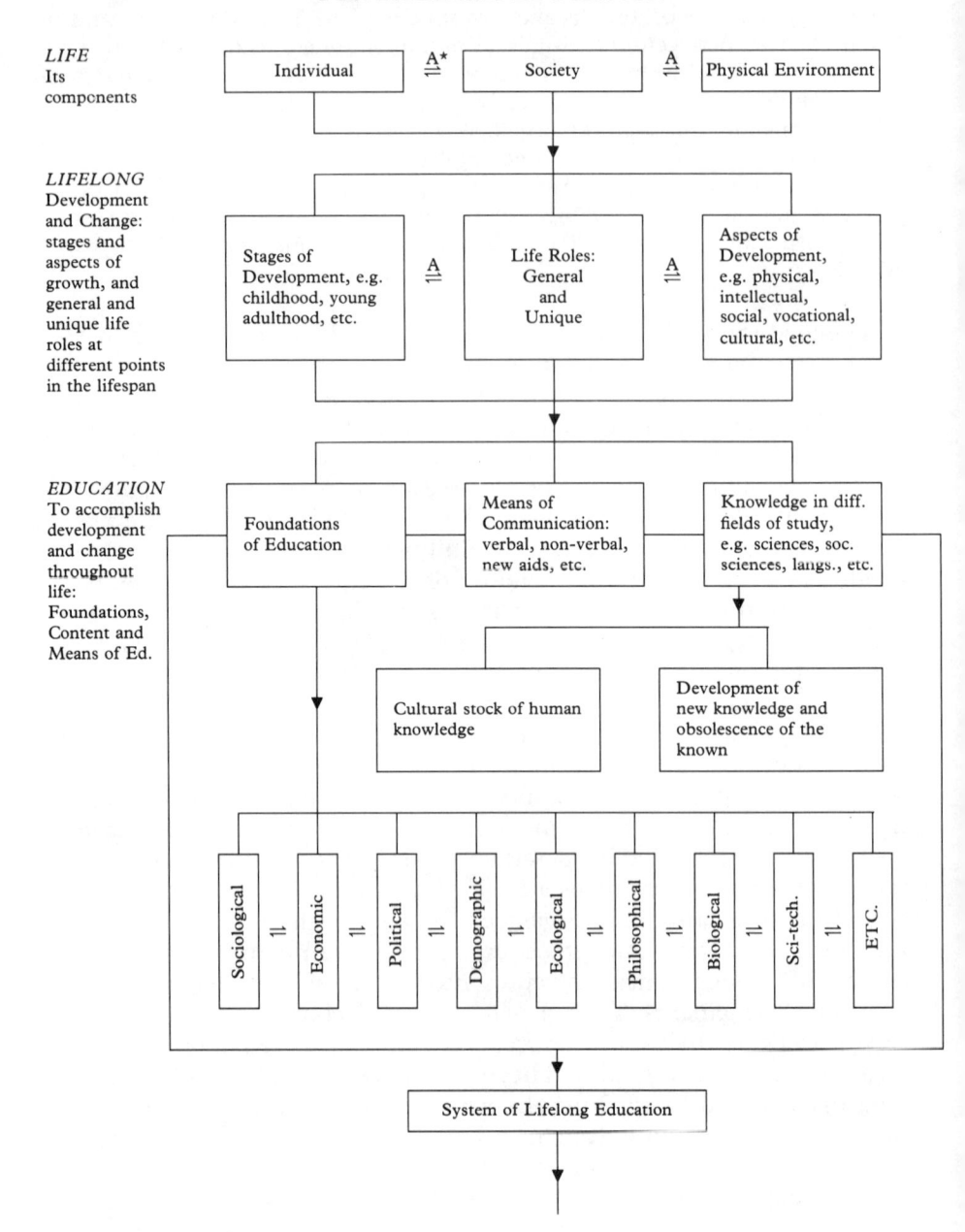

LIFE
Its components

| Individual | $\stackrel{A*}{\rightleftharpoons}$ | Society | $\stackrel{A}{\rightleftharpoons}$ | Physical Environment |

LIFELONG
Development and Change: stages and aspects of growth, and general and unique life roles at different points in the lifespan

| Stages of Development, e.g. childhood, young adulthood, etc. | $\stackrel{A}{\rightleftharpoons}$ | Life Roles: General and Unique | $\stackrel{A}{\rightleftharpoons}$ | Aspects of Development, e.g. physical, intellectual, social, vocational, cultural, etc. |

EDUCATION
To accomplish development and change throughout life: Foundations, Content and Means of Ed.

Foundations of Education

Means of Communication: verbal, non-verbal, new aids, etc.

Knowledge in diff. fields of study, e.g. sciences, soc. sciences, langs., etc.

Cultural stock of human knowledge

Development of new knowledge and obsolescence of the known

Sociological $\rightleftharpoons$ Economic $\rightleftharpoons$ Political $\rightleftharpoons$ Demographic $\rightleftharpoons$ Ecological $\rightleftharpoons$ Philosophical $\rightleftharpoons$ Biological $\rightleftharpoons$ Sci-tech. $\rightleftharpoons$ ETC.

System of Lifelong Education

* The sign $\rightleftharpoons$ means interaction between two entities, and the sign $\stackrel{A}{\rightleftharpoons}$ means interaction among all entities.

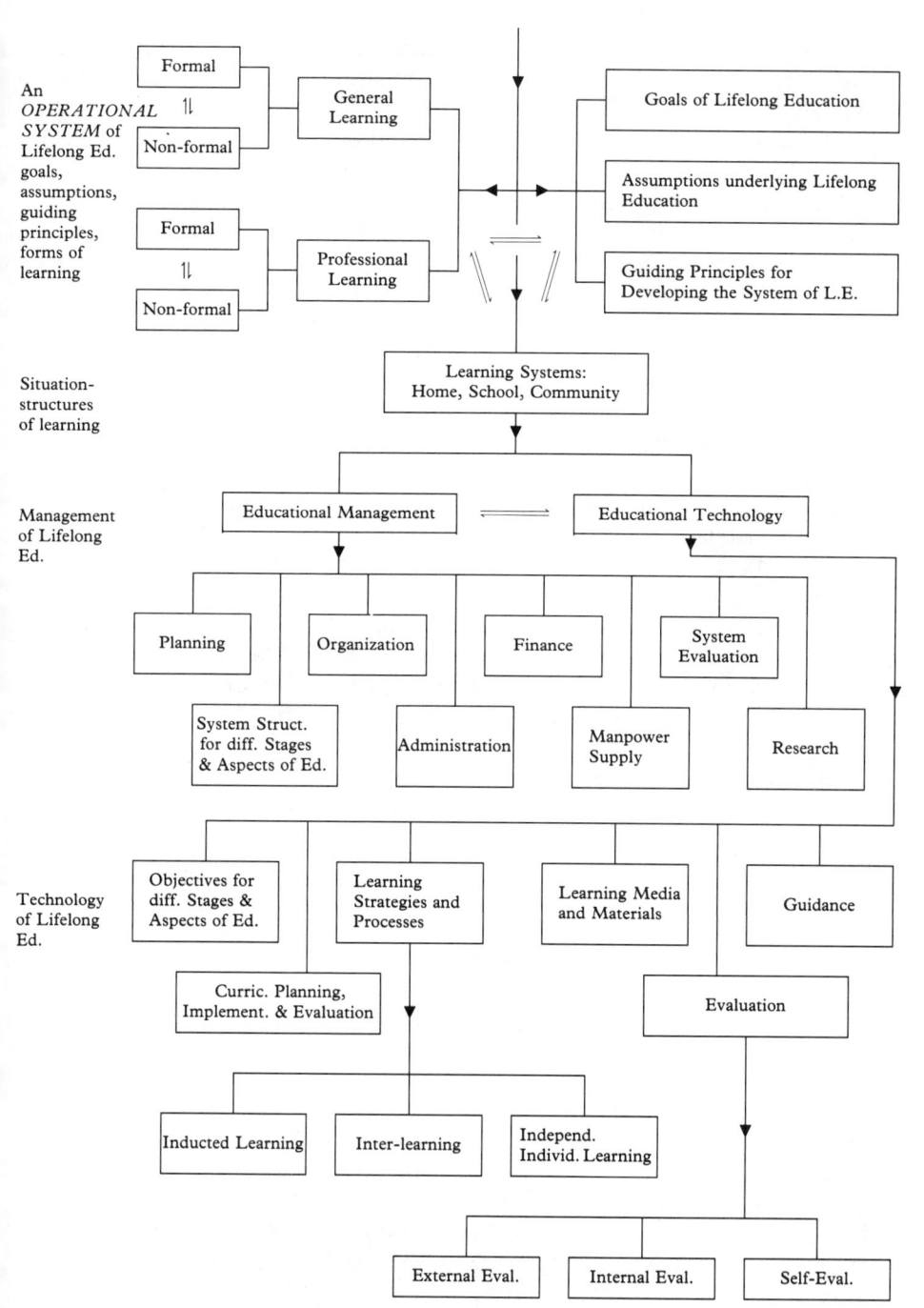

An OPERATIONAL SYSTEM of Lifelong Ed. goals, assumptions, guiding principles, forms of learning	Formal ⇅ Non-formal → General Learning Formal ⇅ Non-formal → Professional Learning	↔	Goals of Lifelong Education Assumptions underlying Lifelong Education Guiding Principles for Developing the System of L.E.
Situation-structures of learning		Learning Systems: Home, School, Community	
Management of Lifelong Ed.		Educational Management ⇌ Educational Technology	
	Planning	Organization	Finance	System Evaluation
	System Struct. for diff. Stages & Aspects of Ed.	Administration	Manpower Supply	Research
Technology of Lifelong Ed.	Objectives for diff. Stages & Aspects of Ed.	Learning Strategies and Processes	Learning Media and Materials	Guidance
		Curric. Planning, Implement. & Evaluation		Evaluation
	Inducted Learning	Inter-learning	Independ. Individ. Learning	
		External Eval.	Internal Eval.	Self-Eval.

Source: DAVE, R. H., *Lifelong Education and School Curriculum. Interim Findings of an Exploratory Study on School Curriculum, Structures and Teacher Education in the Perspective of Lifelong Education.* Hamburg, Unesco Institute for Education, 1973. (UIE monographs, 1.) (fold-out, between pp. 28 and 29)

Lifelong Education and School Education': L. Topa (Romania): 'La didactique dans la perspective de l'éducation permanente'; Salazar Bondy: 'On Educational Reform in Peru'.

Discussing the reform launched in the state of Tamil Nâdu, Adiseshiah highlighted its main objectives: 1. to provide all children and adults with minimum training that will help them in the learning process: improvement of textbooks, access to libraries, etc.; 2. to link the right to education with the right to work; 3. to extend education beyond the confines of the school and university, through evening and correspondence courses, radio and television courses, etc.; 4. to reform structures and make them more flexible, with the aim of providing a range of different 'exit points' and modernizing the curriculum and the evaluation subsystem.

This UIE seminar also provided the occasion for Japan to announce the basic principles of a reform inspired by the concept of lifelong education and the measures to be taken ('Human Development in a New Industrial Society: Ideal Education from a Long-Term Viewpoint'). It is worth noting that the authors of this essentially future-oriented project, drawn up between 1968 and 1972, were a prominent figure in the economic world, Mr Toshio Doko (President of the Toshiba Electric Company) and Dr Masunori Hiratsuka (1907–81), Director of the National Institute for Educational Research (NIER). Indeed, heads of major corporations such as Doko, Honda, and Ibuko are frequently found initiating projects or schemes of an educational nature, and this marriage of the economic and educational worlds constitutes a guarantee that the projects will be carried out. The document presented to the 1974 seminar in Hamburg set out five principles: 1. The reform of education to be undertaken in Japan must take lifelong education as a key principle; generosity of spirit must constitute the basis of all education; Japanese education must give particular prominence to aesthetic, moral and religious instruction, albeit without jeopardizing the development of creative intelligence. 2. The reform of education cannot be limited to problems of structures, content and methods, since education is based on a relationship between individuals; it must accordingly strive to develop desirable attitudes among educators, parents and leaders of the economy. 3. A further principle must be to reconcile (and integrate) traditions and innovations in the domain of education. 4. Companies should improve their education policies; at a broader level, the Ministry of National Education, the principal agency responsible for reform, must review its policy in regard to educational administration. 5. Japanese education must seek to enable all citizens to contribute to the promotion of peace and to the progress of humankind. The project also comprises measures designed to define in clearer terms the roles of the family, of the school and of social education and to ensure a better relationship between their respective spheres of influence, to improve the training and remuneration of teachers, and to enhance co-operation between education and industry, etc.

Finally, mention may be made of the importance attached to the general issue of lifelong education in Romania, where a national symposium, Simpozionul Educatia Adultilor: Cercetare si Actiune Culturala, was organized in 1968 by the State Committee for Culture and the National Institute for Educational Research, with Unesco assistance. In his introductory report, George Vaideanu pointed out that

Pupils learn for the future, but that future consists mainly in entrance tests and final examinations, that is, in strictly limited targets. Moreover, teachers regard themselves as being responsible rather for the teaching of a specific subject than for the all-round training of their students, and their preparation for lifelong education. In its turn, adult education does not represent a continuation, in new guises, of the formal education which precedes and renders it possible; it appears to be concerned rather with limited occupational tasks. This hiatus between the two types of education—school/formal and adult—is at variance with the increasingly powerful movement towards lifelong education.[4]

In 1973, the principle of lifelong education was enshrined in an important decision taken by the government. In 1976, a case-study entitled *Lifelong Education in Romania* was prepared at Unesco's request. From 1980 on, a specific theme—lifelong education: concept and impact—has been included in the education curriculum provided for the in-service training of all teachers. Whereas previously the topic had been dealt with in education courses in a somewhat dispersed way, a chapter has been devoted specifically to the subject in the most recent course.[5]

These examples illustrate the considerable effort that has been made at both national and international levels to realign education systems and the whole teaching/learning process so as to give them a lifelong education focus.

As far as educational thinking and practice are concerned, these efforts have generated a current of ideas, a number of improvements, a broader vision of the ultimate goals of education (one might even say a new philosophy of education), but also and above all a new awareness of the complexity of the problems to be solved. The different stages in its development and the experiments involved, the errors committed and the limits identified have all helped substantially to clarify and enrich the concept of lifelong education. While the idea is a simple one, its consequences are such that, according to Charles Hummel, the formulation of the concept of lifelong education, comparable to the Copernican revolution, is one of the epoch-making events in the history of education. He further argues that education is capable of generating a genuine educational renascence.

The very lively discussion from which the concept of lifelong education as a fundamental principle of education emerged testifies to the fact that a concept benefits by being questioned and interpreted in the light of concrete situations, and that the clarification of its import and the awareness of errors to be avoided in its application can render valuable service to educational authorities, research workers and educators. Initially, the evolution of the working world and the advent of new occupations led to the idea of continuing vocational education for everybody, either in the form of periodic refresher courses or in the form of permanent self-instruction. Along these lines, Sweden launched in the 1960s the concept of 'recurrent education', which proved particularly fruitful (CERI, 1973*b*). Very soon, the magnitude of the changes affecting all socio-economic and cultural sectors led to a new step in the direction of lifelong education with the concept of the continuing and comprehensive education of adults. It then became apparent that the continuing and comprehensive education of adults regarded as a supplement to formal schooling posed difficult problems. How is it possible to provide an education which aims to be comprehensive and continuing if the adult has not been prepared for a mode of learning which calls upon intellectual qualities such as self-reliance and judgement? Hence the fruitful and revolutionary idea of an overall reform of education systems enabling education in all forms and at all levels to be integrated and co-ordinated in the light of the principle of lifelong education. How can educational goals, objectives, content and methods of evaluation be reformulated? What modifications must be made to the subsystem of the training of teachers and educators? Consideration of these questions and experience acquired revealed a series of particularly interesting characteristics of lifelong education.

Lifelong education is of a *global* nature; it embraces the whole of the population and relates or co-ordinates all structures (subsystems) which have educational functions.

Lifelong education is *continuous*, hence it covers the entire life-span of the individual; it is *integral*, providing everyone with possibilities of retraining and improvement: occupational training, socio-cultural training, etc.

In the framework of an open and dynamic system of lifelong education, every individual is called upon to participate; to identify sources of training and to learn from them, so that in his turn he becomes an educational source for others. The *co-ordination* and *integration* of all forms of education make it possible for work and training to be constantly associated.

The advances made in the application of a system of lifelong education coincide with those in the *democratization* of social life, and lifelong education reduces the disparities between those who are knowledgeable and capable of continually improving their knowledge and those who remain paralysed by ignorance and the fear of complex situations.

Based essentially on intellectual autonomy, on a set of learning techniques and on the capacity for self-evaluation, lifelong education is the opposite of 'perpetual schooling', which moreover supposes the segregation of a population into pupils and teachers who remain so permanently, as shown by a collective work prepared under the auspices of Unesco and whose title itself raises a problem: *Education or Permanent Alienation* (Pineau, 1977, p. 83).

Along the same lines, two Polish philosophers (Suchodolski and Kuczynski, 1982) have strongly emphasized the link between permanent education, in its widest sense, and creativity.

But while it may be asserted that lifelong education is a powerful trend and an active principle, it should immediately be added that its application remains an open problem. One example comes to mind: the school textbook, that fundamental instrument of the pupil whose influence is self-evident. How many countries are able to provide textbooks designed as instruments of an ongoing training based on the capacity for self-instruction and self-evaluation, centred on codes of reference and codes of interpretation, giving pupils a taste for innovation and participation, indicating sources of information, etc.?

THE NEW TRIAD OF EDUCATIONAL OBJECTIVES

We have already referred to the impact on educational content of the rapid and constant growth of the volume of information and knowledge circulating in social life. In particular, this impact makes it increasingly difficult to select and organize contents: to bring out fundamental concepts, to organize learning in function of practical problems to be solved, etc. Indirectly, but forcefully, this overwhelming and confusing volume of information points up the importance of attitudes and abilities which can help the individual to find his bearings, and to select and use scientific and technological data. Hence the idea that education might not in the future be confined to giving the learner a sound stock of knowledge and cultivating an interest in further learning; it must also establish attitudes and skills, and cover the spiritual life of the individual. Characteristics such as discretion, sense of responsibility, generosity, sensibility and the spirit of independence are just as important as intellectual capacities such as the ability to identify a central issue, to generalize relevantly, to distinguish between ends and means, to relate cause and effect, and so on.

The increasing importance of attitudes and skills has been highlighted also by other trends: the rapid evolution and mobility of the working world, the increasing number of practical problems to be solved, etc. There have been swift reactions to such changes and demands, and in many cases educators and curriculum builders have been influenced. This pressure from outside the system is combined with another, from inside, acting in the same direction: pupils, parents and those teachers who are capable of seeing beyond the horizon of their own subject are increasingly feeling the need for a learning centred not only on fundamental concepts, but also on attitudes and skills which can ensure the mastery of the knowledge acquired, its enrichment and its renewal. This trend or concern has been clearly expressed first and foremost at the level of educational goals and objectives; it is encountered in different but convergent forms. It may be recalled here that the common core of compulsory schooling established by the British authorities includes a training placing strong emphasis on values and attitudes: spiritual education (OECD, 1983a). The Japanese authorities feel that values and the formation of attitudes (generosity, responsibility, moral and aesthetic sensibility, etc.) must in future occupy a more important place. They specify that giving priority to spiritual values and the formation of attitudes does not and should not mean ignoring either useful information or the promotion of creativity.

But traditionally the school regards the teaching/learning process in terms of a conventional triad of educational objectives, a triad which gives precedence to the acquisition of knowledge and which is firmly established wherever examinations, competitive or otherwise, consist of an evaluation of the quantity and conformity of knowledge acquired. To simplify somewhat a process that is extremely complicated and diversified, we may represent the new trend towards giving priority to the formation of attitudes as a reversal of the traditional triad of educational objectives.

Traditional triad
(in order of importance)
I   Knowledge
II Know-how
III Attitudes and skills

New triad

I   Attitudes and skills
II Know-how
III Knowledge

This reversal of priorities calls for a number of comments and further clarification. Far from underestimating the ever-increasing quantity of information circulating at the different levels of social life, the new order of importance corresponds to the evolution of knowledge itself and its effects on society and on the life of individuals. We know nowadays that the person who possesses soundly established attitudes (an interest in changes and innovation, a critical outlook, a sense of solidarity, a sense of responsibility and moral autonomy) and who, if need be, knows how to find new information from libraries or computers, is best prepared to receive and renew his cultural and occupational training. Furthermore, attitudes and skills are formed in the process of assimilating and applying knowledge.[6]

In some countries, this new order of importance is more than a strong trend; it is, as we have seen, a conviction on the part of the leaders of the economy, a style of activity on the part of teachers, and a concern on the part of evaluators. In other countries, it is more of a transformation in progress, or judged desirable. Quite obviously, such an evolution where objectives are concerned becomes an educational reality only as a result of a long-term effort and a systems approach to the components of the education system:

Reshaping of the goals and operational objectives of education, and the promotion of a new philosophy of education.
Selection and organization of content, in the light of the new objectives.
Adaptation and enhancement of school textbooks, learning methods, teaching methods, techniques of evaluation, school furniture, etc.
Systematic retraining of teachers: courses, individual study, demonstrations, collective and individual applications and exercises, etc.
Training of evaluators, administrators, etc.

This is why such reforms are spread over periods of five to eight years. But when the change has been effected, the teacher has the satisfaction of playing the role of an educator and not merely of an over-burdened repository and a weary transmitter of information.

Let us not overlook the fact that teachers, depending upon the freedom of action which they are allowed, are able to remodel the learning process themselves in the light of the new goals. It may be remarked that, in a very short lapse of time by comparison with corresponding changes in previous centuries, teachers realized—as did research workers before them—the need to reconsider the ends (general objectives) of education, that is to say they went beyond acquired information (lectures, refresher courses) and established a link between educational theory and practice. However, this awareness does not necessarily involve an observable transformation at the level of educational practice, for it may remain a concealed trend for a long time. At the risk of repeating what is already familiar, we may establish a list of objectives advocated by research workers in the 1960s and taken up by teachers in the 1980s.

1960s	*1980s*
Learning to learn	Learning to learn and to self-evaluate. Achieving intellectual autonomy.
Learning to be	Learning to be and to develop; to initiate and control change.
Learning as much for its own sake as for passing examinations	Learning as a means of self-realization and participation in the development of society and the ongoing education of fellow-citizens.

The examples which follow show that the new objectives are compatible with the imperatives of society and are calculated to improve the contribution of the school to socio-economic and cultural development.

In his study of the reform of the curriculum in Hungary, Szebenyi notes first of all that the new document is entitled 'Schooling and Teaching Plan', whereas the former was entitled 'Curriculum'. Previously, the school was simply the place where the teaching/learning process took place; in other words where knowledge was assimilated; it must now become more of an institution which ensures the total development of the personality. The new curricula place particular emphasis on individual work and the development of thinking for one's self. Learning will be organized in function of fundamental scientific concepts. Previously, points out Szebenyi, the teaching of chemistry tended to consist of presenting the phenomena involved correctly, and ensuring that they were memorized. In the new curricula, emphasis is on the understanding of atomic structure and atomic links, and the exploration of the bases of and the reasons for the phenomena which occur. The transformation of what was formerly called 'practical work' is a good example of the new curricula; the term 'technology' is now used, indicating that it is no longer a question of teaching the know-how necessary for day-to-day living, but of building up pupils' technical knowledge and abilities. Other subjects in the curricula reflect the same orientation. Music and singing will not be confined to teaching pupils to sing songs; they will be given a basic musical education, thereby laying the foundations of a universal aesthetic culture. Painting aims to develop a 'visual culture', physical training to develop harmony of movement and a healthy life-style. All these orientations and objectives reflect the concern with enabling the school to accomplish its mission as an institution of general education, that is to say an institution which ensures the full development of the child's personality. The school previously placed emphasis on the preservation and reproduction of traditional values; without ignoring the latter, the reform recently undertaken in Hungary stresses the importance of creativity and the personality. The objectives to be attained are more clearly specified, and this formulation, influenced by Bloom's taxonomy, also makes allowance for performance levels: *minimal* levels necessary for the continuation of studies, and *optimal* levels for gifted children, who it is assumed will reach a higher level. The differentiation of curricula and objectives reflects the intention of requiring teachers to pay more attention to pupils' interests and aptitudes.[7] The author points out that not only has this reform begun to be put into effect, but the educational authorities and educational research workers are working on a project designed for the year 2000.

In Japan, 20 years ago, the development of the country was explained principally or entirely by certain characteristics, such as the modest life-style of the people and national cohesion. The economic performance moreover often overshadowed the at least equal importance of the switch from an authoritarian regime to a parliamentary democracy, the agricultural reform, or the ability to ensure continuity in change in all fields (family life, work, urban living, architecture, etc.). It was rarely noted that the majority of leaders of the economy presided over associations of an educational nature, and that their attitude to the content of education was far from being confined to utilitarian considerations. For some years past an increasing number of economists, political scientists and management specialists have considered that education has played an important role in the development of contemporary Japan. In France, discussions on the strategies of industrial modernization during the years 1983–84 (notably the discussions arising from the closure or restructuring of the Talbot factories) made reference to the functions of education in Japanese society, to the percentage of pupils enrolled in secondary schools from the age of 12 (more than 90 per cent), and hence the cultural level of the workers, the importance attached to moral education, etc. In Japan in particular, the performance of the education system is explained by what lies behind the curricula or syllabuses: a certain attitude to moral and aesthetic values and to national priorities, the special importance attached to traditions, to family life, national fêtes and festivals, etc. One may observe the place occupied in the training of youth by *ikebana* or the 'tea ceremony' when one visits schools, students' and pupils' hostels and centres, and also out-of-school cultural centres, for contemporary educational systems are very complex and their content and mechanisms are sometimes concealed and unobtrusive.

Confining ourselves here to the educational objectives of the Japanese system, we shall refer to the proposals submitted by the Curriculum Planning Council in 1976 at the request of the Ministry of Education, Science and Culture, concerning the revision of primary school curricula.

In its report, submitted in December 1976, the council suggested that curricula be revised with a view to promoting pupils' ability to think for themselves and to make correct decisions. At the same time, the council considered it necessary to underline the importance to be attached to the following points in the revision of curricula:

1. Enthusiasm and a taste for study on the part of pupils.
2. A more relaxed and satisfying school life.
3. The acquisition of basic knowledge and the matching of education to the personality and capacity of each pupil.
4. Where enthusiasm and a taste for study are concerned, pupils must: (a) acquire creative knowledge, know-how, and the ability to think for themselves; (b) develop their love of nature and of human beings; (c) develop a strong will and an independent mentality; (d) acquire a taste for work; (e) develop a sociability based on awareness of social solidarity and the desire to make themselves useful; (f) cultivate a love for their family, their home town and their country, and also become worthy and respectable citizens of the world.
5. To make school life more relaxed and satisfying, the volume of standard lessons by subject-matter must be reduced, and flexibility of timetables must be allowed depending on the situation of the school and the region in question.
6. The objectives and content of each subject laid down in the curricula must be confined to essentials, in order to enable each school and each teacher to make optimum use of its or his own methods.

In conclusion, it may be said that the importance of intellectual attitudes and abilities is recognized to an increasing extent, and that though the new order of priority of educational objectives which we have proposed is perhaps excessively schematic, it reflects an evolution which will manifest itself more and more markedly in the coming decades.

THE CRITICAL RECEPTION OF SCIENTIFIC AND TECHNOLOGICAL ACHIEVEMENTS

Under the heading of the fundamental or exact sciences we group both mathematics and the natural sciences. As some specialists indicate, the gradual integration of mathematics into physics and chemistry cannot be challenged. Furthermore, a number of fields of mathematics have been created or developed by physicists. According to Baez (1977, p. 16): 'The natural sciences include astronomy, physics, chemistry, biology and the sciences of the earth and space. Mathematics is a special case, but whenever I refer to science education I shall implicitly include mathematics.'

Nor can one ignore the interactions between science and technology, though opinions on this subject may differ. Baez (1977, p. 16), for example, links science with applied science, but on the other hand makes a clear distinction between science and technology:

Although they are intimately linked, science and technology differ.... In both natural and applied sciences, the process involves research and the product is a set of ideas, theories and principles which man may organize in particular ways. Using the above criteria, technology is not a science. It consists, rather, of the practical knowledge of what can be done and how. It is not a body of theoretically related laws and principles.

D. Osborne, a professor of physics and astronomy, adopts another point of view:

Research in the basic sciences is dictated by technology! Although technology may be thought of as 'applied science' it is true also that science is applied technology. Historically, the discovery of the electron may be attributed to improvements in vacuum technology (and the fascination of studying electrical discharges through gases). The engineer's concept of information, derived from work in telecommunications, was fundamental to the discovery of DNA [Osborne, 1980, p. 420].

It is not our job to settle this problem of scientific philosophy, and we are tempted to give equal weight to both science and technology. Firstly because, as specialists point out, the trend towards the application of scientific theories and ideas is becoming more marked in all the sciences, which is perhaps why we find a considerable number of mathematicians (research workers, or students with an obvious bent for this subject) in polytechnic institutes. Secondly, because what we are considering here is essentially the attitude to be established towards science and technology, whose discoveries have had and will have a profound impact on the life of human beings.

As we shall indicate in the next chapter, dealing with desirable or foreseeable contents, scientists are not satisfied with the progress accomplished up to the present by the exact sciences in educational institutions; moreover, university teachers frequently consider, or tell their students in their introductory lectures, that the best thing they can do when entering university is to forget what they have learned about algebra, geometry or physics in the secondary school. We cannot always be sure whether they wish thereby to stimulate new students or to incriminate the 'conservative' nature of pre-university education. However, by reason of their accomplishments and their presence in day-to-day life, the sciences—whether theoretical or applied—have had and continue to have a strong attraction for young people whose thinking is profoundly influenced by the discoveries and changes which have occurred in the scientific field in recent decades. Furthermore, the exact sciences are at the origin of most reforms or innovations of the curriculum, or more precisely of contents and sources of the courses in which they are contained. Most taxonomies of objectives, work on learning or evaluation relate to examples borrowed from the exact sciences. As stated in a consolidated study of trends where content is concerned:

Mathematics have come to play a role in the selection of pupils—a role previously played by the humanities. This selective role is omnipresent, though in varying degrees. Its influence varies according to the political and social situation of the region in question, but in general it can be said that the degree of facility of the acquisition of mathematics is a determining factor of differentiation and discrimination, so that for example future doctors are selected from among the pupils who do best in mathematics rather than from among those most gifted in biology or the natural sciences [International Symposium . . ., 1980*a*].[8]

Here we have a complex approach or situation, and in any event a tendency to be encouraged (the learning of modern mathematics, learning to think in terms of probability, etc.); an error to be avoided or an exaggeration to be noted (the naïve idea that mathematics provides the key to the approach to all complex situations); a balance to be maintained between the exact sciences and the human sciences; and in particular an attitude to be established to the achievements and the applications of the exact sciences.

Both consolidated studies of an international nature and case-studies—either national or covering certain sciences (see the general bibliography)—provide evidence of innovations and advances achieved in the teaching of the fundamental sciences (or rather the exact or natural sciences). In Unesco's *Second Medium-Term Plan (1984–89)*, the programme entitled the 'Teaching of Science and

Technology' is the subject of an overall approach and is based on the principle of lifelong education.[9]

Science and technology are an integral part of contemporary culture. In its various forms, science has become an essential means of understanding the world through knowledge of the laws of nature ... Scientific and technological development can be carried on only with the support of an interested and informed public. Public interest in and understanding of science and technology should therefore be increased by means of all forms of educational action and in co-operation with the mass information media [Unesco, 1983c, p. 123].

In fact, the teaching of the exact sciences is increasingly considered as an essential component of the general culture that everyone must possess. All countries make efforts to provide a scientific training for the mass of the population, even when, particularly in developing countries, 'science introduces attitudes, techniques and methods which tend to upset the tradition which previously dominated technical activity and social life' (Dieuzeide, 1983). New concepts and new theories have been and continue to be brought in to school curricula, the effect of which, as in the case of the theory of sets, is to trigger reactions which vary depending on the quality of the strategies employed: the in-service training of teachers, the promotion of active methods, etc. All these innovations have also highlighted the role of parents and of the information of parents, who are sometimes thwarted by the fact that they are no longer in a position to help or control the individual work of their children on the basis of their own educational experiences. Innovation where contents are concerned has been combined with a bolder promotion of active methods and modern techniques of learning; formal lectures have to an increasing extent been replaced by dialogue, learning by 'discovering', consulting libraries, etc. Though the method of exposition, which moreover possesses certain specific advantages, has not entirely disappeared from educational institutions, it has undergone a worthwhile change by being combined with other methods and by relying more on audio-visual methods. But priority is given to heuristic methods which can develop the attitudes to which we have referred under a previous heading: curiosity, a critical attitude, creativity, responsibility in the face of the consequences of the application of scientific and technological advances, etc.

Henceforward, the scientific training of young people is concerned less with the acquisition of formal theories than with the approach to practical problems, the observation of facts, laboratory work, and the analysis of real situations. 'Thus it can prevent errors which were previously prevalent: lags in technological learning in developing countries, wastage of energy in developed countries, lack of awareness of problems of nutrition, hygiene, pollution of the environment, etc.' (Dieuzeide, 1983).

Lastly, whereas scholars representing the different sciences previously attempted to formulate school curricula separately or to confiscate them in the name of their scientific prestige, educational authorities nowadays increasingly recognize that the content of education is a matter of pedagogy and policy which calls for teamwork and for careful decision-making.

The case-study of Chinese education mentions a number of interesting approaches adopted in recent years. It begins by pointing out that the promotion of talent is essential for the country's development; at the same time, it seems evident that the development of talent is conceived in the democratic spirit which characterizes the education policy, whose main aim is to train all young people to take an active part in social life.

General education in China has a twofold task: to train students for entry to higher education establishments, and to train pupils at the preparatory and intermediate levels. The rapid advance of science and technology creates an urgent need for talented people at different levels for the country's socialist construction. For this reason, general education has been assigned a very important role. The development of science and technology changes not only material production, but also social life. It demands a constant renewal of the content of general education. Traditional knowledge must be carefully selected, because it still constitutes the principal stock of basic knowledge. Modern knowledge, enriched and renewed, has to be selected with even greater care. Theory must be associated with practice, not only because this stimulates the student's desire to learn and master basic knowledge, but also because it greatly helps him to develop his aptitudes and to analyse and solve problems.

Being the basis of scientific and technical progress, mathematics occupies a predominant place in the curricula of general education in China. The teaching of this subject will have to be modernized at the secondary level by reason of the rapid development of science and technology, and notably the growing importance of computers. Traditional content will be simplified and new content, allowing for modern advances, will be introduced so as to combine theory and practice and confirm the fundamental, innovative and action-oriented nature of mathematics teaching. Thus the curricula will include such subjects as analysis, probability, operational research and mathematical logic, and great prominence will be given to information technology. Where the natural sciences are concerned, the aim will be to develop pupils' ability to learn for themselves and to make use of their knowledge in practical situations. Fundamental concepts and laws should form the core of this instruction, whose content should be carefully chosen so as not to overload the curriculum, and constantly updated. The methods employed should aim to develop an aptitude for scientific research, notably through practical and experimental work in and out of school, and pupils should be trained to apply their knowledge in day-to-day life, in productive activities, and in social life. A special place should be made in the curricula for certain major problems of contemporary society such as energy and the environment, and for other interdisciplinary fields.

This study, which clearly confirms the trends previously referred to, calls for some remarks. Special importance is attached to the democratization of education, and implicitly to compulsory general education, whose purpose is to train all young people to participate in the construction of a 'highly civilized and democratic socialist country'. The education authorities highlight the ideal of a complete and harmonious moral, intellectual, physical, etc., training. For a country with a thousand million inhabitants, this is a redoubtable task. The idea is that the education system can and should prepare, precede and back up social, economic and cultural development and respond to the demands of that development by a process of continuous adaptation; the education system, in turn, benefits from the role assigned to it in a development based essentially on the training of individuals. The identification and the early development of talent is a fundamental task in a democratic system; there is a complementarity between the specific education received by clever and exceptionally gifted pupils and the help provided for pupils who lag behind. The diversification and differentiation of education mean that all categories of needs and possibilities are more fully satisfied.

In the studies already referred to, we find a relatively new concern which signifies a reaction to a problem or a danger created by the impact of science and technology on the life of men and women. The 'ambivalence' of these activities has been discovered, along with the difficulty of resolving certain dilemmas posed by contemporary research. Osborne (1980, p. 418) outlines the dimensions of this new preoccupation. He quotes Ralf Dahrendorf:

The discovery that science is morally ambivalent, that its creative force is balanced by its destructive force, has changed fundamentally the readiness of people to regard 'rational' as synonymous with 'good' ... there are examples of the attempt to reinstate the irrational in its place, and to curb scientific discovery and technological innovation ... A 'scientific-technological world' is not a very agreeable place to live in: but one in which scientific discovery is supported and applied where it serves human beings, is very desirable indeed.

Osborne (1980, p. 422) himself adds:

Disillusion with science ... arises from excessive claims that have been made for science in the past and a fear that science may dominate our lives ... We need a balanced valuation of the worth, benefits and dangers of science, and a commitment to the truths with which it is concerned.

This discovery of the ambivalence of science and technology has already been expressed in contemporary literature and philosophy, in certain films, and in the programmes of certain very active and bold political parties.

In the near future, men and women may be required to express their opinion by national referenda on the different prospects opened up by biology or chemistry, or on the options offered by technology with regard to energy, food, the use of space, etc. To avoid errors, manipulations, or the transformation of this mistrust of, or critical attitude to, science and technology into hostility, young people must be better informed and trained on the subject. What is meant by establishing a *relevant attitude* to science and technology? Even when we add the word 'relevant' the problem appears extremely complicated and open. Is it a matter simply of correctly and fairly indicating the risks and dangers incurred by various discoveries? How is it possible, during schooling, to follow true educational lines of action which seem to be mutually exclusive: arouse or maintain interest in science and technology, whose role is fundamental for the survival of the human race, and cultivate lucidity or give young people the necessary criteria for a correct evaluation of the effects of different scientific methodologies, possible solutions, dangers to be avoided, etc.? For such criteria rarely derive from the actual science that is taught; their scope is philosophical and ethical. So who should shape, and how, this complex attitude to science and to the exceptional role which it plays in our life? The concern not to confine the teaching of science to the assimilation of knowledge and know-how and to establish an attitude to its achievements and applications, is evident, and strongly felt; introducing this goal into school curricula, the training of teachers and the learning process seems to be an open problem whose solutions depend not only on pedagogic research but also on political and economic factors. From the theoretical point of view, the positions are quite coherent, and a recent study of the pressures exerted on the school by technology reaches a conclusion which seems to us to be relevant:

competition or integration? Refusal or acceptance? The exploring child deserves to be guided out of the magic and ludic undergrowth and to be armed as early as possible against the reality of a technological world ... the new technological literacy training is not linear; it has to use a combination of methods and a diversification of procedures. The active young television viewer is also a user of Logo; multiple possibilities of development are offered. Let us create others. In doing so, let us assert irreducible values. Let us find ways of forming without conforming. Let us encourage seriousness and effort. What is in question is neither more nor less than the future of society. We do not want the citizen of the year 2000 to be either a confused cripple surrounded by prostheses, or the hopeless hostage of technical slaves, we want him to be free [Dieuzeide, 1983].

The picture presented by studies on this subject is that of an educated and informed man capable of appreciating values of the highest order, of distinguishing between ends and means, and of mastering and developing a technology placed in the service of development. This is the neo-humanism of our age, which has emerged as a reaction to the imbalances and dangers generated by the exceptional and uncontrolled expansion of contemporary technology, which should be reinforced in educational curricula and in the minds of learners. In this connection, the reader is referred to the sub-section headed 'Methodological framework of a curriculum'.

RENEWAL OF INTEREST IN MORAL VALUES AND MORAL EDUCATION

Can one tackle such a problem in a study of an international nature, in view of the fact that moral codes vary greatly from one country to another, from one local community to another, and that the new generations are, if not dissidents, at least influenced by non-traditional systems of values? Furthermore, in a given national community, there is neither one single category of aspirations nor one single religion, even though there are many moral convergences which form the basis of national unity. In the face of this diversity and complexity, teachers—and notably those whose training includes few elements of the social and human sciences—tend to ignore the problems posed by moral education; in many situations it is the family, the local community, the church, etc.—hence 'informal' out-of-school education—which offer pupils responses, options, or standards to conform to.

One of the authors contributing to the issue of the *International Review of Education* devoted to the problems of moral education makes some useful distinctions before concluding:

To avoid tackling the problem fundamentally, it is tempting to describe such a situation in terms of crisis. A crisis of authority, a crisis of values, a crisis of society; there is impaired functioning which has to be remedied. Sure enough, the very notion of a changing society, if not a society in the throes of growth or mutation, explains and justifies in advance the axiological vicissitudes which necessarily characterize it. On the one hand, major material changes, if they are lasting, are bound to have psychological, moral and spiritual repercussions on those who undergo them. On the other hand, collective awareness of transformations in progress generally produces a series of contradictory reactions.

For all these reasons, rather than waste time describing the supposed temporary eclipse of moral reflexion in terms of a crisis situation, a situation of change, or of the hazards of cultural development, or announcing, more radically, the disappearance of a form of critical reflexion that has become impossible, it seems preferable in our view to consider what is in the process of change in terms of where we stand, collectively and individually, in relation to questions of an ethical nature. . . . Doubtless the most important factor in our experience lies in awareness of the complexity [Ardoino, 1980, pp. 120 et seq.].

Adding that the awareness in question bears on *the complexity and the socio-economic and political importance of moral values*, we shall attempt to make a series of distinctions and subsequently to indicate significant attitudes or measures which may demonstrate the interest taken in moral education.[10]

In 1978, Unesco organized the first meeting of an international nature devoted to the analysis of the relationship between the curriculum and moral values. The meeting of experts on 'Educational Institutions and Moral Education in the Light of the Demands of Contemporary Life' (Sofia, 1978) focused attention on the idea that, traditionally, moral education was organized in the light of national codes of communities living together in a given country. Response to the demands of the contemporary world has been relatively recent, and the co-ordination between universal and national codes is not easy to achieve. Furthermore, in the preparation of this first international meeting on the relationship between the curriculum, national moral values and the 'universal moral code' which is gradually establishing itself as an imperative and a common denominator, an anticipatory evaluation was made of the difficulties to be overcome and the possibility of arriving at a certain consensus; not without reason, certain Unesco specialists expressed the fear that this meeting might be likened to the Tower of Babel and accentuate conflicts and disparities. The participants received: 1. A recapitulatory list of the problems and objectives of Unesco for the years 1977–82, which was also included in the final report; 2. A table showing the status of moral education in 15 countries of Asia, and another concerning priority moral values; 3. A table of the aims and objects of moral education courses provided in Belgium; 4. A list of fundamental concepts. After very lively discussions, the participants reached agreement on many problems. The *Final Report* of the meeting (Meeting of Experts on Educational Institutions..., 1978) defined in particular the social forces influencing the quality of moral education, without however having the same impact on individual countries:

Scientific and technological development may erode traditional belief systems and confront people with unfamiliar moral choices.

Urbanization that often threatens traditional family structures can foster alienation and promote the formation of youth sub-cultures with competing values.

Rapid population growth that alters the age distribution in a society, perhaps changing the sources of authority.

Growing disparity of wealth among the nations that fosters feelings of exploitation, anger, and despair on the part of the poor nations and promotes reckless consumption of resources or insensitivity on the part of the rich nations.

The report points out that the content of moral education has both cognitive and affective aspects:

The content... consists of the knowledge, attitudes and skills students must acquire to become morally mature individuals... various skills are needed. Communication skills are one type of skill required by a socially mature person. These skills include those associated with leadership, participation and decision-making [p. 7].

Our purpose is to show that the interest taken in the promotion of moral values in school and social life manifests itself not only in the form of discussions, research, and conflicts of axiological systems, but also in the form of recommendations made by the educational authorities or in the form of educational activities. The 1978 meeting on the relationship between moral values, the curriculum and the demands of contemporary life was designed as a platform and as an opportunity of taking stock of the situation in this field.

The United Nations sent a cable of encouragement:

On behalf of the Secretary-General of the United Nations, I wish to congratulate Unesco for its initiative in convening this important international meeting... we are especially encouraged by the fact that education on international cooperation has become an integral part of moral and civic education in an increasing number of countries... the questioning of systems of values in the industrialized societies, the conflicts between and within societies with different social, ideological and economic systems, the tremendous problems of developing countries, the dread of a nuclear holocaust and the many forms of injustice and discrimination, conjure up feelings of frustration and anxiety in peoples. The traditional values must thus be reexamined in terms of the benefits not only to individuals but to the world as a whole [Annex IV].

The meeting led to a comparative study of the place of moral values in educational programmes by Mehlinger (1984). Furthermore, the problems dealt with by the meeting were presented in the *International Review of Education* by Vaideanu (1979)[11] as a result of which the editors of that journal published a special issue in 1980 on the teaching of moral values. Still on this international level, mention may be made of a significant paragraph which participants representing the natural sciences, the social sciences, culture, the arts, etc. at the first International Symposium on the Evolution of the Content of General Education over the next Two Decades (Paris, 1980) felt it necessary to introduce into the *Final Report* (International Symposium..., 1980a). Even though they were mainly concerned with the problems posed by the natural sciences, they added, after underlining the importance of mathematics, a sound knowledge of the environment, etc., a reference to the teaching of values and to the importance of hard work, loyalty, responsibility, justice and other values in the general education of the individual.

Equally significant are the results of the analysis made in 1983 by a Romanian cultural journal, *Almanahul Contemporanul*, which presented the justifications of the committee responsible for the attribution of the Nobel Prize for Literature in the course of the years; criteria of a moral nature are seen to be very important, if not even more determining than purely aesthetic criteria.

The growing interest in the integration of moral values in the curriculum or the 'co-curriculum' is also seen at the level of the formulation of education programmes and the teaching/learning process. Two strategies may be identified.

Firstly, that which seems to be gaining ground and which consists of introducing into school timetables or into out-of-school (co-curricular) activities specific lessons or activities assigned to teachers of philosophy or pedagogy. Though not alone in adopting such a strategy, Asiatic countries set a good example. Various documents on the subject indicate the objectives, the organization of in-school or out-of-school activities, the values incorporated in school curricula, the methods of evaluating pupils' progress, and the problems arising. The report of a meeting on moral education held in 1980 and attended by participants from 16 countries states that the majority of the participating countries have a definite time allotted to the teaching of moral education. This allotment ranges from 1 to 6 periods per week of 20 to 40 minutes per period at elementary level and from 1 to 5 periods a week of 40 to 50 minutes per period at secondary level. Co-curricular activities are widely used in the promotion of moral education in all the participating countries. The values emphasized in moral education programmes of the participating countries fall into the following categories:

1. Social values: co-operation, cleanliness, kindness, filial piety, social justice, respect for others, public spirit, social responsibility, cosmopolitanism, universal brotherhood, respect for human dignity, respect for human rights, dignity of labour, etc.

2. Values pertaining to self: truthfulness, honesty, discipline, tolerance, cleanliness, orderliness, peace of mind, perfection of self, etc.

3. Values pertaining to country and the world: patriotism, national consciousness, loyalty to the king and the crown, peaceful citizenship, international understanding, human brotherhood, awareness of the interdependence of nations, etc.

4. Process values: scientific approach to reality, discrimination, search for truth, suspension of judgement, etc.

Among the problems mentioned in the same publication are: the dichotomy between moral precept and moral practice (recalling Ovid's words: 'Video meliora proboque deteriora sequor');[12] the conflict between traditional values and modern life-styles; moral education: independent subject or integrated subject?, etc.

Another strategy, one which seems to be employed by the majority of countries, assigns the task of moral education to all teachers, on the basis of the fact that all subjects have a role to play in this connection. This strategy has advantages and drawbacks. Sometimes the teacher chiefly responsible for the class acts as a catalyst and an adviser *vis-à-vis* his pupils. Particularly in socialist countries, youth organizations are fully committed to the moral, civic and political education of pupils. But this, based on the contributions (uneven and sometimes contradictory) of all the teachers, raises two questions: how can different knowledge acquired under very different circumstances be organized into a coherent moral culture able to provide a basis for pupils' options and decisions? And what is the ethical and axiological training to be given to the teachers to enable them to make an effective contribution to the moral training of their pupils? The case-study on the Chinese experience published by Lian Jian-Sheng (1980, p. 200) provides a good example of this strategy:

To take a middle-school as an example, the forms and methods by which moral education is taught are generally of four kinds:
First, well-delivered lectures are given in the courses on politics; that is to

say, pupils are given clear and necessary concepts of politics such as the 'five loves' (love for the fatherland, people, manual labour, science and public property).

Secondly, teachers of no matter what subject are asked to make themselves responsible for the task of ideological education, mainly to discover the internal, not the external elements in the teaching materials which are connected naturally and organically, and are very clear in their aim.

Thirdly, 'regular' education must be firmly grasped; that is to say, pupils must be asked to act in accordance with the contents of the pupils' 'Rules and Regulations'.

Finally, pupils' communist ideology and moral character must be fostered through various activities such as doing good deeds for the people, actively helping with their lessons those pupils who have missed classes on account of illness, and helping old people who can no longer manage for themselves on account of age, by fetching water, sweeping the floor and cleaning the house, and by taking an active and positive attitude in lending a hand to whoever is in difficulty.

Referring to the work of the Institute of Moralogy in Tokyo (represented by a group of observers at the Unesco meeting in 1978) J. Lauwerys sees in moralogy the only attempt to establish a veritable moral science. The institute was founded in 1928 by Chikuro Hiroike (1866–1938) as the first attempt to establish moralogy as a new science. The founder's son, Sentaro Hiroike, at present directs this celebrated institution which has both a theoretical and practical vocation. There is now a whole literature on the institute, whose role in the construction of modern Japan is seen to be important. The institute has offshoots in different regions of the country, and also a university associated with a secondary school. Its activity has two aspects: one theoretical, dealing with moral problems, and the other practical, concerned with the systematic analysis of the quality of family life and the life of different communities. The work of this institute, whose role and life-style are exemplary, has particularly strongly highlighted:

The importance of spiritual values in the development of contemporary societies based essentially on the progress of science and technology.

The weight of the moral factor in the formation of the individual.

The balance to be maintained in the moral field between continuity and change, between tradition and innovation.

Young people's responsiveness to moral problems and their spiritual need to find their bearings in the light of a moral ideal.

The importance of moral values in day-to-day life and the unity to be achieved between moral teaching and the quality of school life (the atmosphere of the school, the style of teaching, and especially the quality of relations between pupils and teachers, between pupils themselves and between teachers themselves, etc.).

It appears significant that for some years past specialists in management and economics who are concerned with the performance of the West have paid increasing attention to the moral factor and have tried to evaluate its role in the development of Japan.

Bousquet has said that in Japan the quality and functions of education are such as to prepare, make possible and promote development, and that conversely the sector of the economy which helps to promote an education system conforms to what is required. Indeed, the personnel requirements and policies of large companies systematically confirm educational goals and criteria of educational evaluation. The example of Japan shows that placing education in the service of development answers a twofold question: what education, and for what development?

The discussions, research and even the hesitations of education authorities and teachers' representatives show that while the promotion of moral education in school curricula seems to be increasingly necessary, the implementation of such a measure constitutes for many countries both a priority and an open problem which arises not only at the level of curriculum design but also in the process of teacher training; any educator inadequately prepared to engage in discussions of an ethical nature will have reservations precisely because he considers the undertaking at one and the same time important, complicated and strewn with ambushes. A distinction should therefore be made between hesitation and indifference, or between the time required to master the change of values and a presumed eclipse of morality and moral education.

It is true that the dialogue between adults and young people is not always very constructive, and that young people sometimes display a certain indifference to social traditions and demands, but there is no symmetry between their desire for independence and their sense of responsibility, etc. It is also true that some young people are easy to manipulate[13] and that their enthusiasm may be directed along negative lines of action. Sometimes their desire for independence and new experiences and the rejection of taboos goes too far and may annoy adults or generate conflicts. But before rejecting these experiences, attitudes or values advocated by young people, one should realize that in their origins lies a fund of frankness, sincerity, justice and a desire to innovate. Referring to this problem, G. de Landsheere (1976a, p. 132) appeals to teachers in these terms: teachers of the year 2000 must be prepared to encounter young people who will continue to struggle with serious psychological problems and to oppose institutions, standards and morals which they feel to be foreign and vitiating, and who hold to values often far removed from those prevailing in the twentieth century. Contrary to the claim of certain detractors of youth, these new values often have a great deal of coherence. D. Yankelovich, for example, advances the hypothesis that the values which predominated (in 1972–73) on American university campuses find their unity in a belief that a new relationship must be established with nature and the natural. This general trend may be centred around three principal themes: 1. More emphasis is placed on the community than on the individual—co-operation takes precedence over competition. 2. Sensory experience takes precedence over conceptual knowledge; truth is sought more through direct experience than through detachment and objectivity. 3. Emphasis is placed on the sanctity of nature (open-air life, the protection of the environment) as against economic growth and technology.

As we see, while it is true that increased attention to moral values and moral education is a strong trend, it has to be recognized that the problems to be solved are exceptionally complicated. In this field, more so than elsewhere, the formation of attitudes calls for a wisely conceived and long-term educational effort.

THE INTEGRATION OF TECHNOLOGY AND PRODUCTIVE WORK IN GENERAL EDUCATION

Here we have a good example of the strong trend towards the assimilation of a new type of content in general education. There has been, and still is, a degree of hesitation or resistance; but in all or almost all countries technology and socially useful productive work are beginning to become in-school or out-of-school activities and to make use of the services of a new category of teachers: engineers and foremen or, in other situations, non-teaching educators such as museum guides, librarians, cultural leaders, tourist personnel, etc. The example of socialist countries has frequently been cited, and rightly so; but about twenty years ago some of them had ten- or eleven-year general secondary schools which made no provision for any manual or technological activity; general education at that time meant mathematics, physics, literature, philosophy, etc. The change has been very rapid, and education authorities and research workers now express the issue in different terms; it is not a question simply of introducing a new subject, but of reconsidering and relocating the school in the dynamic context of contemporary society. It is not merely a matter of identifying the educational virtues of work, but of associating work, technology and culture and of integrating these components in the curriculum as a whole.

Current developments

Experience acquired in different countries or regions has been the subject of a series of analyses which have made it possible to identify both common trends and the diversity of socio-economic situations and possible solutions, and to specify the concept of productive work and the pedagogic demands to which it gives rise.

In 1979, Unesco published *Learning and Working*, which begins by identifying the problem:

If there is . . . a problem where all the others tend to intercept, it is certainly the problem of determining and establishing in educational practice the connecting link between the process of general education and the world of work. As things stand, it is as if these two universes—education and work—were fundamentally indifferent to each other [Unesco, 1979, p. 8].

The problem receives a dialectical and extremely nuanced approach which reveals the complexity of the field and the variety of situations. A. Visalberghi (Italy) deals with education and the division of labour in the developed world, and M. Sinclair with the introduction of work-experience programmes in the Third World. B. Schwartz writes of the problems and prospects of alternation, while L. Emmerij examines the question: education and work—in succession or recurrent? The work includes a series of national case-studies: India (M. Adiseshiah); Senegal (V. Tara); Panama and Honduras (S. Lourié); the United Republic of Tanzania (G. Mmari); Cuba (A. Prieto Morales and M. Figueroa Araujo); USSR (N. Semykin); polytechnical education in the German Democratic Republic (G. Neuner); seminary education and recurrent education in Sweden (G. Bergendal); and the course in technology at the Open University (J. Sparkes). In 1981, in preparation for the thirty-eighth session of the International Conference on Education organized by Unesco in Geneva, the IBE also produced a series of studies and documents under the title *Interaction between Education and Productive Work*.

The document prepared by Unesco in co-operation with the ECA and OAU for the Conference of Ministers of Education and Those Responsible for Economic Planning in African States, which took place in Harare in 1982, examines the application of the concept in the African context:

In Africa, where rural production activities constitute the principal basis for economic and community development, the majority of educational productive work projects concern agricultural production. Although the concepts adopted and practices followed vary greatly according to the local socio-economic and political structures, two main trends emerge. First of all, there have been a number of experiments in which, the plan being that the school should become a production unit, the link education–productive work constitutes the backbone of an overall reform of educational systems. The application of this reform is accompanied by the establishment of appropriate structures at the national level. Examples of this are the Tanzanian experiment in 'education to promote community self-reliance' and other projects launched in Burundi in primary schools, in Benin with the 'New School' and in Guinea with the 'revolutionary education centres'. A number of experiments are also being developed which, without aiming at a global reform of the educational system, affect one part of this system or some branches of specialized training. The pilot projects offering agricultural or crafts prevocational training programmes may be quoted in this category. The Bunumbu project in Sierra Leone for the training of teachers for rural development, the 'polytechnic villages' in Kenya and the Nianing Centre in Senegal, intended for young people who have not attended school or who have dropped out of school, are examples of educational innovation for rural development [MINEDAF, 1982, pp. 47–8].

The seminar of socialist countries on education for and through work, organized in Bucharest in 1976 with the participation of Unesco, dealt among other subjects with the 'polytechnization of education' and the polytechnic school; the principle of unity between education, research and production applied in Romania; and the methodology of the integration of productive work in the curriculum. Emphasis was laid on: 1. The need to make use of progress in ergonomics and industrial design in the organization of productive work. 2. The need to associate education for and through work systematically with moral and aesthetic education (valorizing local craft traditions, etc.). 3. The need to proportion the work in the light of the possibilities of each age-group (see Simonescu, 1980; Vaideanu, 1976).

Apart from these consolidated studies, the literature on the subject includes a number of case-studies setting forth the specific experiences of certain countries, such as the 'countryside scheme' for secondary schools in Cuba, or the Swedish 'recurrent education' system, one of whose noteworthy features is its flexibility of organization, which makes it possible for pupils to prepare for either future studies or future work, whichever they prefer. The Romanian experiment is presented by Vaideanu in the following terms:

The fundamental principle governing the educational process in Romania is the unity of teaching, research and production. In the light of this principle, school and university learning is in permanent and open contact with the methodologies and achievements of research and with the demands of the evolution of production (*lato sensu* socially useful activities). Thus learning means assimilating in order to apply what is assimilated, or understanding in order to act and bring about improvement.... Practical courses are incorporated in school timetables, applying this principle; they are a form of learning, and their content is established in function of the pupils' age and capacity for work, the socio-economic profile of the locality, and the profile of the secondary school: mathematics and physics, chemistry and biology, Romanian language and literature, etc. The time allotted to practical activities varies: 1 hour a week in primary school, 2 hours a week in the fifth and sixth years, 3 hours a week in the seventh and eighth years, and 10 to 13 weeks a year in secondary school. It represents about 30 per cent of the total time allotted to pupils' education [Vaideanu, 1982b, pp. 211, 215].

On the conceptual level, we may be thankful for the relinquishing of narrow views which linked the promotion of productive work in schools with the early occupational training of pupils, thereby reserving productive work for a certain category of children: those not possessing the material possibility of going on to higher education. The spectrum of the objectives of education for and through work has been broadened by making provision not only for the assimilation of a stock of know-how and knowledge, but also through the formation of suitable attitudes to the world of work, to technology, and to the impact of the latter on the life of human beings.

Lastly, there has been a clearer realization of the fragility of the moral and political training of a child who, destined for an intellectual or management career, receives general education (primary and secondary) without having any knowledge of the industrial, agricultural, commercial or socio-cultural life of the community to which he belongs. As stated in a Unesco study (Busshoff et al., 1981, p. 307):

It really makes no sense to accept as self-evident and propagate such formulae as 'science for all', 'sport for all' and 'art for all' and at the same time reserve work chiefly or solely for certain categories of children ... learning and working are, increasingly and everywhere, inseparable activities ... work experience proves essential in the intellectual, moral, civic and political training of young people.

Analysis of the latest trends in this field shows that whereas in an initial stage education authorities were concerned with the quantitative dimensions of the promotion of productive work in general education, the attention of research workers and decision-makers is now centred mainly on qualitative problems, the more so since the introduction of information technology in industry and other sectors of social life is making rapid strides in many countries, opening up new prospects and partially modifying the terms of the problem. Here are some of the questions which are currently under discussion:

How can technology and productive work be effectively integrated into the contents of in-school and out-of-school education as a whole? In certain situations this new content is 'stuck on' rather than integrated.

What are the prejudices of a moral nature to be overcome within the school (teachers of conventional subjects, pupils) and outside the school: the prejudices of parents, prejudices fuelled by certain religions, discrimination between boys and girls, etc.? If little progress has been made in certain countries, even though the relevant recommendations have been adopted by the Conferences of Ministers of the regions in question, it is because prejudices demand a special pedagogic treatment: they must be gradually dissipated and not uprooted authoritatively.

What is the minimum amount of technological knowledge to be introduced into the training of all teachers in order to make possible and effectively establish correlations, and furthermore to promote interdisciplinarity in the learning process?

In what framework, and by whom, should training be provided for teachers of general technology and/or foremen who in certain countries are called on to run practical courses for pupils in industry?

What methods and techniques should be used for evaluating the performance of children in this new field? The question is pertinent wherever specific, observable and measurable objectives have already been formulated. Moreover, the establishment of a method of teaching productive work is a priority both at the level of certain Member States and in the programme of Unesco for the coming years.

How is the link between the school and productive work to be conceived in countries where rural production represents the principal source of economic and social development? In Africa, for example, there is a great diversity of formulae and experiments; but certain conclusions have already been reached.

How is productive work to be introduced into the school without ignoring the educational goal of any in-school activity and the physiological and psychological particularities of the children? Methods of working which ignore the specificity and the pedagogic demands of education cease, indeed, to be an educational resource.

NEW WAYS OF ORGANIZING CONTENTS

The quest for a greater relevance of content in function of both the characteristics of pupils and the demands of society has become a permanent concern of educational authorities, curriculum planners and teachers. In previous decades, content remained stable over long periods; one and the same curriculum could be defined, particularly in centralized systems, at the national level for all pupils of a given level. As a result of the multiplication of the expectations and aspirations of individuals and the diversification of the environment, this somewhat simplistic approach, consisting of promulgating uniform curricula, has given way to more flexible approaches. In most countries, both decentralized and centralized, the tendency today is to make a distinction between two parts in the content of general education: on the one hand, a common core, a compulsory minimum for everyone; and on the other hand various options. The common core includes knowledge, concepts, know-how and values which the society in question considers necessary for all its members. The options constitute a series of specific contents which may be determined in the light of the aspirations, interests and aptitudes of the pupils and in the light of the needs of the socio-economic and cultural environment. This approach maintains the fundamental unity of the education system and hence preserves equality of opportunity while at the same time making it possible to provide a better response to individual expectations and to development demands. The co-ordination of specific contents and of a common core makes it possible, particularly at the level of primary education, to mitigate the serious drawbacks which result from an authoritative and uniform definition of identical contents whatever the prevailing environment, notably in countries where rural zones are widely separated from urban areas. The OECD (1983a) considers that it is the core of all modern systems of education; in all countries, it constitutes the main body of formal education for virtually all children and the whole of formal education for a large percentage of them.

As a new form of organization of the content of compulsory schooling, the common core and the system of differentiation provide a response to the various expectations of learners and to the demands of contemporary societies; among the latter, the following may be noted:

The need to make learning more effective and to ensure an effective democratization of education, notably from the point of view of access to, and the successful completion of, studies.

The need to provide the whole population of the country with a basic education conceived as a basis for moral and intellectual autonomy and for ongoing self-instruction.

The determination to prepare all young people to take an active part in the socio-economic development and the socio-cultural life of the community in which they live.

The composition of the common core and the content of the options vary from one country to another. We have already had occasion to refer to the components of the common core in countries such as

Hungary and the United Kingdom, and we shall revert to this in a later chapter. We would like at this point to present the content of a future common core which J. van Bruggen has analysed in his study. He considers that compulsory schooling will have to qualify all young people for three sorts of activity: *communication, occupational orientation* and *participation*. The qualifications necessary for communication with other people and within large or small groups include skills such as spoken and written communication in the mother tongue and in at least one foreign language, the ability to communicate through images and body movements (dancing, mime, photographs, films, video, etc.), the ability to seek and make use of information in all its forms, the capacity to identify values and standards and to master possible conflicts between them, and receptivity and responsiveness to others. The qualifications necessary for an *effective social life* include skills in calculation and the use of information technology, basic knowledge in certain fields which are seen to be important in a given national or regional environment among which may be mentioned biology, geography, chemistry, economics, physics, history, psychology, technology and sociology; the content of curricula is confined to that which necessitates a systematic presentation so as to allow for subsequent possibilities of more thorough study, and special attention should be paid to future developments and to all sources of subsequent self-instruction. The qualifications necessary for active participation in social life at the level of the local, regional and national community include the skills of day-to-day life (the preparation of meals, the repair of clothing, maintenance of the home, management of the family budget), skills in sport and leisure activities, education through the media, aptitude for self-instruction, and also the development of democratic attitudes, respect for minorities, initiative, and a minimum knowledge in the field of civic life and international relations.

This common core of knowledge, know-how and basic values which van Bruggen predicts for the future also reflects a concern with enhancing the contribution of education to the social, economic and cultural development of our societies.

Other approaches to the organization of educational contents have also been proposed by those responsible for the design of curricula and by teachers (see in particular D. Lemke's (1981) idea of the flexible curriculum; teachers themselves have a fairly considerable margin of freedom in this connection: while criteria of a policy nature are actively involved in the phase of the selection of content, the establishment of goals, the determination of timetables, etc., they are somewhat less obtrusive when it comes to organizing this same content in the form of teaching activities. This is probably one of the reasons why teaching as it is experienced from day to day by pupils and teachers sometimes differs from the model laid down in official texts; and this difference, resulting from teachers' initiative, should be considered as an advantage and not a defect.

Analysing educational strategies, methods and media, Berger and Brunswic (1981d, pp. 79–91) have recourse to four possible initial conceptions for developing the systems approach and for determining the organization of content and methods. They are the content-centred conception, the learning-centred conception, the relationship-centred conception, and the conception centred on process and situation.

The first three are particularly interesting from the point of view of the organization of content, and the fourth places emphasis on the conditions of implementation.

The content-centred conception is based on the *a priori* definition of a curriculum. It is a linear approach, and to some extent a deductive one. The crucial role is played by the curriculum, defined as the subject-matter to be taught and its predetermined breakdown in terms of the amount of time allocated for each part of the course. The learning-centred conception is founded on the analysis of learning behaviour and on the definition of certain *terminal profiles* (or qualifications). The relationship-centred conception is of relatively recent date, and particularly suited to adult or lifelong education and training situations. The curriculum becomes a component of the teaching/learning situation governing the interplay of personal relationships; it may be reviewed at any time and is thus subject to continuous negotiation.

In the field of the natural sciences, Unesco, which is customarily very cautious in proposing models, has gone a long way in this connection—and rightly so. For instance, in a Unesco publication on biology teaching we find a table of the 'aims of biological education in schools' which seems to us to be quite relevant:

1. Fostering and sustaining interest in learning the scientific process and sustaining interest in a comprehension of the causes of events.
2. Training in the skills and attitudes of the scientific method.
3. Imparting factual knowledge.
4. Imparting motor skills.
5. Stimulating pupils to maintain a science component in higher education.
6. Stimulating application of the principles and skills of science to relevant areas outside science.
7. Promoting understanding of science in the cultural life of the individual and society, and thereby promoting the breakdown of the so-called two cultures (arts-based and science-based).

8. Training for specific careers in biology [Unesco, 1977, p. 20].

The authors then propose a rating scale for priorities among objectives in order to ensure the necessary flexibility in the teaching process (objectives which are to be pursued intensively and in depth, objectives which are to be pursued in depth but not intensively, objectives which are to be pursued as the opportunity arises, etc.) and organize them in accordance with known taxonomies (cognitive, affective and psycho-motor fields). However, they introduce some useful nuances:

It is accepted that all three domains are often involved together in acts of learning ... it is also to be noted that the will to do something (cognative domain) is not the same as knowing about it, knowing how to do it, and feeling like doing it [p. 22].

A more flexible organization of contents (modular organization, multiple and combinable options, etc.), making it possible at one and the same time to pursue objectives and to differentiate the learning process, is gaining ground at all levels of education (Lemke, 1981).[14] This approach is gradually establishing itself in the field of the social and human sciences, but this trend calls for two remarks.

When it is a question of formulating observable and measurable objectives and promoting a rigorous didactic technology in the learning of values, ideas and matters stemming from subjects such as literature, philosophy, ethics, etc., varied reactions are triggered; or in any case, many reservations. This is a point to which we shall revert in connection with the training of teachers.

Research workers have difficulty in organizing and presenting the content of the human and social sciences in the form of precisely and rigorously formulated objectives. They have to resort to more flexible formulae and always aim at a good philosophical and aesthetic training of teachers; indeed, only those who possess a sound general culture will be capable of making use of progress achieved in the taxonomies of objectives, the systems approach and the technology of education without being overwhelmed or confused by them.

A very useful distinction which has asserted itself forcefully for some time past has also helped to improve the organization of content. We have already referred to the pressure exerted on content by the exceptional mass of information which is produced, accumulated and put into circulation in the different fields of science, technology and culture as a result of the development of traditional and modern media of communication. And the distinction between *information* and *knowledge* which we made in the introduction to this part provides teachers with a valuable criterion for making a perspicacious and wise selection from among the growing flood of information.

Organizing the information contained in school curricula around fundamental concepts in order to provide pupils with terms of reference and with instruments to master information and co-ordinate in-school and out-of-school information seems to be a widespread concern among those responsible for curriculum building. It needs boldness and perseverance to centre knowledge around fundamental concepts and to jettison ballast from school curricula.

Not only pedagogic and epistemological principles are involved in the organization of contents. Training learners to take an active part in social life also means taking into consideration and reconciling two categories of demands or expectations; those of society, with the working world at the centre, and those of individuals, their aspirations and interests. The problem is a big one, and there are no simplistic solutions to it. A school which ignored the demands, changes and priority problems of contemporary society, aligning itself uniquely with the expectations and interests of children and adolescents (whose interests are moreover not always clearly defined) would temporarily satisfy learners—and possibly parents—but it would isolate itself, and would justify the doubts and criticisms formulated recently by authors such as Jencks and felt by all those who take an interest in the future of the school. For example, the importance assumed by the teaching of mathematics in compulsory school education is, to a large extent, the expression of a social demand, or more precisely of the evolution of the world of work. But it often happens that some pupils, before making the effort to learn the subject, and taking advantage of the availability of options, announce other 'interests' in order to avoid having to cope with mathematics at the upper secondary or higher education level. Hence the multiplication of sections or faculties slanted towards literature, social studies, the law, etc., producing large numbers of young people who are incapable of fitting into active life—or more precisely, into those sectors of it where mathematics are necessary. It cannot be denied that mathematics is part of the general culture which everyone must possess; on the other hand, the idea must be promoted that all pupils should benefit from teachers, textbooks, teaching materials and resources which can facilitate the learning of mathematics; and that any improper utilization of mathematics to influence pupils' choice, to discourage or confuse them, is prejudicial and contrary to the principle of the democratization of education.

The contrary situation is to be avoided also, because a school which ignores the aptitudes, interests and intellectual possibilities of children and which strictly confines itself to meeting social demand (sometimes defined out of perspective and by questionable methods) ultimately does not properly meet either the expectations and aspirations of individuals or those of society; on the one hand because motivation plays a decisive role in any occupational activity, and on the other hand because the progress of any society supposes a systematic development of all talents, in all fields. The spectrum of demands in a modern society is broadening, and the diversity of types of activity offers structures which leaves scope for all categories of interests. But reconciling these two worlds—youth and the world of work and of socio-culturally useful activity—is not a task which can be solved separately either by the education authorities or by the leaders of the different sectors of economic and social life.

Examining this problem, a study of the evolution of the contents of general education over the period 1970-80 identifies, on the worldwide level, four types of relationships between economic imperatives and the play of natural faculties, each type with its advantages and limitations.

Some countries have set up an educational system that corresponds to the requirements of national development. Pupils are steered through such a system by selective examinations which in successive stages draw upon the heterogeneous mass of pupils in order to supply, from year to year, the requisite numbers and categories of workers and supervisory grades considered necessary. Educational activities designed to ensure the fulfilment of the individual remain independent of this selection process and are aimed at training the individual as a citizen who will contribute to his country's development whatever his qualifications and his job.

In other countries successive and varied options enable each pupil to choose from among different fields of knowledge and activities those which seem to correspond to his tastes and preferences. In this type of organization, pupils are steered through the system individually; it corresponds to their motivation in that it enables them to exercise and develop their aptitudes in the fields of their choice.

Other types of organization seek to reconcile economic imperatives and natural faculties. Pupils are steered through different sections of studies which themselves follow on an undifferentiated teaching. This orientation takes into account not only the purely scholastic aptitudes of pupils, but also their intellectual faculties and their practical capabilities. It is seen as a concerted and carefully thought out procedure designed to enable each individual to engage, at the level corresponding to his abilities, in activities which conform to his preferences and are socially useful.

Lastly, there are countries which, as a consequence of recent accession to independence or of a change in regime, are still seeking the best form of scholastic organization. In a perspective which combines the future of the economy and the future of citizens, thought is given to problems of literacy, universal primary schooling, and secondary education. Some of the systems which have been set up are based on an existing model; others have drawn upon initiatives and derive from an original creation [International Symposium..., 1980a, p. 2].

These four strategies, and especially the third, remind us that the provision of satisfactory schooling and the development of the intellectual and moral potential of young people call for a measure of generous investment and of patience where the expectation of results is concerned.

THE EMERGENCE OF NEW CONTENTS IN CURRICULA

We refer here to content which has been introduced in response to the demands of the contemporary world (the protection of the environment, the defence and promotion of peace, the promotion of a new international economic and ethical order, the teaching of human rights, etc.), which themselves express an awareness of the importance of the problems of our world and of our time for the survival and progress of mankind. Admittedly, one may wonder quite simply why contemporary world problems are not taught as a subject in itself. On certain serious problems such as underdevelopment or the deterioration of the environment, there is fairly broad agreement both as to the nature of the problem and as to possible solutions.

But complications arise when we consider that on other problems, points of view and interpretations differ greatly, and may even clash. It is obvious that terms such as 'democratization', 'human rights', 'the defence of peace and education for peace' do not have an identical meaning everywhere. Furthermore, even though we may manage to agree in approving resolutions in favour of peace at the level of teacher training and educational practice, we find few practical measures and activities which may be classed unhesitatingly under the heading 'training for the promotion of peace'. This disparity between the seriousness of the problems involved and the modesty of practical actions, between unanimously approved resolutions and the weakness of relevant measures, clearly indicates the global nature of 'contemporary problems' and the interrelations between the problems covered by that notion, which has become somewhat commonplace. Agreement on solutions to be put into effect in order to solve a certain problem is blocked by contradictory approaches to another problem, and sometimes by a lack of sincerity, resulting in mutual mistrust which plays a baneful role. Otherwise, why is it that we do not yet read engraved over the portals of educational institutions or inscribed

Current developments

on the flyleaf of textbooks of history and literature, the opening sentence of the Constitution of Unesco, approved by all Member States: 'Since wars begin in the minds of men, it is in the minds of men that the defences of peace must be constructed'; or the even more pregnant phrase proposed by the World Association for the School as an Instrument of Peace: 'Disarm the mind to disarm the hand'? However, we shall attempt to show here, with the aid of a few examples, that the process has been initiated: the contents of the curricula or the co-curricula of certain countries are beginning to respond to the demands of the world in which we live, and this may lead other countries to take an interest in the possibility of such contents contributing to the preparation of a better future.

It may be noted that Unesco has published a useful study for curriculum designers and teachers entitled *World Problems in the Classroom* (Unesco, 1982b). After describing the United Nations, the study deals with: peace and security; disarmament; human rights and fundamental freedoms; population; poverty and economic progress; the environment; the seas and sea-bed; social justice for workers; food and hunger; health; children's welfare; education, science and culture.

Each chapter proposes or indicates definitions of fundamental concepts (human rights, peace, disarmament, etc.), gives an overall view of the problem and the data relating to it, replies to possible questions, highlights the common goals which could make co-operation between individuals, peoples and states more effective, and proposes subjects for study and discussion. In raising questions and in encouraging discussion, the study is calculated to arouse pupils' interest and give them an idea of the dimensions and gravity of world problems, leading them to adopt an appropriate conception and attitude. For example, where health is concerned we find questions such as: 1. 'Should we support WHO's goals of better health for all the people in the poorest countries?' Some people argue against this. This is followed by arguments for and against support of the WHO's activities. 2. 'Why are the control of disease and the improvement of health considered to have international aspects?'

On the subject of environmental education, in 1975 Unesco launched, in co-operation with the United Nations Environment Programme, a coherent International Environmental Education Programme (IEEP) in response to a recommendation of the United Nations Conference on the Human Environment in 1972.

Along the same lines, the International Workshop on Environmental Education was organized in 1975 and adopted the Belgrade Charter, a global framework for environmental education. This was followed by meetings in all the regions, culminating in the ministerial-level Intergovernmental Conference on Environmental Education held in Tbilisi in 1977 (Unesco, 1980a). In 1982, Unesco convened in Paris an International Expert Meeting on Progress and Trends in Environmental Education since the Tbilisi Conference. The newsletter *Connect* (Unesco/UNEP, 1983) presents the principal results which can be attributed to the actions of the IEEP in three complementary domains:

1. The development of a general awareness of the necessity of environmental education, achieved through a series of international and regional meetings, comparative studies, consolidated studies, etc.

2. Development of concepts and methodological approaches in this sphere, with emphasis on the interdisciplinary and problem-solving approach which enables the environment to be regarded as a totality.

3. Efforts to incorporate an environmental dimension into the educational processes of Member States, through international and regional seminars for school curriculum builders and teacher educators, through methodological guides and textbooks, and through a series of modules designed for the training of teachers.

Research in this field relates to the incorporation of environmental education in different levels or categories of education (primary, secondary, higher, etc.), or in the content of various groups of subjects or activities: biology, geography, civic education, out-of-school education, etc. Unesco has initiated and continues to follow up many pilot projects: in Colombia (for rural populations), in France (methodologies for secondary schools), in Guatemala (for rural schools and the general public), in Ghana (for primary level teachers), in India (for primary schools), in Egypt (for youth clubs and associations), in Czechoslovakia (for the school system), and in Senegal (for the adult population of the Sahel).

Still at the international level, Unesco has adopted a comparable approach (studies, pilot projects, training seminars) to nutrition education (Davadas et al., 1982; Ingle et al., 1982; Srinivasan and Peters, 1983; Unesco, 1983a, 1983b), aimed in particular at developing countries.

A similar effort is being made in the field of population education, a field which ties in with those of socio-economic development, nutrition, health and the environment. In Asia in particular, this effort to use educational resources to solve an extremely complex and tricky problem is being systematically undertaken in very different forms: case-studies, comparative studies, exchanges of experience, discussions and seminars, consolidated publications, etc.[15]

At the level of individual countries, these new types of content are beginning to be introduced into school curricula and timetables, in particular environmental education, population education, nutrition education, and modern domestic economy. In his study of trends and prospects in education in Latin America and the Caribbean Blat Gimeno (1983, p. 56) indicates significant innovations:

New material is being included in curricula on questions of contemporary interest or which have never been given adequate attention, despite their importance, such as environmental education, population education, sex and family education, and education in health and nutrition. But attempts to bring about renewal have, perhaps, been most evident in the reform of syllabuses for the sciences and their technological applications.

In China, population education has special significance, touching as it does upon one of the most important problems. Courses in this subject are included in general education; their purpose is to present the importance of population control in a scientific manner, in order that pupils may properly understand the relation between population growth and the development of production and adopt an appropriate attitude to this problem.

In Africa, as indicated in the document prepared by Unesco for the Conference of Ministers of Education and Those Responsible for Economic Planning in African Member States held in Harare in 1982, new contents are also beginning to appear in curricula:

New disciplines belonging to different sciences are being introduced into the curricula in nearly all African countries. These include nutrition, health education, education related to the environment, agriculture and animal husbandry ... the placing of emphasis on African cultural roots does not, of course, preclude opening the door to other cultures nor the appreciation of universal cultural values. With a view to encouraging an interest in the outside world, while remaining committed to the policy of promoting the cultural specificity of Africa, eighteen countries of the region have already begun to develop, particularly at the primary school level, teaching that aims to promote education for international understanding, co-operation and peace and education concerning human rights and fundamental freedoms [MINEDAF, 1982, pp. 45 and 46].

Thus, even though much remains to be done, the progress achieved in all—or almost all—countries, this responsiveness to world problems, is promising, and represents a step towards more effective co-operation at the regional and international levels. This progress clearly shows that isolation is dangerous, that nations cannot ignore one another, and that openness and sincere co-operation are the lines to be followed. The situation may be said to be promising.

Current developments

SUMMING UP

A review of discussions, projects and achievements leads us to the conclusion that on the threshold of the twenty-first century rigorous and resolute thought is being given to the future of education, and that the warning 'do not neglect education' (or 'education and culture') can no longer be ignored by all those whom this field concerns: policy-makers, parents, educators, employers, etc. Furthermore, this warning has been uttered twice in the United States in the course of recent decades, and upon each occasion this country, which is keenly competitive and does not like being outdistanced, reacted positively. In 1957, when the Soviet Union launched the first artificial satellite and when certain political authorities were considering increasing the funds allotted to American space programmes or launching an investigation into the causes of the United States' lag in this field, NASA specialists were the ones who gave the signal: 'do not neglect education'. And we may pay tribute to the wisdom of the scientists of this distinguished body whose gaze is turned towards the twenty-first century, and assert that this appeal was the most intelligent satellite they have so far launched, and the one of greatest use to the world community. Subsequently, in 1983, the American Congress, faced with the Japanese challenge, particularly felt in computerization, approved as a relevant measure an increase in teachers' salaries and in the funds allotted to the improvement of the teaching process.

We have indicated a number of trends which will probably continue and even become more pronounced, developing into clear educational orientations or realities. Similarly, we have indicated promising developments which are seen as applications of the achievements of pedagogic research, manifestations of a forward-looking attitude, reactions to actual or possible mistakes, etc. But the dialectic is such that trends or successes must throw light not only on the lines to be followed but also on existing inadequacies and unsolved problems. So let us begin by pointing out certain deficiencies where educational goals and objectives are concerned.

The response of educational contents to contemporary world problems and to the recommendations of various international conferences or agencies remains selective, partial and hesitant. Admittedly, there are encouraging examples in many countries (OECD, 1983a). The special number of the *International Review of Education* (Unesco Institute of Education, 1980) briefly describes some examples of the introduction of education for peace into in-school and out-of-school activities in countries such as the Federal Republic of Germany, the United Kingdom, Belgium, etc. The 'Code of Peace' proposed by the

World Association for the School as an Instrument of Peace is taught in certain schools in Europe and Africa. The International Association of Educators for World Peace has organized a pilot school in Jassy, Romania, and initiated research on the subject. A number of peace research institutes, universities and academies are active, some of them even extremely active. Mention should also be made of the Associated Schools Project, organized and run by Unesco. And there is no lack of studies on fundamental concepts and difficulties to be overcome, evaluations of an economic or political nature of the advantages of a process of disarmament, guides for teachers and teacher educators, etc. (World Congress..., 1980). But if we compare the efforts made at the international level between the Recommendation adopted by all the Member States of Unesco in 1974 and the Intergovernmental Conference on the same subject in 1983 (Intergovernmental Conference, 1983) with practical measures relating to the curriculum and to the training of teachers, we cannot fail to realize what meagre progress has been accomplished. As specialists observe, at the level of educational practice organized on the basis of official documents, there have been few significant experiments susceptible of widespread adoption. It is sometimes said that 'nationalism' or national interests are an obstacle to the promotion of education for peace, and it should perhaps be recognized that mistrust, national egoism, political ambition or outdated political thinking delay the application of a series of wise and realistic recommendations, even though they have been unanimously approved.

In the early 1980s, education for the future acquired concepts and methodologies which could be introduced into the training of teachers and into educational practice. More than twenty years ago, the Polish philosopher and teacher Bogdan Suchodolski (1962) wrote:

Education for the future expresses the conviction that the present reality is not the only reality and that, consequently, it is not the only criterion in education. The future reality is another. In defining this future reality, historical necessity coincides with the realization of our ideals. This necessity is a protection against utopia; action is a protection against fatalism.

The fact that the principle of education for the future means breaking out of the narrow horizons of the present is of great significance.

And yet there are few countries which can provide examples of education for the future or of the promotion of exercises of a forward-looking nature in the curriculum. We may wonder what form should be taken—firstly at the level of goals and subsequently in the learning process—by pedagogic solutions to such imperatives as: (a) training young people to detect, identify and discourage all forms of extremism or fanaticism; (b) providing all adolescents with a basic culture in order to help them to select information, to reject the utilitarianism and commercialism of the mass media; (c) teaching young people the cultural and ethical significance of sport in order to prevent sporting contests becoming violent or politically slanted; (d) promoting the moral values essential for the progress of mankind and, under the specific socio-political conditions at the close of the present century, waging the extremely difficult struggle against individual and collective egoism which is at the origin of so many ills, and training adolescents to be generous, sincere and honest.

Progress in the real democratization of the school has been modest—even very modest in certain countries—despite the fact that there is much talk of it in official documents and declarations. But the contemporary school no longer claims to be above politics or social struggles; it plays an essential role in the life of every society and every individual; it can perpetuate disparities and inequalities, just as it can open up prospects for all children and provide greater equality of opportunity. This is a subject of lively discussion, and the criticisms seem relevant. In many countries, for example, examinations—competitive or otherwise—rarely assess the aptitudes, attitudes and creative abilities of candidates, but remain centred on the volume of knowledge acquired and how faithfully it can be reproduced. And in this case, preparing for a difficult entrance examination means benefiting from all the conditions necessary for devoting three to four hours a day for two to four years to the assimilation of the content of the subjects set.

Educational authorites are concerned with the real democratization of education, and it is the subject of sustained research.

The comparative study by the OECD (1983*a*) of compulsory schooling in a changing society contains a chapter on equality of opportunity and the examination of measures to ensure equality and to provide back-up programmes for underprivileged children; the questions to be solved are dealt with. Schaeffer's study prepared for the symposium organized by Unesco in 1980 on the evolution of the content of general education, wondered whether the school was an instrument of authority or whether it could have a moral inspiration, a spiritual dimension and a civilizing influence. Referring to the same problem, and recalling the principles adopted by African countries for their socio-educational and economic development—namely 'authenticity' and 'endogeneity'—Lê Thành Khôi (1984)[16] points out that these two principles must be combined with the democratic nature of development in order to satisfy the expectations of the whole population and not merely a minority. Development, including the development of education and culture, must benefit the people; but neither authenticity nor endogeny can on their own ensure the democratic nature of development. So here again we have an open problem (see Tanguiane, 1977).

One series of criticisms concerns the quality and relevance of content, as adopted in the curriculum or taught in school. The disparities and lack of communication between the contents of in-school education and informal education are increasing, and becoming a problem for the school; a large part of the extremely varied information, lacking coherence and of uneven value, acquired outside the school forms an inactive deposit; another part, useful and up to date, corresponds to the interests of pupils but is only rarely referred to or taken advantage of by teachers. When there is a contradiction between these two types of information, the situation is even more disquieting. Teaching continues to follow the tradition of compartmentalized and juxtaposed subjects; the connections between the subjects are slight, teachers being more concerned with defending their own subject-matter than with promoting, in its different forms, the principle of interdisciplinarity. Despite certain measures adopted and research undertaken in various countries with the idea of giving pupils an overall view of knowledge and reality, the specific nature of the subject-matter resurfaces, as G. Gozzer (1982) has remarked. But without being a panacea and without doing away with subjects, interdisciplinarity is a modern and effective means of learning; we shall revert to this question in the next chapter when we deal with interdisciplinarity as a solution to be encouraged. Along the same lines, reference should be made both to the lack of coherence between different educational levels, classes and subjects, both horizontally and vertically, and to the asymmetries and imbalances between groups of subjects. Teachers and pupils feel the need for a more global and more realistic approach to science and technology, but we are far from having a paradigm to apply effectively to school curricula and the training of teachers.

Curricula are so heavily loaded, and sometimes classes are so large, that pupils cannot easily find an opportunity to engage in dialogue, to discover their latent resources and to assert themselves as individuals with their own interests and aspirations. The insignificant place occupied by reading (reading accompanied by meditation) and by reflection on complex problems in contemporary education reminds us of Pascal's celebrated phrase: 'All human ills stem from man's inability to stay quietly in a room.' While dynamism and a practical attitude are admirable qualities, fruitless agitation, idle chatter and the perpetual quest for external information and ideas are anachronistic and dangerous. In any event, when they leave school young people must know, among other things, how to organize themselves intellectually and avoid mental destabilization.

We have acclaimed the promotion of environmental contents in school curricula as a successful line to follow. Here it is a question of the infusion of ideas, facts and events into the activity of teachers and the subjects taught; it is a positive approach, because the problems of the environment are of an interdisciplinary nature. But these problems constitute a whole, and in order that an awareness and an attitude may be created, they demand a holistic approach. At present, pupils manage to acquire a certain quantity of information or knowledge where the environment is concerned (and also on nutrition, population, etc.), but not an overall view.

It happens that reflection and research sometimes provide the solutions to problems. But as J. Bruner has observed, even if a pedagogic theory is correct, relevant and applicable, it can be ineffective in educational practice if it does not correspond to the priorities or urgent demands of a given society.

Like other authors, we have highlighted the pressures exerted by society on the school, making this traditional institution a dependent rather than an independent variable, a resource or an instrument of society rather than an end. But schooling covers an extremely rich and delicate period in the life of every individual; it must be, and remain, a privileged territory, conducive to learning, to experience of a moral nature, to reflection, to the quest for truth, to self-instruction. Like the authors of the work on compulsory schooling (OECD, 1983a), we wish to make the distinction, sometimes neglected, between an open school and an institution which may lose its specificity and its pedagogic goal. 'It is important not to overlook one of the most fundamental yet simple goals of compulsory schooling—that schooling itself should be worthwhile not only in a future but also in a present context.'

How can reforms or innovations be conceived, and how can there be a response to the problems of the contemporary world, without maintaining schools in a state of permanent and confusing trepidation? How can social demands be introduced and apportioned while at the same time allowing children and adolescents the time to reflect, to find their bearings and to develop?

NOTES

1. Friedrich Froebel, the German educationist (1782–1852), invented sets of building boxes of different shapes and colours for use in infant schools which were long considered an indispensable teaching aid.
2. In his doctoral thesis for the University of Jassy in 1984, Y. O. Sid Ahmed pleads in favour of multi-dimensional, balanced and integrated content within the context of lifelong education. Against this background he gives an interesting

case-study on 'Les Mahedras chinguittiennes ou universités à dos de chameau'. Chinguitt is an ancient town which played a considerable cultural role in the history of Mauritania. In 1981, the Director-General of Unesco, Amadou-Mahtar M'Bow, visited the town and launched an appeal for the safeguarding of the ancient cities of Mauritania. The expression '*à dos de chameau*'—'on camelback'—indicates that this type of education was linked with the wanderings of the camels from place to place in search of pasture in accordance with the pattern of rainfall. Through the centuries this peripatetic system of schooling has produced educated individuals and ensured the cultural and linguistic unity of the people. The author deals with its programmes, its teachers, its pupils, its costs and finally its future.

3. For example: Meeting of Experts on the Content of Education in the Context of Lifelong Education (Paris, October 1975); Meeting of Experts on the Methodology of Curriculum Reform (Paris, December 1976); Expert Committee Meeting on the Co-ordination of the Content of Pre-University Education at School with that of Post-Secondary Education in Europe (Paris, June 1978); Regional Meeting of Experts on Examinations and Other Procedures for the Evaluation of Educational Achievements and Experiments in the Context of Lifelong Education in Europe (Paris, December 1978).
4. The proceedings of this symposium, published in Bucharest in December 1968, contain, abstracts in English, French and Russian. The majority of the communications are centred on the problems of lifelong education.
5. This is based on a two-volume guide for teachers, published by the University of Jassy in 1982 under the editorship of George Vaideanu.
6. Wincenty Okon is a remarkable didactician who has greatly contributed to the renewal of the teaching-learning process in his country, Poland. He has promoted a coherent approach to the curriculum co-ordinating objectives, content, learning methods, and methods and techniques of evaluation. He gives great prominence to the formation of intellectual attitudes and abilities, placing learning in the perspective of lifelong education. For the past three decades, he has strongly advocated active methods, and has made a special study of the learning of cultural and artistic values.
7. Almost the same approaches can be found in the latest reform of the educational system in Yugoslavia. See: Juhas Mihailo, *Education and its Reform in Yugoslavia*, Belgrade, 1975.
8. The authors also ask in this paper (p. 15), referring to the teaching of mathematics:

How are teaching curricula and methods influenced by cultural patterns and attitudes? How do children acquire a knowledge of mathematics? These are the questions which must be answered if we want to explain the swing of the pendulum in recent years: the abandonment of traditional mathematics in favour of the 'new maths' based on Gaussian theory, followed by a reversion to the previous system ... Though there has been a tendency towards the achievement of a balance over the past two or three years, this trend does not mean that an identity of points of view has been reached (p. 10). In the process of modernization, young children, or those less inclined to scientific studies, have often been subjected to contents and approaches which are valid for older people who are better motivated for scientific studies.

9. The programme entitled 'The teaching of science and technology' is part of the Major Programme 'Education, training and society' designed in liaison with another Major Programme, 'Science, technology and society'. The importance of the teaching of science and technology is highlighted: 'The application of science and technology can make a decisive contribution to improving living standards and

conditions. Some of the essential tasks of education, therefore, are to impart the basic scientific and technological knowledge necessary to prepare the younger generation for the practice of an increasing number of occupations, especially in the productive sector ... and to foster awareness among young people and adults of the interrelationships between science, technology and society' (Unesco, 1983c, p. 123).
10. A. S. Makarenko, (1888–1939), the Soviet educationist whose activity was centred on the moral training of young people and adolescents, through his research and experiments highlighted: (a) the role of the collective in the training of individuals; (b) the importance of the aesthetic factor in the effectiveness of moral influence; (c) discipline as an initial condition for character-building; (d) the role of 'hidden contents' in this extremely tricky and complex process: the attitudes of the educator, non-verbal methods, etc.; and (e) the training of the teacher as an educator.
11. The author notes that the desire of contemporary youth to express itself and to participate in the improvement of the life of the local community and the international community is evident. It may also be recognized that, through their taste for innovation and their aspiration for social justice, young people can make a specific contribution to the promotion of moral values in the future and to a more equitable and more democratic political and economic order. Furthermore, young people are not hostile to traditional moral values (modesty, tolerance, sincerity, etc.), but rather to their misuse, and hence to the hypocrisy of certain sectors of society. However, the taste for innovation and the desire for change do not constitute values in themselves. At present: (a) the moral objectives of the school are out of step with the complexity of contemporary socio-moral life; (b) moral maturity or autonomy comes later than intellectual maturity; (c) one cannot ignore the existence of compartmented groups of young people who have their own code and jargon, refuse to work, and may influence youth as a whole; (d) societies seem reluctant to offer adolescents and young people the possibility of participating effectively in the improvement of cultural and moral life, and to accept an open dialogue; (e) where moral education is concerned, the training of teachers (their ethical, sociological and pedagogic training) is inadequate.
12. I see right, I approve it, and I do wrong.
13. It is difficult to say, for example, whether the music promoted by David Bowie and Boy George, presented as the 'triumph of the third sex' responds precisely to an aspiration, to a spiritual need, of young people, or whether it has been encouraged and launched, with the aid of talented youngsters, by certain mass media. Moreover, youth (or part of it) is sometimes oriented in a certain direction, and subsequently research workers study the 'spontaneous and objective orientations of youth', using irreproachable techniques of social psychology.
14. In this connection, the reader is invited to compare two conceptions concerning the modular organization of content: that of Professor L. D'Hainaut (Busshoff et al., 1981) and that of the Indonesian authorities (Unesco, 1974).

D'Hainaut devotes a chapter to modular organization, and before attempting a definition (a conception) he highlights the characteristics of the traditional organization of content which has survived over the years: the concentration of studies at the beginning of life, to the exclusion of all other periods; the division of study possibilities into a small number of streams or ladders which are in turn divided into as few sub-streams as possible; relative lack of contact between the streams and diploma prerequisites governing admittance; continuity within a stream or sub-stream; horizontal division into years and breakdown of pupils according to age-groups; overall certification at the end of a cycle by means of a diploma; collective teaching; a common timetable, almost always full time. D'Hainaut than defines the four fundamental criteria of the educational module.

It must: (a) present or define a set of learning situations; (b) have its own carefully specified function and be directed at clearly defined objectives; (c) include tests designed to guide the learner and/or teacher and provide them with feedback; (d) be capable of fitting into a variety of learning paths or itineraries, methods and situations. Lastly, the author gives a series of diagrams to clarify the organization of a system of modular learning.

In the case-study of Indonesia already referred to, this country's option is presented and justified: the modular organization of content. Experience has shown that it is not easy to train a large number of teachers in a short time. At present, Indonesia is faced with the problem of training teachers, notably in the science field. By adapting the modular system of instruction to the school, it is hoped that the quality of the pupils' training will not be over-dependent on the quality of the teachers. The modular system of teaching and learning has the following characteristics: (a) it places emphasis on self-instruction; (b) it allows for individual differences in learning; (c) it uses multi-media and a set of methods; (d) it requires the active participation of learners; (e) it provides a feedback of learners' performance; (f) it applies strategies of mastery learning, or complete and sound learning. The option of the authorities seems fully justified; however, in promoting this form of organization of content and learning they perhaps rely too much on the virtues of educational technology.

Furthermore, Lemke (1981) referring to philosophical and psychological confrontations where learning and the curriculum are concerned, proposes a flexible curriculum designed in function of the needs and interests of pupils and the problems to be solved; he underlines the importance of educational research for the identification of learners' needs. His study indicates the steps to be taken to establish a flexible curriculum expressed in terms of 'integrated learning units'.

15. Dealing with the same problem, Christopher Dede is concerned in particular with the impact of demographic changes (which differ greatly from one country to another) on education: 'Overall, demographic changes will have primarily qualitative impacts on educational policies in nations with low rates of population growth and quantitative effects on countries with continuing high fertility . . . The size of student population and the geographic distribution of demand will be the major source of change in developing nations, resulting in a very large increase in educational demand and associated problems of scale in providing services.'

16. Indicating his agreement with the conception of authenticity promoted by African countries, the author makes some interesting remarks. 'It places emphasis on the specific activity of the people, who seek in their ancestral values those which contribute to their development, while at the same time being responsive to other people's culture. This conforms to the original meaning of the Greek word "*authenthes*", meaning "one who does something with his own hand". The idea that emerges is that of autonomy of action. Authenticity is the opposite of mimicry or sham: in legal language, an authentic deed or instrument is one which originates from the person to whom it is attributed, and not another. In this sense, authenticity is close to endogeneity, another fashionable concept. "Endogenous", which also comes from the Greek, means "produced from within".

'In both cases, what is emphasized is the origin, the provenance, and not the content of the action. Here we have the major inadequacy of the two concepts when applied to development. Because development, as everyone agrees, must benefit the whole population and not a minority. But neither authenticity nor endogeny guarantee this. Similarly, an individual may be "authentically" democratic or reactionary, just as an "endogenous" development, if it is only that, may take conflicting directions.'

8
Future prospects

EDUCATION UNDER GROWING PRESSURES: CONSERVATISM OR CHANGE?

In the face of the economic, social and cultural pressures described in the first part of this work, and the new developments in education[1] referred to in the previous chapter, the capacity of education systems to react depends on a series of factors that vary from one country to another—such as the quality of educational tradition, the availability and quality of educational publications, the cultural and educational level of teachers, their material and moral status, and the quality of curricula, textbooks and teaching aids. It is important, in any case, to hold on to two ideas: (a) education systems should not be subject to constraint or harassment by the various forces acting upon them; (b) by accommodating the new sources of contents and the demands of the modern world, education systems can play an enhanced role in the exploration and solution of the social, political and moral problems of our time. The reason why some authors arrive at pessimistic conclusions and others propose radical solutions with regard to educational reform is because of a certain resistance to innovation, which can become a formidable obstacle compromising the future of a whole national community. What seems clear to us is that changes are widespread, that they exert pressures on education systems and that these systems sometimes behave in a 'reactive' manner,[2] and in other cases in a 'proactive' manner—i.e. *by anticipating, which is a reflection of their independence and should be encouraged.*

The responses or strategies to which new educational developments (or, more precisely, the new contents) have given rise are broadly threefold. The essentially conservative systems have initiated a limited modernization process, based on the traditional contents of mathematics, physics, history, etc. The authors of curricula reflecting this strategy point out that the new contents are already inherent in various forms in the ultimate goals or the substance of traditional contents;

thus, it is claimed that, by modernizing the subject-matter of traditional disciplines such as physics, biology, history and geography, the new demands have been satisfactorily met. This conservative approach is condemned by many critics.

At the opposite extreme, one encounters a kind of educational radicalism. The proponents of this strategy contend that the authorities should abandon traditional content forthwith and develop a new curriculum. Edward Cornish (1978) for example, in his chapter 'The Coming Revolution in Education', considers that scholars have a remarkable capacity for ignoring the present as well as the future; backward-looking and incapable of analysing what is around and ahead of them, they exert a strong influence on teaching. Advocating 'futurism' as the 'secret weapon' of an educational revolution, the author proposes six objectives—objectives and not a list of disciplines to be taught—for a 'total curriculum'.

Access to Information: Reading; listening and seeing; direct experiment; libraries and reference books; computerized data-retrieval; data from newspapers, businesses, government agencies, etc.; asking experts; judging reliability; managing information overload.

Thinking Clearly: Semantics, propaganda and common fallacies; values clarification; deductive logic; mathematics; analytical problem-solving; scientific method; probability and statistics; computer programming; general systems; creative problem-solving; forecasting and prediction.

Communicating Effectively: Speaking informally; public speaking; voice and body language; cultural barriers to communication; formal and informal writing; grammar, syntax, and style; drawing, sketching, still photography, film making, etc.; graphic design and layout; outlines, flow-charts, charts, tables, and graphs; organization and editing; handwriting, typing, dictating.

Understanding Man's Environment: Astronomy, physics, and chemistry; geology and physical geography; biology, ecology, and ethology; genetics, evolution, and population dynamics; fundamentals of modern technology; applied mechanics, optics, and electronics.

Understanding Man and Society: Human evolution; human physiology; linguistics; cultural anthropology (including history and the humanities); psychology and social psychology; racism, ethnicity, and xenophobia; government and law; economics and economic philosophy; changing occupational patterns; education and employment; issues in human survival; prospects for mankind.

Personal Competence: Physical grace and coordination; survival training and self-defense; safety, hygiene, nutrition, and sex education; consumer education and personal finance; creative and performing arts; basic interpersonal skills; small group dynamics; management and administration; effective citizen participation; knowledge of best personal learning styles and strategies; mnemonics and other learning aids; biofeedback, meditation, mood control; self-knowledge and self-motivation.

The author goes on to note that 'futurism' enables teachers to make a genuine link between education and life. 'Futurizing' the curriculum implies orienting young people towards the future instead of the past. This vision of educational contents, far from being a wild flight of fancy, comes from a country which is currently moving towards the post-industrial age (or, as we prefer to say, towards the age of a strong and humanized industry); it does not seem very realistic, but it could, with some modifications, represent an alternative to be pursued at a given juncture. We accept the idea that streamlining the curriculum could involve jettisoning part of the current subject-matter of history, literature, philosophy, etc. But it is not so much knowledge of the past which stands in the way of education for the future; it is rather the style of analysis of the past which is in question. How can a future-oriented approach be possible unless one takes the past and present as one's terms of reference? How can one make reason the supreme authority of life without having regard to the examples of history?

Shane and Tabler (1981) establish a comparison between the traditional subject-centred curriculum and a learner-centred curriculum. Before proposing this alternative, they stress the idea that education for the new millennium, taking place in a period of tension and upheaval, should highlight all the values that have been confirmed throughout history and have guided mankind over long periods.

None of the national projects known to us and mentioned previously have to our knowledge set out to achieve a radical transformation of the contents of education during the 1980s and 1990s; even where the term 'revolution' is employed, one cannot talk of a truly revolutionary strategy with regard to decision-making or educational practice. On the other hand, as we have said, many countries have adopted an 'infusional approach' to the integration of new contents; this is a way—or so it is hoped—of avoiding the overloading or imbalance of curricula. Recalling, for example, the case-study on the prospects for Hungarian education, it may be said that, while there is a certain awareness of the problems of the modern world and the future, it still remains hesitant and selective.

In addition to the conservative and the radical approaches, there is also a middle way, which, while it might be said to be excessively cautious, undoubtedly reflects a certain realism: its aim is to achieve what is possible in current socio-political circumstances. Whatever the reasons for their existence, the gaps between countries seem fairly large and backwardness in some cases assumes alarming proportions. However, the bold strategies proposed by some authors cannot be filed away under the heading of Utopias or projects for a distant future. Some of the factors influencing social change can become very

Subject-centred curriculum	Learner-centred curriculum
1. Introduces learners to the cultural heritage.	1. Releases the teacher from the pressure to follow a prescribed scope and sequence that does not invariably meet all learners' needs.
2. Gives the teachers a sense of security by specifying what their responsibilities are for developing given skills and knowledge.	2. Has a positive influence on learners as they find instruction varied to meet individual needs and purposes.
3. Reduces repetition or overlap between grade levels or different sections of the same class.	3. Encourages teacher judgement in selecting the content deemed most suitable for a group of learners.
4. Increases the likelihood that learners will be exposed to knowledge and develop skills in an orderly manner.	4. Increases the likelihood that content has relevance to learners.
5. Permits methodical assessment of pupil progress; assumes that knowledge is the only measurable outcome of learning experiences.	5. Modifies instruction to accommodate developmental changes and behavioural tasks as individual differences are identified and monitored.
6. Facilitates co-operative group planning by educators in allocating the scope and sequence of learning experiences.	6. Allows much more latitude for creative planning by the individual teacher.

active, and change very rapid. Educational research should not hesitate to remain firmly in advance of the relatively slow changes in systems and to contemplate fresh alternatives, so as to be able to provide decision-makers and planners with approaches that could prove relevant over the next decade.

REMARKABLE ACHIEVEMENTS AND
FORWARD-LOOKING SOLUTIONS

The impact of self-instruction and self-evaluation on educational contents

In an earlier sub-chapter, we described lifelong education as a possible key to reform and useful avenues of approach. We outline below some repercussions of continuing self-instruction on educational content.

Future prospects

To the extent that education effectively encompasses an individual's whole existence, constitutes a continuum, it becomes possible *to effect transfers* between the school and post-school context. These transfers could in the future represent an effective way of streamlining curricula and promoting an innovatory, participatory and highly differentiated form of learning. So far, educational authorities and teachers have shown little inclination to follow such a course; but there seems to have been some progress in this area in decentralized systems, the Scandinavian countries and, more generally, those countries with regular educational radio and television broadcasts. At present, it is all too common to find the various categories of teachers battling to ensure that the time devoted to their subject in the school timetable is maintained or even increased; but this battle, together with that waged by the representatives of new fields such as environmental studies and the new international order, can only result in curricula becoming overloaded and pupils overwhelmed, ultimately jeopardizing any attempt to bring about the genuine democratization of education. On the other hand, it is perfectly true that transferring knowledge to a post-school setting in the name of continuing self-instruction could compromise pupils' basic education until such time as lifelong education has become a socio-educational reality. One is faced then with an interlocking set of problems to which solutions can only be found through co-operation between educational authorities and the various social groups. What is needed is: (a) to create facilities and sources of information geared to the cultural and occupational needs of the population as a whole; disparities between urban and rural areas, in particular, need to be reduced to a minimum; (b) to ensure that educational radio and television broadcasts are of a high technical and educational quality; (c) to pay special attention to popular universities, open universities,[3] libraries and documentation centres, etc.; (d) to provide modern teacher training for all non-teaching educators such as museum guides, librarians, activity organizers in cultural centres, sports activity organizers, etc.; (e) to determine which knowledge could be transferred to a post-compulsory-schooling learning phase without jeopardizing the coherence and soundness of initial training conceived from the standpoint of lifelong education; (f) to promote an economic policy and legislation favourable to continuing self-instruction; what is important is, firstly, free time for study and, secondly, recognition of learners' progress and achievements; (g) to ensure that all those completing their compulsory education have a solid educational grounding.

On the other hand, certain kinds of information and knowledge usually acquired after school—relating to hygiene, political or family life, information technology, etc.—should be transferred to the period of compulsory schooling. Before reaching maturity and holding a job, the adolescent should understand what is meant by such notions as democracy, solidarity between peoples, and participation in social life.

Lifelong education makes its main impact on education systems through the educational objectives corresponding to economic and socio-cultural demands and the aspirations of young people. Once specified, these objectives determine syllabuses, curricula, educational technology and assessment procedures. Ideas such as the ambivalence of science and technology, the relativity of knowledge, the rapid obsolescence of technological information, the diversification of information sources and the global multidisciplinary character of world problems should be reflected in goals and objectives, leading eventually to new approaches to the teaching–learning process. While the application of the principle of lifelong education can lead to a genuine 'revolution', this revolution should take place in the classroom and in places of learning; it is a quiet revolution which has to be pursued daily as part of an extremely fragmented process and which is strongly influenced by the technological and educational culture of teachers. Yet the transformation in question is a very radical one which could increase equality of opportunity and make people better equipped to cope with and resolve the problems of the future. A proper awareness of the pitfalls to be avoided is as important as a thorough understanding of the changes to be brought about. The introduction of the idea of the relativity of knowledge or the ambivalence of science and technology must not lead to useful information and knowledge being neglected, but rather to a new system of assimilation, selection, storage and use of information. Education for creativity must not signify recourse to abstract exercises unrelated to life or the knowledge included in curricula. Finally, training for lifelong education and self-evaluation involves *a reinforcement of educability* and the shaping of a new attitude to the learning process: rather than experiencing it as an imposed task or burden to be borne throughout life, the young school-leaver should regard continuous learning as a way of life and as a means of enhancing his prestige, his social role and his adaptability.

Minda Sutaria's case-study on the probable evolution of the content of education in the Philippines contains some interesting facts and forecasts concerning the application of the principle of self-instruction. The author notes that pupils are currently ill-equipped to deal with the complex problems of change and the future. She forecasts an increased emphasis on self-instruction over the next two decades; in this connection, pupils will be more highly motivated and greater attention will be paid to the acquisition of learning-to-learn skills and to development of performance, self-assessment ability and of initiative. Teachers will increasingly fulfil the roles of group leaders, guides and organizers in the learning process; they will be more concerned with turning to account knowledge acquired outside school in a great variety of situations.

The contribution of information technology

Information technology has had a notable impact on education; change has been very rapid, and it seems likely to become even more rapid and to extend to all education systems. Fifteen to twenty years ago, the computer inspired a science-fiction type of approach which worried teachers: they saw it as a dangerous rival, as an educator endowed with secret qualities or, alternatively, a narrow-minded, monotonous and even stupid teacher. It is now clear that the computer has a great many uses in education, the use that concerns us here—computer-assisted learning (CAL) and, more generally, the introduction of pupils to information technology—being only one of them. In virtually all countries, the computer is used in one field or another: (a) the management and administration of education systems; (b) documentation; (c) computerized continuous assessment; (d) simulation; (e) non-programmed teaching; (f) programmed teaching; (g) educational research; (h) education for creativity (see France, 1981). A number of factors have favoured and accelerated the use of the computer in the teaching–learning process: the rapid development of information technology and its increased role in development; the rapid computerization of the various sectors of economic and social life, particularly industry; the continuing reduction in the size and price of computers; and the convincing results of educational research and the role that computers could play in combating failure at school (Council of Europe, 1983, Nos. 1 and 2).[4] All these factors have played a part in the development of a positive attitude to computers on the part of teachers, and not only science teachers. It is now recognized that the computer helps, facilitates and accelerates learning; it is becoming, if it has not already become, a technique essential to modern, effective and democratic education.

In Denmark, for example, the computer has in recent years captured the interest of all categories of teachers. Moreover, 'the interest of the upper secondary schools in computer science is not only overwhelming, but also shows a remarkable change in the traditions of the upper secondary schools and the development of new attitudes among teachers. Whole teaching staffs have applied to participate, and it is more often teachers of languages, history or religion who have taken the initiative than teachers of mathematics and physics' (Council of Europe, 1983, No. 2). What is occurring is in line with the forecasts and hopes of Seymour Papert (1980, pp. 38-9) who, in a chapter entitled 'Mathophobia: The Fear of Learning', wrote:

I have already suggested that the computer may serve as a force to break down the line between the 'two cultures'. I know that the humanist may find it questionable that a 'technology' could change his assumptions about what kind of knowledge is relevant to his or her perspective of understanding people. And to the scientist dilution of rigor by the encroachment of 'wishy-washy' humanistic thinking can be no less threatening. Yet the computer presence might, I think, plant seeds that could grow into a less dissociated cultural epistemology.

The advantages and limitations of the computer and computer-assisted learning are now apparent. Many European countries have in recent years adopted policies aimed at the systematic introduction of information technology into education.

Certain developing countries in Latin America and in Asia have recently undertaken experiments in this field and a fair number of them are planning measures in this area over the next two decades. Indeed, the computerization of the various sectors of social life and computer studies in schools should go hand in hand. As J. van Bruggen points out, 'computeracy' is destined soon to become part of the common core of general culture required during compulsory schooling. In this field, the help of those countries possessing technical and educational experience could prove very useful to the developing countries.

New educational methods

The democratization of education remains no more than a promise or no more than fine words so long as schools do not possess the necessary resources to increase the efficiency of the learning process and to pave the way for the success of all children. Of course, schools cannot by themselves solve a problem which has its roots in multiple causes—physiological and moral, family and economic, etc. However, one certainty has emerged from the educational experience and achievements of the last two decades: the school, as a specialized institution that occupies children for four, six or eight hours a day and which works in co-operation with the family, is becoming the key factor in the success of young people. By changing the outlook and working habits of teachers, applying new learning strategies and methods, promoting a formative style of assessment and encouraging healthy competition and a positive atmosphere in all phases of the school and out-of-school teaching process, the school could, towards the end of this century, achieve an extraordinary thing—levelling from above and the elimination of failure at school.

This most important advance, which truly deserves to be called an 'educational revolution', is very much dependent on the quality of the initial and in-service training of educators (teachers and non-teachers), which should be particularly focused on methods. The teaching process was long dominated by a restricted number of methods, if not by a single one. Modern education theory cultivates the idea of the variety and relevance of learning strategies. In order to succeed, all pupils should learn by a variety of methods, situations and techniques appropriate to the goals pursued and to their individual characteristics. They may find themselves in traditional classes (25 to 30 pupils), in large groups of 90 to 150 pupils (to see an instructional film or listen to a talk), in small groups of 4 to 6 pupils (to draw up scientific reports, analyse specific problems, etc.), or they may work individually in the classroom, the library or the laboratory with textbooks or programmed workbooks, reference works and, if possible, audio-visual or computer programmes.

Schools employing a single method—i.e. a predominant method—are a thing of the past, even if some researchers and teachers still try to uphold the virtues of a certain traditional or modern learning scheme. Differentiation, variety and flexibility should prevail over monotony and rigidity in the learning process.

Hidden contents

A series of experimental studies and international surveys has highlighted the educational role of hidden contents (see Barnes, 1982, Ch. 2), of the quality of school life and, in this context, of the non-verbal inputs of teachers; all these findings should serve to enrich the training of teacher-trainers, administrators, evaluators and, naturally, educators themselves.

Educating for success, which has been the subject of a series of studies, mainly by American educationists, implies a conception and organization of learning aimed at eliminating, or substantially reducing, failure at school. In this connection, it is essential that the educator learns to conduct the learning process optimistically and to maintain learners' confidence in themselves. This idea, although widely accepted, still has its opponents, and is still frequently ignored. However, it is known that the mistrustful and grudging attitude of teachers and the various forms of treatment, all to a greater or lesser extent humiliating, with which poor results are penalized give rise to lasting inhibitions and represent obstacles for pupils who require remedial teaching or who are disadvantaged (see Rosenthal and Jacobson, 1985).

As such findings and ideas find their way through teacher-training into educational practice, we may hope to see a spectacular reduction in failure at school, in other words, a democratization of education, and, above all, of educational success. A change in the style of teaching activity is the *sine qua non* for achieving the transition from a traditional form of learning, in which a substantial section of the pupils were condemned to failure, to a participatory, formative and rounded learning process:

Traditional learning process	*Formative and rounded learning process*
Learning under pressure (rapid pace)	Differentiated and intensive learning
Imposed learning	Participatory learning, corresponding to the pupil's interests
Learning process that is frustrating for a sizeable proportion of the class	Learning process beneficial to all
Learning oriented towards examinations and competitions	Learning oriented towards achievable goals and performances
Learning focused on the assimilation of knowledge	Learning centred on the application of knowledge and the shaping of attitudes

We should not lose sight of a fact corroborated by all teachers in educational practice: pupils who possess a good intellectual ability and good working conditions need only limited educational help whereas the others, so long as they receive systematic support from teachers, can achieve comparable performances.

Linking of formal, non-formal and informal education

We have already referred to the tensions or rivalries that can exist between these three types of education or contents.

Future prospects

The contents of formal education are determined by the school authorities; pupils are under the obligation to assimilate them, and their performance is systematically evaluated. These contents represent, or should represent, a digest of material significant to the aims of education and to the information used in social life. Learning in school is systematic and to a greater or lesser extent coherent and concentrated, since it is conducted by specialists on the basis of educational standards and school timetables; examinations or competitions govern access to certain levels at given stages of the process.

The contents of out-of-school (non-formal) education are represented by the totality of options or optional (rarely compulsory) activities organized by the school, youth organizations, the school in co-operation with parents or cultural associations, the pupils themselves, etc. (Vaideanu, 1982, pp. 221–4). These 'post-classroom' activities take place in school (groups concerned with particular subjects and themes or multidisciplinary groups, cultural or sporting competitions, commemorations and festivities, etc.,) or outside, taking the form of visits, excursions and nature classes, or, in the socialist countries, in the Young Pioneer centres.

The contents, methods and duration of these activities are, in principle, decided by the pupils; helped by the teachers, whose role changes in relation to teaching activities, pupils are in charge of the debates,

Types of education

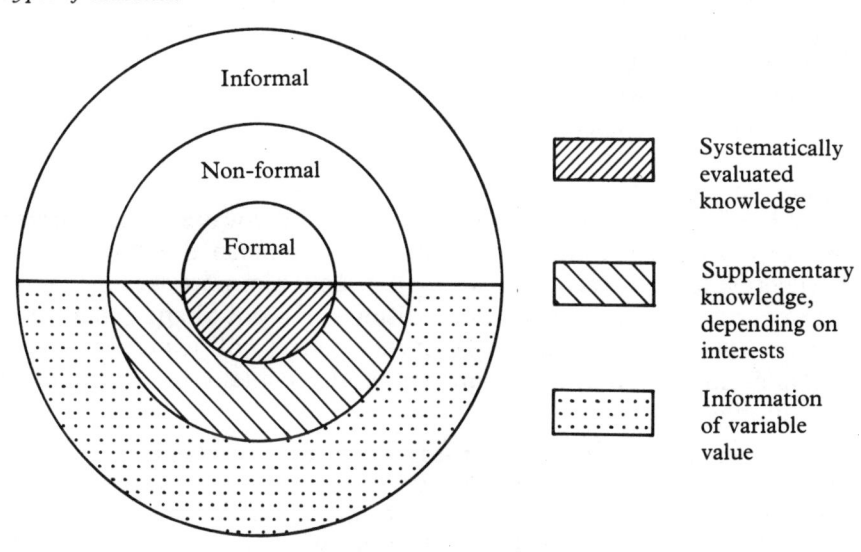

Fig. 2.

competitions, excursions etc. Non-formal activities, which supplement formal activities and are more flexible and more varied, play an important role in the identification and shaping of talents (in the USSR, as in other socialist countries, many scientists, including cosmonauts, are former members of scientific or technological clubs in the Young Pioneer centres), in the promotion of interdisciplinary learning and in the approach to specific problems. It is significant that out-of-school activities are in many countries the entry point for new forms of education, such as environmental education, and contribute to the democratization of education. It was probably for this reason that Unesco, in its 1984–85 biennium, devoted a subprogramme to 'better co-ordination between formal and non-formal education and greater continuity between the various parts of the education system' (Unesco, 1984a). Mention should also be made of an event that marks an important stage in the development of learning structures and methods: in 1901, it was the adolescent pupils of the secondary school in Steglitz, near Berlin, who got together and called for a programme of excursions and for school activities placing greater emphasis on nature; the proportions assumed by their demands alarmed the authorities at the time, but fortunately the association set up in 1901 on the pupils' initiative (*Wandervogel* from *wandern* = to travel + *Vogel* = bird) managed to establish itself and to promote new forms of education. The success of the pupils in this instance may also represent an important date in the democratization of education.

The contents of informal (parallel) education are constituted by the mass of information received, for example, through the media, within the family, at weekends and in sports competitions—information which, though substantial in volume, is very uneven, varied and variable as between pupils; it includes images and ideas on the recent findings of science and technology, information on the past or on possible future developments, facts about very diverse countries, regions or phenomena, etc.

Such information is of uneven quality, and the way it is interpreted and its moral impact are in any case dependent on the cultural and intellectual level of each individual; the same film provokes different, even contradictory, reactions and attitudes. Harold Shane (Shane and Tabler, 1980, pp. 444, 446) suggests the concept of 'experience compression' to describe and characterize the content of this parallel education.

All of us living in the 1970s and 1980s . . . have been influenced at least to some extent by experience compression. Probably its permeating power has been more profound than most humans realize . . . experience compression, due to rapid change and the electronic magic of the media, is complicating and accelerating the areas of research in sociology and in anthropology.

Future prospects

The author considers that this experience compression, initially generated by the media, results in: a loss of temporal congruity, a loss of geographic coherence, information overload and overstimulated sensory circuitry.

In the view of some specialists (or futurologists), parallel education is becoming more important, more democratic and more open than school. However, the majority of specialists, particularly those in charge of projects launched in various countries, are concerned with the problem of *better linkage* among the three types of education. How can school become more responsive to the messages of parallel education, how can it turn to account some of the extensive and varied information acquired or perceived outside school? Interest in the problem has been triggered and prospects opened up by the principle of lifelong education, which by definition effects syntheses, co-ordinates, establishes relations and eliminates barriers between the various levels and types of education. We shall confine ourselves here to showing by way of a few examples that the linking of school and out-of-school education is at the forefront of the concerns of education authorities everywhere.

For some years now the problem has been coming up at regional conferences of ministers of education, who are beginning to analyse the advantages of better linkage, particularly for underprivileged groups. In Latin America, for example, 1979 was 'the first time that a ministerial conference held in the region had dealt explicity with the problem of linking school and out-of-school education. It was undoubtedly a response to the remarkable development in recent years of out-of-school educational programmes' (Romeo-Lozano, 1980, p. 237). The intergovernmental conferences or meetings held subsequently in the region (1981, 1982) paid special attention to the problem by treating it as an application of the principle of lifelong education and by linking it directly with the aims of the Major Project adopted in Quito in 1981.

In Africa, efforts towards linkage are guided by the principles of authenticity and endogenous development, which should be at the basis of any reform project; a particular effort is being made to put a premium on oral traditions, African cultural values and the useful know-how and knowledge acquired over centuries in rural areas.[5]

The case-study on the prospects for Hungarian education identifies as a major preoccupation the extension of education beyond academic disciplines and activities so that it may include leisure, local community and socially useful activities.

The Danish project on education in the 1990s adopts the principle that

The isolation of the school with regard to all the things that take place outside the classroom should be broken up.... Furthermore, it is important that teaching creates a connection with the sum of experience of the individual person. General knowledge becomes more important by being related to the concrete knowledge of the individual, and many skills are best learned in connection with the practical tasks which all persons are constantly faced with.... We propose that a special report be made on the role which radio and TV have acquired in the imparting of knowledge and attitudes, and the repercussions this has on the work of the school [Denmark, 1978, pp. 193–7].

The studies already mentioned and others suggest various ways of turning to account the information acquired by pupils outside school: consolidation of the basic concepts as terms of reference for the selection and organization of the contents of informal education; strengthening of evaluative criteria; debates on themes of general interest; debates organized by teams of teachers with different and complementary backgrounds; and discussions on major cultural, economic and artistic events.

Lifelong education: a mode of being and becoming

Possible convergence of the various parallel forms of education

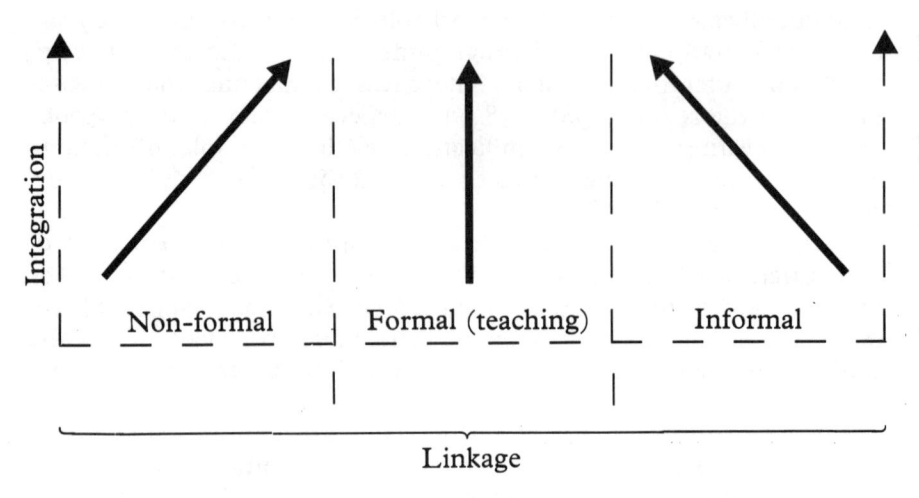

FIG. 3.

GENERAL INDICATORS OF THE RELEVANCE OF CONTENTS

Interest in the *relevance of contents* has visibly increased in recent years. The English word 'relevance' is approximately equivalent to the French word *'pertinence'*.[6] The relevance of educational content may be regarded as describing its relationship to and conformity with a twofold set of requirements represented, on the one hand, by the whole range of sources of contents and societal values and, on the other, by the needs, interests and intellectual and physical abilities of learners. The experience of the 1950s and 1960s with regard to contents served only to increase the attention paid by curriculum designers, teachers, personnel in cultural fields and non-teaching educators to the characteristics and quality of the contents of education. That experience confirmed certain conclusions and, at the same time, highlighted errors to be avoided. For example, patriotic education has sometimes been undervalued or neglected in the name of international education, which has contributed to a sense of rootlessness among young people; in other cases, patriotism has been confused with nationalism or chauvinism. Under some political systems, a pragmatic philosophy of education (i.e. educating active, practically minded individuals with the capacity to identify and resolve problems) has been confused with utilitarianism and the abandonment of spiritual values. Some countries have taken the view that preparing young people for development could be reduced to increased emphasis on the natural sciences and technology, thereby adopting a simplistic approach that might jeopardize the idea of a comprehensive and harmonious development beneficial to all; others have overlooked, and continue to overlook, the educational importance of productive work or, at the other extreme, have gone so far as to confuse productive work in school with the exploitation of child labour.

Interest in the relevance of contents is not confined to certain developing countries in search of a form of education in keeping with their traditions and aspirations. The Third Conference of Ministers of Education of the Member States of the Europe Region (1980*a*), organized by Unesco in 1980, paid special attention to this problem and formulated a series of basic questions.

The problem of defining the content of education has probably never been so complex and so pressing as it is now. In view of the increasing number of demands made on education systems by the modern world and its rapidly changing nature, *what can be done to guard against the overloading of curricula and the increase in the number of subjects and disciplines taught at the different levels and in the different types of education, particularly general education?*

According to what criteria should the subjects and disciplines to be taught be chosen in each case? How can a judicious balance be ensured between the different subjects that appear important and on the basis of what criteria? What can be done to select for each subject that which is fundamental and essential and to discard that which is less so in order, in particular, to give curricula a minimum 'expectation of life' and to avoid over-frequent and over-hasty modifications? What are the advantages and limits of the interdisciplinary approach and what can be done to put it into effect? How is educational content likely to be affected by the growing trend towards lifelong education and the democratization of education? What are the possibilities and the limits of individual teaching under the curricula for the different levels and types of education? What ways and means could be adopted to strengthen the links between theory and practice in educational content? How can curricula and textbooks be reformed and revised in such a way as not to impair the necessary continuity of the educational process? How can the content of education be made to take account of the increasing number of messages conveyed by the mass media and of their effects?

From the point of view of the scale of the approach, a distinction can be made between comprehensive measures, taking in all the sources of contents and the contents as a whole, and isolated or specific measures designed to produce criteria and techniques either for the evaluation of a given discipline or else for the evaluation of all contents in the light of a given criterion, such as coherence, education for peace or humanism, etc.

It has been suggested that education should be characterized by:

(1) prospective orientation; (2) individual and social relevance; (3) orientation toward the nation and the world outside; (4) fostering efficiency in the skills required for communication; (5) orientation toward the achievement of a common quality of life; (6) orientation toward a liberating education; (7) being directed toward equality of opportunity [Herrera, 1976, p. 81].

These criteria, which relate mainly to contents, are worth noting, but it seems to us that, although comprehensive in character, they derive mainly from a socio-political approach to education which—be it said—is fully justified by the needs of the region. Still on the subject of a set of general indicators, it may also be noted that Unesco's programme for 1984–85 included a subprogramme (4.2.2) concerned with 'improvement of the content of education' and that a paragraph is devoted to promotion of interdisciplinarity, coherence and balance in the content of general education programmes (Unesco, 1984*a*, para. 04227). While the accent in this subprogramme, which represents only a fraction of the Organization's medium-term programme, is placed on certain educational and epistemological indicators such as interdisciplinarity, coherence and balance, other indicators are to be found in other subprogrammes concerned with education.

Future prospects

As has been said, contents can be conceived or evaluated from a very precise and restricted standpoint: the emphasis can be put either on the requirements of society or on the aspirations and needs of youth; it is thus possible to talk of relevance in, for example, social, psychological, economic, historical and other terms. Some specialists try to evaluate contents employing the temporal criteria of past, present and future, an approach which is all the more useful since errors in this area are relatively frequent; the needs or pressures of the present seem rarely to be neglected, but the values of the past or the problems and requirements of the future are sometimes forgotten. Below is a set for analysing a reader based on three axes (socio-cultural, scientific and educational) and three categories of indicator (rapid, quantitative analysis and qualitative analysis). The following variables are proposed for quantitative socio-cultural analysis: the individuals concerned (sex, age, race, nationality and social status); spatio-temporal settings (geographical context, reference periods, technological environment and everyday objects, etc.); social context (representation of work, socio-professional categories represented, etc.); situations and themes.

The same document proposes as variables for a qualitative analysis: accuracy and authenticity; balance (with particular reference to the following: representation of the national culture, representation of other cultures, type of explanation, underlying ideology, etc.); contribution to peace and international understanding; relationship between individual values and collective conceptions of moral values.

These different sets of criteria or indicators may prove satisfactory in certain situations, but the multidisciplinary and indissociable nature of the sources of contents and the goals of education calls for a comprehensive approach and a synthesis between internal requirements (of a specifically educational character) and external requirements. The relevance of contents as a set of values, knowledge and know-how is a basic initial problem confronting curriculum designers, teachers and evaluators alike. They must perceive the very close connections between the various characteristics of the contents, which cannot be balanced unless they are coherent, responsive unless they are flexible, and so on. The list of general indicators which follows is intended to be representative, while not setting out to be exhaustive and definitive.

1. *Receptiveness to scientific and technological progress.* We would point out firstly that the updating of contents cannot be conceived either in terms of the extrapolation of the latest scientific findings or in terms of an undertaking that would put a strain on schools. What is required is rather: to seek an epistemological harmony between the spirit and methodologies of modern science and the contents of edu-

cation; to include basic concepts in school curricula and to organize knowledge in relation to those concepts; to be receptive to new disciplines or sciences and to their impact on socio-economic development and the spiritual life of the community. On the occasion of the International Symposium on the Evolution of the Content of General Education over the Next Two Decades, organized by Unesco in 1980, Osborne (1980, p. 422) noted that 'there is a time lag between new developments in the basic sciences and their effects on the content of general education'. He considered that 'the complexity of the sciences has led to needs for less rigidity in our thinking: reflected even in the language of theoretical physics where the standard categories of laws and theories have been supplemented by new terms such as "conspiracies"' (Osborne, 1980, p. 420). However, this time lag is shorter today than it was previously; it should therefore be used to ensure that changes (in school textbooks, evaluation tools, audio-visual aids, etc.) are better analysed, devised and prepared and that teachers are better informed and trained for their new tasks.

2. *Axiological harmony with culture, art and the aspirations of the people.* With regard to values and the teaching of cultural, artistic and ethical values, harmony should be sought both in the preparation of curricula and textbooks and in the teaching–learning process. The level of culture of teachers and their attitudes to values are the key to achieving such harmony, and non-verbal behaviour is sometimes as crucial as verbal inputs. Herein lies the importance of the approach to teaching as a cultural process and of cultural training for prospective teachers. In the view of G. De Landsheere (1976a, p. 129), 'education is impossible unless the notion of values is central, and axiology is fundamental to all teaching'.

3. *Receptiveness to the problems of the modern world and to the needs of the local or national community.* This twofold receptiveness needs to be constantly borne in mind when updating educational content in relation to present priorities and future requirements. Traditionally, schools are national in character, although they open windows on the universe through literature, painting, history, etc. However, the scale of world problems, highlighted on a number of occasions in this work, demands that this receptiveness be wider and better organized. The example of certain developing countries which, after borrowing their educational contents from other countries, set out to discover their national identity, is worth noting. Meanwhile, in the industrialized countries, élitist schools too often remain insufficiently responsive to the life of the local community and the needs of the people; in this connection, the assessment of a French specialist seems to us significant.

What then is the position of France in this major movement that is calling the traditional school into question? Turning its back on the sociological criticism that originated in France alongside the peaceful movement of May 1968, the country has recently sought to make the specialized branches of study—ostensibly abolished—more narrowly subject-based and more selective, having previously made a show of absorbing such truly progressive reform projects as the post-war Langevin-Wallon plan, which opened the way to a more egalitarian and more creative school, and Freinet's 'co-operative classroom' scheme, which established a dynamic relationship between teacher and pupil in the context of a genuine integration with the environment. Consciously or otherwise, our current educational thinkers, with the possible exception of Bertrand Schwartz, base their ideas on the classical model of the Jesuits and their secular disciple the philosopher Alain. It is in the Third World that the inheritors of the tradition of Rousseau are to be found—Illich, who wishes to de-school society by basing it on 'conviviality', and Paulo Freire, the advocate of the education of the oppressed and of 'conscientization' of the illiterate popular masses [Champion, 1983].

The difficulty in achieving this dual form of receptiveness is due to the fact that it involves reconciling and co-ordinating objectives and contents that were previously, if not in conflict, at least separate: national objectives and universal objectives or those of neighbouring countries, national history and the history of other peoples, etc. Needless to say, Unesco and the other United Nations agencies are very well placed to promote such receptiveness to a set of imperatives that are fundamental for the future and survival of mankind.

4. *Aligning contents with the intellectual and physical needs and abilities of learners.* Educational research—and we are thinking in particular of the work of Bruner and of Bloom and his team in the Chicago experimental schools—have demonstrated something of exceptional importance: that all children can learn and that success in school is not reserved for an élite. Moreover, complex scientific, literary and economic facts are accessible to children at all levels of education. The consequence is well known: teaching the theory of sets at the primary and even pre-school level; the introduction of pupils to foreign languages at the age of 7, and even 3; and, finally, the spectacular case of pupils dialoguing with and programming computers in secondary, primary or even pre-primary school.

What an excellent demonstration of the intellectual qualities of children to find that the best 'teachers' for adults following computer training courses are adolescents aged 13 to 15! But this educational principle, which should help to increase success in school and to promote the democratization of education systems, has been perceived and applied in very different ways. On occasion the right approach has been adopted by improving curricula and the training of teachers in the light of firmly applied psycho-educational criteria. In other instances, the measures adopted have created formidable difficulties for learners. These include: the overloading of curricula through the introduction of new scientific or literary theories and new scientific concepts or findings without reviewing the volume and quality of the whole body of knowledge taught; the general introduction in secondary or lower secondary curricula of subject-matter—in physics, mathematics, chemistry and biology—previously dealt with in higher education, frequently without analysis and adaptation to the intellectual interests and potential of adolescents; the presentation of phenomena which are in fact of general interest—such as development, the new international economic order, the problem of outer space, etc.—in an abstract way, thereby engendering indifference rather than interest on the part of pupils. At the same time, entrance examinations have been geared to the assimilation of a large body of complex knowledge, which discourages many pupils.

In this way, a principle which should contribute to the democratization of education from the point of view of access and success sometimes produces the opposite results. Some countries have extended or are thinking of extending the period of compulsory education to ten, eleven or even twelve years without posing the problem in new terms: what should be the goals, contents and methods of learning in such a school for the masses? What is wanted is not to introduce a 'cut-price education', which would be both expensive and illusory, nor to ignore talent and produce a levelling down that could ultimately discourage all pupils, but rather to apply effectively a set of principles and the findings yielded in recent decades by educational research in curriculum design, the training of teachers and the organization of the learning process.

5. *Balance in the design of curricula and organization of the learning process.* The idea here concerns the internal organization of content both from the quantitative standpoint (size of the workload represented by a particular subject in relation to the whole) and from the qualitative standpoint (convergence of values as between the various types of content, relationship between theories and examples, etc.).

Content balance seems to be one of the most sought-after characteristics, perhaps in response to the growth in the pressures exerted on contents and perhaps also because of the fact that the many changes made to the curriculum over recent decades have resulted not only in the revision of curricula and textbooks but also in an increase in discontinuities and imbalances which have affected the efficiency of the work of the teacher and, above all, that of the learner. Balance is sought in relation to the ultimate goals of education. Thus it is possible to analyse the balance between:

1. The different groups of objectives (cognitive, affective, psycho-

motor), in the light of the needs or interests of pupils and to the principle of the all-round development of the personality.

2. The different groups of disciplines, bearing in mind that the temptation to downgrade certain subjects remains strong in all those countries that identify development with economic growth and the natural sciences as the only suitable preparation for active life and a career.

3. Theoretical elements and those that are immediately applicable, or between conceptual aspects and exercises.

4. The distribution of the various types of content between levels, from the primary (or pre-primary) level and to higher education.

5. The distribution of disciplines or contents between school and out-of-school education (education relating to the quality of life and the environment, education for peace, etc.), recognizing that certain forms of education are sometimes more appropriately introduced in a non-formal rather than a formal context.

6. National (specific) values and universal values likely to foster communication between peoples and individuals.

7. The various modes of learning—conventional classes, small groups, large groups, etc.

8. The emphasis placed respectively on words and images at the various educational levels.

Unesco's programmes pay particular attention to balance, stressing the importance of the social and human sciences and indicating the need to accommodate new contents (education relating to the quality of life and the environment, peace and human rights education, etc.) whose relevance to education is highlighted by the development of contemporary world problems. The same concern is to be found in many recommendations and comparative studies: for example, a study on compulsory schooling (OECD, 1983a) identified the following broad areas of experience to form the foundation of a core curriculum—'aesthetic/creative, ethical, linguistic, mathematical, physical, scientific, social/political and spiritual'.

Bearing these considerations in mind, we would point out that some subjects are occasionally downgraded either in the syllabus and curriculum or else in the actual teaching process, in which context some subjects—sometimes termed 'career subjects'—exert a strong attraction or pressure on pupils. In this respect we would mention:

History—understood as knowledge of the past experience of mankind and of the conclusions to be drawn from it for the present. Arguing for the effective teaching of history, H. Shane recalls the saying of Cicero to the effect that not to know what has happened before one's own birth is to remain always a child.

Domestic science—understood as a training in the economics, hygiene and aesthetics of family life and as an indirect but vital preparation for working life; before taking up a job, the individual should know how to organize his own life. It seems significant that this activity is given its proper place mainly in the industrialized countries, whereas it is often neglected in the developing countries, where its role is even more important.

The arts and art education—which, in some countries, does not extend beyond primary or compulsory schooling. It is worth recalling here the view of certain leading figures in the Japanese economy that *ikebana* has made as important a contribution to present-day Japan as have computers.

Physical education and sport—which, while fully justifying their place in the curriculum by virtue of their objectives and content and constituting an irreplaceable means to individual development, are rarely given their rightful place in the curriculum or the necessary resources (such as gymnasia and sports grounds, qualified teachers and equipment).

It should be remembered that the sources of content imbalance are numerous and that the expansionist trends of certain subjects are often defended with seemingly convincing arguments, but let us not forget either the educational meaning of the metaphor used to explain an extremely complex socio-economic phenomenon, namely that 'present-day Japan is a synthesis of *ikebana* and computers', nor the fact that creativity is the result of a total and harmonious development of the personality.

6. *Coherence of content.* The term 'coherence' has a logical or epistemological ring about it, signifying a close relationship of consonant ideas and hence an absence of contradiction. Coherence can be understood diachronically—in the sense of an absence of contradiction in the development of studies within a particular stage of education or between one stage and another—or synchronically, implying continuous linkage and non-contradiction in the acquisition of knowledge between the various subjects. When a physics teacher is disagreeably surprised to discover that pupils do not know certain vital and essential facts about algebra, this means an absence of coherence. When pupils, at the beginning of a new school year, have difficulty in making the connection between the various elements of a subject taught over two, three or more years, this also means an absence of coherence; and these discontinuities or contradictions are even more apparent and disturbing in the case of a transition from one educational level to another. When at the end of the school year pupils and teachers have difficulty in organizing and mastering the information included in curricula and textbooks, we are once again dealing with the same

shortcoming. This indicator of relevance needs then to be looked at very closely at all stages in the design of contents—in preparing the overall project, in drawing up syllabuses, timetables and programmes, in designing school textbooks and choosing teaching methods, in organizing the work of teams of teachers by level and by class, etc. It is possible then to analyse: the quality of the philosophy on which the selection and organization of content is based; the structuring of subject-matter over two, three or more years; the vertical or horizontal linkage between the various subjects; the quality of the linkages between ultimate goals, general objectives and operational objectives; the operation of the relationship of complementarity between school and out-of-school education; the effectiveness of the measures adopted by the school to ensure that the miscellaneous information unevenly acquired by pupils outside school is turned to better account. It may be noted that some countries have done interesting experiments in this area—open debates on questions raised by the pupils, discussions of major cultural events and teaching in small groups focused on pupils' experience in such areas as the environment, astronomy, etc.

7. *Contents capable of stimulating effort and sustaining the pleasure of learning.* Psycho-educational research has shown that learning calls for great effort. The learner must cross thresholds and cope with hidden or half-concealed obstacles which cause anxiety or provoke crises; there are also leaps forward and unrivalled satisfactions to be gained (see Bloom, 1981; Pinillos, 1981; Unesco, 1978a). In the preface to *Pygmalion in the Classroom. Teacher Expectation and Pupils' Intellectual Development* (Rosenthal and Jacobson, 1985), the point is made that for centuries the emphasis in schooling was placed on the serious efforts to be made and, in some instances, on the basic difference between school and life. The idea of making education interesting and attractive was put forward diffidently. The only acceptable attitudes seemed to be to make high demands and even to be severe and intolerant. However, carefully conducted research, carried out on the basis of representative samples and over long periods, to which we have already made or shall make reference, has highlighted: the influence of the aesthetic component[7] on the effectiveness of learning; the exceptional educational resources of learning games and of learning by play; the stimulating role of encouragement of the pupil and of the satisfaction produced by even modest success; the key role of the atmosphere in which teaching takes place, of patience and of an optimistic attitude on the part of the educator.

The initial need is to reconcile these two theses: learning involves an effort, but this effort does not exclude play and is all the more effective in so far as it draws on the learner's manifest or latent potential. The second requirement is to transfer and incorporate findings on the learning process into the initial and in-service training of teachers; the research to which we have referred shows that training for 'successful behaviour' calls for systematic exercises of an innovatory kind and presupposes specific training for teacher educators.

8. *Giving a forward-looking and democratic slant to contents and learning.* The need to orient the curriculum in this direction is dictated by socio-political and educational considerations. The process should find expression in certain characteristics of contents and learning such as may increase equality of opportunity: flexibility of contents, structures and linkages between levels; multiple and combinable options as a way of diversifying learning and satisfying the diversity of pupils' interests and abilities; promotion of active methods and computer-assisted learning as a way of increasing the rate of success at school and preparing pupils for intellectual independence and creative, independent and continuous learning; the provision of a sound, full education enabling learners to communicate, evolve, participate and have a sense of freedom so that the pupil learns at school not only to learn but also to live and develop; provision of opportunities for the education and personal development of gifted pupils, in which connection we consider it vital that attention should be paid not only to the 'traditional' areas (music, painting, literature, mathematics and sport) but also to all those areas in which performance is possible and useful—foreign languages, marketing, management, industrial occupations, tourism (catering, hotels, guide services, etc.), agriculture, health work, etc.

The socialist countries have established 'olympiads' for all sorts of occupations and subjects; these competitions begin at the local authority level and extend up to the national level, thereby involving thousands of pupils in each field.

INTERDISCIPLINARITY

In the early 1970s, many organizations, research institutions and specialists turned to interdisciplinarity as a way of organizing contents and developing learning. In 1970, Unesco organized an African seminar for lecturers in teacher-training colleges on ways of introducing interdisciplinarity into teacher-training programmes and, subsequently, primary education (Seminar for the Training..., 1970). In 1970 (Colloque Nationale de Pédagogie, 1970) and in 1972, the National Institute of Educational Research in Romania held two national symposia—but attended by foreign participants—on the same subject, the promotion of interdisciplinarity in the approach to education and the organization of contents. The institute brought together for these symposia not only specialists from the ministry but also members of the Romanian Academy, the Academy of Social and Political Sciences, etc. In 1972, a volume was published on interdisciplinarity (Seminar on Interdisciplinarity in Universities, 1972) based on the results of a seminar organized at the University of Nice in 1970 by the Centre for Educational Research and Innovation (CERI) with the collaboration of the French Ministry of Education.[8] At that time, many specialists had some experience in this field; at the same time, Unesco launched pilot projects in this area with a view to the integrated study of science (see Jegede, 1982; Lutterodt, 1981; Stenhouse, 1980, Ch. 14; Vaideanu, 1974).[9]

Today, one can point to a whole host of projects and attempts to promote interdisciplinarity in the learning process, as well as to evaluations and critical reflections. The time would seem to have come to take stock of what has been done before proceeding to more realistic and more effective measures. Two opposing tendencies may be observed: one seeks to minimize the impact of the principle of interdisciplinarity on the working out of curricula and teaching–learning methods, while the other considers that school education should move towards a total integration of traditional subjects.[10] Everything points to the fact that there is a movement towards an operational approach. The relevant concepts (inter/multi/transdisciplinarity) are more clearly defined;[11] however, as regards the promotion of interdisciplinarity in general education, practical considerations are more crucial than theoretical progress: the *problems of the world of work and daily life* are increasingly multidisciplinary in character.

In the light of recent studies, interdisciplinarity emerges as a way of designing curricula and/or of organizing the learning process; it is neither a new form of education (even if certain authors speak of 'an educational philosophy of unity or totality') nor an educational or epistemological panacea. Moreover, pupils (learners) feel the need both for an overall, unifying vision to which facts and details can be subordinated and for a knowledge and mastery of the specific characteristics of different fields. Teachers are called upon to co-ordinate and integrate, while avoiding both the juxtaposition of subjects and their mere confusion. Unesco's Second Medium-Term Plan perhaps points the way forward:

In view of the complex requirements and the need to avoid overloading curricula, the solution would seem to be not to add new elements to the existing content but to integrate them organically into new, composite wholes, taking into account the complementary nature of the disciplines concerned and the educational objectives in view' [Unesco, 1983c, para. 4025].

Future prospects

In any event, we take as our premiss the idea that the old philsophical thesis of the unity of the sciences is still relevant, although it today assumes new forms.

Introducing interdisciplinarity. Some examples

In the projects being carried out in various countries or in the context of experimental research, the promotion of interdisciplinarity is sometimes obscured by such expressions as 'modules', 'mixed or combined syllabuses', '*activités de synthèse*', 'subject linkage', 'project work', 'co-ordinated' teaching, etc. In all probability, the point of such a cautious approach is not to upset teachers.

With reference to the curriculum represented in Figure 1 (page 132), it should be said that all the components of a curriculum (A → I) can become points of entry for interdisciplinarity; in practical terms, school activities no less than out-of-school activities (I → F) provide teachers with the opportunity to integrate or co-ordinate more closely the contents of a given class or level. We shall confine ourselves here to just a few possible points of entry.

Curricula (A and C) or, more precisely, the objectives and contents of education; it is for curriculum designers to define the type of integration (interdisciplinarity, transdisciplinarity, infusional approach, etc.), the degree of integration by level, the scale of the process, etc.

The organization of the teaching–learning process (D, E, F, G) which, by employing the basic concepts common to a number of subjects, manages to establish systematic correlations and to give pupils a 'bird's eye view' of the knowledge acquired; such an approach is very dependent on the teachers of a particular level or class being willing and able to form a unified team.

Out-of-school (extracurricular) activities (F ⇌ I) which can not only constitute the entry point for new contents (e.g. environmental education) but also help to break down compartmentalization between subjects.

Evaluation of pupil performance (H) which, depending on the quality of the methods and techniques used, could encourage pupils to establish connections between subjects and to discover the unity of the natural and/or human sciences.

We have already seen that in Denmark the computer encourages teachers to establish new forms of co-operation and to take advantage of a number of points of convergence between subjects; the same promising phenomenon is reported in other countries such as the

United States and the Netherlands, which have been successful in using the computer as a teaching resource. There are, however, many other ways of pursuing interdisciplinarity.

Hungary: The case-study mentioned on a number of occasions refers to a set of seven educational groupings or modules which is replacing, or will replace, the loosely coherent cluster of isolated disciplines. It is explained that the concern to develop co-ordinated curricula, thereby strengthening the horizontal connections between subjects belonging to the same category, represents a way of integrating knowledge. This concern has as its chief focus the following fields: development of basic mental operations and of communication and learning skills; development of a scientific attitude and the ability to employ methods of scientific investigation; development of a socio-historical view of the world and appropriate methods for investigating socio-historical phenomena; development of receptiveness to aesthetic values and the capacity for self-expression; balanced physical development; development of a positive attitude to technology and manual skills; development of the ability to 'coexist' with computers and electronic data-processing techniques.

Proceeding from the fact that the vertical and horizontal coherence of the curriculum is basically the responsibility of the public authorities, particularly in countries where education is centralized, Louis D'Hainaut (1980) has launched a project going by the name of 'instrumental transdisciplinarity'. He defines this concept as follows:

Instrumental transdisciplinarity, also known as structural interdisciplinarity, is an approach to education in which, through various subjects, an attempt is made to provide the pupil with instruments and attitudes of thought and reflection that have a very wide field of application ... For example, he is introduced to concepts such as transformation, criterion, system, etc. ... The prefix 'trans' indicates that these notions are valid *through* a number of disciplines.

The coherence or integration of the various types of knowledge included in curricula

requires a concurrence of views which is impossible with the disciplinary approach, with its prestige struggles between subject specialists. What is needed is a curriculum centred on the learner, developed in a transdisciplinary framework by commissions made up of those responsible for the curriculum and teachers not only at the level involved but also from other levels. These commissions should also seek the collaboration of representatives of the community and the world of work. For example, the Ivory Coast authorities responsible for the secondary school curriculum, on the proposal of the principal official concerned in the Office for the Reform of Secondary Education and with the help of Unesco, have just set up a multidisciplinary team working together with those responsible for primary education, to develop secondary school syllabuses which are both centred on the learner and interdisciplinary [Busshoff et al., 1981, p. 228].

Early results seem promising and activities have been under way for a number of years.

Scotland: In her article on 'Scottish Integrated Science' Sally Brown provides a systematic report on this research project under the following headings: (1) innovatory aspects of the course; (2) integration; (3) evaluation of the course; (4) concluding remarks. She writes that teachers and administrators have, to a large extent, accepted the innovation (proposed by the project) and have attempted to implement it. However, such information is of little use unless supplemented by answers to other questions such as: have teachers understood what was intended by the authors of the project, and have they found it possible to implement those intentions? The widespread adoption of the Integrated Science Course in Scottish schools, the influence it has exerted on curricula in the Caribbean, Asia and Africa (as witnessed by Unesco publications) are compelling measures of its success. However, a close look at the pedagogical changes that have been introduced reveals them to be very modest.

Spain:

The curriculum for so-called basic schooling in Spain, i.e. the eight years of compulsory schooling with a common curriculum at primary and secondary levels, also deals with the problem of the new arrangement of educational content by devising a pattern subdivided into areas: linguistics; mathematics; social and natural sciences; expression in the plastic arts (draughtsmanship and basic technology); dynamic self-expression (music, physical education); religion. It is primarily the so-called 'social and natural sciences' area that achieves a truly 'composite' structure, by combining traditional subjects such as history, geography and civics, with 'new aspects of economics, sociology, politics and anthropology...' [Gozzer, 1982, p. 283].

But these new syllabuses and curricula, the author observes, include no reference to interdisciplinarity; it is rather a question of grouping subjects together.

France: Francine Best begins an article on interdisciplinarity with the statement that 'interdisciplinarity is understood here in its broad— even imprecise—sense, no distinction being drawn between pluri-, multi-, and bi-disciplinarity' (Legrand, 1983). It is more practically useful to outline a typology of interdisciplinary activities in the lower secondary school. Taken as a whole, these activities serve a twofold purpose: (a) they help pupils to understand that subjects are not separate, juxtaposed islands and that all human activity draws on methodological sources and on knowledge from a number of scientific domains; (b) where those involved are already motivated, such activities boost this initial motivation. It is possible to distinguish three main types of interdisciplinary activity in the secondary school: (1) *activity projects:* pupils' needs and requests are at the origin of such projects; (2) *learning and interdisciplinarity:* a better understanding of certain phenomena often calls for inputs from two or three overlapping subjects; (3) *extension workshops in specified subjects:* the term 'extension' (*prolongement*) does not imply in this instance that such workshops take place subsequently to teaching and learning in a given subject. It is very often useful for study of a given subject to be preceded by so-called 'workshop' activity. The author mentions that all the examples given reflect experiments carried out and then analysed in terms of their basic principles and their effects by lower secondary school teachers.

Italy: According to Giovanni Gozzer (1982, p. 284):

A slightly different path was taken by those who prepared the lower secondary curriculum in Italy (from the sixth to the eighth year of schooling), which was approved in 1979 and came into force the following year. The Italian model runs along two parallel tracks, so to speak. In the specific formulation of curriculum content, it retains the traditional distinction between subjects (Italian language, mathematics, history, geography, etc.). However, in the general instructions that precede this classification of content, indicating 'theoretical and practical educational planning' as the line of approach, the various disciplines are to some extent 'unified' under the common heading 'branches of education', these branches being: language, history, civics and geography, mathematics, science and health, technical skills, art, music, physical education and religious instruction. In this case, rather than expressing an interdisciplinary approach, however vague, as was mentioned earlier, the same set of instructions justifies terminology that unifies the subjects while separating them into branches of education, stating: 'In their various specialized branches, the disciplines provide the means and the opportunity for the united, integrated and complex development of functions, knowledge, abilities and tendencies that are indispensable to the growth to maturity of responsible human beings who are capable of making choices.' The aim is clearly, therefore, a relative 'weeding out', or at least a pruning of the autonomy of the subject as such, so as to replace their straightforward juxtaposition by a plan, design or project that should predetermine what is finally achieved, imposing overall unity at an early stage.

Romania: In the period 1962–65, Vaideanu carried out experimental research on the promotion of interdisciplinarity in the study of the arts (literature, music, painting, the theatre, etc.). At the time, he called these activities 'mixed-profile groups'; they were conceived as out-of-school activities, but linked to school curricula. Use was made of transdisciplinary aesthetic themes or concepts, the applications (illustrations) referring to the various arts; the study was both theoretical and applied in character. In the chapter entitled 'General aesthetics as the basis for an integrated aesthetic culture', the author pointed to certain advantages of interdisciplinarity:

The themes and categories of general aesthetics open the way to fruitful comparisons between the arts and to the organization of mixed-profile groups (literature-music, painting-music, etc.). Through the *integration of knowledge*, general aesthetics is helpful in the study of the arts; its analyses and applications highlight the *unity and specificity* of the arts and the rules governing the *integration of beauty* in the various categories of human activities and products [Vaideanu, 1967, p. 335].

After 1980, the author renewed this research using the concept of transdisciplinarity ('transpecificity') and taking in all school subjects. The research has been carried out at the lower secondary level of two secondary schools in Jassy (Liceu Naţional and Liceu D. Cantemir). The stages accomplished in the school years 1981/82 and 1982/83 were the following: (1) working out of the research hypothesis and choice of pilot schools and classes; (2) briefing of teachers (which proved more complicated than expected); (3) study of curricula (sixth and seventh grades) to identify the basic concepts by discipline, and the drawing up of lists; (4) comparative study of the lists to identify the basic common concepts (ideas, principles); (5) systematic observation of the teaching process (pilot and control classes) to identify the incidence of correlation between disciplines, the meaning given to fundamental concepts, etc.; (b) preparation of a teachers' guide and definitions of basic concepts (trans-specific and specific acceptations by discipline). Co-ordination between the team of teachers is essential for the success of such research.

The advantages of interdisciplinarity

Approaches vary and so do evaluations. In some cases, it is thought that integration should lead to the disappearance of traditional subjects, at least from the learners' point of view. However, most countries seem to adopt the other point of view: *inter- or transdisciplinarity does not do away with specificity*, but rather it breaks down the compartmentalization between subjects. Although movement in this direction is still cautious and a major problem—namely the training of teachers in interdisciplinarity—still has to be resolved, it is possible to identify the advantages of organizing contents and/or learning in this way. Coupled with other approaches or principles such as lifelong education, the application of research findings on the learning process and the use of computers, interdisciplinarity could help in the future:

(1) to open the way to the introduction of new contents, particularly education for peace and democracy, education relating to the quality of life and of the environment and education for development;

(2) to streamline curricula and the learning process;

(3) to democratize education from the standpoint of pupil achievement;

(4) to promote a problem-centred approach which would strengthen the conviction among learners that science serves to solve real problems. These are substantial advantages which will assume increasing weight in the future. However, we shall now attempt to pinpoint some of the more specific advantages of this new approach to learning:

An interdisciplinary organization of the contents to be studied, by building bridges between subjects without detracting from their specificity, is appropriate both from the *objective* standpoint (the development of contemporary science, the multidisciplinary nature of the specific problems to be solved, etc.) and from the *subjective* standpoint (learners' needs). To put it another way, unity genuinely exists in diversity, but its discovery through systematic mental effort will constitute an intellectual achievement. The perception of the unity and diversity, or specificity, of things thus represents an ultimate goal of the learning process and corresponds both to a need in the learner and to a concrete reality, and such a discovery is accompanied by a not inconsiderable intellectual satisfaction, since it can make for more effective learning.

Implicit within this increased relevance of the organization of contents to the characteristics of contemporary science and the psychological and philosophical needs of the learner is a solution to another genuine problem, i.e. the unfortunate 'slicing up' of general culture into separate parts; interdisciplinarity is a way of overcoming the drawbacks arising from the juxtaposition of isolated subjects.

A good many researchers and educators rightly look to a reorganization of subjects from the standpoint of interdisciplinarity as a way of increasing the efficiency of the learning process. It has been pointed out that expanding the links between subjects points up the key ideas of contents, eliminates a certain amount of redundancy and, thereby, simplifies the learners' task.

The promotion of interdisciplinarity in curriculum development and the learning process makes for greater flexibility of content, thereby favouring both the introduction of new elements and the application of knowledge. Authors such as Francine Best, Sally Brown (Stenhouse (ed.), 1980, Ch. 14) and Louis D'Hainaut, speak of an observable growth in the operational character of knowledge acquired by pupils.

Interdisciplinarity is associated logically with other principles or characteristics of a relevant content, i.e. coherence, balance, the pleasure of learning, a forward-looking approach and the spirit of lifelong education; such qualities are currently the focus of a special research effort, which is also a feature of Unesco's programmes. In this context, interdisciplinarity thus reveals itself as an approach that makes it possible not only to streamline curricula but also to promote active methods and formative evaluation.

Seen in relation to the educational process, the promotion of interdisciplinarity is a way of co-ordinating the various types of contents—formal, non-formal and informal; the strengthening of the connections between subjects helps to strengthen the role of codes of reference and codes of interpretation—these become focal points around which the information acquired outside school can be organized and turned to account. So long as the school learning process remains compartmentalized and too much centred on the preoccupations of individual subjects, the discontinuity between formal and informal education will remain almost total; the experience acquired outside school will represent a mass of vague images and ideas which is seldom referred to.

There are then both theoretical and practical advantages—already identified or to be verified in educational practice—that argue in favour of interdisciplinarity. Interdisciplinarity opens up new prospects not only for researchers and those responsible for curricula but also for educators and teacher educators.

The limits of interdisciplinarity

A complex field such as education, which demands not only substantial investments but also long time-spans to prove its efficiency and effectiveness, by definition excludes simple approaches and miracle methods. Yet the temptation of expecting everything or too much from some new approach is at times apparent among those in charge of education, and even among researchers and educators. It is a difficult thing to admit the complexity of a field or a profession; it has often been the case in the history of education that promising educational approaches—e.g. the active methods or the project work idea launched by Dewey—have resulted in some countries or schools in failure by being carried too far or over-simplified. Setting limits means guarding against possible errors; however, only applied research can establish how an innovation should be incorporated into the education system as a whole.

Study of the discussions and proposals on the subject readily leads one to the conclusion that the promotion of interdisciplinarity must reconcile very diverse requirements: it must take account not only of the specific development of each science but also, increasingly, the unity of contemporary science (transferable methodologies, basic common concepts, etc.); it must offer a relevant response to a twofold need of learners: the need to acquire an overall view of reality and to master complex problems; and the need to grasp the classification of phenomena and to distinguish the different spheres of knowledge, working life and culture; it must include elements of *scientific method* and basic concepts (codes of reference and codes of interpretation) and must provide pupils with sufficient examples and useful and precise knowledge (e.g. in learning the mother tongue, arithmetic or foreign languages).

The originality sought at any cost by some specialists who have advocated a form of education free of subject boundaries (without specifying conditions to be met or the stages to be gone through to arrive at such a content) has put some educators on their guard. It therefore seems appropriate to state yet again that the promotion of interdisciplinarity respects subject divisions, and that the degree of integration and the combinations among disciplines have to be determined in relation to specific situations. There are, first of all, the limits imposed by existing structures, namely, the levels of education and types of secondary schools, the relationship between formal and non-formal structures, school timetables, etc. Some structures favour the promotion of interdisciplinarity and others hinder it: for example, an early vocational option, which obliges pupils to choose a certain type of vocational or technical school at fourteen years of age becomes an obstacle, whereas the existence of a common core of general education pursued to the age of fifteen or sixteen is a factor favourable to the promotion of interdisciplinarity.

Other limits may be imputable to the philosophy underlying the organization of contents, which may result in the provision of; multiple and combinable options or compulsory subjects only; a solid common core of general education at the secondary level, or marked specialization; and a last secondary grade that is career-oriented or one that sets out to provide a final interdisciplinary overview. The quality of teacher training is a decisive factor in the promotion of interdisciplinarity. One can point to a number of alternatives in this

Future prospects

field: the existence of a common core in the training of teachers, or single-subject specialization; the presence or absence of a philosophy component in the training of prospective teachers; pedagogical training favouring or hindering an interdisciplinary approach.

It can be noted also that in certain countries prospective secondary-school teachers are trained in institutions of a pedagogical character (*Ecole normale supérieure*, School of Education, Pedagogical Institute, etc.) while in others they receive a very specialized training alongside future researchers (in biology, physics, etc). In the latter case, the obstacles become formidable.

THE SHAPE OF A POSSIBLE SYLLABUS

All the foregoing thoughts and suggestions culminate naturally in the venture to be undertaken here, since the important thing ultimately is the practical use to which they can be put in terms of educating individuals. So, after a few observations on the goals and shape of subject-matter in the 1980s and 1990s, we shall put forward by way of a general conclusion to this chapter a methodological framework for a syllabus, intended to serve not as a model but as something to be borne in mind by, or a source of suggestions for, curriculum designers.

The goals of education: divergences and convergences

The regularity with which the various international bodies and regional conferences of ministers of education underline the desirable goals of education is in our view not only a sign of a growing awareness of the path to be followed (humanism, co-operation, solidarity, democracy and human rights, etc.) but also the expression of the popular will; we are dealing here not with mere wishes but with increasingly strong expectations, constant aspirations derived from a series of distressing experiences. We recognize that education subsystems can only react to the imperatives of the modern world in terms of the socio-political systems of which they are a part; we also recognize that these goals, insistently proclaimed at the highest level, are not always apparent in educational practice and that, in some instances, the meanings attached to the above-mentioned concepts are different if not contradictory; and yet, before pointing to the divergences in goals, we think it right to underline that the desirable in education can become a fact of life.

It therefore seems necessary that, in the content of its curricula, in the spirit in which it is dispensed and in the methods it uses, education should help to inculcate at all levels not only certain values, for example a sense of responsibility, honesty and uprightness, loyalty, tolerance towards others and respect for life, but also attitudes likely to encourage family-mindedness, a sense of human solidarity, the spirit of peace, respect for human rights and understanding between peoples [Unesco, 1983c, para. 5009].

Sharing these ideas, we implicitly subscribe to the thesis of a committed school (perhaps we should say committed in the right direction), a thesis which is opposed to the educational neutralism preached by some researchers or practised, officially or on the quiet, by some educators.

Not without reason, many specialists warn us against dangerous trends, which could lead us to overlook the basic common goals which alone are capable of ensuring that education serves the cause of the co-operation and progress of mankind. The main alternatives are as follows:

- Democracy, or authoritarianism and totalitarianism? The report of the International Commission on the Development of Education (Faure et al., 1972) rightly placed great weight on a belief in democracy. It is democracy as a socio-political system and way of life that renders possible participation, the deployment of human spiritual resources, creativity and the expression of talent; it is likewise democracy that ensures socio-economic and cultural development and peoples' participation in international life. In the view of some specialists, the latter part of the century could see an expansion of totalitarianism and in this case, in some countries at least, education will be directed to other goals than those usually recognized, and will even tend to 'fanaticize youth'. On the other hand, the early 1980s have witnessed a certain advance of democracy, particularly in Latin America, and the 'belief in democracy' has continued to find expression in other countries.
- A humane and harmoniously developed world, or a world blindly dominated by science and technology?
- Mankind reconciled with itself, or a divided world, tension-ridden and plagued by wars and upheavals?
- Development for the benefit of all, or a widening of the gaps and inequalities between the developed and developing countries?
- Agreement on certain basic principles such as human rights and fundamental freedoms, social justice and equity, independence and co-operation, or false interpretations, disputes and political chaos?
- Growth in the role of the United Nations and other international governmental or non-governmental agencies or organizations, or the clash of political ambitions, tendencies towards domination, national self-interest, etc.?

- The affirmation of reason, the rational spirit and moral values, or the unleashing of religious, political or other kinds of fanaticism?
- A protected and humanized environment, or galloping desertification?

Most authors who refer to disquieting trends conclude their remarks by putting forward solutions and/or underlining the possible and beneficial role of a school inspired by goals that go against these trends. Our comments on the goals of education over the next two decades take account, in the first place, of the obligation incumbent upon all international organizations to react against the dangers threatening mankind, to propose solutions and to pursue the application of the relevant recommendations adopted by Member States, and their opportunities for doing so; and it may be that the United Nations and its agencies, dealing with specific and difficult situations, could show greater initiative and resolution. Such a path is clearly charted in the programmes of Unesco, and an illustration may be in order here:

As all communities are more and more gathered together within one and the same network of vital relationships and even mutual dependence, the prospect at last gleams ahead of a world community joined in unity of purpose and finally reconciled with itself, where all will be sure of the means to live a better life, unhampered by fear, and where there will be an ever fuller flowering of freedoms and creative faculties [Unesco, 1983c, para. 1].

Secondly, we do not forget the right and duty of education systems, particularly the subsystems of educational research, to point to possible dangers and errors, to boost teachers' confidence in education and to steer young people in the direction of universally valid spiritual values. It is encouraging to see a philosopher such as Suchodolski, who contemplates the future of the world in the light of seven decades of activity in which he has experienced different socio-political systems, opposing ideologies and the tragedies and injustices brought about by two world wars, pleading for a world approach to the problem of goals:

Despite the differences between continents, in particular on the north/south axis, and between the developed and the developing countries, and despite cultural and ideological differences, the goals of the struggle for a new future in the world are the same everywhere. Defending peace, guaranteeing education to all human beings, overcoming the menace of famine, protecting health, conserving the wealth of the natural environment and preserving the cultural identity of all human groups are universal activities. A stop must be put to fanaticism and terror; the respect of human rights and the opportunity to participate in social and political life must be assured to all [*Educational Goals*, 1980, p. 165].

There are then a set of goals[12] deriving from the indivisible problems confronting the contemporary world which require a joint effort on the part of all nations and the participation of every individual. No country can remain on the sidelines waiting for the others to solve the joint problems; there is no possibility of splitting this indivisible whole into parts, for example by accepting technological aid and rejecting the principle of democracy, or accepting co-operation with regard to the protection of the environment while avoiding commitment to the promotion of peace.

Opening education up to world problems and to common goals does not mean cancelling out the specific character of each system, or diminishing the importance of patriotic education, or creating discontinuities between tradition and modernity. The interpretation of these goals in specific situations and the place assigned to each of them will always remain a prerogative of the national authorities, exercised on the basis of a philosophy, explicit or otherwise. However, it is the task of the various international bodies and of the institutions and specialists engaged in the struggle for the future of mankind to point out possible or existing errors committed in the name of autonomy, authenticity, independence, etc. Referring to the universality and specificity of the goals of education, one of the authors of the collective work already quoted puts us on our guard against totalitarianism and points to two errors to be avoided:

> One can imagine the amount of harm, some of it irreparable, that is done by cure-all and dangerously levelling formulas which are only an atrocious caricature of educational goals. The advocates of maintaining local traditions come-what-may are always able to demand 'a return to origins' as the only guarantee of authenticity. According to them, specificity and authenticity are antidotes for the commonplace and the loss of identity. . . . Educational goals should not be a trap or snare. When defining them one must avoid both a reduction through an excess of universalism and solecisms through an excess of focusing. This grave and dual requirement is thus characteristic of the debate on the universality and specificity of educational goals [*Educational Goals*, 1980, pp. 109–10].

Being as they are the main point of entry for the requirements deriving from science, culture, the world of work and socio-political developments, educational goals have become considerably more diversified in their range—hence the dual preoccupation of specialists with grouping them and integrating them. The goals are interlocked, and each of them is to be found in all the various subjects or types of objective—cognitive, affective and volitional, or psychomotor (on the problem of the transition from educational goals to educational objectives, see Busshoff et al., 1981; D'Hainault, 1977). Grouping of the goals helps teachers to identify the range of sources of modern educational contents, the interrelations among subjects and the connections among the various orders of objective—operational objectives, objectives by educational level or grade, general objectives, and ultimate goals. Some goals relate mainly to contemporary world problems; others to the cultural and artistic life of society or to sociopolitical life; some link education directly with the world of work, others with the findings and spirit of science and technology; some are more the expression of social needs (protection of the environment, new international economic order, etc.); others raise to the level of goals the aspirations of individuals and of learners—creativity, solidarity, freedom, etc. It is for this reason that a reform of contents should be based on a philosophy of education and an explicit table of relevant goals.

For some time, general surveys and national studies or projects have stressed integration of goals or, to borrow Roller's expression (*Educational Goals*, 1980, p. 208) the 'goal of goals'. Roller himself at the beginning of his study quotes Bertrand Russell to the effect that we must have some conception of the kind of person we wish to produce before we can have any definite opinion as to which education we consider best. His interest in a supreme value capable of integrating all types and registers of objective, finding expression in educational practice, and finally, of mobilizing both the manifest and the latent energy of learners is a healthy reaction against a kind of education which was fairly widespread in the 1950s and the 1960s—soulless education divided up into compartments or sectors, which offered learners no spiritual model or ideal, education that left young people halfway along the road, that provided them with divergent information rather than answers capable of mobilizing their energies in the service of action and values unanimously recognized as beneficial. Speaking of the educational function of such a 'goal of goals', of 'painting a portrait of man', Roller notes that goals are precise functions and are of such great importance that without them education will be condemned to failure and bring about its own downfall as well as that of mankind. And the supreme goal, the goal of goals, is that which, assuming different forms according to the periods in the history of mankind, expressed itself fully in the period of economic and spiritual effervescence—Greek or Roman Antiquity, the Renaissance, the Enlightment: it is man with his fundamental dimensions and aspirations; it is man fully and harmoniously developed, it is 'Man, the Essential Value' in the words of Roller, who adds: 'Education has only one goal—that of educating man' (*Educational Goals*, 1980, p. 214).

Towards a multidimensional and integrated content

On the characteristics of contents for the school of the future, there is, if not full agreement, at least little divergence between what is desirable and what is predictable, in other words, between recommendations or studies of a normative character and the projects launched in various countries—China, Denmark, Hungary, the Philippines, etc.; these convergences are clear in the case of the natural sciences.

In the first place, there is agreement in the premises, or sources, of a relevant content (see Frey, 1978). Specialists highlight the proliferation of sources, the complex and global nature of the problems to be solved and a series of developments which should not escape the attention of the designers of school curricula or educators:

• The world will experience trends and countertrends; even the strongest trends may weaken for a time, then will reassert themselves; the future will be a succession of surprises and individuals should be prepared for such changes, which will not be uniform or rectilinear. Dangerous developments or actions can occur suddenly, spread rapidly and temporarily disturb the life of the national or international community. In its contents and methods education should include responses (i.e. form attitudes) to such situations.

• Communication between peoples, groups and individuals will become faster and easier; communication satellites, information technology, etc. will facilitate exchanges and, thereby, knowledge of the different cultures and problems of other regions. We all know how quickly and faithfully music, fashions in clothes, vocabulary, behaviour, etc. spread at the present time, particularly among the young. This trend will influence the contents of education and conversely should find a backing in educational contents—foreign languages, an open and critical attitude, communication know-how, historical culture, geography, etc. (see Castarède and Sur, 1980).

• A richer cultural life embodying broader participation will constitute a favourable context for the democratization of education and education for peace and co-operation. If culture comes about through education, education in its turn should be very responsive to cultural activities and developments in the local community or in the various regions of the world. On the one hand, the school could take advantage of the increasingly varied range of original cultural activities (shows, museums, complex multi-functional cultural centres such as the Centre Pompidou in Paris) and, on the other hand, it should offer pupils cultural training. In France, for example, there is much appreciation of the educational services rendered to schools (and to the public in general) by the radio station France Musique, whose programmes place the emphasis on classical music. In many countries, Colombia for example, the school in co-operation with other institutions trains and involves pupils in activities involving the protection of cultural values and property. In nearly all countries, pupils are educated, in or out of school, for cultural tourism (knowledge of values, mankind, the past, etc.).

Secondly, the emphasis is on a multi-dimensional content, made necessary by this proliferation of sources of contents and these varied and rather unpredictable developments (see International Symposium, 1980*b*, 1980*c*, 1980*e*, 1980*f*, 1980*g*, 1980*h*, 1980*i*, 1980*j*; Osborne, 1980).

With regard to the basic or natural sciences, we may begin by noting a series of characteristics or recommendations of a general nature:

• Although the latest findings of science do not have an immediate impact on curricula, the contents of general education should reflect the ongoing development of science.

• Greater use should be made of the notion of probability, drawing on examples from daily life.

• Curricula should include a simple introduction to the theory of communication—channels of communication, binary units of information (bits), bandwidths, etc.; such knowledge would be useful also in social science education.

• Science teaching should highlight both the advantages and the dangers involved in the application of the findings of the natural sciences.

• The problems of energy and the environment and the applications of computers to the various sectors of activity or to research will have a profound influence on the development of the basic sciences and, consequently, on the contents of education.

• Science teaching should place greater emphasis on experimental work, practical work and everyday applications—weather forecasts, road traffic and accidents, the development and incidence of certain illnesses, etc.

• An introduction to logic could facilitate and simplify learning in the natural sciences; this module could also include information on contemporary scientific method. Problem-oriented teaching, highlighting alternatives and the practical value of solutions provided by the sciences, should replace axiomatic tendencies.

• There is a need to develop the capacity to transfer concepts and techniques from one science to another.

With regard to the social and human sciences, specialists continually stress their educational and socio-political functions and the role they

could play in the maintenance and progress of democracy, in the development of healthy co-operation between nations based on sincerity and generosity, in the promotion of culture and in efforts to combat violence, terrorism, etc.
- The social sciences teach us that civilization is a product of co-operation, to which almost all peoples have made their contribution. Civilization is a legacy to be defended and developed, it is 'our common heritage and debt'.
- In the future, we shall not be able to reduce world civilization to European civilization or that of a few developed countries.
- The social and human sciences should help all men to understand that ambition, the desire to obtain advantages at the expense of others and wealth greatly in excess of needs can only encourage instability, fuel selfishness and violence, and engender conflict. In tomorrow's world, moral criteria should play a more important role in the election of leaders at all levels of society.
- In the social and human sciences in particular, learning should be personalized; teachers have a duty to make the distinction—a particularly important one—between learning and indoctrination.
- Knowledge of man and society acquired by a direct approach (psychology, sociology, etc.) or indirectly (history, literature, philosophy, etc.) is becoming vital for every school leaver.
- Exceptional intellects and outstanding talent should be encouraged so as to prepare the way for ordinary mortals. One proviso should however be made: education should try to reduce differences with regard to the ability to communicate more clearly.
- The young fully realize that the Euro-American type of affluent society will no longer be able to go on developing as we approach the limits of the planet's natural resources. The powerful motivation of personal gain will thus be less strong; it will be necessary, for education, to find ways of motivating people (see International Symposium, 1980*i*).

However, the emphasis placed on the social and human sciences in curricula varies between different countries; it is, for example, greater in Japan and the United Kingdom than in other countries.

With regard to aesthetic education, it should be noted that the links between the arts are becoming more numerous, and inter- or trans-disciplinary aesthetic education is today possible. Experimental research has shown that all peoples can participate in creative activities, that their artistic resources manifest themselves before the infant school. To neglect this form of education will be to neglect an essential component of the human spirit.

Thirdly, studies, recommendations and projects reveal *a concern to integrate*, focus and achieve better co-ordination of contents. The proliferation of sources and new forms of education is giving rise to a fear that school may become an overloaded, bloated institution, accumulating subjects to be taught just as television accumulates programmes (see International Symposium, 1980*h*). This anxiety is obviously well founded, but it is also constructive in the sense that all the projects we have considered have evinced the desire to avoid disorder, dispersion and overloading and to promote a relevant content that is more goal-centred, better co-ordinated and more adapted to the needs of the different school age-groups. Inter- or transdisciplinarity, the infusional approach or holistic approach, the concept of paradigm, the concern with achieving a better linkage of goals, objectives, curriculum contents and learning methods, all constitute a reaction to a danger and different ways of integrating a multi-dimensional content. Among the solutions proposed in this connection, mention may be made of the project for the redistribution of working hours, launched in the USSR (Kostyashkin, 1980), where the concern to avoid overloading and to rationalize studies has led to a reorganization of daily learning timetables. In the previous chapter we have already described Unesco's efforts to promote interdisciplinarity in general education curricula and syllabuses and education relating to the quality of life and the environment embodying previously fragmented contents: environmental education, population, health and nutrition education, education for drug abuse prevention, etc.

Methodological framework for a syllabus

Most studies on the education of the future or its contents stop short, not unreasonably, at the level of goals or general objectives, placing the stress on new forms of education, i.e. the types of contents called forth by contemporary world problems. In an international survey such as this, we could have confined ourselves also to that approach, since to define a possible syllabus is to involve oneself in questions relating to socio-cultural and school situations, priorities and very diverse financial and educational resources.

However, the work of those who design curricula, syllabuses and school timetables, school principals and teachers does not stop with the analysis of the sources of new contents; they also have to organize the teaching–learning process in the light of a very large number of variables specific to each national community or each establishment. Any demonstration of the importance of the natural sciences or technology and of the emphasis to be placed on spiritual education, modern domestic science or future-oriented exercises has to take ac-

count of very different socio-cultural, demographic and economic realities; these realities very often amount to limitations and difficulties that have to be taken into consideration. Let it be said in the first place that school learning takes place in a more or less rigid institutional framework:
• A weekly school timetable of 5 to 6 hours daily for 5 to 6 days a week.
• Classrooms assigned to a single set of pupils or occupied throughout the day by two sets of pupils (morning and afternoon) and sometimes by evening classes.
• Flexible and effective co-ordination between the various levels of education (pre-school, primary, secondary, university) or discontinuities that do not facilitate the promotion of new contents, principles and methods of learning.
• Teachers whose weekly teaching commitments are reasonable or which go beyond what can be regarded as reasonable, having regard to out-of-school obligations, tests and examinations, remedial work etc.
• Teachers trained according to a subject-based approach or one favouring interdisciplinarity.

Add to this the fact that the socio-political context in which the school learning process is organized and takes place is sometimes encouraging and sometimes constraining or even harmful:
• Because of their professional commitments, and their economic, cultural and social difficulties, many parents are not able to participate effectively in the education of their children, to provide them with adequate help at the various stages of school life, or to maintain systematic contact with educational institutions; and it is very likely that these difficulties will continue over the next two decades in many countries.
• The developed countries are unable to control and reduce the moral damage produced by commercialistic mass media; rather than benefiting from the inputs from parallel education, schools are consequently confronted by an influence that is difficult to counteract.
• In some cases, the aggressiveness and dogmatism of certain types of dominant religious or political bias constitute a formidable obstacle to the promotion of spiritual or humanist education, a genuine moral education or education for peace and co-operation among peoples.

There can be no question of our proposing here a single syllabus or school timetable, which would be open to criticism on several grounds. The methodological framework presented here is intended not as a model or as an ideal to be achieved over the coming decades but rather as a platform or reminder for political authorities, curriculum

Methodological framework for the contents of general education

Subject groupings and/or subjects—formal and non-formal education[1]	Importance of informal education[2]	Goals; remarks[3]	Observations; possible options
I. *Education for and through the natural sciences*[1] Mathematics Computer science and/or CAL Physics Chemistry Biology Knowledge of the earth and space: geography, geology, astronomy, etc. Non-formal activities and national and international competitions to identify and encourage talent[2]	Important: to link up formal and informal education (see sub-chapter VI.2: forms of linkage)	1. Providing a basic training in the sciences: basic concepts, theories, methodologies and outlooks, mathematical tools to be used 2. Training young people in the use of computers 3. Enabling young people to utilize sources of information available in society 4. Preparing pupils for continuous and creative self-instruction[5]	1. Different modes and degrees of subject integration 2. Infusional approach:[4] education relating to the quality of life and environment, the problems of development and underdevelopment
II. *Social and human sciences* National, regional and world history National and world literature Philosophy and philosophy of life Understanding of man, of society and the future	Important: apply procedures at school for linking formal and informal education	1. Humanist education 2. Fostering a critical spirit 3. Conclusions on the development of societies, on social inequalities and injustice 4. Knowledge of different societies and acceptance of their diversity 5. Improvement in the quality of school life and the life of the community	1. Infusional approach: education for democracy and participation 2. Introduction of future-oriented exercises or courses 3. Emphasis on the role of the family 4. Possibility of introducing contents pertaining to education for peace, education relating to the environment and the quality of life

228

III. *Education for and through technology and work* In relation to the needs, resources and prospects of each national community. In keeping with the computerization of all sectors of social life. School and/or out-of-school activities	1. A proper attitude to work; respect for work 2. A technological culture; a critical interest in and attitude to technological progress 3. Training of active individuals and inculcation of know-how 4. Preparing pupils to adapt easily to changes in the world of work	1. Open to boys and girls; options 2. Conceived as a component of general culture[6] 3. In keeping with the dynamics of the world of work
IV. *Mother tongue and foreign languages* Important role of the media and cultural exchanges	1. Sense of belonging to a given culture; national dignity 2. Means of communication and knowledge of other cultures; open-mindedness 3. Critical analysis of the quality of the messages carried by the media	1. Systematic teaching and preparation for continuous self-instruction 2. Possibility of fitting in education for peace and co-operation
V. *Moral and civic education* Courses and exercises or debates (cf. the experience of Asian countries), or indirect moral education involving the participation of all teachers Religious education. Greater consultation and/or involvement of the family	1. Cultivating an interest in the ethical quality of life and in social equality and justice 2. Inculcating moral values likely to further co-operation and participation 3. Defusing aggressiveness, self-interest, racism, etc.	1. Can include education for democracy and participation and sex education[7] 2. Non-verbal teaching inputs to be taken into account

Subject groupings and/or subjects—formal and non-formal education[1]	Importance of informal education[2]	Goals; remarks[3]	Observations; possible options
VI. *Spiritual and cultural education* Helping young people to steer a course in the world of material and spiritual values and to combat dehumanization. Improving the quality of relations: pupil–pupil, teacher–pupil, etc.	Important role of the family and youth organizations Importance of traditions and of the cultural training capacity of the local community	1. Distinction between ends and means 2. Respect for values and talent 3. Giving cultural values priority in life 4. Combating the possible moral disintegration of society	1. Ensuring balance between the cognitive and affective 2. Educating young people to make rational decisions and choices 3. Possibility of fitting in education for development and international co-operation
VII. *Education for and through the arts and manifestations of beauty* Special emphasis on music and the visual arts Multiple and combinable options Importance to be given to artistic events	Very important: hence the need to guide pupils and utilize in the school the aesthetic experience acquired out of school Role of the family	1. Development of aesthetic taste and acquisition of criteria of judgement 2. Preparing pupils to participate in the artistic life of society 3. Organizing creative artistic exercises 4. Identifying and encouraging talent	1. Possibility of linking different arts or integrating education in the different arts through common aesthetic concepts; means of expression, styles, etc. 2. Possibility of fitting in education for peace and co-operation
VIII. *Education for and through sport and leisure* Non-formal activities organized by the school (clubs, competitions, excursions, nature classes, etc.) should have an important place	Linkage between formal and informal education is important	1. Knowledge and know-how with regard to sports and leisure pursuits 2. Developing a sporting outlook 3. Cultivating interest in the various competitions seen as sporting and ethical events 4. Fostering enjoyment of life	1. Possibilities for incorporating new types of education

IX. *Modern domestic science* The home (furnishing, *ikebana*, etc.) Family life Nutritional education Family budget Formal and/or non-formal activities	It is essential to involve parents	1. Preparing pupils for marriage and family life 2. Indirect preparation for future parenthood 3. Indirect preparation for working life: knowing how to organize one's own life	cf. the experience of Japan, the Netherlands, the Federal Republic of Germany, etc. Possibility of introducing population education
X. *The new forms of education and contemporary world problems*[8] Environmental education. Education for democracy and participation Education for a new international order Education for peace and co-operation Population education, etc.	Informal education is very important here, and not always in accordance with the aims pursued in school	1. Goals coinciding with those of sections I, II, IV, V, VI and IX. 2. Giving pupils a relevant view of world problems 3. Devising exercises as an approach to specific problems of a global and multi-disciplinary nature 4. Improving the quality of school life and relationships 5. Highlighting interdependencies and the responsibilities of each individual 6. Cultivating the idea of the solidarity of modern man	1. Infusional approach or separate subjects: depending on needs and traditions, the characteristics of the initial and in-service teacher training subsystem, etc. 2. In the case of an infusional approach, one subject should have a co-ordinating role

NOTES TO METHODOLOGICAL FRAMEWORK

1. Understanding (education for) and training (education through); subjects are at one and the same time the aims and the means of education.

$$\text{Learner} \underset{\text{through}}{\overset{\text{for}}{\rightleftarrows}} \text{aims + means}$$

   Education for = understanding the methodologies and principles of science, values, the languages of art, etc. and assimilating know-how.
   Education through = being educated to act and participate with the help of the educational resources of the various subjects. Education in these two senses does not take place in clearly separable phases.
2. *Non-formal activities* organized by the school or youth organizations may or may not be included in school timetables; they are often elective or optional and they are also often multi- or interdisciplinary. In Europe, 'olympiads' in the various subjects—mathematics, physics, chemistry, etc.—are starting to play an important role. The international phase is preceded by phases at the national level (towns, departments, etc.) involving thousands of pupils. In Romania, national competitions are organized in all subjects (literature, geography, music, etc.) and all occupations.
3. Under this heading, we offer some comments on the goals or major concerns without attempting to give an overall view of the general aims of education.
4. *Infusional approach* = expression used in Unesco's programmes to designate the promotion of the contents of a new type of education in curricula or the process of learning the various subjects; applies in particular to education for peace, environmental education, etc., i.e. interdisciplinary objectives and contents.
5. Every learning process should be geared to lifelong education, that is to say, should prepare pupils for creative and continuous learning and for realistic self-evaluation.
6. Education for and through technology and work helps to provide pupils with educational and career guidance without imposing unduly early specialization; productive (socially useful) work should be regarded as a means of training and not as a purely economic activity.
7. Possible options in relation to specific social and educational situations.
8. We have tried to avoid making the list of subjects too long; however, to avoid edging out or eliminating some subjects, we have opted to include ten groups of subjects in school timetables; the subjects could no doubt be grouped in a different way, but the important thing is that they should be included as contents of learning.

---

designers and educators. This framework is meant to be comprehensive in relation to the sources of contents and the aspirations of young people and relevant with regard to the indicators listed above. Being aimed at an all-round, integrated education, it links education of the mind and of the body, computer science and sport, patriotic education and receptiveness to world problems. It also indicates some essential educational goals and linkages to be achieved between formal, non-formal and informal education. For a given type of content (education for peace, nutritional education, sex educaton, etc.) several

Future prospects

points of entry are suggested with the aim of providing curriculum designers with a choice in accordance with specific educational situations.

NOTES

1. Listing the new forms of education described or proposed by international agencies and the various authors, or as yet inadequately defined at the conceptual level, is a major task; there are few surveys (educational studies, educational encyclopedias or dictionaries, etc.) dealing with the new forms of education which, over the last two decades have found their way into Unesco's programmes and into the literature on educational innovation. Mention may be made, however, of the *EUDISED Multilingual Thesaurus* (Viet and Van Slype, 1984). Published in English, French, German, Spanish and Dutch, this work employs an up-to-date teminology. In addition, the Council of Europe has for some years published interesting educational literature, organized educational meetings and promoted exchanges of information between European countries. The emphasis placed on education and the educational sciences by the Council of Europe in its activities underlines once again the role that education plays and could play in the organization and development of any socio-cultural or political enterprise. We employ the information provided by the Council's newsletter on computer assisted learning (CAL).

2. Negative reactions to change are sometimes explained by the fear that the new contents will overload the curriculum. The list of new contents which are rightly forcing their way into the traditional curriculum and the volume of the information to be learnt are formidable. Moreover, whereas traditional contents are subject-based, the new contents constitute complexed wholes. As John Oxenham (1982) points out:

   Underlying the NIEO are several educational disciplines or subject areas: morals, ethics, politics, economics, law, human behaviour. There are also key concepts like resources, property, sovereignty, production, markets, exchange, negotiation, equality/inequality, self-reliance, interdependence. How these are to be interpreted, harmonized and organized into learning programmes for different learners is at the heart of any education about the NIEO.

3. In this connection, mention should be made of the value as a model acquired by the Open University in the United Kingdom. Established in 1969, it is a key element in British higher education and has led to the creation of similar universities in all continents. The courses and publications of the Open University are widely used by other institutions of higher education. A comparison between traditional universities and the Open University highlights the cultural impact of this new type of university.

Traditional university	*Open University*
—Entrance qualifications required	—No entry qualifications
—Full-time studies following enrolment	—The student can pursue his studies whenever he wishes throughout his adult life
—Full time	—Part time
—In a specific institution	—Anywhere in the United Kingdom

Future prospects

4. No. 1 outlines the development of instruction in computer science and computer assisted learning in Norway. The Norwegian Minister of Education is quoted as saying that today all young people need some knowledge of computers and should preferably have some personal experience in using them. Computer science studies will become available shortly for all pupils in the upper secondary school. At present, instruction in computer science is provided at 200 comprehensive schools and 275 upper secondary schools. In Denmark, measures have gone further:

> The Directorate for Upper Secondary Education has registered an enormous interest from schools all over the country for experimental teaching in and about computer science. From the beginning of the coming school year over a third of the upper secondary schools—50 out of 142—will be involved in these experiments.... All pupils should have a knowledge of computer science. The object is not to make pupils expert in this subject, but to teach them how to use computers.... In the first year pupils should have a common course of about thirty hours.... Teachers, in particular of history, social sciences, religion and languages, should introduce pupils to the interplay between computer science and the individual, culture and society, and explain the possibilities and limits of computer systems [Council of Europe, 1983, No. 2].

Introductory courses for teachers of all subjects are planned in co-operation with the universities to train some 500 teachers over three years.

5. Sanwidi (1981) writes that 'One of the first things noted is that this underdeveloped country is very backward with regard to schooling (a rate of 13 to 14 per cent) and that its population is 95 per cent illiterate and rural.' The author analyses an experiment carried out by the Rural Radio Service, functional literacy work, etc., before going on to examine educational reform as a framework for the convergence of formal and informal education.

The problem of effective communication between school and the cultural life of a community is one addressed by many African specialists in the light of the principle of authenticity and endogenous nature of education (see Dongala, 1981; Yerodia, 1981).

6. In a recent French dictionary, the following general definition of the concept (French: *'pertinence'*) is given: 'Relevance. 1. The fact of an object's being more or less important in relation to the objectives of an individual or a group, of being within the scope of their preoccupations, aims and interests; 2. The standpoint adopted by the scientific approach and coherence from this stand-point' (Mialaret, 1979, p. 340; see also Page et al., 1977).

7. One can also point to educationists who posed this problem sixty years ago, such as Scharelmann and Gansberg in Germany (1926) and, more recently, Hausmann (1959). It may be noted that, according to Rabindranath Tagore (1861–1941), learning should always be a source of joy to the child.

8. This work has become a classic. On page 106, definitions are proposed for concepts such as multi-, plural-, cross-, inter-, and transdisciplinarity. It would seem that the concepts of 'interdisciplinarity' and 'transdisciplinarity' have in particular been exploited and used by educationists in their research.

9. Jegede evaluates the results of the Nigerian Integrated Science Project after ten years of practical experience. A great variety of ways have been used of collecting all possible data from the teachers involved and also from a sample of students using these books throughout the country. Results show that teachers of integrated sciences are not well disposed to the project because of a lack of appropriate training; the cognitive attainments are less than predicted; however, most of those involved acquired a positive attitude to science as a result of this project. The areas that need to be looked at again when the project is revised have been

identified, which could be of interest to those responsible for the development of similar projects.

Lutterodt (1981) discusses the rapid spread of integrated science courses throughout the world should not hide the difficulties facing teachers using these courses, in particular the tensions between the scientific and educational principles underlying them. Discovery learning, adapted to pupils' level of intellectual development, should bridge the gap between the knowledge derived from everyday experience and awareness of the unity of the sciences. The very different environments determining everyday experience complicate the solution of these problems. The evaluation of the Integrated Science Project in Ghana points to three problems facing teachers using integrated science curricula: (1) how far is it possible to incorporate experience without sacrificing conceptual unity? (2) How does one ensure that pupils understand the theoretical implications of practical activities? (3) How can the different outcomes of the experience of each pupil be adapted to effective teaching of the objectives included in the curriculum? These questions highlight the need for a realistic assessment of the experience of integrated science teaching over the last decade in order to arrive at greater conceptual precision and more enlightened decisions.

Vaideanu (1974) underlines that interdisciplinarity does not cancel out individual subjects but enables their points of contact and interactions to be highlighted more clearly. He also (1982) deals with the linking of various types of contents (formal, non-formal, informal) and subjects. In this context, he reports the relaunching of a research project carried out twenty years previously, which had led him to propose integrated teaching of the arts (literature, music, painting, etc.) in his book *Cultura estetica scolara* (1967). This time, he invokes transdisciplinarity (common basic concepts) as a way of linking school subjects more closely.

Dario Antiseri (1975) sees interdisciplinarity as a way of transcending both the blinkered specialist and the encyclopedically informed amateur. Interdisciplinarity presupposes and recognizes subject divisions and can be brought into play whenever a problem has to be resolved in an explanatory or interpretative fashion. Interdisciplinary work is a collaborative enterprise involving various specialists with a view to explaining a fact, predicting an event or interpreting a text.

10. See D'Hainaut (1980), who describes instrumental transdisciplinarity as a working method for teachers; without modifying curricula, teachers are invited to highlight basic concepts common to a number of subjects—system, criteria, transformation, etc. The author has carried out research on the subject in Côte d'Ivoire.

Gusdorf (1977) quotes a speech by the French historian J. Michelet in 1825 to show that interdisciplinarity is not something absolutely new invented in our own times nor a panacea. Michelet pointed out that, in the Ancient World, the Muses were sisters and knowledge was not fragmented; man can perceive the harmony and unity of the sciences and wishes to do so; he will thus discover the progress of the human mind and the path that leads from science through sciences back to science.

Ravagioli (1975), an anthology including texts by Hegel, Comte, Cassirer, Mialaret, etc. In the introduction, the author deals with 'multidisciplinarity and interdisciplinarity' and 'limits to the classification of the sciences', ending with a sub-chapter entitled 'Towards transdisciplinarity'.

Semeraro. (1982) deals with the following subjects: I. Towards a new concept of interdisciplinarity. II. Interdisciplinarity and new curricula. III. Possible interdisciplinary curricula. Annexes: 1. First-year secondary-school interdisciplinary syllabus 2. Second-year secondary-school interdisciplinary syllabus

3. Third-year secondary-school interdisciplinary syllabus. (See also Jantsch, 1980.)

11. Mialaret's *Vocabulaire de l'éducation* (1979) gives the following definition of interdisciplinarity:

> Interdisciplinarity. This term was created to designate the new realities brought about by the decompartmentalization of subjects in the treatment of new problems. The aim of any interdisciplinary movement is to create a 'sufficiently broad and precise formalism' (P. Delatre) to express, communicate and pursue research in fields explored by researchers from different disciplines which would otherwise remain isolated. The result is better integration of knowledge and a more effective and realistic development of action and research.

Unesco (1983e), p. 9 suggests that

> The first thing is to establish a distinction between interdisciplinarity, understood in a strict sense, and transdisciplinarity. The first implies the meeting and co-operation of two or more disciplines, each possessing (in the realm of theory or of empirical research) its own conceptual frame of reference, its own way of defining problems and its own research methods. The second implies that contact and co-operation between various disciplines has occurred essentially as the result of their coming to adopt the same set of basic concepts or certain similar approaches to research—in more general terms, the same paradigm.

12. *Educational Goals* (1980) is the outcome of a programme on educational goals initiated by the IBE in 1974, it provides an interesting and ultimately stimulating view of the problems. As C. Fitouri points out in the Introduction (p. 13), it attempts to avoid a series of snares:

> It was necessary to avoid both the mythology of presenting the problem in terms too theoretical, and the pitfalls of a short-sighted policy sticking too closely to reality. It was further noted that along with explicit goals—the fruit of philosophical and pedagogical deliberations—social and educational realities almost always contained implicit goals, which one must know how to identify and analyse and to which the greatest amount of attention must be paid if one desires to promote advances in educational thought.

Following studies devoted to the regions of Africa (N'Sougan Agblemagnon), Latin America (R. Nassif), Asia (J. P. Naik), the Arab States (M. A. El-Ghannam), the USSR (D. V. Ermolenko), Western Europe and North America (J. A. Lauwerys and R. Cowen), the work devotes a number of chapters to an overall approach to goals, e.g. 'Universality and Particularity of Educational Goals' (A. Bouhdiba), 'For a World Approach to the Problem of Goals' (B. Suchodolski), 'Goals of Education: Generation and Re-generation' (S. Roller).

9
The path of innovation

In the foregoing chapters we have called for a thoroughgoing transformation of educational contents in the light of a future whose demands and characteristics are becoming increasingly clear. Yet one sometimes hears advice to 'leave well enough alone'. Let us accept this saw—but take it to mean that what is better, i.e. innovation or reform, even if right in theory, becomes a threat to what is well enough if it is not backed up by proper implementation—and let us, accordingly, turn our attention to the ways and means of educational innovation (see Debeauvais, 1974; Havelock and Huberman, 1978; Lourié, 1974).

TOWARDS RELEVANT METHODOLOGIES

The methodology of educational reform is a thread that, implicitly or explicitly, runs through all studies of a forward-looking nature. In the 1970s, Unesco, for example, organized a series of meetings and seminars on this topic. It is considered from various points of view by a number of authors or publications. We have chosen the term 'methodology' to encompass the set of principles and methods for the preparation, implementation and evaluation of a reform, because more than other terms it connotes the sort of comprehensive and coherent approach which matches a philosophy of education.

The successes achieved in certain cases, and the setbacks noted in others, have merely served to stimulate interest in the quality of the methodologies used by curriculum planners and designers, researchers and educators. The idea that developing countries, for example, with their scanty resources, could make do with improvised and less costly procedures has been rejected, along with the idea of 'cut-price education'. A relevant methodology is not necessarily sophisticated and/or costly; real wastage and errors spring from improvisation, superficiality and anti-democratic procedures.[1] One of Unesco's meetings on curriculum reform strongly emphasized this idea:

It is important to recognize that systematic organized curriculum development does not connote the evolution of ideal, unrealistic specifications.... Curriculum development is an aspect—a critically important aspect—of educational management. The solutions sought must, of necessity, lie within the framework of constraints imposed by the availability of trained staff, other human resources, finance and materials, and, most important of all, time. The more limited these resources are, the more compelling it is to use them to the best advantage. The developing countries are faced with acute problems in this context.... It was the conviction of the group that the application of systematic procedures will in the main ensure high returns on investments made [Meeting of Experts on Curriculum..., 1968, p.5].

Interest in the methods to be used, the factors to be taken into account and the stages to be passed through—hence in what we term the methodologies for bringing about a real transformation of the teaching–learning process, the quality of life in schools and the results obtained by the pupils, has been strengthened by the collection of evidence furnished by specialists and conclusions reached by those responsible for education.

Certain original and attractive schemes have met with success on paper but have been a disappointment in the classroom; both educators and decision-makers have learned that it is better to be realistic than to overdo things, even if this is less exciting than seeking to be original at any price. The problems of education must be seen in terms of complexity:

The education system needs to be seen as part of the network of complex interactions that binds it to society as a whole, and the educational act must take this complexity into account from the outset ... so we must therefore seek to understand and foster a conscious synthesis at the level of determinate societal units (regions, nations, groups of nations, etc.), between an economic and technological logic (which is predominantly global), a social logic (which is already distinctly more national) and a cultural logic (still more local) [Reiffers and Sylvestre, 1985, pp. 101, 103].

We would add that the same economic problem sometimes has different repercussions on the content of different education systems. In the countries of the Third World, the approach to the general issue of underdevelopment will focus on the right attitudes and methods to adopt in combating drought, famine and disease, or in making use of their natural resources, etc. The industrialized countries, on the other hand, will seek to sensitize young people to the problem of underdevelopment, to the campaign against wastage, to the need for a sense of responsibility and solidarity, etc. Without evading the pressures of the day, a reform should be implemented in accordance with an overall methodology that takes account of future requirements and traditions, and the need for change and the need for continuity, and treats the school as an institution capable of securing both social mobility and social stability.

Certain authors have a tendency or a habit of presenting changes as a kind of threat. When they talk of a 'change of society' before the end of this century, they appear to be thinking more of collapse than of the construction of a new, more humane, more democratic and more equitable system. The fact is, any in-depth change in education means involving educators in a constructive effort to attain the model desired by the people, and not prophesying an upheaval which will achieve nothing.[2] At all events, the worst course is to make teachers fearful about the demands of the future.

The traditional methodologies have in some cases proved satisfactory, but, with the growing complexity of the task of planning content, their omissions have become more manifest and more bothersome. In the traditional approach, content development was rarely comprehensive, covering all levels, disciplines and forms of education; this shortcoming was in fact the chief source of breakdowns and contradictions. Committees set up for each discipline, working more or less independently and in virtual isolation, form a structure that hinders from the outset the promotion of balance, coherence and interdisciplinarity. Without a comprehensive and coherent approach, one loses sight of the goals and ultimately neglects broad areas of objectives and content. By encouraging the 'each to his own discipline' mentality one makes it very difficult for teachers of the same school or the same class to work together.

The periodical revisions of educational contents, planned and carried out in every country, are only rarely based on a pertinent analysis of the totality of the *sources* on which the syllabuses should draw. The committees for each discipline or level (primary education, upper secondary, etc.) are concerned on principle with enriching the curriculum on the basis of the inheritance of the past, and not in the light of present and future circumstances and demands. Such a piecemeal and incoherent approach, adopted by committees following their own whims and ignoring the fact that the sources of a particular content are indivisible, has negative repercussions on pupils' learning and performance and on plans to update the training of teachers, etc. It is therefore worth while to remind researchers, planners and especially senior education officials that education is so complex that it rules out any simplistic or inflexible approach. The difficulty of predicting the outcome of a particular measure or innovation is greater than in other areas of activity; the results are often unforeseen or contrary to expectations. Moreover, the success of a reform of educational content depends to a great extent on the dialectical association of apparently contradictory qualities: boldness and realism, a critical outlook and trust in human nature, receptiveness to worldwide experience and respect for national distinctiveness, rigour and flexibility, generosity and economic efficiency.

In speaking of 'methodologies' in the plural, we wish to make it clear from the start that, although a number of successes or experiments are to be noted, there is no single valid universal methodology for all situations. On the other hand, there have been some interesting experiments which deserve to be analysed as socio-historical phenomena and the product of a series of research projects. There is undoubtedly much to be learned, for example, from the impressive traditions and from the influence of educational theory in countries such as Denmark, Belgium and Sweden, even though their populations are small. The most interesting aspect of the Danish U 90 project (Denmark, 1978) is its methodology: the stages it has passed through, how it has sought out contributors with relevant interests and resources and enlisted the active participation of various national organizations and social groups, etc. Educational reform is, and should be, a national event: the involvement of the entire population in the discussion creates a general awareness of the innovations and constitutes a first step towards success. From this point of view, the moment for launching a project must be chosen with great care. We cannot afford to disregard the technical, critical and constructive role played by specialists and especially by educational research in the preparation of reform projects, the checking of certain key hypotheses, the implementation of the project and the evaluation of its results.

The characteristics of a relevant methodology have been revealed by experience, that is to say, by successes and failures; they are comparable to those which ensure the relevance of educational content, and we shall do no more than recall a few of them. A relevant methodology must be as follows:

Comprehensive, including all levels and all forms of education and all the subjects taught; this will make it possible to give formal education the extra dimension of lifelong education and to ensure proper training for all the categories of educators (teachers and non-teachers).

Coherent, i.e. based on a philosophy that is relevant to the social realities, clarified by researchers and presented in the form of guides to assist all those involved in the preparation, analysis and implementation of a reform. This philosophy will help teachers to think in terms of the ultimate goals of education, and will help the various social groups to participate in the education of children and the democratization of education systems.

Geared to national objectives, to the circumstances of the school and society and to financial resources. Its adjustment to real factors and constraints should not be any obstacle to coherence and rigour in the methods used.

Interdisciplinary, i.e. capable of combining and guiding, for educational purposes, the work of specialists in different fields such as sociology and ergonomics, anthropology and genetics, futurology and history, etc. In order to benefit from all these different approaches, with the many suggestions and wide-ranging experience that they represent, an interdisciplinary and coherent methodology must integrate all this work with the teaching function, while asserting the specific role of education and treating the school as an independent variable.

Receptive to contributions from all the parties concerned by a reform, and in particular to the findings of educational research and experience throughout the world.

Realistic in regard to the complexity of the problems and the obstacles to be overcome; the actual stages of the reform, the timetable to be allowed for its implementation and the methods to be used in explaining profound changes to pupils, parents, etc., all call for a sense of realism.

Forward-looking, i.e. capable of tackling present-day problems in the light of the obvious or foreseeable demands of the future.

Examples and observations

All the case-studies so far mentioned contain ideas on methodologies to be used in future or already in use. The case-study on the modernization of education in China states the fundamental principles of this socio-political and educational undertaking. The study on Hungary devotes a chapter to the new curriculum development strategies which are wholly in keeping with the considerations outlined above. Christopher Dede and Johan van Bruggen, for their part, stress the difficulties to be overcome; both researchers and education officials should be prepared to confront difficult and unexpected situations, and in order to be able to cope with these, decision-makers should be able to draw on a varied store of alternative solutions.

The case-study on the evolution of the content of education over the next two decades in the Philippines lays particular stress on '*the forecasting of content*'. Six criteria are taken into consideration which, as a whole, attest to the determination of this country to take an effective part in the race for the third millennium, in which all or nearly all countries are taking part as the present century draws to an end. The criteria for determining the prospective value of curriculum content are: national objectives and the goals of education and development; trends in the economy; probable social changes and their implication for education; the development of patriotism as an indispensable prerequisite for the growth of international solidarity; changes in educational methods and techniques.

In addition, the study devotes a chapter to the relationship between change and stability in the development of education over the next two decades.

EDUCATIONAL RESEARCH: STRUCTURE AND ESSENTIAL ACTIVITIES

In their quest for endogenous and multidimensional development, a great many countries—particularly in Africa and the Arab world—are much exercised by problems concerning the relevance of education to their particular traditions, needs and aspirations. But 'relevance' is achieved through research and the use of a certain methodology: it is the long view that pays dividends, not improvised decisions. Thus the political authorities find themselves faced with a fundamental problem: what machinery is most likely to produce appropriate systems of education, relevant content and teaching/learning methods that are up to date and democratic?

Despite frequent assertions to the contrary, educational research has amply proved its effectiveness and justified its place in present-day education systems. After the Second World War, the growing importance of education for the development of contemporary societies and expansion of education systems led most countries to step up their research in the field of education. The older educational research laboratories or institutes in the developed countries and faculties of educational psychology have become bigger, or at least more active and with a more important role in national and/or international life. The socialist countries have their Academies of Pedagogical Sciences (USSR and the German Democratic Republic) or national research institutes in educational psychology.

For the developing countries, educational research has gathered strength in the general context of national affirmation. Having won their independence, in most cases during the 1960s, the great majority of the former colonies set ambitious tasks for education with a view to closing, in a relatively short space of time, the gap that separated them from their former mother countries. At that time their major preoccupation was to carry through a technological and cultural transfer that was expected to help them to put a rapid end to their economic and social backwardness. The European model of development, together with its instrument, the education system, was regarded as potentially very well suited to African circumstances. Transplanted lock, stock and barrel, however, these models turned out not to work, and in many cases their imposition complicated the situation inherited from the colonial period. These countries then realized that the road to development lay through the search for authenticity and the twofold adaptation of education both to local circumstances and to progress in science and culture. At first sight this road seems not only longer, but also precarious, since it requires them to design, put into application and assess the operation of their own models, and this requires time as well as human and financial resources. In the last analysis, however, it is proving less costly and even less long than the straightforward introduction of foreign models, an alternative which attracted many countries but which in the end, as the 1976 Conference of Ministers of Education of African Member States (1976) observed, yielded deplorable results in the 1970s.

In a study on educational reform in the United Republic of Cameroon, E. Bebbé-Njoh (1985) states that African countries have been prevented from making satisfactory decisions by a lack of reliable data on their own educational situations. For instance, decision-makers in African countries often suffer from a shortage of information in such essential areas as numbers of pupils, resources or the structure of the population. Even more serious reforms in Africa during the 1970s were often attempted without any real prior evaluation or analysis of the problems to be solved and without a clear definition of objectives. However, a coherent education policy involves more than the mere proclamation of a few important guiding principles. It must result in an appropriate strategy that determines what needs to be done in the light of the actual situation in the context and any difficulties that may arise in the future. This transition—from the political to the strategic phase of an educational reform—is impossible without the backing of a network of research units to gather and analyse relevant data on the problems in question, map out the general programme of action, introduce the proposed changes and monitor the results. In the developed countries these tasks are handled by educational research institutions, which include national institutes for educational research, curriculum development centres, university laboratories for experimental pedagogy, institutes for educational research and development and, in certain countries, academies of pedagogical sciences.

In recent years, almost all the developing countries have established research structures as part of their national reform programmes. This is an extremely encouraging trend, since the research makes it possible to rethink what education should be in the context of the new conditions created by political independence. It allows national objectives to be defined and the long-ignored traditional cultures to be fostered. It leads the way to a genuine 'acclimatization' of the reform, enabling the individual to feel at home in the heart of his cultural tradition and to arrive at an understanding of who he is and how he became the person he is. When not confined to devising ready-made solutions with a view to administrative decisions, educational research makes it possible for the political authorities or a community to give thought to its present condition and its future.

Expansion of research

One of the features of present-day education is the much broader range of people now benefiting from educational research. Teachers at all levels, administrators and politicians, pupils and students, parents and the leaders of adult groups are more and more often faced with educational problems for which research is needed. But the use and assimilation of its results and the benefit derived from it when individual or collective decisions are to be made depend to a large extent on the traditions of the users and their attitudes to reflection and to experimental research, which, combined, lead to educational improvements and innovations. This attitude may waver, from one country, community or period to another, between confidence and distrust or between indifference and rational exploitation.[3] In fact, it could be said that the demand for educational research is a reliable indicator of decision-makers' general attitude to change, of their degree of confidence in the internal possibilities of their education systems, of their familiarity with teaching problems and, ultimately, of their faith in humanity.

In every field of knowledge, revolutionary progress has been made in the last few decades. When we measure their impact on everyday life, the advances made in educational research are admittedly less spectacular than those of technological, physical or biological research. Being an extremely long and fragmented process, education is difficult to observe and evaluate. But there can be no denying the importance of the progress made thanks to certain theories or the fruits of reflection and experimental research, such as the concept of life-long education, steps forward in the area of learning processes and evaluation, etc.

As a distinct branch of theory, pedagogy parted company with philosophy before certain other philosophical disciplines such as aesthetics or ethics: Comenius (1592–1670) marks the watershed. Experimental research in education, which began around 1900 in the laboratories of experimental pedagogy of W. Lay and E. Meumann

(Germany), Binet and Simon (France), Claparède (Switzerland), Thorndike (United States) and Schuylen (Belgium), or in experimental schools (J. Dewey, 1896), was at that time an extension of the personal interests of researchers and a consequence of advances in experimental psychology and child psychology rather than of the explicit needs of education officials and educators. Those benefiting from this research came from within a narrow circle of researchers, and its findings were very seldom transferred or put into practice.

After the Second World War, interest in human problems in general and spectacular advances in science and technology gave fresh impetus to research in education. Almost all the universities of the industrialized countries were provided with educational research laboratories or centres. National institutes for pedagogical research were set up in a great many countries. Countries such as the United Kingdom, the United States, Japan, Sweden, the Soviet Union, etc. provide significant examples of this extraordinary upsurge of educational research. In the Soviet Union, the Academy of Pedagogical Sciences (whose President holds the rank of Deputy Minister of Education) has several thousand researchers and a number of specialized institutes: institutes for the general problems of education, general psychology, general pedagogy, study of the contents and methods of instruction, school equipment and technical educational aids, work training and vocational guidance, pre-school education, vocational and technical education, child and adolescent psychology, general adult education, special education, education in the arts, in-service training for teacher educators and teaching of the Russian language in non-Russian schools. Similarly, the German Democratic Republic has established an Academy of Pedagogical Sciences which comprises several specialized institutes.

In Japan (Kida, 1981, p. 50), there are some 960 institutions or organizations engaged in research, surveys and in-service teacher training. Over 500 of them are autonomous and more than 50 are attached to universities. There are also 60 research sections attached to administrative bodies and 330 universities and university colleges with pedagogical faculties or sections. Lastly, more than 220 teaching establishments are also working in the field of educational research. In the next ten or twenty years few developing countries, even those with appropriate research facilities established several years ago, are likely to build up a technical potential comparable to that of the developed countries mentioned above. But this does not mean that the role of their national institutes in the effort to promote relevant and original forms of education is negligible. As stated in the *Final Report* of the International Colloquium on Research and Practice in Education, these institutes can serve as relay stations for the findings of pedagogical research obtained from elsewhere, selecting and adapting them for local needs; secondly, they should offer methodological assistance to teachers who are engaged in research on their own initiative, in order to ensure that their efforts are well directed and that their findings contribute to the gradual improvement of educational practice (International Colloquium..., 1981).[4]

More important still are the new attitudes to educational research. In the well-known phrase of Cronbach and Suppes (1969, p. 21), 'conclusion-oriented research' has now given way to a new type of research in education: 'decision-oriented research'. Instead of concentrating on reaching conclusions (theories, general ideas, etc.), educational research lays greater stress on the problems to be solved and on the needs of the decision-makers and educators who are frequently consulted or asked to collaborate in the research. This is the R&D model, which focuses more on the clients and their interests than on the theoretical interests of the researchers. It starts with the assumption that the user has specific needs and that it is the task of research to satisfy them. In many countries, in fact, as is shown by a European Cultural Foundation survey (Malmquist and Grundin, 1975, p. 282), decision-makers appear to encourage 'policy research' rather than 'conclusion-oriented research'. For example, the National Institute of Education (NIE), established in the United States in 1972, serves an explicitly operational purpose: its three fundamental tasks are the development of education (learning), study of education policy and organization in the various states, and the dissemination of research findings and improvement of teaching.

In Sweden, a country often mentioned for its receptiveness to pedagogical research and its avant-garde reputation, the 'rolling reform' launched in 1962 was prepared by a research and development body specially set up for the purpose, the National Council for Education (Skölverstyrelsen), with a great many researchers taking part at both national and municipal levels (see Husen and Boalt, 1968; Vielle, 1981).

As we have seen, certain developing countries have also set up institutions which can, among their other functions, serve as relay stations for research findings and exchanges of experience. These institutions may operate at the national level, as in the case of China's National Institute for Research in Education, India's National Council of Educational Research and Training (NCERT), Mexico's Centro de Estudios Educativos, Nigeria's Educational Research Council and Peru's Instituto Nacional de Investigación y Desarrollo de la Educación, etc.; or they may take the form of facilities for educational research set up within governmental bodies, as is the case for the Centres of Curriculum Development in Singapore, Malaysia, Sri Lanka, Ghana, etc.

People often speak of the need to transfer technology to developing countries. Where pedagogical research is concerned, experience shows that the possibilities for such transfers are still insufficiently exploited. We are thinking of shared facilities for the training of researchers, in the context of regional projects or centres, of the transfer of research tools, and of the broader dissemination of experience and findings, etc. To this end, Unesco has encouraged the setting up of regional or subregional networks of educational innovation for development which link together innovatory institutions: the Network of Education Innovation for Development in Africa (NEIDA), the Caribbean Network of Educational Innovation for Development (CARNEID), the Asian Programme of Educational Innovation for Development (APEID), etc. Even greater support for their activities would be desirable, through the broader participation of the governments concerned, the more rapid dissemination of tested innovations, the adoption of joint programmes of broad interest (especially in curriculum development, teacher training, pupil assessment, the training of researchers, educational planning, etc.). The pedagogical traditions and culture of a nation take the form of certain mental outlooks and attitudes which are expressed in public opinion and participation. Clearly, countries with traditions and experience of this kind will find it easier to master the processes of innovation. But this does not mean that developing countries have to follow precisely in the footsteps of the developed countries or that the transfers can take place in one direction only, from North to South or from Europe to Asia; on the contrary, they can and should be reciprocal.

Types of research to be developed

One cannot avoid being struck by the extreme disorder that reigns in the terminology used to denote the various types of educational research. In the management of research and its related literature, *basic research is distinguished from applied research*. But other, more or less relevant, contrasting pairs of terms are also to be found (see De Landsheere, 1979, pp. 228–32; Suppes, 1978).

The concept of basic research is usually defined in opposition to that of applied research. Both concepts are important, but the distinction between them is not clear. What should be understood by 'basic' and what by 'applied' where educational research is concerned? Basic research is an activity in which researchers seek greater knowledge about a phenomenon without considering the immediate practical application of their discoveries. By contrast, applied research has a specific practical purpose.

In contrast to this somewhat narrow distinction we have the distinction between conclusion-oriented research and decision-oriented research, to which we have already referred. However, the term 'conclusion-oriented research' is equivocal, since a decision is also a conclusion based on information obtained through various channels (including research).

Lastly, mention should be made of the emergence of a new pair of contrasting terms, with a distinction between *systematic research*, conceived and carried out by specialized researchers in a context of programmes lasting for several years, and *spontaneous research*, conducted in educational institutions by teacher-researchers with or without the assistance of professional researchers; in the latter case, the person conducting the research is at the same time the primary user of its findings.

In education, needless to say, as in other fields of activity, innovations do not spring into being spontaneously, through some kind of pedagogical 'illumination' as to how the complex problems of human education and training can be solved. They have to be worked out, prepared, nurtured, compared and introduced in such a way that they are accepted in educational practice as the best solutions. 'Systematic research' seems a closer definition of this long and difficult work of pedagogical innovation and development; on the other hand, spontaneous research can have a 'snowball' effect and give educators encouragement and assistance.

However, it is also true that teachers, parents and other people concerned with education in general often feel the need for self-improvement. This sometimes leads to ad hoc, spontaneous innovations; as such efforts have the advantage of being more directly related to actual practice, they are worth incorporating into systematic research projects or at least monitoring from the methodological point of view. Hence the importance of encounters between specialized researchers and 'classroom' teachers or researchers in the form of *participatory research* or *action-oriented research*. This kind of research closely relates theory and practice, and its users and initiators as well as the researchers themselves are involved in it, whether the research itself is 'conclusion-oriented' or 'decision-oriented'; it also combines scientific rigour with the desire to solve a particular problem; such comparing of notes is particularly important and effective when the subject is innovation in educational contents. Participatory research is beyond the possibilities of pedagogical services and institutes of the traditional type, but it could be entrusted to bodies made up of a series of 'scientific workshops'.

One example of action-oriented research is Project II of the National Institute of Education of Yaoundé (United Republic of Cameroon), in which the new school curricula have been prepared jointly by specialist researchers (educational psychologists, epistemologists, etc.) and teachers representing all the subjects taught (Bebbe-Njoh, 1985).

The findings of research and the introduction of new contents

The view that reflection on education and experimental research should precede and determine any innovation, even at the risk of seriously holding back decisions, may be contrasted with the view that education systems develop independently of theories and research findings, which leaves scope for improvisation and arbitrary decisions. In fact, the exploitation of research findings (often produced by researchers working with educators) in the classroom or at the decision-making level has been going on for decades; it is a slow but continuous process which has produced positive results. The work of Bloom on teaching objectives, for example, has had a very substantial influence on curricula. The fundamental and far-reaching idea of Bloom and his collaborators has become a genuine tool for the designers of school curricula or textbooks, for decision-makers and for educators. Nearly everyone now knows that the first step is to determine the goals and objectives of education and then, in the light of those goals and objectives, to select and organize content, work out methods of learning and of evaluation, etc. Everyone is beginning to realize that the efficiency of the teaching–learning process owes a great deal to the *unity* of the curriculum (objectives, content, learning methods and methods of evaluation). It may be argued that the time-lag has been excessive, but educational practices (school curricula and learning methods, teaching style and materials) cannot be transformed as easily as a technological process used by an industrial firm. In this case, optimism is a realistic attitude.

In practice, incorporating a research finding into the real world of education means promoting a new pedagogical value and thus transforming not only some part of the education system but also the context, consisting of the attitudes of pupils and parents, way of life at school, style of education, etc. Information and training are therefore necessary, and educators' support for the pedagogical innovation must be secured; the next step is to help educators gradually and systematically to introduce the new method or technique into their system of teaching by assessing the results and making the necessary adjustments. This has a number of consequences:

It is necessary but not sufficient to inform educators about a given finding by providing them with documents and films, etc.; in order to change their way of working, they need to try things out and to practise. For this purpose the pilot schools and laboratory schools scattered through the various regions of a country form an indispensable support network.

The timing for the introduction of an important innovation is not decided by the researcher himself:

> Naturally, more often than not the results of psychological and educational research are only integrated into educational practice to the extent that they converge, or are at least compatible, with the ideas, beliefs and values which lie behind the philosophy of education and educational policy at any given time [Busshoff et al., 1981, p. 40].

According to information from a study on the use of educational research in the United Kingdom and United States (Huberman, 1982), the findings are utilized in the first place by the designers of curricula and then by teacher educators, other researchers, documentation services, research organizations, educational publishers and the general public. This remark is not surprising, since the contents of education (knowledge, know-how, ethics and citizenship) are the aspect of education that arouses strongest feelings, is the most talked about and is the most exposed to multi- and interdisciplinary investigation. Rapid progress in knowledge, technology and working methods and procedures, together with the spectacular results of educational psychology and epistemology and changing social priorities and demands, all oblige the designers of curricula to take frequent stock of the current state of research.

This particular dynamism can be illustrated by a significant example. In 1962, Thomas Kuhn (1967) introduced the concept of 'paradigm' as a broader and more operational term than 'theory'. For him, a paradigm is both a body of knowledge accepted by a scientific community and a certain way of utilizing those data. It is therefore a representation, a prevailing conception concerning a phenomenon, but at the same time a mode of action determined by that representation. A change of paradigm entails a change in the modes of action of the community concerned (in our case, the community of researchers and users of educational research). Getzels (Suppes, 1978, pp. 477–521) gives an interesting example of a change of educational paradigm under the influence of basic research in education. This is the case of changes in school architecture, particularly the physical arrangement of the classroom under the impact of different theories of learning. This example confirms that it is always worth while for authors of courses and textbooks and teams responsible for curriculum design to start from a sound theoretical position on the learning process and some basic knowledge about other educational processes such as socialization and interpersonal communication.

The truth is that a high proportion of educational research has repercussions on educational content. Sometimes the findings of the research prove of immediate use, as in the case of research on the minimum requirements to be met by compulsory education, learning how to perform logical operations with the assistance of a computer, forming concepts, analysing verbal interactions in the classroom, teaching moral values, teaching young children to read by means of pictures, etc. Other research projects prove useful in the long term, after a period of evaluation and public information. For example, research on programmed teaching has facilitated subsequent advances in educational technology such as modular teaching, computer-assisted teaching, epistemological and pedagogical analysis of content, behavioural analysis, ongoing evaluation, etc.

Where the theory of educational contents or 'curriculum development' is concerned—this being an interdisciplinary field deriving its principles, subject-matter and methodologies from didactics, epistemology, psychology, etc.—neither the designers of syllabuses nor teachers can afford to ignore advances in areas such as: methods of determining the goals assigned by each society to its education system and of working out teaching objectives; analysis of the sources of educational contents, which should determine its nature; principles and methods used for the selection and organization of contents (by level, type of institution, etc.); analysis of the specific educational value of each type of content; components of a common core curriculum for the training of teachers and non-teaching educators; specific needs and educational resources for different age-groups: children, pre-adolescents, adolescents, young adults, working adults and the elderly.

The above is occasionally disregarded; when this happens, it is for financial or political reasons or because of the gap between research and decision-making.

Obstacles to be overcome and machinery to be set up to improve communication between researchers, decision-makers and teachers

As we have seen, there is communication and a flow of results between the levels of research, decision-making and actual teaching, but that communication is sometimes irregular, incomplete or disrupted by blockages or conflicts. How can a country provide itself with a mechanism or strategy that will make good use of research findings and, even more importantly, steer research towards the preparation (design), analysis (verification) and implementation of an educational reform that is geared to the country's possibilities and specific resources? Situations vary greatly from one country to another; in some countries it is a matter of improving what already exists (committee, methodology, strategy, etc.), whereas in others it will be necessary to set up an appropriate, flexible structure with a suitable status designed to guarantee healthy communication between all the parties involved in educational reform, and in particular between research, decision-making and educational practice.

In every country, specialists who wish to set up efficient machinery encounter problems left over from the past and obstacles between researchers and educators or between researchers and administrators among which the following can be mentioned:

Psychological divergences: different attitudes towards innovation, a more marked concern with change or with continuity, etc.

Pedagogical divergences: different interpretations of new guidelines or different attitudes to traditional teaching methods and the demands of the future, etc.

Shortcomings of a cultural or linguistic nature: many difficulties are due to the fact that researchers do not adapt their reports or publications to those who will read them; in addition, there is the even more regrettable tendency of some researchers to use a sophisticated vocabulary for the sole purpose of masking the barrenness of their work or the flimsiness of their arguments.

Loopholes in the system for dissemination of research findings: absence of laboratory schools or of documentation and demonstration centres, etc.

Weaknesses in the methodologies used by researchers, loss of contact between researchers and educators at various stages of research, such as design, execution and dissemination, etc.

Omissions in the training of researchers (in administration, economics, etc.) and in the training of educators (philosophy, research methodology, etc.).

In order to establish continuous and effective communication between researchers, decision-makers and educators, the obstacles have to be identified but something also has to be done about the causes of the difficulties which can arise at any moment. Here we are at the education policy level and touch implicitly upon a fundamental problem: who can establish efficient machinery in a centralized or decentralized system? Researchers and educators should be involved in the design and introduction of a mechanism or strategy of this kind, but the chief role falls to the education authorities: it is they who ensure that their policy is coherent and effective (Busshoff et al., 1979, pp 44–49; International Colloquium . . ., 1981, pp. 124–31). Research, by definition, has a forward-looking and constructive stance: like any reflection or investigation, its duty and its right are to forge ahead of current practice, to look boldly into the future and to give free rein to its hypotheses. Narrowing the gap between the themes and hypotheses of research and educational needs does not mean suggesting solutions to the researchers or asking them for arguments to support measures that have already been taken; on the contrary, it means giving them the opportunity to investigate priority problems, to keep a finger on the pulse of life in schools and, at bottom, to derive satisfaction from their work. Closer links between research, educational practice and decision-making require a coherent and relevant set of measures designed:

1. *In research:* to improve the system of recruiting researchers; a good specialist in teaching methods, for example, should begin his or her career as an educator or spend long periods working in schools; to improve the training of researchers, particularly in the economics and administration of education; to provide researchers with opportunities to spend short periods in educational institutions and in the administration of education; to persuade researchers to involve educators in their work at all times and at all stages of research;
2. *In educational practice:* to improve the training of educators, particularly in educational psychology and the philosophy of education; to encourage reflection on teaching practices, exchanges of experience and innovatory initiatives; to reward educators who take an active part in research, and especially in the propagation of new approaches to teaching or education; to enhance the cultural and pedagogical life of schools and to foster educators' interest in the future of education;
3. *At the decision-making and administrative levels:* to involve administrators in the launching of research projects and in the analysis of their results; to enable administrators to spend short periods in educational research institutions; to assist senior officials and administrators in the management of education; to make administrators more interested in forward-looking studies in education etc. (International Colloquium . . ., 1981).

In considering the list of obstacles to be overcome in order to increase the impact of research on educational practice, which had been drawn up by the Bucharest Colloquium in 1980, the International French-language Seminar on the Dissemination of Educational Research Findings (Paris, 1984; Unesco, 1985a) on the same theme discussed, among other things, the general problem of the dissemination of research findings, and sought means of improving the situation; the proposals put forward by the participants focused on the training (for research) of educational personnel, documentalists and researchers, the planning of research dissemination processes, and 'relay' structures and institutions.

Unesco: crossroads for exchange in education

As an intergovernmental organization whose programme gives special prominence to education and educational research, Unesco is well placed to encourage and direct the efforts of its Member States, to point out errors to be avoided and to sustain healthy and beneficial cultural and educational competition. The hundreds of requests for educational expertise received by the Organization each biennium testify to the increased interest which educational authorities are showing in the experience of other countries and the findings of research. Unesco has become a major clearing house for the recording and circulation of research findings and for exchanges in the field of educational innovation or reform. Lastly, the establishment after the Second World War of numerous non-governmental organizations with education-related interests is evidence not only of a certain anxiety and need to communicate on the part of specialists but also of the development of reflection and applied research.

INITIAL AND IN-SERVICE TRAINING OF TEACHERS

The teacher in a traditional school, in the years preceding the Second World War, for example, knew that educational contents (curricula, textbooks, etc.) would remain stable over long periods. At that time, out-of-school education carried neither influence nor prestige, and the methods were typical of a teacher-centred pedagogy. The performance of the learners did not pose a socio-economic and political problem; changes in schools were slow and the atmosphere was serene.

Even more striking than the growth in the number of teachers (30 million in 1980) were the increasing demands made on the teaching profession. A few decades ago teacher trainers liked to recall the accepted idea that the teacher was an exceptional being not for who he or she was but for what he did, a view that should be interpreted not as a slur on the individual but as a eulogy of the profession. Nowadays, with the changes in education and the hopes placed in it, there are many people who think that teachers should epitomize the conscience of the nation, or even the conscience of the world community, a demand that carries immense obligations. The objectives to be attained, the content to be mastered and the methods to be used have all rendered the work of a teacher more complicated; for one thing, educational practitioners are keenly aware of the pressures brought to bear on content, and, for another, the task of the teacher—whether that of guide or group leader, and even when blessed with a propitious environment—is no easier than it was in the 1940s and 1950s. If we feel obliged to touch upon this complex and relatively distinct problem of the training of teachers, it is because the effectiveness of any reform of educational content depends on the full support of teachers for its objectives and upon the relevance of their training. There is a vast literature on this subject and a variety of possible approaches.[5] Our own approach is to consider the training of teachers in relation to foreseeable innovations—new types of content, application of the principle of lifelong education, promotion of interdisciplinarity and greater concern for the success of learners, etc.—because we subscribe to the idea that there can be no forward-looking approach to the training of primary school teachers unless there is first a forward-looking approach to education.

Reform and the status of teachers

All the foreseeable trends so far presented affect or ought to affect the initial and in-service training of teachers. To avoid both conservatism and the hasty introduction of ill-prepared schemes, the education authorities and teacher trainers must pay careful attention to all the problems connected with the training of the practitioners of education. Here are some of the issues which they are obliged to confront:

Teaching has become one of the most difficult professions, which will steadily increase in complexity and mobility. Do teachers and the people who train them enjoy psychological and material status commensurate with their exceptional role? To cope with the emerging cultural demands and respond to the expectations of young people, educators need an appropriate social status, psychological and material resources, prestige and good health, the means of continuing their own education (travel, books, educational resource centres, etc.) and spare time.[6]

We have mentioned the tendency to regard the teacher as 'a technologist of education'. We have also seen the considerable advantages of approaching the teaching/learning process in terms of complexity and flexibility. Teachers have or should have their individual *teaching styles*; the teacher can set high personal standards in the art of teaching. How can teachers be trained to master educational technology without becoming its slaves?

Recent studies have shown the importance of certain qualities such as flexibility, modesty, imagination, cordiality and willingness to enter into dialogue and communication, etc. A comparative study by OECD attempts to list these favourable qualities.[7] How should teachers be recruited and trained so as to evince such attitudes, which are stimulating for pupils and beneficial to all concerned?

The effectiveness of the educational process seems to depend to a large extent on how much latitude is given to teachers in interpreting instructions, apportioning and adapting contents and selecting appropriate methods and solutions. At present, however, as the above-mentioned study points out, the degree of autonomy allowed to schools and teachers varies considerably, even in countries with firmly established traditions in education:

There are marked distances among OECD countries in the extent to which the curriculum-in-action (classroom practice) is circumscribed by regulations issued from higher levels in the administrative hierarchy of a national school system. In some countries e.g. Sweden, Norway and France, central authorities exert strong influence. In the Federal Republic of Germany, much regulating authority is vested in the government of each *Land*. In most states in the United States many regulations governing the work of the schools originate at the school district level. In the United Kingdom, each school has a considerable autonomy in framing its own curriculum within the tangible constraints posed by external examinations and other factors [OECD, 1983*a*, p. 55].

We have observed that the preparation of educational content, in the broad sense, is now guided by the idea that the fostering of certain attitudes, aptitudes and skills, which takes place during the learning process, is in fact more important than the assimilation of knowledge (see in particular what has been said on the inversion of the triad of educational objectives). Basing teacher training on study in a particular discipline with a view to passing on a consignment of knowledge is now, rightly, out of date. On this point we are in agreement with M. Goldschmid (1983), who observes that 'the majority of teachers are appointed on the basis of their specialist knowledge or scientific qualities rather than their gift for teaching' and that 'the saying that a clear grasp of one's subject is all that is needed in order to teach it to others has had its day; the content-based attitude to education, which aims not at the all-round education of the individual but at the mere transmission of theoretical knowledge, is out of date.

Full command of the subject is admittedly indispensable, but it is not enough. Exclusive concentration on the subject itself is no longer acceptable'.[8] (See also Chiesa Azzario, 1983; International Symposium . . ., 1980c; Porter, 1983.)

Taken in this sense, the 'content-based attitude' is an obstacle to innovation in contents. However, it must be said that some countries keep to the traditional system, which provides for scientific training (in one or two disciplines) and a theoretical and practical introduction to the educational sciences (educational psychology). Referring to the content of the training courses for teacher educators, Vandevelde (1983, pp. 26–7) observes:

The training of a teacher educator manifestly consists of two separate kinds of content: 1. Subjects which the teacher educator will be called upon to teach. . . . 2. Subjects which form part of the specifically pedagogical preparation of the teacher educator. These subjects are sometimes subsumed under the generic term 'educational sciences' and broken down into various disciplines: pedagogy, psychology, statistics, didactics, etc. In reality, this breakdown is virtually a replica of the traditional divisions found in schools.

These two groups of disciplines (scientific training and pedagogical training) occupy different proportions of the university timetable from one country to another, but these proportions are always at variance with the new roles expected of teachers. In certain cases the scientific part of the training takes up 70 per cent of the course, in others 90 per cent or even more, so that the future teachers are trained more as researchers in their disciplines than as pedagogues with the task of organizing creative, participatory and formative learning. Nevertheless, some promising research has been done, and there are already a number of subsystems for in-service training which succeed in providing regular refresher courses for all teachers. For several decades, for example, all the socialist countries have possessed structures of this kind, usually known as 'further training subsystems for teachers'.

Here we shall simply argue that the new philosophy which is beginning to influence the determination of goals, objectives and content (taken broadly to include the learning process) should also influence the initial and in-service training of teachers. This is not merely a matter of juggling with the proportions of training given over to the scientific and pedagogical parts of the curriculum or of adding a new discipline (e.g. the theory of communication); it is a question of achieving complete harmony between the objectives, the educational content and the teacher-training subsystem. As Pauvert (1983, pp. 34–5) notes, Unesco has sought in recent years to promote the idea of a common core in the training of all categories of educators:

The origin of the notion of common core may be considered to lie precisely within this ideal of participation, from which moreover parallel or subsequent specializations should not be excluded. This was already expressed in the notion of 'basic education, the common fund of humanity' which emerged when the Organization came into being.

Teacher training therefore makes it possible to promote the inclusion of current world problems (undeniably global and indivisible in scope) in school curricula, is conducive to learning that is more closely in keeping with the purposes of education and provides fresh opportunities for the encouragement of interdisciplinarity and the use of research findings to improve education.

The training of teachers of general subjects does not form a separate subsystem; on the contrary, it can be conceived only in terms of the needs peculiar to that type of education. In the light of foreseeable innovations in objectives and content and on the basis of the methodological framework for a syllabus proposed in the previous chapter, we have attempted to determine which groups of disciplines ought to be included in a common core of initial training for teachers. In view of what has already been said on new educational trends and the proliferation of new forms of education, we shall merely give a straightforward list together with a few comments.

Components of a common core for the training of teachers in educational psychology

1. *The impact of current world problems on education*
    1.1. Environmental education.
    1.2. Education for peace, co-operation and the promotion of humanism in relations between peoples and individuals.
    1.3. Education for democracy, participation, development, etc.
2. *The philosophy of education*
    2.1. Educational axiology and the purposes of education.
    2.2. The purposes (creativity, development of critical faculties, etc.) and the taxomony of educational objectives.
    2.3. The lessons to be learned from education in the past.[9]
    2.4. The philosophy of science as a basis for the incorporation of the scientific disciplines.
3. *General aesthetics* (as a basis for the incorporation of the arts), and design; various combinations according to needs (for teachers of human sciences and the arts).
4. *The impact of management* and systems theory on formal and non-formal education.

5. *Knowledge of the learner*, of human relations and of the quality of life in schools.
6. *The teaching–learning process* in the context of lifelong education and interdisciplinarity.
   6.1. Lifelong self-instruction as the future approach to learning.
   6.2. Curriculum: theory and practice.
   6.3. Experience gained from the learning process; eductational performance.
   6.4. Educational and vocational assessment and guidance: theory and practice.
   6.5. Promotion of stimulating patterns of behaviour: theory and exercises.
   6.6. Audio-visual and computer facilities.
7. *Pedagogical research*
   7.1. The methodology of research.[10]
   7.2. Systematic research and spontaneous research.
   7.3. Application of research findings to educational practice.
8. *The impact of informatics* and communication theory on learning.

We should once again state that a list of this kind is simply a foundation, a minimum to be achieved by approximately the year 2000 and not a model that can meet the needs of every country. A common core of this type should represent between 35 and 40 per cent of the time allocated to the initial training of teachers (4 to 5 years).

Pedagogical training of teacher educators

In certain countries teacher training is carried out by specialized institutions: teacher training colleges, Schools of Education attached to universities, Universität für Bildungswissenschaften (Austria and the Federal Republic of Germany), postgraduate pedagogical courses lasting for one or two years (Federal Republic of Germany), 'pedagogical institutes' with 4- to 5-year courses in the USSR, etc. In such cases the student teachers experience the atmosphere of their future profession from the very first year, and learn in instructive and stimulating surroundings. We may assume that the academic staff, whatever their discipline, also have a great deal of teaching experience and are well informed about the nature and purposes of education today. However, they have no choice but to maintain the existing situation: teaching compartmentalized into disciplines, a school more or less deaf to the messages of the local community and the aspirations of young people, a system of assessment which sets up barriers, etc. In other countries, the teachers who work in pre-university education are trained in the universities alongside future economists and lawyers, with the inevitable result that their pedagogical training and its updating take second place.

Everything that has been learned about organization of contents, ranking of objectives and remedial teaching is passed on or should be passed on by those who train teacher educators. Their work has a multiplier effect that is made even more decisive by the fact that, in certain countries, it is they who are responsible for both the initial and the in-service training of teachers. During a series of meetings organized by Unesco's European Centre for Higher Education in Bucharest, it was the university academics themselves who drew attention to the need to provide all teachers in higher education with pedagogical training; this was particularly important for those who would be responsible for the training of schoolteachers for the coming decades. To bring out more clearly the decisive role of teacher educators in making educational innovations we shall take an example from the book already mentioned entitled *Pygmalion in the Classroom* (Rosenthal and Jacobsen, 1985). In presenting their hypothesis and the results achieved, they emphasize a few particularly eloquent facts.

By observing the work of a great many educators, they singled out many counter-productive, anti-pedagogical and inhibiting patterns of verbal and non-verbal behaviour. From the standpoint of their hypothesis it would have been desirable to discover whether the favourable or unfavourable prejudices of the teachers could bring about a corresponding improvement or deterioration in the intellectual performance of the pupils. For ethical reasons, however, it was decided to test only the hypothesis that favourable prejudices in teachers could raise the intellectual standards of pupils.

To obtain a higher success rate at school, the researchers worked with the teachers. Their programme of educational change was aimed directly at the teachers and indirectly at the pupils; they improved teachers' attitudes to learners by eliminating certain types of behaviour and encouraging others.

The retraining of the teachers chosen for the experimental schools was long and difficult, and some of the teachers were unable to change their attitudes.

Summing up, the authors observe that it is through what he or she says, how and when he says it, the expression on his face, his gestures and perhaps his physical contact that the teacher is able to communicate to the experimental group that he is hoping for an improvement in their intellectual performance. Such communication may have helped the child to learn by changing his or her previous view of himself, his confidence in his own potential, his way of learning and his aptitudes. But what strategy should be adopted to ensure that these discoveries are taken up in the first place by those who train teacher educators, so that through the work of teachers they eventually become part of educational practice?

This example alone lends weight to two fundamental assertions which the whole of this section has sought to defend: the school contains within itself important resources that can contribute to a genuine democratization of education, and the success of an innovation or reform depends on the adoption of a comprehensive, coherent approach.

NOTES

1. During the 1970s, one of the authors of this study encountered experts working in developing countries who, forgetting that they were by definition standard-bearers of progress in educational thinking and research, argued that the Third World countries had no need for consistent methodologies or for research findings.
2. According to Adams and Chen (1980, pp. 270–1): '(a) The initial acceptability of an innovation is a function of the rhetoric used. The more the rhetoric conveys the impression of difference between the innovation and the status quo, the greater the likelihood of rejection. (b) Persistence of an innovation is a function of the innovation's credibility. The greater the gap between promise and performance, the less the credibility. The less the credibility, the less the likelihood of persistence.'
3. On the fiftieth anniversary of the Institute of Psychology and Educational Sciences, Liège (1979), G. De Landsheere made some interesting remarks on attitudes to the human sciences, to the effect that the human sciences, among which psychology plays a central role, are felt by many people as a threat, a source of disruption of the status quo and a hotbed of revolutionary agitation. And they are not wrong. For one thing, as psychology discovers more and more about the developing human being, about the origins of intelligence and personality, it unearths mechanisms and responsibilities that it is often more comfortable to disregard. At the same time, it brings to light sources of alienation and processes of manipulation.
4. This colloquium had repercussions in almost every region. One of the recommendations which the participants addressed to Unesco, namely, that it organize training seminars for researchers, has been carried into effect in Asia by APEID, in co-operation with the National Institute for Educational Research (Tokyo), and has yielded interesting results; among other topics, the seminar dealt with 'the philosophy of education', 'the professional ethics of research', 'research technques', etc.
5. On the training of teachers, see, *inter alia*, De Landsheere (1976), Pauvert (1983). The latter is a summary report based on the programmes of Unesco in this field. In summing up the results of a consultation held in 1983, the author discusses, among other things, approaches and experiments and questions of terminology, agreement and convergence. One section is devoted to future prospects and to the Unesco programme for 1984–89. See also Frey, 1978, where one chapter deals with the repercussions of curriculum reform on the training of teachers.
6. In his study on the United States of America, Christopher Dede raises the prob-

lems of the teacher's status, the attractiveness of the teaching profession and a reform of teacher training.
7. 'The behavioural implications for teachers ... may be summarized as follows:
    (i) they must pay greater attention to the affective development of their pupils;
    (ii) they must be able to diagnose individual learning problems and to invoke the expert assistance of other colleagues or outside specialists or both;
    (iii) they must devise curricula and methods that are adapted to pupils individually or collectively or to both;
    (iv) they must collaborate with colleagues and, where appropriate, with outside experts in determining the school's specific objectives, its general curriculum, plans for using resources and available time, teaching and learning strategies, the evaluation of achievements—what may be described as the concerns of the 'teaching team';
    (v) they must co-operate with parents, representatives of the local community, managers of other socio-cultural activities—the concerns of the 'educational team';
    (vi) they must maintain a continuing dialogue with pupils not only so as to get to know them better but also to make the validity of the curricula and teaching methods fully comprehensible;
    (vii) they must be capable of objectively analysing methods and results and proposing solutions to problems as they arise' [OECD, 1983a, p. 103].
8. In this study, Goldschmid, of the Lausanne Université Polytechnique, proposes a series of eight modules to cover the common core of pedagogical training for teachers. An indication is given of the units that each module comprises.

I *Administration of training*	4 units
II *Self-knowledge, personal aptitudes and skills*	6 units
III *Psychology of trainees*	4 units
IV *Human relations*	4 units
V *Pedagogical relations*	4 units
VI *Teaching/learning strategies and methods*	6 units
VII *Resources, facilities and teaching aids*	6 units
VIII *Learning, assessment and evaluation of training*	5 units

9. Stefan Barsănescu has been training teachers and conducting research for over 60 years. In two editions of his work on the unity of contemporary pedagogy as a science, the second published 40 years after the first, he presents a broad and comprehensive picture that brings out a few fundamental ideas: 1. The scientific character of pedagogy is becoming increasingly evident. 2. The expansion and diversification of pedagogy have not destroyed its unity. 3. Teachers need a general pedagogy (an overall approach to the educational sciences) that is forward-looking and critical; the lessons of the history of education should not be overlooked.
10. G. Mialeret (in De Landsheere, 1976b, p. 12) has written: 'Education is an art and will always be an art. This claim does not conflict with the fact that part of pedagogy is becoming increasingly scientific'. The author of the book also writes: 'Progress in pedagogy suffers from a lack of communication between the researchers and the practitioners of education, the latter being the consumers of research findings.' In many cases, teachers also collaborate with the specialist researchers.

Conclusions

SUGGESTIONS

In the first part of this work we attempted to provide a general analysis of world problems. Such an analysis cannot be expected to win unanimous support on all points because of the diversity of philosophical and political options throughout the world, but it is not the detail of our diagnoses and forecasts which is essential: what matters is that educational objectives, contents and activities in and out of school should be defined on the basis of this type of analysis. An education system which shuns such an analysis and the changes which it implies would be in danger of becoming isolated from the world and thus giving rise to concern and tension. This was the thinking behind our 'methodological framework for a syllabus'.

The constantly increasing speed of change is one of the main aspects of the problems of the modern world. That change is due, specifically, to technological developments and, as we know, it is very difficult for education to keep pace with them. General education must therefore provide *a solid grounding* (a common core of general culture) on which to base any further training, at work or elsewhere. This means that schools must be able to live with change and prepare pupils for change. Because of these two requirements, there must be sufficient flexibility in contents and in the structure of the future school and permanent contact must be ensured between schools and the outside world, between schools and the cultural and economic life of the national and international community. In some countries, it has proved possible to interest heads of businesses in the content of technical education. A similar relationship may be imagined between general education and the civil or political authorities, academies and learned societies.

However valuable the knowledge built up by the natural sciences and by technology, it will not be able to satisfy all aspirations and guarantee the happiness of mankind. Men and women must also learn to control their own personalities and their own history on the basis of a new ethic. This new ethic could perhaps be described as *neo-humanism*, in the sense of a reassertion of human dignity, receptiveness to spiritual values, the stepping up of human activities aimed at the full and balanced development of the individual, an attachment not only to traditional values (such as loyalty towards the local, regional and national community) but also to the values of our times such as international solidarity, respect for other communities, democratic relationships and, finally, a feeling of confidence and responsibility in relation to the future of human society. It is particularly important that education systems, inspired by this sort of approach, ensure that it is translated in terms of educational contents and the educational environment, that is to say, not only curricula but also the quality of school life, learning methods, the verbal and non-verbal behaviour patterns of the teaching staff, relationships between teachers and learners and all types of instructional activities.

In fact, content and environment are in constant interaction at the school level and the question of the content of education cannot, therefore, be dissociated from all of the influences originating in the school and out-of-school environment as a whole. Moreover, schools cannot be attuned to world problems merely by including in the curriculum a few facts about democracy and participation, human rights, peace and disarmament, ecology and the environment, etc. All aspects of school life, the training of teachers and the management of educational institutions must also be modified in the light of educational goals. It should be borne in mind that the content of education is not wholly programmed or explicit. The implicit or latent content also plays an important role, which is considerably more important than the one traditionally attributed to it by teachers. However much a teacher may talk of high ideals, it is certain that if his or her non-verbal behaviour (acts and attitudes to values and to the children) conveys an impression of personal indifference to those ideals, the explicit content will not have the desired effect.

We had these ideas in mind in attempting to define what would or should be the contents for tomorrow's school, the criteria and the solutions which should be applied in order to develop a relevant curriculum, the factors and stages in any reform. This is not the place to list the components of the desirable content of education, but it should be remembered that their number is inevitably growing and this makes it more than ever necessary to organize a multi-dimensional, balanced and integrated content. This is what we have tried to do, and the reader will have observed that we have tackled the problem without accepting the idea of a gradual reduction in the importance and functions of the general school or the idea of dropping certain traditional contents such as history or the history of literature, systematic learning of the mother tongue or of arithmetic, etc.

We were aware of the difficulties involved and looked for indicators of the relevance of content and for solutions which could help educators in their task. It should be said immediately that *indicators* form an indivisible set devised in accordance with the dynamics of science and culture, the requirements of the learning process and, always, the ultimate goal; the educational ideal of each education system, conceived in the light of the prospects and requirements of the world of tomorrow. It is therefore impossible to proceed by way of exclusion, adopting either the idea that learning is a matter of effort and accordingly transforming examinations into inhibiting and, hence, antidemocratic tests, or else the idea that modern learning should be seen as an endless game, an agreeable, optional and leisurely stroll from one subject, one school and even one country to another. Serious endeavour does not exclude play and, vice versa, play does not eliminate the need for perseverance and sound learning. As for the *solutions* which will increasingly help those responsible for the design of explicit contents, teachers and learners to master the explosion of information, the extraordinary impact of technology on human life and school learning and also the various problems of the modern world, we should like to draw special attention to: *the promotion of interdisciplinarity* in the organization of contents and the design, execution and evaluation of the teaching–learning process; the relevant application of the principle of *lifelong education*; the contribution of *informatics* and computer-assisted learning; the assistance provided to the school by *parallel education* and, particularly, the mass media; educational television channels could take over increasingly important educational tasks in the future, throughout the world; a better division of tasks between *school and out-of-school education* and the promotion of open and flexible structures (multiple and combinable options); *the infusional approach* for the promotion of the new types of education in the teaching–learning process.

Finally, it seems to us that: any curriculum reform depends to a great extent on the quality of the preparation which precedes it and the pedagogical standards prevailing in the school environment. The task of carrying out the *experiments* which should, normally, precede any reform and that of raising the *awareness* of those actively involved in this reform fall to *educational research* in the broad sense of the term; the *initial and in-service training of teachers* should develop and adapt to the new requirements of a relevant curriculum. In many countries, this problem most probably concerns the in-service training of teachers or the pedagogical training of teacher educators.

Conclusions

But, while paying special attention to these two subsystems—educational research and teacher training—we do not overlook the other factors and agents contributing to a reform of the contents of general education: pupils and parents, learned societies and associations of philosophers, cultural societies and sports associations, representatives of the different sectors of social life such as industry, agriculture, commerce, tourism, social services, etc.

OBSTACLES

Throughout this work we have attempted to demonstrate that the problems confronting educational decision-makers and teachers are formidable in terms of their complexity and the pressures to which they give rise. Education systems are not insensitive to the national and international environment, and an awareness of the problems is not in itself sufficient to produce change, however much change is desired. In the world of education, as elsewhere, any rational approach to the future runs up against a certain number of passionately held ideas, vested interests and misconceptions that stand in the way of change or innovation. Planners and decision-makers in the education sector will have to overcome many difficulties and much resistance in order to adapt the contents of education to the requirements of tomorrow's world.

We shall only mention four major difficulties here:

1. The difficulty of forecasting the socio-political, scientific and technological future in a world in which the speed of change is increasing.

2. A certain almost natural resistance to change on the part of education systems.

3. The inadequacy of the financial, human and technological resources available to educational decision-makers for large-scale changes.

4. The divergent or incompatible ideas and interests of the various agents of change in the educational world: decision-makers, administrators, teachers, parents, pupils, etc.

The problems are obviously not restricted to those which we have listed. For example, many countries are at present in a state of armed conflict and it is unlikely that they will be able to prepare for the future while the present gives so much cause for concern.

We shall not dwell further on the first point, the relative unpredictability of the future, having already devoted so much attention to it that the entire first part of our work may be considered as an attempt to reduce the area of unpredictability. We shall merely point out that the future is doubtless easier to predict and to control in societies where there is a community of values and objectives and where the population is extensively involved in the preparation and implementation of decisions than in those where the population has not made its own the values and objectives of its leaders.

A certain resistance to change may be said to be inherent in education systems since education is essentially the transmission to the new generation of the knowledge, know-how and attitudes of the previous generation. Teachers, having received their training in years gone by, do not always have an opportunity to update their professional knowledge. Hence the natural conservatism of the system which is not easy to overcome.

Other factors have recently contributed to education systems' resistance to change.

First, the quantitative expansion of the 1950s and 1960s was accompanied by an expansion on the administrative side and a trend towards bureaucracy, entailing a rational approach to management, a trend towards the standardization of procedures, the distribution of power on a hierarchical basis, the limitation of opportunities for genuine participation and the stifling of initiative to a greater or lesser degree.

Second, the failure of qualitative reforms in many countries in recent decades has generated a certain degree of apathy on the part of the systems towards new activities.

Third, since 1973, and the recession which began at that time, the education sector gives the impression of having been relegated to a low level of priority and neglected in favour of sectors regarded as being more immediately important such as the economy, defence, promotion of technology, etc. This loss of priority has prompted education systems in certain countries to withdraw into themselves.

In connection with the inadequacy of financial and other resources, we have shown elsewhere that the unit costs of education have tended to stabilize or increase very slightly over recent decades. One consequence in some countries has been a reduction in the purchasing power of teachers, which has dealt a heavy blow to their social and professional status. This state of affairs has not helped to stimulate the creativity of this important category of the *dramatis personae* of education.

Technological progress has admittedly increased the resources available to teachers but here again, with the exception of a few particularly wealthy countries, most schools in both the Third World and the industrialized countries have not managed fully to exploit these new resources. Financial factors, sometimes compounded by a lack of know-how, are responsible for this under-utilization.

Conclusions

Several changes must be noted in relation to human resources:

1. The ageing of the teaching staff, due, in particular, to the unwillingness of administrators to recruit new teachers after the feverish years of explosive growth, and to the preference of young people today for professions other than teaching (a difficult and relatively poorly paid profession in some countries).

2. The difficulties which some countries experience in providing adequate training for teachers hastily recruited during the years of euphoria between 1950 and 1970 without sufficient preliminary training.

3. The political stance adopted by teachers in some countries which has earned them the mistrust of governments. The latter problem has not helped teachers to obtain greater access to the financial and technical resources they require in order to improve their teaching.

Our list of obstacles to be overcome includes the differing ideas and interests of the agents of change in education. In this connection, let us recall several by no means unexpected assertions confirmed by the research undertaken by R. Adams (Adams and Chen, 1981).

The widespread acceptance of an innovation will depend on the extent to which it may be perceived by certain groups as infringing on their power—the less threatened that power appears, the greater the acceptance of the innovation. Similarly, its acceptance will depend upon the extent to which the resultant advantages seem to outweigh the disadvantages incurred (relative costs). Finally, an innovation's chances of success depend on the stability of the personnel responsible for its implementation.

This last assertion reminds us that some plans for innovation or reform have suffered as the result of very frequent changes of government officials, the viewpoint and interests of the new educational decision-makers or officials often being different from that of their predecessors. A period of four to five years and sometimes longer is often needed before a reform can be put fully into effect, during which time any major change in the composition of the body of decision-makers produces a situation that is frequently unfavourable to the reform, as the experience of the international development financing agencies has shown.

Lastly, we should like to draw attention to something on which views very often differ, the relationship between school and out-of-school education. While traditional teachers remain attached to the development of schools and formal education, other, non-formal modes of education such as the media, on-the-job training, in-service training, etc., are becoming increasingly important. Teachers' inadequate information about the educational potential of the new media is one of the factors in their resistance. A reduction of national spending on formal education in order to promote non-formal modes of education, such as vocational training to bolster rural employment, does not seem to enjoy the support of the middle and upper classes. The relatively privileged classes give even greater emphasis to the promotion of education at the higher levels, which obviously costs much more than primary or adult education.

It may be said, in conclusion, that each society gets the schools it deserves. If the values pursued by society are different from those taught in schools, the latter will become isolated institutions, sources of illusions and naïve Utopias.

HOPES

Our study may have raised more problems than it has solved, in spite of our efforts to maintain a balance between unsolved problems and possible solutions. In our own defence, we would say that the works we consulted, although generally instructive on the critical level, seemed to us to be much more reticent when it came to making suggestions or working out new and viable formulae. Another reason is that we have deliberately avoided giving our study a normative character; rather than make statements of principle we have preferred to give a range of examples which are probably more convincing to planners and educators. Similarly, we have perhaps paid more attention to those of the works consulted that appeared to us more realistic. This does not mean that we would be unhappy if future developments confirmed forecasts which seemed to us to be, if Utopian, at least optimistic, and invalidated those which foresaw catastrophe!

Educational research covers a huge area today. In each particular field, there are different approaches and different conclusions. The many fundamental concepts are periodically subjected to analysis and reappraisal, and it is not always easy to distinguish between realism and Utopia, between originality at any price and the type of originality which foreshadows what is probable or possible. Decision-makers, planners and educators need balanced and critical information digests and guides. Works of this type, which could provide correct and relevant information to the different social groups concerned by educational reform, should be published regularly and made available to these groups. As regards the new educational themes (education for peace and human rights, for a new international economic order, for participation and democracy, etc.), we should like to express the hope that all the agencies in the United Nations system and all the international and national institutions concerned will show greater decisiveness and perseverance in applying the recommendations adopted by the international community.

Our research has convinced us that education could and should play a fundamental role during the next two decades; by virtue of its goals and its quality, it is education that could lead mankind towards healthy co-operation and a peaceful life, prosperity and culture. Designers of general education curricula and educators must not be daunted by the immensity of the tasks they have to face in order to prepare the younger generation for a constructive role in the future of the world: for what is at stake is the very survival of mankind and of the values essential to each individual.

The present world crisis is not superficial and temporary, limited to the economic sector or any particular aspect of life and human activity. It has very varied sources or causes and is primarily due to the unsuitability, in relation to needs, of structures, relationships and attitudes, of the order prevailing in the world and the relationships between nations; it calls for a reappraisal of the international socio-economic order and at the same time of ideas, values and behaviour. The depth and scale of educational activity mean that education has a very large role to play in this period of great transformations. It must prepare people to cope with unpredictable situations but also to set desirable changes in motion. It must develop a critical spirit to counter anti-educational influences but it must also create and reinforce attitudes capable of leading the world in the direction of peace and co-operation. The contents of education are of particular importance for the success of this mission. They must provide the necessary knowledge and know-how for life in a world which is deeply influenced by science, but must also promote appropriate attitudes towards science, in order to restore the balance between science and ethics, the material and the spiritual.

Annex

The study of the future: an outline

BASIC CONCEPTS

Various designations have been applied to research on the future development of mankind. The terms most frequently encountered in English and French are: futurology (*futurologie*), forecasting (*prévision*), futuristics (which does not seem to have an exact French equivalent), *prospective* and *futuribles* (French terms).

The term, 'futurology', which was coined in the United States by Ossip Flechtheim, seems unsatisfactory as the future cannot be the subject of a scientific investigation in the strict sense of the term. It has often been said that the future contains an element of necessity, a random element and an element of volition. It is possible to make forecasts about 'marked trends', predetermined phenomena and the necessary; options and actions which have been deliberately undertaken may be discussed beforehand; but there can be no rigorous forecasting in respect of the random element (see Cornish, 1978, pp. 254 et seq.)

The English term, 'futuristics', which, as yet, has no French equivalent, seems more appropriate in that it defines the activity not in terms of methodology but with reference to its subject or field of investigation—'things to come'—albeit rather vaguely.

The term 'forecasting' (*prévision*), is employed very frequently but contains a hint of the 'prophetizing' which is just what today's analysts of the future are rightly trying to eliminate from their approach.

The term, *prospective*, is more apt. It was proposed by Gaston Berger at the beginning of the 1950s and is derived from the Latin, *prospicere*, 'to look forward'. This look at the future differs fundamentally from a *rétrospective*, which deals with established facts while the future has yet to be created. For its proponents, *la prospective* is an art or a method rather than a science. Pierre Massé, who was an active member of Berger's Centre International de Prospective and was later the French Commissaire Général au Plan, has written that 'It is a search for a new type of knowledge which views all future situations as the consequence of our actions, free or otherwise, and of the reactions, predictable or otherwise, of the rest of the world.' Another thinker in the same group, J. de Bourbon-Busset, has said that its aim is not to guess the probable nature of the future but to prepare a future which is desirable and, going even further, to make it probable. Thus, it is clear that, unlike futurology and forecasting, *la prospective* implies a commitment to action, as the anticipation of future trends enables man to guide developments, assisting and hastening or else obstructing them. The participants in the International Symposium on the Evolution of the Content of General Education Over the Next Two Decades, which was held in Paris in July 1980, correctly declared in their *Final Report* that, 'in contrast with forecasting, future studies [*prospective*] are the methodical investigation of the future starting from an approach that favours change and newness while avoiding, unlike futurology, a break between the past and the future'.

In the 1960s, Bertrand de Jouvenel, a compatriot of Gaston Berger, invented the term, *futurible* to designate a subject of research on the foreseeable future. The term is used in the plural (*futuribles*) to mean the range of possible futures. According to the *Encyclopaedia Universalis*:

Futurible as seen from the present designates a future which may be achieved with a specific scientific and technological base and socio-political context. Thus, series of different *futuribles* are established at any point in their formulation; the march of time eliminates some and reveals others, exposing the 'foreknown' elements of the dominant processes that forecasters refer to as 'marked trends'; top-level decision-makers are then brought together to assess social priorities, co-ordinate expectations and construct alternative models.

A cursory examination of the literature concerned with this type of reflection and research shows that the most neutral and, consequently, the most appropriate term is 'study of the future' (*étude du futur* or *étude des futurs*). It should be added that the idea of a certain future is losing ground nowadays as may be seen from the title of a well-known publication published by the OECD in 1979:: *Facing the Future: Mastering the Probable and Managing the Unpredictable*. Some writers have treated the present or the immediate future as an age of uncertainty. Professor Edmund J. King, of the University of London, was editor of a book with a most significant title: *Education for Uncertainty* (1979). When the idea of a certain future is dropped, it becomes possible to see the future in various ways. In his introduction to *Futurism in Education: Methodologies* (Hencley and Yates, 1974). E. C. Joseph draws a distinction between several types of future: a feasible future, a probabilistic future, a forecastable future, a plannable future, etc.

MAJOR TRENDS IN THE STUDY OF THE FUTURE

It may be asserted without fear of contradiction that concern with the future is as old as religion, which has always paid great attention to the future of the individual and the community. The religious works with which we are familiar present two conflicting concepts of time: a linear view of history held by the Zoroastrians and encountered in Judaeo-Christian religions and a cyclical view which lies at the heart of Hinduism and Buddhism. The first view usually sees the ultimate future of human communities in terms of the appearance of a new city, the advent of a kingdom of God from which death, war, injustice and evil will be banished forever. The cyclical view of history does not exclude the idea that history, while moving in circles, may advance spirally in a certain direction, as Toynbee explained in *Civilization on Trial* (1948).

After the religious views, brief mention should be made of philosophical views of history: the Utopianism of Plato, Thomas More and Campanella, the evolutionism of many nineteenth-century thinkers among whom the supporters of the idea of 'limitless progress' occupy an important place; the Marxist materialist and dialectical interpretation of history, which also implies a belief in the ultimate achievement of socio-economic justice, etc.

Two different movements in the modern period have been concerned with the study of the future: firstly, there was the development of a new literary genre, science fiction, whose most famous representatives were Jules Verne (the author of sixty fictional works from 1863 to 1903), H. G. Wells and Aldous Huxley; then, the scientific or para-scientific approach which has developed since the end of the Second World War.

Scientific study of the future was started in the United States of America in the 1950s by the researchers of the Rand Corporation. Initially, these studies were concerned with military and technological issues. It was not long before Herman Kahn's team began work. Kahn managed to free future studies from the limits imposed by the earliest researchers. Thereafter, it was not only the development of science and technology (including the art of war) which attracted interest, but also the development of the economy, society and culture. Since the 1970s, this interest has also extended to the physical and natural environment of human societies and its future development. Forecasting methods and techniques have been considerably improved since 1945. The Rand Corporation had already employed the Delphi method, based on the periodic consultation of experts through questionnaires and repeated brainstorming sessions which led to contrasting scenarios reflecting different trends. Other methods were soon added such as projection and extrapolation, the preparation of 'maps' of the future, modelling, games, simulations, etc. The use of computers will eventually enable future-oriented studies to make a great leap forward.

It is important to point out that the new technique of building models of the future involves a volitional element as well as forecasting. These models generally revolve around one central idea, target, value or goal. For example, the World Order model (1973) was directed towards the three major objectives of peace, well-being and identity. Bariloche's model was guided by the idea of justice and drew on the image of an egalitarian society (see Cole, 1977; *Futures*, 1982). The International Development Strategies in the three declarations relating to the United Nations Decades for Development (1960, 1970 and 1980) may be included in this same category of 'voluntarist forecasting'. The Declaration of the Third Decade reaffirms the determination of the international community to establish the New International Economic Order, to promote the economies of developing countries, to reduce the inequalities between rich and poor countries and to eradicate poverty and dependence. The GNP of developing countries should achieve an annual growth of the order of 7 per cent (agricultural production: 4 per cent and industrial production: 9 per cent) according to this new International Development Strategy. Efforts should be made at world level to achieve the following objectives by the year 2000: food self-sufficiency, full employment, health and education for all. The United Nations model constructed by Leontief (1977), which draws its inspiration from the organization's International Development Strategy, envisages halving the per capita income gap between rich and poor countries by the year 2000 while preserving the quality of the world's physical environment.

Few organizations were engaged on future research before 1960. Many 'futurologists' were 'militant prophets' or isolated theoreticians. But a new stage of joint reflection and research on a national or even international scale began nearly two decades ago.[1] Among the many practitioners of this new trend, mention may be made of the Club of Rome, the Association Internationale de Futuristes, the International Association Futuribles, the World Future Society and the OECD 'Interfutures' group.[2]

A systematic account of the recent development of future studies was provided by Sam Cole in *World Futures, the Great Debate* (Freeman and Jahoda, 1978, pp. 9–50). It deals with the years 1965–76 and shows the decisive influence which the political climate in each period had on the general direction of work done by those engaged in future research. The first period (the 1960s) was marked by a desire for continued economic growth and a certain optimism in relation to technology. Its most prominent representatives were Arthur C. Clarke, Colin Clarke, B. Fuller and Herman Kahn. Towards the end of the 1960s, the population explosion and the deterioration of the environment caused serious concern. A new neo-Malthusian school was born. Joseph Spengler warned the poor countries about overpopulation. Ann and Paul Ehrlich spread the concept of an ecological disaster. Dennis Meadows and his team took over the model created by Forrester and reached the conclusion that the rapid exhaustion of non-renewable resources necessarily placed limits upon growth. According to Sam Cole, the third period in the development of future studies was characterized by a realization of the need to live with the constraints and limits of nature and ecology. R. Dumont and E. F. Schumacher represent this new current of thought. We now come to a fourth period characterized by models which Sam Cole considers as belonging to the 'second generation', such as the model of a strategy for survival advocated by N. Mesarović and E. Pestel (1974); the world input-output model of W. Leontief (started in 1973); the Japanese model of world development put forward by the team of Yoichi Kaya which advocates a rethinking of the international division of labour; the model designed to satisfy essential needs by redistributing wealth within each region, put forward by the Bariloche team; and, finally, the RIO (Reshaping the International Order) model put forward Jan Tinbergen (1977). At the end of his account, Sam Cole also mentions the 'Soviet point of view on growth' which is particularly critical of Western futurology.

The following is a brief description of several general trends which are apparent in the recent development of future studies.

1. Many researchers are attempting to escape from the conservative 'extrapolationism' of the early work in this field, which saw the future as the

continuation of the present and the past ('a future without surprises'), and are moving towards a critical or radical revolutionary form of future study (see Bengtsson, 1975). Many works are distinctly pessimistic and sometimes 'catastrophist', particularly those which have appeared in the last decade, although there is also no shortage of realistic work.

2. There is a growing awareness of the impossibility of achieving complete objectivity in future studies. Willis Harman, one of the representatives of this new trend of thinking, is correct when he writes (Boucher and Amara, 1977) that all future studies and forecasts somehow or other have a normative aspect, which may be explicit or concealed. He is not bothered by the normative nature of these studies; he merely considers that, from the point of view of scientific objectivity, it is necessary to define from the outset one's position, that is to say, the norms and values underlying one's definition of the future and one's plan of action.

3. While the first futurist studies generally produced unilinear forecasts, consideration is increasingly being given to alternative futures based on different normative modes or models. The costs and benefits of each option under consideration are then analysed to produce conclusions relevant to the choice of subsequent action.

4. Recent future studies reveal an acute awareness of the existence of world crises: in population, energy, the environment, food, North–South relations and many other fields. These crises have since caught the attention of the media and have become a part of day-to-day discussions. The very scale and depth of these crises have produced an important change in public perceptions, transforming momentary or short-term interest and preoccupation with this type of problem into a long-term view and concern.

5. Another change worth mentioning concerns the preparatory *training* of *future researchers*. Scientists (physicists and mathematicians) and engineers initially led the way in future studies, but more recently, at least in the United States, contributions to the progress and expansion of the new 'discipline' have come mainly from researchers with different backgrounds (social sciences, humanities and behavioural sciences).

6. Finally, it should be noted that, for some time, future studies have no longer been the preserve of professionals. They have given rise to a certain number of *social movements*, such as 'the future is in our hands' movement which has sprung up in the Scandinavian countries. Pacifists, ecologists, civil rights and other movements are now also interested in future studies and have contributed to reflection in this area.

Many public and private institutions have been set up in order to conduct studies of this type. For over fifteen years the development of research has been assessed by several international conferences concerned with the study of the future (Oslo 1967, Kyoto 1970, Bucharest 1972, etc.). A World Future Studies Federation (WFSF) has also been in existence since 1967. Major conferences within the United Nations and its Specialized Agencies have kindled interest in reflection and action in response to the problems of today and the challenges of tomorrow. In 1974, the United Nations Institute for Training and Research (UNITAR) organized in Moscow a conference on the United Nations and the future. The major world conferences of the

United Nations have always had a forward-looking dimension, such as, for example, the United Nations Conference on the Human Environment in Stockholm (1972), the World Population Conference in Bucharest (1974), the United Nations Conference on Human Settlements (Habitat) in Vancouver (1976), the World Conference on Employment in Geneva (ILO, 1976), the World Food Conference in Rome (FAO, 1974), etc.

THEORIES OF THE FUTURE

The actual content of writers' conclusions about the shape of the future may be said to fall into three major categories: many writers stress the major trends which are shaping the future of mankind; others highlight the problems which mankind must tackle and for which it must find satisfactory solutions; a third group of thinkers concentrate on the promises of the future and the hopes it might fulfil.

We shall quote two present-day writers, one American and one French, on the subject of long-term trends. The former, John Naisbitt, aims to describe the new American society which is now being formed. The latter, Gérard Bonnot, attempts to define major world trends.

For Naisbitt, current trends are away from the industrial society towards the computer society, from 'forced' technology towards high technology, from a national economy to a world economy, from the short term to the long term, from centralization to decentralization, from institutionalized assistance towards self-help, from representative democracy towards participatory democracy, from hierarchical organization towards network organization (Naisbitt, 1982; Sachs, 1984).

According to Bonnet (1983), the new world trends are: the demise of economic nationalism, power-sharing, the return of man with the computer age, the ascendancy of temporary occupations (as against careers) and of provisional technologies, etc., the trend towards short periods of study within the context of lifelong education and, finally, the rediscovery of the body and the discovery of a new *joie de vivre*.

With reference to the perception of problems, W. W. Harman and M. E. Rosenberg distinguish between two types of problems which will have to be faced in the future in a study for Unesco (1971) on the methodology of future studies in education: social problems and metaproblems of society. Attention is drawn to the following problems in the first category: social instability, unequal distribution of wealth and income between individuals and peoples, dehumanization of individuals, threats to freedoms and individual rights, breakdown of the balance of ecosystems, the global threat of mass destruction of human beings and nature.

In discussing the metaproblems of society, the writers refer to: the crisis in the image of man and society, the crisis of authority and legitimacy in social institutions, the crisis relating to the effectiveness of social structures, the crisis of management and government.

Another view, equally pessimistic, regards the future in terms of three explosions (the population explosion, the explosion of knowledge and that of rising expectations), three problems (war and peace, man and the environment, culture and technology), three conflicts (between the soul and the external world, between science and spirituality, between individual liberty and social organization), and, finally, three gaps (between the developed and developing countries, between knowledge and wisdom, between power and love).

Problems are referred to more often than positive trends in the list of features of the modern world drawn up by Ervin Laszlo:
1. Emergence of interdependence.
2. Underdevelopment and overdevelopment of various regions of the world.
3. Overexploitation of resources.
4. Impoverishment of the physical environment and ecology.
5. Exhaustion of fossil fuels.
6. Considerable reduction of forests nurtured by rain and fertile soil.
7. Desertification.
8. New geographical distribution of mankind (85 per cent of the world's population will soon live in the poor countries).
9. Problem of the gap between various countries.
10. Collapse of old cultures and the crisis of Westernization.
11. Excess population growth.
12. Disparity in research and development (95 per cent of research capacity is located in a few developed countries and research is controlled by the multinational and transnational companies).

On the promise of the future, reference may be made to the works of those for whom the progress of science and technology is central to history. Thus, many writers see the future in a particularly favourable light (in terms of computers and information technology, the colonization of space and other forms of scientific and technological progress) (see Berry, 1974; Stine, 1975).

Diverging trends?

Some predictions are based on a clear distinction between societies which are said to be egalitarian and those which are considered as non-egalitarian. The work on the future of education by Bengtsson (1975) is based on this distinction.

Other researchers such as Willis Harman make a distinction between economic and post-economic rather than between equal and unequal. According to Harman, the future may see the emergence of two contrasting types of society: a society in the third stage of industrial development or, more precisely, a post-industrial society, to use Daniel Bell's terminology; and a society based on the individual in which new humanist and post-economic values will appear and be institutionalized.[3]

The determining factor in the first type of society is technology. The process of change would be continuous whereas human considerations have pride of place in the second type of society and change involves a break with the past.

It is likely that change in advanced societies (egalitarian or otherwise) will occur between these two extremes under the combined effect of these two major trends. We see the future of developed societies in terms of a permanent dialectic between the economic and the post-economic, between the material and the cultural, between machines and man, and between the institutional and the personal.

STUDIES ON THE FUTURE OF EDUCATION

Many future studies which are global and general in nature pay little attention to the position of education in tomorrow's society. Their forecasts are more concerned with more easily quantifiable sectors such as population and the economy. Nevertheless, several studies of this type such as those by A. Toffler (1970, 1974, 1981) and A. Herrera (1976) deal at length with the future of education.

Specific studies on the future of education may be arranged in five catagories according to their sponsors.

The first group is composed of works dealing with the future of education in a specific country carried out in connection with the preparation of long-term development plans; for example, in Denmark, in France and in several countries of the Third World.

Secondly, several non-governmental, regional and international organizations have also been very active in the field of studies of the future of education. One thinks for example of the work of the European Cultural Foundation (established in 1954), which has devoted several major works to the future of education in the region since 1968 under its Plan Europe 2000 (see Bengtsson, 1975; Fragnière, 1976; Schwartz, 1973).

Mention should also be made of the interest shown by the Club of Rome in the future of education, which finds expression in its well-known publication: *No Limits to Learning, Bridging the Human Gap*.

In the United States, where the Federal Government has a very limited role in socio-economic planning, the Carnegie Foundation for the Advancement of Education set up in 1967 a special commission to consider the vital questions which must be tackled by higher education in the United States as the year 2000 approaches. The Carnegie Commission for Higher Education produced some 21 reports between 1967 and 1973 which are summarized in a digest published in 1974. The Carnegie Foundation has also engaged in other activities. The Carnegie Council on Policy Studies in Higher Education continued the work of the commission and published a series of reports leading up to a *Final Report* (1980).

The reasons why Americans, in their studies of the future of the educational sector, have been more concerned with higher education than with education at other levels appear to us to be quite clear. With the launching of Sputnik, America awoke from a relatively long sleep, abandoning easy solutions, and began to consider how to catch up in the teaching of science and technology, particularly at the university level. Recent interest in projects relating to 'excellence' derives partly from this same political concern.

Another private organization interested in the future of education in the

The study of the future: an outline

United States of America is the Aspen Institute for Humanistic Studies, which, in 1976, organized a conference on 'The future of institutionalized schooling'.

Thirdly, Unesco, as an international organization, has made a major contribution to the promotion of the idea of educational planning and also to the advancement of certain guidelines for the formulation of educational policies. The best example of this second type of effort was the publication of the report of the International Commission for the Development of Education, *Learning to Be* (Faure et al., 1972), which certainly had a major impact at world level. Unesco was also responsible for the organization of several meetings at regional and international level for the purpose of thinking about 'the future development of education' (see Unesco, 1985*b*); the last of these was an international meeting held in November 1980 in Paris. Equally important was the organization by Unesco of a major 'International Symposium on the Evolution of the Content of General Education Over the Next Two Decades' (Paris, 7–11 July 1980). This symposium was one of the major sources of inspiration for the present work and gave rise to many studies both before and after the actual meeting.

The International Institute of Educational Planning (IIEP) which has played a significant role in disseminating the idea of planning within countries of the Third World, contributed to thinking about the future of education through the organization of two seminars in Paris: one in October 1978, which resulted in the publication of a large collection of articles (IIEP, 1980); the other, on the theme of 'Education in the 1980s; some key problems', in May 1981, during which discussions centred on a document prepared by Philip Coombs (1981).

Furthermore, the IIEP held a seminar on 'Prospects of educational planning related to contemporary development problems' (Paris, October 1983) at which certain contributions were connected with our theme.

Fourthly, also at the intergovernmental level, the OECD has produced many interesting studies in the field of manpower and educational planning. In 1973 it published a work on *Long-range Policy Planning in Education* following a conference held in Paris in June 1969 on experience in, and prospects for, this type of planning in the industrialized countries. The OECD has been responsible for several valuable works on the future of education in the industrialized countries.[5]

A fifth type of study consists of individual reflections on the future of education. These may also be placed in several major categories:

1. Studies on the methodology of educational forecasting (by writers such as J. S. Armstrong, R. G. Davis, G. M. Dobrov, B. Hudson and J. Bruno, R. W. Hostrop, S. P. Hencley and J. R. Yates, etc.). It is worth recalling that an article which takes stock of studies on the methodology of educational forecasting was prepared for Unesco in connection with its international symposium (1980*k*).

2. General studies of the future of educational systems. The following are among the many authors responsible for major works of a general nature which have appeared in recent years: C. Hummel (1977), T. Husen (1979); P. A. Coggin (1979); P. Coombs (1981). There are so many studies of this

sort that some writers have produced descriptive bibliographies, running at times to several hundred pages (see Glines, 1979) and collections of documents including one published by the World Future Society, which is the product of the first conference on education held by that society in the United States (Kierstead, et al., 1979).

3. Future studies of education which are of a general nature may be classified in terms of the authors' approach. Some writers are particularly interested in the contribution of education to social change or economic development. Others examine the relationship between education and culture as a whole or certain aspects of culture such as science and technology, communication and the media, ethics, etc. The demographic aspect of education has always attracted the attention of many future analysts, as has the role which education plays or could play in the achievement of certain national objectives such as the equalization of opportunity, the democratization of society, full employment, etc. Interest in many of these goals has grown with the crisis which began in 1973. A selective annotated bibliography of studies of this type was produced by Rosemary Di Carlo (1980) for Unesco's Division of Educational Policy and Planning. It was only a few years ago that researchers began to be interested in the present and future role of education in tackling the major problems of mankind: education and international understanding, education and the safeguarding of the natural environment, education and the renewal of ethical and spiritual values and, finally, education and the new international order. A recent article entitled 'L'education comparée et l'éducation internationale' (Comparative Education and International Education), by Angel Diego Marquez (in the journal, *Education Comparée*, No. 31, May 1983, which is devoted to the future of educational sciences and is published by the Association francophone d'éducation comparée) offers an extremely interesting overall view of this new trend in world education. There is also a special number of the *International Review of Education*, Vol. 28, No. 4, 1982, which deals with education and the New International Economic Order.

4. The new economics of education. The economic crisis in recent years and the pressure which it has exerted on educational budgets in many countries have led a number of researchers to consider a form of education for the future which is more economical in the use of human and financial resources. One popular theme with economists is the evolution of educational expenditure. The following are among the many studies on this theme: Charles Benson, *Education Finance in the Coming Decade*, 1978; Philip H. Coombs (Coombs and Chaudhury, 1981); J. C. Eicher (1982); G. Carcelles, 'Development of education in the world' in the *International Review of Education*, Vol. 15, No. 2-3, 1979. Another concern of educational economists, as can be seen from a recent general article in the journal *Futuribles* (Sachs, 1984)[6] is the mobilization of new resources for education, particularly at the local level.

5. Some future-oriented studies of education deal only with one specific type or level of education (technical education, university education, etc.). A selective list of these studies is provided in the bibliography by Ulrika von Haumeder (1979).

6. No discussion of the future of education could fail to mention certain

current studies on accelerated learning and the raising of the intelligence quotient (IQ) and learning readiness of young people by various scientific techniques (including biotechnology). Some of the works and articles mentioned by Di Carlo (1980) under the title 'Education and the Individual' deal precisely with this particular theme (see Chall and Mirsky, 1978; Lozanov, 1979; Schwartz, 1980; Unesco, 1978a).

7. Johan van Bruggen, in his case-study has concentrated on what he refers to as reasonable expectations in relation to society in the first two decades of the twenty-first century. It is worth pointing out, without going into detail, that other researchers before him have employed this method. H. Shane (1977) refers to future changes in the contents of education as forecast by teachers, learners and others interested in education.

The role which education could play in preparing young people to tackle the challenges of the future more effectively has been the subject of discussion for several years. This type of future-oriented education has already been introduced in some countries, including the United States of America. Ossip Flechtheim, a professor of political science, wrote an essay in 1943 in which he called for the teaching of futurology as an independent discipline or subject. Alvin Toffler was one of the first teachers (1966) to give a course on future studies at the New School for Social Research in New York.

A series of surveys conducted by H. W. Eldredge, professor of sociology at Dartmouth College (Canada), shows clearly that at least 475 courses were being taught in various institutions on this type of subject at the beginning of the 1970s. A rapid increase in this type of education has been observed since that time at secondary and primary levels as well as in the universities (see Cornish, 1978, pp. 212 et seq.).

In Europe at the beginning of the 1960s, Robert Jungk was advocating the establishment of workshops for the exploration and construction of the future in which ordinary citizens would play an active part. Alvin Toffler laid great stress on the importance of developing the aptitudes and skills of learners which would help them to face the future: imagination, anticipation, innovation and creativity (see Rassekh, 1983). Kauffman (1976) produced a future-oriented educational guide.

The currents of thought which we have just discussed principally concern the Western world. Studies exploring the future of education are much less common in the developing countries, although Shiva Lingappa (1979) has devoted forty pages to this based on existing material on the subject.

Several conferences have been held in the major developing regions on the future of education in those regions. For example, a conference was jointly organized in July 1977 in Dakar by UNITAR and the African Insititute for Economic Development and Planning (IDEP) on the theme of 'Africa and the problems of the future'. Several papers submitted for that meeting dealt with the future of education in the region. Another interesting example is provided by the discussion group meeting on Reflection on the Future Development of Education in Asia and the Pacific (Thailand, September 1980). A table summarized the forces promoting or obstructing the future development of education and also the effects and reactions of education as an independent variable (of social change).[7]

The study of the future: an outline

NOTES

1. In 1973, the 'Futures' group in the United States listed 850 to 900 organizations and associations active in this area of research, i.e. having recently undertaken at least one major research project. Over 500 of these bodies were based in the United States; over 200 were located in Western Europe (see Boucher and Amara, 1977, pp. 4–5).
2. A list of these organizations and associations is contained in *The Future, a Guide to Information Sources*. (World Future Society, Washington, D.C., 1979, pp. 1–122), which provides succinct information on no less than 450 future analysts, 230 institutions and associations active in this area of study, 116 research projects, 400 books and reports and 107 periodicals. A considerable number of films, video cassettes and tapes are also listed.
3. The idea of such a society is particularly close to thinkers such as Fromm, Maslow, Jungk, Roszak, Reich, etc.
4. The authors (Bodkin et al., 1979) defend what they refer to as innovative learning, which is characterized by participation and anticipation as opposed to maintenance learning and what is termed 'reductionism', i.e. the learning of certain fixed rules which are wrongly considered as applicable to all situations.
5. In particular CERI (1972). *Future Educational Policies in the Changing Social and Economic Context* (1979) is the report of a meeting of the Ministers of Education of the Member States on 9 October 1978. Reference may also be made to more recent meetings of the OECD's Education Committee and its work, such as for example: *Compulsory Schooling in a Changing World* (OECD, 1983a); Intergovernmental Conference on Policies for Higher Education in the Eighties, Paris, October 1981 (various documents published later under the title: *Policies for Higher Education in the 1980s.*)
6. The article deals with the search for local solutions to global problems of mankind. The study of the 'cost of education' conducted for several years by IIEP (Unesco) could contribute to efforts to rationalize expenditure and reduce wastage in this area.
7. At the level of society these forces include (1) population growth, urbanization and the pressure of the environment; (2) 'illusory' urban economic growth accompanied by rural poverty, socio-economic disparities; (3) the process of democratization; (4) the failure of economic planning, which used to be considered as a scientific discipline; (5) the concentration of power at the central national level; (6) the inability of governments to manage increasingly complex social systems; (7) the phenomenon of information overload; (8) excessive dependence on imported science and technology and the resultant phenomenon of structural unemployment; (9) the gradual transfer of responsibility for the well-being of the individual, his family and himself to society as a whole; (10) the rapid exhaustion of natural resources combined with 'stagflation'; (11) incompatibility of different incentives, for example, material profit and consumption on the one hand and the quality of life on the other; (12) international conflicts and tensions, the persistence of an unjust economic order in spite of an increased awareness of the interdependence of peoples and nations; finally, the insufficiency of marginal aid for education.

References

ADAMS, D. K. 1977. Development Education. *Comparative Education Review* (Chicago, Comparative and International Education Society), Vol. 21, No. 2/3, pp. 296–310. (Special issue on 'The State of the Art'.)
ADAMS, R. S.; CHEN, D. 1981. *The Process of Educational Innovation: An International Perspective*. Paris/London, Unesco/Kogan Page. 284 pp.
ANTISERI, D. 1975. *I fondamenti epistemologici del lavoro interdisciplinare*. Rome, Armando.
ARDOINO, J. 1980. Les avatars contemporains de la morale. *International Review of Education*, (Hamburg, Unesco Institute of Education), Vol. XXVI, No. 2, 1980. (Special number on 'Problems of Teaching Values in a Changing Society'.)
BAEZ, A. V. 1977. *Innovation in Science Education—World-wide*. Paris, Unesco. 249 pp.
BARNES, D. R. 1982. *Practical Curriculum Study*. London, Routledge & Kegan Paul. 510 pp.
BEBBE-NJOH, E. 1985. Problems of Disseminating Educational Research Findings in Cameroon. In: Unesco, *International French-language Seminar on the Dissemination of Educational Research Findings, Paris 1984*, pp. 120–23, Paris, Unesco. 133 pp. (Unesco doc. ED-85/WS/17.)
BELL, D. 1973. *Coming of Post-industrial Society: A Venture in Social Forecasting*. New York, Basic Books.
BENGTSSON, J., et al. 1975. *Does Education Have a Future?* Boston, Kluwer. 134 pp. (Plan Europe 2000, 10.)
BERGER, B.; BRUNSWIC, E. 1978. *Eléments pour un examen critique des manuels scolaire*. Paris, Unesco. 33 pp.
BERRY, A. 1974. *The Next Ten Thousand Years: A Vision of Man's Future in the Universe*. New York, Dutton.
BEST, F. 1973. *Pour une pédagogie de l'éveil*. Paris, Armand Colin. 239 pp. (Bourrelier Education, 10.)
BIRZEA, C. 1982. *La pédagogie du succès*. Paris, Presses Universitaires de France. 152 pp. (L'Educateur, 79.)
BLAT GIMENO, J. 1983. *Education in Latin America and the Caribbean. Trends and Prospects*. Paris, Unesco. 190 pp.
BLOOM, B. S. 1956. *Taxonomy of Educational Objectives. The Classification of Educational Goals. Handbook 1, Cognitive Domain*. New York, D. McKay.
———. 1981. *All our Children Learning*. New York, McGraw-Hill.
BONNEFOUS, E. 1982. *Le monde en danger*. Éditions du Moniteur. 272 pp.
BONNET, G. 1983. Sept directions que prend le monde. *Le nouvel observateur*, No. 2228. (Special issue on the future.)

References

BOTKIN, J. W., et al. 1979. *No Limits to Learning; Bridging the Human Gap; A Report to the Club of Rome*. Oxford, Pergamon Press, 159 pp.
BOUCHER, W. I; AMARA, R. 1977. *The Study of the Future, An Agenda for Research*. Washington, D.C., National Science Foundation, 315 pp.
BROWN, L. R. 1972. *World without Borders*. New York, Random House. 395 pp.
BUSSHOFF, L., et al. 1981. *Curricula and Lifelong Education*. Paris, Unesco. 360 pp. (Education on the Move, 1.)
CANADA. PROVINCE OF QUEBEC. MINISTRY OF EDUCATION. 1974. *L'éducation de demain*. Quebec.
CARNEGIE COMMISSION FOR HIGHER EDUCATION. 1974. *A Digest of Reports: with an Index to Recommendations and Suggested Assignments of Responsibility for Action*. New York, McGraw-Hill. 399 pp.
CARNEGIE COUNCIL ON POLICY STUDIES IN HIGHER EDUCATION. 1980. *Three Thousand Futures: The Next 20 Years for Higher Education; Final Report*. San Francisco, Jossey-Bass. 439 pp.
CARRON, G.; TA NGOC CHAU. 1981. *Reduction of Regional Disparities: The Role of Educational Planning*. Paris/London, Unesco/IIEP/Kogan Page. 126 pp.
CARRON, G.; TA NGOC CHAU (eds.). 1980. *Regional Disparities in Educational Development: Diagnosis and Policies for Reduction*. Paris, Unesco/IIEP. 409 pp.
CASTARÈDE, J.; SUR, J. 1980. *La communiculture: pour une culture de la communication*. Paris, Stock. 295 pp.
CEPII (CENTRE D'ETUDES PROSPECTIVES ET D'INFORMATIONS INTERNATIONALES). 1983. *Economie mondiale: la montée des tensions*. Paris, Economica. 314 pp.
CERI (CENTRE FOR EDUCATIONAL RESEARCH AND INNOVATION). 1972. *Alternative Educational Futures in the United States and in Europe: Methods, Issues and Policy Relevance*. Paris/London, OECD/HMSO. 214 pp.
——. 1973a. *Case Studies of Educational Innovation. I: At the Central Level; II: At the Regional Level; III: At the School Level; IV: Strategies for Innovation in Education—A Synthesis*. Paris, OECD.
——. 1973b. *Recurrent Education. A Stretegy for Lifelong Learning*. Paris, OECD. 91 pp.
CHALL, J. S.; MIRSKY, A. (eds.). 1978. *Education and the Brain. The Seventy-seventh Yearbook of the National Society for the Study of Education*. Part II. Chicago, University of Chicago Press. 413 pp.
CHAMPION, J. 1983. L'école demain en France et dans le monde: un essai de futurologie. *Education comparée* (Sèvres), No. 31/32, pp. 15–18.
CHIESA AZZARIO, M. P. 1983. *Étude de deux experiences de formation d'educateurs qui se développent actuellement à Turin et qui mettent en œuvre des 'troncs communs de formation'*. Paris, Unesco. 82 pp. (Unesco doc. ED/HEP/TEP.)
COGGIN, P. A. 1979. *Education for the Future: The Case for Radical Change*. Elmsford, N.Y., Pergamon Press. 170 pp.
COLE, S. 1977. *Global Models and the International Economic Order*. Oxford, Pergamon Press, 80 pp.
COLEMAN, J. S., et al. 1974. *Youth, Transition to Adulthood*. Chicago, University of Chicago Press. 193 pp.
COLLOQUE NATIONALE DE PÉDAGOGIE (Bucharest, 1970). 1970. *La recherche interdisciplinaire de l'enseignement*. Bucharest, Institut des Sciences Pédagogiqies (ISP).
CONFERENCE OF MINISTERS OF EDUCATION OF AFRICAN MEMBER STATES (Lagos, 1976). 1976. *Final Report*. Paris, Unesco. 98 pp. (Unesco doc. ED/MD/41.)
COOMBS, P. H. 1981. *Future Critical World Issues in Education: A Provisional Report of Findings*. New York, International Council for Educational Development (ICED). 79 pp.

References

────. 1982. Critical World Educational Issues of the Next Two Decades. *International Review of Education* (Hamburg, Unesco Institute of Education), Vol. XXVIII, No. 2, pp. 143–57.

COOMBS, P. H.; CHAUDHURY, K. 1981. *World Trends and Prospects for Educational Costs and Expenditures, 1960–2000.* Essex, Conn., International Council for Educational Development (ICED). 85 pp. (Mimeo.)

CORNISH, E. S. 1978. *The Study of the Future; An Introduction to the Art and Science of Understanding and Shaping Tomorrow's World.* Washington, D.C., World Future Society. 307 pp.

COUNCIL OF EUROPE. DOCUMENTATION CENTRE FOR EDUCATION IN EUROPE. 1983. *News-letter/Faits nouveaux* (Strasbourg).

CRONBACH, L. T.; SUPPES, P. (eds.). 1969. See: National Academy of Education, Committee on Educational Research, 1969.

CROPLEY, A. J. (ed.). 1979. *Lifelong Education: A Stocktaking.* Hamburg, Unesco Institute for Education, 115 pp. (UIE Monographs, 8).

D'HAINAUT, L. 1977. *Des fins aux objectifs de l'éducation; l'analyse et la conception des politiques éducatives, des programmes de l'éducation, des objectifs operationnels et des situations d'enseignement.* Paris, Fernand Nathan. 400 pp.

────. 1980. *Ébauche d'un guide pour la transdisciplinarité instrumentale (Rapport de mission en Côte d'Ivoire, Abijan, 1980).* Paris, Unesco.

DAVADAS, R., et al. 1982. *Nutrition Education. Case Study in School.* Paris. (Nutrition Education Document Series, 1.) (Unesco doc. ED.82/WS/112.)

DAVE, R. H. 1973. *Lifelong Learning and School Curriculum.* Hamburg, Unesco Institute for Education. 90 pp. (UIE Monographs, 1.)

DAVY, C. 1961. *Towards a Third Culture.* London, Faber & Faber. 178 pp.

DE CORTE, M. 1949. *L'essai sur la fin d'une civilisation.* Librairie de Médicis. 252 pp.

DE LANDSHERRE, G. 1976a. *La formation des enseignants demain.* Paris, Casterman. 297 pp.

────. 1976b. *Introduction à la recherche en éducation.* 4th ed. Paris, Armand Colin.

────. 1979. *Dictionnaire de l'évaluation et de la recherche en éducation.* Paris, Presses Universitaires de France.

DE LANDSHEERE, V.; DE LANDSHEERE, G. 1975. *Définir les objectifs de l'éducation.* Paris, Presses Universitaires de France. 293 pp. (Pédagogie d'aujourd'hui.)

DEBEAUVAIS, M. 1974. The Popularity of the Idea of Innovation: A Tentative Interpretation of the Texts. *Prospects, Quarterly Review of Education* (Paris, Unesco), Vol. IV, No. 4, pp. 494–504.

DENMARK. MINISTRY OF EDUCATION. CENTRAL COUNCIL OF EDUCATION. 1978. *U90. Danish Educational Planning and Policy in a Social Context at the End of the 20th Century.* Copenhagen. 365 pp.

DI CARLO, R. 1980. *Reflection on the Future Development of Education: A Selective and Annotated Bibliography.* Part 2. Paris, Unesco. 70 pp. (Reports and Studies [on Educational Policy and Planning], S.87.)

DIEUZEIDE, H. 1974. Educational Technology for Developing Countries. *Seventy-third Yearbook of the National Society for the Study of Education.* Chicago, University of Chicago Press.

────. 1983. *L'école et la pression du milieu technologique.* Paper presented to the Congrès de l'Association Générale des Institutrices et Instituteurs des Écoles et des Classes Maternelles Publiques (Lyons, 23 June).

DONGALA, J. B. 1981. *Using the African Oral Heritage for Educational Purposes.* Paris, Unesco. 24 pp. (Unesco doc. ED.81/WS/125.)

DORE, R. 1984. Unity and Diversity in World Culture. In: H. Bull and A. Watson (eds.), *The Expansion of International Society.* Oxford University Press. 496 pp.

References

DUCROCQ, A. 1984. *Le futur aujourd'hui 1985–2000, les quinze années qui vont changer votre vie quotidienne.* Paris, Plon. 280 pp.

Educational Goals. 1980. Paris, Unesco. 231 pp. (IBE Studies and Surveys in Comparative Education.)

EICHER, J. C. 1982. What Resources for Education? *Prospects, Quarterly Review of Education* (Paris, Unesco), Vol. XII, No. 1, pp. 57–68.

EICHER, J. C., et al. 1984. *The Economics of the New Educational Media.* Vol. 3: *Cost and Effectiveness: Overview and Synthesis.* Paris, Unesco.

ESSLEMONT, J. E. 1980. *Bahá'u'lláh and the New Era: An Introduction to the Bahá'í Faith.* 4th rev. ed. Wilmette, Ill., Bahá'í Publishing Trust.

Exploring New Directions in Teacher Education: Experiments in the Preparation and Training of Teachers in Asia. 1976. Bangkok, Unesco Regional Office for Education in Asia. 251 pp. (Teacher Education, 1.)

FALK, R. A. 1972. *This Endangered Planet, Prospects and Proposals for Human Survival.* New York, Random House. 495 pp.

———. 1975. *A Study of Future Worlds.* New York, Institute for World Order/Free Press. 506 pp. (Preferred Worlds for the 1970's.)

FAO (FOOD AND AGRICULTURE ORGANIZATION OF THE UNITED NATIONS). 1981. *Agriculture: Toward 2000.* Rome, FAO. 134 pp.

FAURE, E. et al. 1972. *Learning to Be. The World of Education Today and Tomorrow.* Paris/London, Unesco/Harrap, 313 pp.

FELDEN, M. 1981. *21e siècle; les nouvelles dimensions du futur.* Édiitons Entente.

FERKISS, V. C. 1969. *Technological Man: The Myth and the Reality.* New York, Braziller.

FITOURI, C. 1983. *Biculturalism, biliguism et éducation.* Neuchâtel/Paris, Delcahaux & Niestlé. 300 pp.

FOULQUIÉ, Rev. P. P.; SAINT-JEAN, R. 1961. *Dictionnaire de la langue philosophique.* Paris, Presses Universitaires de France. 776 pp.

FRAGNIERE, G. G. (ed.). 1976. *Education without Frontiers.* London, Duckworth. 207 pp.

FRANCE. COMMISSARIAT GÉNÉRAL AU PLAN. 1980. *Demain, La France dans le monde.* 1980. Paris, Documentation Française. 192 pp. (Preparer l'avenir.)

FRANCE. 1981. *L'Éducation et l'information de la société: rapport à M. le Président de la République,* by J. C. Simon. Paris, Fayard. 275 pp.

FREEMAN, C; JAHODA, M. (eds.). 1978. *World Futures, The Great Debate.* London, Robertson. 416 pp.

FREY, K. (ed.). 1978. *Curriculumreform unter europaïschen Perspektiven.* Frankfurt am Main, Diesterweg.

FREY, K. et al. 1975. *Curriculum-Handbuch.* Vols. I, II and III. Munich, Piper-Verlag.

Futures (Guildford). 1982. Vol. 14, No. 2.

GABOR, D.; COLOMBO, U. 1981. *Beyond the Age of Waste, A Report to the Club of Rome.* 2nd ed. Oxford, Pergamon Press. 239 pp.

GARAUDY, R. 1977. *Pour un dialogue des civilisations: l'occident est un accident.* Paris, Denöel. 233 pp.

———. 1978. *Comment l'homme devint humain.* Paris, Jeune Afrique. 335 pp. (L'épopée humaine.)

GELPI, E. 1984. Éducation permanente: créativité et résistances. *Paideia* (Warsaw), Vol. XI, pp. 277–87.

GERSHUNY, J. I. 1979. *After Industrial Society? The Emerging Self-service Society.* Sussex, Humanities Press. 181 pp.

Gleanings from the Writings of Bahá'u'lláh. Rev. ed. Wilmette, Ill., Bahá'í Publishing Trust.

GLINES, D. 1979. *Educational Futures*. Vol. IV: *Updating and Overleaping*. Milville, Minn., Anvil Press.
GOAD. L. H. 1984. *Preparing Teachers for Lifelong Education; The Report of a Multinational Study of Some Developments in Teacher Education in the Perspective of Lifelong Education*. Hamburg/Oxford, Unesco Institute of Education/Pergamon Press. 188 pp. (Advances in Lifelong Education, 8.)
GOBLE, N. M.; PORTER, J. F. 1977. *The Changing Role of the Teacher; International Perspectives*. Paris/Geneva, Unesco/IBE. 234 pp. (Studies and Surveys in Comparative Education.)
GOLDSCHMID, M. L. 1983. *Formation pédagogique des enseignants: essai de définition d'un tronc commun*. Paris, Unesco. 43 pp. (Unesco doc. ED/HEP/TEP.)
GOOD, C. 1973. *Dictionary of Education*. 3rd ed. New York, McGraw-Hill. (Foundations in Education.)
GOODLAD, J. I. 1979. *What Schools Are For*. Bloomington, Ind., Phi Delta Kappa Educational Foundation.
GOODLAD, J. I., et al. 1979. *Curriculum Inquiry; The Study of Curriculum Practice*. New York, McGraw-Hill. 371 pp.
GOZZER, G. 1982. Interdisciplinarity: A Concept Still Unclear. *Prospects, Quarterly Review of Education* (Paris, Unesco), Vol. XII, No. 3. pp. 281–92.
GURVITCH, G. 1958. *Traité de sociologie*. Vol. II. Paris, Presses Universitaires de France. 468 pp.
GUSDORF, G. 1977. Past, Present and Future in Interdisciplinary Research. *International Social Science Journal* (Paris, Unesco), Vol. XXIX, No. 4, pp. 580–600.
HAAVELSRUD, M. 1976. *Education for Peace: Reflection and Action*. Brighton, Humanities Press. 407 pp.
——. 1983. An Introduction to the Debate on Peace Education (Editorial). *International Review of Education* (Hamburg, Unesco Institute of Education), Vol. 29, No. 3, pp. 275–80. (Special issue on 'The Debate on Education for Peace'.)
HAFT, H.; HAMEYER, U. 1975. *Curriculumplanung. Theorie und Praxis*. Munich, Kösel-Verlag.
HALL, P. 1977. *Europe 2000*. New York, Columbia University Press/European Cultural Foundation (Netherlands). 274 pp.
HARMAN, W. W.; ROSENBERG, M. E. 1971. *Methodology of Educational Futurology/Alternative Futures in Educational Policymaking*. Paris, Unesco. (International Commission on the Development of Education, Series B, Opinions, 44.)
HATCHER, W. S.; MARTIN, J. D. *The Bahai Faith, The Emerging Global Religion*, New York, Harper & Row. 226 pp.
HAUMDER, U. VON. 1979. *Reflection on the Future Development of Education: A Selective and Annotated Bibliography*. Paris, Unesco. 74 pp. (Reports and Studies [on Educational Policy and Planning], S.70.)
HAUSMANN, G. 1959. *Didaktik als Dramaturgie des Unterrichts*. Heidelberg, Quelle & Meyer. (Anthropologie und Erziehung, 2.)
HAVELOCK, R. G.; HUBERMAN, A. M. 1978. *Solving Educational Problems: The Theory and Reality of Innovation in Developing Countries*. Paris/Toronto, Unesco/Ontario Institute for Studies in Education (OISE). 308 pp. (Studies and Surveys in Comparative Education.)
——. 1970. *Main Trends of Research in the Social and Human Sciences*. Part I: *Social Sciences*. Paris, Unesco/Mouton.
HAVET, J. (ed.). 1978. *Main Trends of Research in the Social and Human Sciences*. Part II: *Anthropological and Historical Sciences; Aesthetics and the Sciences of Art; Legal Science; Philosophy*. Paris, Unesco. 2 vols. 1,591 pp.
HAWES, H. R. 1975. *Lifelong Education, Schools and Curricula in Developing Countries*.

Hamburg, Unesco Institute for Education. 110 pp. (UIE Monographs, 4.)
HAWKRIDGE, D. 1982. Educational Technology, Present and Future. *Prospects, Quarterly Review of Education* (Paris, Unesco), Vol. XII, No. 3, pp. 325–34.
HAYMEYER, U. 1979. *School Curriculum in the Context of Lifelong Learning.* Hamburg, Unesco Institute for Education. (UIE Monographs, 9.)
HEIDT, E. U. 1979. *Self-Evaluation in Learning: A Report on Trends, Experiences and Research Findings.* Paris, Unesco. 45 pp. (Unesco doc. ED.79/WS/119.)
HEILBORNER, R. L. 1974. *An Inquiry into the Human Prospect.* New York, Norton.
HELY, A. S. M. 1962. *New Trends on Adult Education: from Elsinore to Montreal.* Paris, Unesco. 136 pp. (Monographs on Education, IV.)
HENCLEY, S. P.; YATES, J. R. 1974. *Futurism in Education: Methodologies.* Berkeley, Calif., McCutchan. 510 pp.
HERRERA, A. O. 1976. *Catastrophe or New Society! A Latin American World Model.* Ottawa, International Development Research Centre (IDRC). 108 pp.
HOFMAN, D. 1972. *The Renewal of Civilization. Bahai Faith.* Rev. ed. Oxford, George Ronald.
HUBERMAN, A. M. 1973. *Understanding Change in Education. An Introduction.* Paris/Geneva, Unesco/IBE. 99 pp. (Experiments and Innovations in Education, 4.).
——. 1982. L'utilisation de la recherche éducationnelle: vers un mode d'emploi. *Education et rechercheBildungsforschung und Bildungspraxis* (Zurich), Vol. 4, No. 2, pp. 136–54.
HUMMEL, C. 1977. *Education Today for the World of Tomorrow.* Paris/Geneva, Unesco/IBE. (Studies and Surveys in Comparative Education.)
HUSÉN, T. 1979. *The School in Question; A Comparative Study of School and its Future in Western Societies.* Oxford University Press. 196 pp.
——. 1982. Present Trends in Education. *Prospects, Quarterly Review of Education* (Paris, Unesco), Vol. XII, No. 1, pp. 45–56.
HUSÉN, T.; BOALT, G. 1968. *Educational Research and Educational Change: The Case of Sweden.* New York, Wiley. 233 pp.
IFRI (INSTITUT FRANÇAIS DES RELATIONS INTERNATIONALES). 1984. *RAMSES 83/84; Rapport annuel mondial sur le système économique et les stratégies.* Paris, Economica/Documentation Française. 322 pp.
IIEP (INTERNATIONAL INSTITUTE FOR EDUCATIONAL PLANNING). 1980. *The Future of Education and the Education of the Future. Final Report and Documents of an IIEP Seminar, Paris, 23–26 October 1978.* Paris. 369 pp.
ILO (INTERNATIONAL LABOUR ORGANISATION). 1981. *The Cost of Social Security.* Geneva, ILO.
——. 1984a. *Travail dans le monde.* Vol. 1: *Emploi, revenus, protection sociale, nouvelles techniaues d'information.* Geneva, ILO. 224 pp.
——. 1984b. *World Labour Report.* Vol. 1. Geneva, ILO.
INDEPENDENT COMMISSION ON INTERNATIONAL DEVELOPMENT ISSUES. 1980. *North–South: A Programme for Survival. Report.* Edited by W. Brandt. Cambridge, Mass., MIT Press. 304 pp.
INGLE, R., et al. 1982. *Nutrition Education; Relevance and Future.* Paris. (Nutrition Education Document Series, 5.) (Unesco doc. ED.82/WS/114.)
INGRAM, J. B. 1979. *Curriculum Integration and Lifelong Education; A Contribution to the Improvement of School Curricula.* Hamburg/Oxford, Unesco Institute for Education/Pergamon Press. (Advances in Lifelong Education, 8.)
INTERGOVERNMENTAL CONFERENCE ON EDUCATION FOR INTERNATIONAL UNDERSTANDING, CO-OPERATION AND PEACE AND EDUCATION RELATING TO HUMAN RIGHTS AND FUNDAMENTAL FREEDOMS, WITH A VIEW TO DEVELOPING A CLIMATE OF OPINION FAVOURABLE TO THE STRENGTHENING OF SECURITY AND DIS-

References

ARMAMENT (Paris, 1983). 1983. *Final Report*. Paris, Unesco, 101 pp. (Unesco doc. ED/MED/74.)
INTERGOVERNMENTAL REGIONAL MEETING ON THE OBJECTIVES, STRATEGIES AND METHODS OF ACTION FOR A MAJOR PROJECT IN THE FIELD OF EDUCATION IN THE LATIN AMERICAN AND CARIBBEAN REGION (Quito, 1981). 1981*a*. *Final Report*. Paris, Unesco. 71 pp. (Unesco doc. ED/MD/75.)
———. 1981*b*. *Reflections and Suggestions concerning the Major Project on Education in Latin America and the Caribbean*. Paris, Unesco. 62 pp. (Unesco doc. ED.81/PROMEDLAC/3.)
INTERNATIONAL COLLOQUIUM ON RESEARCH AND PRACTICE IN EDUCATION: HOW TO STRENGHTEN LINKS BETWEEN RESEARCH AND PRACTICE IN ORDER TO IMPROVE GENERAL EDUCATION (Bucharest, 1980). 1981. *Final Report*. Paris/Bucharest, Unesco/European Centre for Higher Education. 144 pp. (Unesco doc. ED.80/CONF.816/12.)
INTERNATIONAL SEMINAR ON FINANCING EDUCATIONAL DEVELOPMENT (Mont Sainte Marie, Canada, 1982). 1982. *Financing Educational Development; Proceedings*. Ottawa, International Development Research Centre.
INTERNATIONAL SYMPOSIUM ON THE EVOLUTION OF THE CONTENT OF GENERAL EDUCATION OVER THE NEXT TWO DECADES (Paris, 1980). 1980*a*. *Contribution to a Study on the Evolution of the Content of General Education, 1970–1980*. By L. Legrand and J. Majault. Paris, Unesco. (Unesco doc. ED.80/CONF.803/4.)
———. 1980*b*. *Le développement probable des arts et des autres formes contemporaine de l'expression visuelle et les contenus de l'éducation*. By E. Fulchignoi. Paris, Unesco. 14 pp. (Unesco doc. ED.80/CONF.803/INF.9.)
———. 1980*c*. *Développement probable des contenus de l'éducation et formation des enseignants pendant les deux décennies à venir*. By A. Drubay. Paris, Unesco. 38 pp. (Information Study, 7.) (Unesco doc. ED.80/CONF.803/INF.8.)
———. 1980*d*. *Final Report*. Paris, Unesco. (Unesco doc. ED.80/CONF.803/7.)
———. 1980*e*. *General Education in India: A Search for Relevance*. By B. V. Doshi. Paris, Unesco. 24 pp. (Information Study, 6.) (Unesco doc. ED.80/CONF.-803/INF.10.)
———. 1980*f*. *The Impact of the Evolution of Exact Sciences on the Curricula during the Next Two Decades*. By M. Malitza, A. M. Sandi and B. Chitimia. Paris, Unesco. 29 pp. (Information Study, 2.) (Unesco doc. ED.80/CONF.803/INF.11.)
———. 1980*g*. *The Impact of the Evolution of Technology on the Content of General Education in the Course of the Next Two Decades*. By A. Koukhartchouk. Paris, Unesco. 25 pp. (Information Study, 3.) (Unesco doc. ED.80/CONF.803/INF.11.)
———. 1980*h*. *Incidence des moyens d'information sur les contenus de l'éducation générale; compte tenu des évolutions*. By P. Schaeffer. Paris, Unesco. 31 pp. (Information Study, 1.) (Unesco doc. ED.80/CONF.803/INF.12.)
———. 1980*i*. *Probable Developments in the Social Sciences and their Consequences for Educational Content*. By. H. G. Shane and M. B. Tabler. Paris, Unesco. 35 pp. (Information Study, 4.) (Unesco doc. ED.80/CONF.803/INF.13.)
———. 1980*j*. *Summaries of Studies on the Evolution of the Content of Education*. By P. Ramseyer. Paris, Unesco. 25 pp. (Unesco doc. ED.80/CONF.803/5.)
———. 1980*k*. *Educational Forecasting Methodologies; State of the Art, Trends and Highlights*. By B. M. Hudson and J. Bruno. Paris, Unesco. 39 pp.
JANTSCH, E. 1980. Interdisciplinarity: Dreams and Reality. *Prospects, Quarterly Review of Education* (Paris, Unesco), Vol. X, No. 3, pp. 304–12.
JAUBERT, A. 1975 *(Auto)critique de la science*. Paris, Éditions du Seuil.
JEGEDE, O. J. 1982. An Evaluation of the Nigerian Integrated Science Project (NISP) after a Decade of Use in the Classroom. *International Review of Education*

(Hamburg, Unesco Institute of Education), Vol. 28, No. 3, pp. 321–36.
JENCKS, C., et al. 1973. *Inequality. A Reassessment of the Effect of Family and Schooling in America.* New York, Harper & Row.
JUNGK, R. 1973. *Der Jahrtausend-Mensch: Bericht aus den Werkstätten der neuen Gesellschaft.* Munich, Bertelsmann.
KAHN, H., et al. 1978. *The Next 200 Years: A Scenario for America and the World.* Abacus.
——. 1979. *World Economic Development; Projections from 1979 to the Year 2000.* New York, Morrow. 519 pp.
KAHN, H.; WIENER, A. J. 1967. *The Year 2000, A Framework for Speculation on the Next 33 Years.* New York, Macmillan. 431 pp.
KASTLER, A. 1983. Introduction. *International Social Science Journal* (Paris, Unesco), Vol. XXXV, No. 1, pp. 3–5.
KAUFFMAN, D. L., Jr. 1976. *Teaching the Future: A Guide to Future-Oriented Education.* Palm Springs, Calif., ETC Publications. (Education Future Series, 4.)
KIDA, H. 1981. Educational Research Institutes in Japan. *Research and Practice in Education: How to Strengthen Links between Research and Practice in Order to Improve General Education.* Paris, Unesco. 146 pp. (Unesco doc. ED.80/CONF.816/12.)
KIERSTEAD, F.; BOWMAN, J. R.; DEDE, C. 1979. *Educational Futures: Sourcebook 1* (Selections from the First Conference of the Education Section, World Future Society). Washington, D.C., World Future Society. 254 pp.
KING, E. J. 1979. *Education for Uncertainty.* Beverly Hills, Calif., Sage Publications Inc.
KLUCHNIKOV, B. K. 1980. *Reflections on the Concept and Practice of Educational Planning and Reforms.* Paris, Unesco. (Reports and Studies [on Educational Policy and Planning].) (Unesco doc. ED.80/WS/104.)
KOSTYASHKIN, E. G. 1980. The School of the Future in the USSR. *Prospects, Quarterly Review of Education* (Paris, Unesco), Vol. X, No. 4, pp. 489–94.
KOTHARI, R. 1975. *Footsteps into the Future. Diagnosis of the Present World and a Design for an Alternative.* New York, Institute for World Order/Free Press. 173 pp. (Preferred Worlds for the 1990's.)
KRATHWOHL, D. R.; BLOOM, B. S.; MASIA, B. B. 1964. *Taxonomy of Educational Objectives: Handbook II: Affective Domain.* New York, David McKay. (French version: *Taxonomie des objectifs pédagogiques: Tome II: Domaine affectif.* Montreal, 1978.)
KUHN, T. S. 1967. *The Structure of Scientific Revolutions.* 2nd ed. Chicago, University of Chicago Press. (Foundations of the Unity of Science, Vol. 2, No. 2.)
LADERRIÈRE, P. 1975. Educational Documentation and Information. *Bulletin of the International Bureau of Education* (Geneva), No. 195. (Special issue on 'Trends and Innovations in Teacher Education' with an annotated bibliography.)
LAUWERYS, J. 1976. *Science, Morals and Moralogy.* Tokyo, Institute of Moralogy.
LE THANH KHOI. 1984. *Revue tiers-monde* (Paris), Vol. XXV, No. 97. (Special issue on 'Culture et Développement'.)
LECERCQ, J. M. 1984. *Le Japon et son système éducatif.* Paris, Documentation Française. 120 pp. (Notes et études documentaires, 4747–8.)
LEGRAND, L. 1983. *Pour un collège démocratique. Rapport au ministre de l'éducation nationale.* Paris, Documentation Française. 376 pp.
LEMA, V.; MARQUEZ, A. D. 1978. What Kind of Development and Which Education? *Prospects, Quarterly Review of Education* (Paris, Unesco), Vol. VIII, No. 3, pp. 295–300.
LEMKE, D. A. 1981. *Steps towards a Flexible Curriculum.* 2nd rev. ed. Santiago,

Unesco Regional Office for Education in Latin America and the Caribbean. 150 pp.
LENOIR, R. 1984. *Le tiers monde peut se nourrir. Rapport au Club de Rome.* Paris, Fayard. 192 pp.
LEONTIEV, W., et al. 1977. *The Future of the World Economy: A United Nations Study.* New Delhi, Oxford University Press (India). 110 pp.
LESOURNE, J. 1981. *Les mille sentiers de l'avenir.* Paris, Seghers. 372 pp.
LIAN JIAN-SHENG. 1980. Moral Education in New China. *International Review of Education* (Hamburg, Unesco Institute of Education), Vol. XXVI, No. 2, pp. 198–201. (Special number on 'Problems of Teaching Moral Values in a Changing World'.)
LINGAPPA, S. 1979. *Directions of Educational Development in the Developing Countries: Outlook for the Year 2000.* Paris, Unesco. 42 pp. (Reports and Studies [on Educational Policy and Planning].)
LOURIÉ, S. 1974. Education and Society: the Problems of Change. *Prospects, Quarterly Review of Education* (Paris, Unesco), Vol. IV, No. 4, pp. 541–8.
LOZANOV, G. 1979. Accelerated Learning and Individual Potential. *Prospects, Quarterly Review of Education* (Paris, Unesco), Vol. IX, No. 4, pp. 414–25.
LUTTERODT, S. A. 1981. Definition, Design, Utilization. Some Problems Associated with Integrated Science Curricula with Special Reference to the Project for Science Integration in Ghana. *International Review of Education* (Hamburg, Unesco Institute of Education), Vol. 27, No. 3, pp. 301–14.
MACKENZIE, N.; ERAUT, M.; JONES, H. C. 1970. *Teaching and Learning; An Introduction to New Methods and Resources in Higher Education.* Paris, Unesco/IAU. 209 pp. (The Development of Higher Education.)
MAHEU, R. 1973. *Culture in the Contemporary World. Problems and Prospects.* Paris, Unesco. 32 pp. (Paper submitted by the Director-General of Unesco to the United Nations General Assembly at its 28th Session. In Unesco doc. A/9227.)
MALMQUIST, E. J. T.; GRUNDIN, H. U. 1975. *Educational Research in Europe Today and Tomorrow.* Lund, CWK Gleerup/European Cultural Foundation. 442 pp.
MARIEN, M. 1976. *Societal Directions and Alternatives; A Critical Guide to the Literature.* Lafayette, N.Y., Information for Policy Design. 400 pp.
MASSARENTI, L. 1982. *Conjuguer les droits de l'homme.* Geneva, Éditions EIP.
M'BOW, A.-M. 1982. *Where the Future Begins.* Paris, Unesco. 118 pp.
MEADOWS, D., et al. 1972. *The Limits to Growth, A Report for the Club of Rome's Project on the Predicament of Mankind.* New York, Norton (New American Library). 207 pp.
——. 1974. *Dynamics of Growth in a Finite World.* Cambridge, Mass., MIT Press. 637 pp.
MEETING OF EXPERTS ON CURRICULUM OF GENERAL EDUCATION (Moscow, 1968). 1968. *Final Report.* Paris, Unesco. 19 pp. (Unesco doc. 67–68/EDM/13.000/13.2111.)
MEETING OF EXPERTS ON EDUCATIONAL INSTITUTIONS AND MORAL EDUCATION IN THE LIGHT OF THE DEMANDS OF CONTEMPORARY LIFE (Sofia, 1978). 1978. *Final Report.* Paris, Unesco. 21 pp. (Unesco doc. ED.78/CONF.631/4.)
MEETING OF THE INTERIM INTERGOVERNMENTAL REGIONAL COMMITTEE FOR THE MAJOR PROJECT IN THE FIELD OF EDUCATION IN LATIN AMERICA AND THE CARIBBEAN (Castries, 1982). 1983. *Final Report.* Paris, Unesco. 122 pp. (Unesco doc. ED/MD/71.)
MEGARRY, J., et al. 1983. *Computers and Education.* New York, Kogan Page/Nichols. 280 pp. (World Yearbook of Education, 1982/83.)
MEHLINGER, H. D. 1984. The *Place of Moral Values in Educational Programmes, In-depth Study.* Paris, Unesco. 212 pp. (Unesco doc. ED.84/WS.22.)

MENDLOVITZ, S. H. (ed.). 1975. *On the Creation of a Just World Order*. Amsterdam, North Holland Publications. 302 pp. (Preferred Worlds for the 1990's.)

MESAROVIC, M.; PESTEL, E. 1974. *Mankind at the Turning Point: The Second Report to the Club of Rome*. New York, Dutton. 210 pp.

MIALARET, G. (ed.). 1979. *Vocabulaire de l'éducation*. Paris, Presses Universitaires de France. 457 pp. (Education et sciences de l'éducation.)

MINEDAF, FIFTH, (Harare, 1982). 1982. *Education and Endogenous Development in Africa; Trends, Problems, Prospects*. Paris, Unesco. 119 pp. (Unesco doc. ED.82/MINEDAF/3.)

NAISBITT, J. 1982. *Megatrends, Ten New Directions Transforming our Lives*. New York, Warner Books. 290 pp.

NATIONAL ACADEMY OF EDUCATION. COMMITTEE ON EDUCATIONAL RESEARCH. 1969. *Research for Tomorrow's Schools: Disciplined Inquiry for Education*. Edited by L. J. Cronbach and P. Suppes. New York, Macmillan. 281 pp.

NEWCOMBE, H. 1974. Alternative Approaches to World Government. *Peace Research Review* (Dundas, Ont., Peace Research Institute), Vol. 5, No. 3.

OECD (ORGANISATION FOR ECONOMIC CO-OPERATION AND DEVELOPMENT). 1979. *Facing the Future: Mastering the Probable and Managing the Unpredictable*. Paris, OECD. 425 pp.

——. 1983a. *Compulsory Schooling in a Changing World*. Paris, OECD. 149 pp.

——. 1983b. *World Economic Interdependence and the Evolving North–South Relationship*. Paris, OECD. 83 pp.

OLIVEIRA, J. B. A. 1982. Making Good Use of Educational Technology. *Prospects, Quarterly Review of Education* (Paris, Unesco), Vol. XII, No. 3, pp. 335–46.

OPHULS, W. 1976. *Ecology and the Politics of Scarcity. Prologue to a Political Theory of the Steady State*. San Francisco, Freeman. 303 pp.

OSBORNE, D. 1980. Basic Science: Learning to Think in Terms of Probability. *Prospects, Quarterly Review of Education* (Paris, Unesco), Vol. X, No. 4, pp. 417–24.

OXENHAM, J. 1982. Education and the New International Economic Order (editorial comment). *International Review of Education* (Hamburg, Unesco Institute of Education), Vol. 28, No. 4, pp. 403–5. (Special issue on 'Education and the New International Economic Order'.)

PAGE, G. T., et al. 1977. *International Dictionary of Education*. New York, Nichols. 381 pp.

PAPERT, S. 1980. *Mindstorms: Children, Computers, and Powerful Ideas*. Brighton, Harvester Press. 230 pp. (Harvester Studies in Cognitive Science, 14.)

PAUVERT, J. C. 1983. *Research concerning Common Cores of Training of Educational Personnel*. Paris, Unesco. 74 pp. (ED/HEP working document.)

PECCEI, A. 1981. *One Hundred Pages for the Future; Reflections of the President of the Club of Rome*. New York/Oxford, Pergamon Press. 191 pp.

PHILLIPS, H. M. 1976. *Educational Cooperation between Developed and Developing Countries*. New York, Holt, Rinehart & Winston. (Praeger Special Studies.)

PICHT, G. 1970. *Mut zur Utopie. Die grossen Zukunftsaufgaben*. Munich, Piper.

——. 1974. *Réflexions au bord du gouffre*. Paris, Laffont, 1974.

PINEAU, G. 1977. *Education ou alienation permanente?* Paris, Dunod. 296 pp.

PINILLOS, J. L. 1981. *The Development of Intelligence: Hope or Reality. Venezuela (Mission)*. Paris, Unesco. 67 pp. (Unesco doc. FMR/ED/SCM/80/177E.)

PORTER, J. 1983. *The Concept of a Common Core Training Applied to Complex Learning Situations*. Paris, Unesco. 54 pp. (Unesco doc. ED/HEP/TEP.)

PRADERVAND, P. 1982. Would You Please Empty your Teacup. Epistemological and Conceptual Aspects of Development Education. *International Review of Education* (Hamburg, Unesco Institute of Education), Vol. 28, No. 4, pp. 449–55.

References

Rama, G. W. 1978. The Project for Development and Education in Latin America and the Caribbean. *Prospects, Quarterly Review of Education* (Paris, Unesco), Vol. VIII, No. 3, pp. 301–5.

Rana, S. (ed.). 1981. *Obstacles to Disarmament and Ways of Overcoming Them.* Paris, Unesco. 233 pp. (Insights.)

Rassekh, S. 1983. L'apport de la futurologie à la connaissance de l'évolution des systèmes de formation. *Education comparée*, May 1983.

Ravagioli, 1975. *Interdisciplinaritá.* Rome, Armando.

Regional Conference of Ministers of Education and Those Responsible for Economic Planning of Member States in Latin America (Mexico City, 1979). 1980. *Final Report.* Paris, Unesco. 113 pp. (Unesco doc. ED.79/MINEDLAC/REF.2.)

Reich, C. A. 1970. *Greening of America: How the Youth Revolution is Trying to Make America Liveable.* New York, Random House.

Reiffers, J. L.; Silvestre, J. J. 1985. An Approach to the Question of Education in Terms of its Complexity. *Educational Planning in the Context of Current Development Problems.* Paris, Unesco/IIEP. 156 pp.

Research, Theory and Practice in the USSR. Interview with Mikhaïl Kondakov, President of the Academy of Pedagogical Sciences. *Prospects, Quarterly Review of Education* (Paris, Unesco), Vol. XIII, No. 3, 1983. pp. 275–98.

Reves, E. 1946. *The Anatomy of Peace.* 8th ed. New York/London, Harper Bros. 293 pp.

Richardson, J. M., Jr. 1981. Global Modelling in the 1980s. *Impact of Science on Society* (Paris, Unesco), Vol. XXXI, No. 4, pp. 401–12. (Special issue on models.)

Riesman, D. 1973. *Lonely Crowd: A Study of the Changing American Character.* New York, Yale University Press. (Studies in National Policy.)

Rigaud, J. 1975. *La culture pour vivre.* Paris, Gallimard. 307 pp. (L'air du temps.)

Romeo-Lozano, S. 1980. The Mexico City Conference. *Prospects, Quarterly Review of Education* (Paris, Unesco), Vol. X, No. 2, pp. 235–40. (Report of the Conference of Ministers of Education and Those Responsible for Economic Planning of Member States in Latin America and the Caribbean, Mexico City, December 1979.)

Rose, B. (ed.). 1972. *Modern Trends in Education.* London, St Martin's Press.

Rosen, S. 1976. *Future Facts.* New York, Simon & Schuster.

Rosenthal, R.; Jacobson, L. 1985. *Pygmalion in the Classroom: Teacher Expectation and Pupils' Intellectual Development.* Enl. ed. New York, Irvington Publications. 265 pp.

Sachs, I. 1984. Développement local et sorties de crise dans la société industrielle. *Futuribles* (Paris, Association Internationale Futuribles), No. 75, pp. 50–6.

——. 1982. The Crisis of the Welfare State and the Exercise of Social Rights to Development. *International Social Science Journal* (Paris, Unesco), Vol. XXXIV, No. 1, pp. 133–48.

Saint Marc, P. 1971. *Socialisation de la nature.* Paris, Stock. 380 pp.

——. 1978. *Progrès ou déclin de l'homme?* Paris, Stock. 414 pp. (Monde ouvert.)

Sanwidi, I. 1981. *Étude sur les relations entre les expériencies d'éducation non-formelle et le système éducatif formel en Haute-Volta.* Paris, Unesco. 44 pp.

Sanyal, B. C. 1982. *Higher Education and the New International Order; A Collection of Papers.* Paris/London, Unesco/Francis Pinter. 242 pp.

Sasson, A. 1984. *Biotechnologies: Challenges and Promises.* Paris, Unesco. 315 pp.

Schaeffer, P. 1980. Mass Media and the School: Descartes or McLuhan? *Prospects, Quarterly Review of Education* (Paris, Unesco), Vol. X., No. 4, pp. 425–40.

Schumacher, E. F. 1975. *Small is Beautiful: Economics as if People Mattered.* New

York, Harper & Row. 290 pp. (Harper Colophon Books.)
SCHWARTZ, B. 1973. *L'éducation demain. Une étude de la fondation européenne de la culture*. Paris, Éditions Montaigne. 333 pp. (Recherches économiques et sociales, RES.)
———. 1980. Qu'est-ce que l'intelligence artificielle? *Education permanente* (Paris, Université de Paris-Dauphine), No. 52, pp. 117–24.
SEABORG, G. T.; CORLISS, W. R. 1971. *Man and Atom: Building a New World through Nuclear Technology*. New York, Dutton. 411 pp.
SEMERARO, R. 1982. *L'interdisciplinaritá nell'insegnamento*. Rome, De Monnier.
SEMINAR FOR THE TRAINING OF TEACHERS IN AND THROUGH INTERDISCIPLINARITY (CÔTE D'IVOIRE, 24 MARCH TO 4 APRIL, 1970). 1970. *Final Report*. Paris, Unesco.
SEMINAR ON INTERDISCIPLINARITY IN UNIVERSITIES (Nice, 1970). 1972. *Interdisciplinarity: Problems of Teaching and Research in Universities* (conference proceedings). Paris, OECD/CERI. 323 pp.
SHANE, H. G. 1977. *Curriculum Change Towards the Twenty-first Century*. Washington, D. C., National Education Association (NEA). 184 pp.
SHANE, H. G.; TABLER, M. B. 1980. The Social Sciences: Current and Foreseeable Trends. *Prospects, Quarterly Review of Education* (Paris, Unesco), Vol. X, No. 4, pp. 441–55.
———. 1981. *Educating for a New Millennium: Views of 132 International Scholars*. Bloomington, Ind., Phi Delta Kappa Educational Foundation. 160 pp.
SHEPPARD, C. S.; CARROLL, D. C. (eds.). 1980. *Working in the 21st Century, 1979, Richmond, Va. Proceedings* [of a symposium]. New York, Wiley. 235 pp. (Wiley Interscience Publications.)
SIMIONESCU, C. I. 1980. Teaching, Research and Production in Eastern Europe. *Prospects, Quarterly Review of Education* (Paris, Unesco), Vol. X, No. 3, pp. 333–9.
SOROKIN, P. A. 1948. *Reconstruction of Humanity*. Kraus Repro. (Facsimile.)
———. 1957. *The Crisis of our Age: the Social and Cultural Outlook*. New York, Dutton.
———. 1970. *Social and Cultural Dynamics*. Abr. ed. Sargent.
SRINIVASAN, L.; PETERS, J. 1983. *Approaches to Non-formal Nutrition Education*. Unesco. Paris. 40 pp. (Nutrition Education Series, 6.) (Unesco doc. ED.83/WS/43.)
STENHOUSE, L. (ed.). 1980. *Curriculum Research and Development*. London, Heinemann Educational Books.
STINE, G. H. 1975. *The Third Industrial Revolution*. New York, Putman.
STUDY GROUP ON PREPARING TEACHERS FOR EDUCATION IN RURAL DEVELOPMENT (Bangkok, 1976). 1977. *Exploring New Directions in Teacher Education. Re-orienting Teacher Education for Rural Development*. Bangkok, Unesco Regional Office for Education in Asia and Oceania. 194 pp. (Teacher Education, 2.)
SUCHODOLSKI, B. 1962. Education for the Future and Traditional Pedagogy. *International Review of Education* (Hamburg, Unesco Institute of Education), Vol. VII, No. 4.
SUCHODOLSKI, B.; KUCZYNSKI, J. 1982. *Permanent Education and Creativity*. Paris, Unesco. (Unesco doc. ED.82/WS/16.)
SUPPES, P. 1978. *Impact of Research on Education: Some Case Studies*. Washington, D.C., National Academy of Education. 672 pp.
TANGUIANE, S. 1977. Education and the Problem of its Democratization. *Prospects, Quarterly Review of Education* (Paris, Unesco), Vol. VII, No. 1, pp. 14–31.
THEE, M. (ed.). 1981. *Armaments, Arms Control and Disarmament—A Unesco Reader for Disarmament Education*. Paris, Unesco. 446 pp.
THIRD CONFERENCE OF MINISTERS OF EDUCATION OF MEMBER STATES OF THE EUROPE REGION (Sofia, 1980). 1980a. *Education in the Europe Region: Trends and Future Outlook*. Paris, Unesco. 74 pp. (Unesco doc. ED-80/MINEDEUROPE/3.)

References

------. 1980b. *Final Report.* Paris, Unesco. 82 pp. (Unesco doc. ED/MD/61.)
THOMAS, J. 1975. *World Problems in Education; A Brief Educational Survey.* Paris/Geneva, Unesco/IBE. 166 pp. (Studies and Surveys in Comparative Education.)
TINBERGEN, J. (ed.). 1977. *Reshaping the International Order: RIO—A Report to the Club of Rome.* London, Hutchinson. 325 pp.
TOFFLER, A. 1970. *Future Shock.* London, The Bodley Head. 504 pp.
------. 1981. *The Third Wave.* Toronto, Bantam Books. 537 pp.
------. (ed.). 1974. *Learning for Tomorrow; the Role of the Future in Education.* New York, Random House. 421 pp.
TOYNBEE, A. 1948. *Civilization on Trial* (essays). New York, Oxford University Press. 263 pp.
TROTIGNON, Y. 1978. *Le monde du XXe siècle, un outil d'investigation de et de compréhension de notre époque.* Paris, Fayard. 534 pp.
TYLOR, E. B. 1974. *Primitive Culture: Researches into the Development of Mythology, Philosophy, Religion, Arts, and Custom.* 2 vols. New York, Gordon Press. (Reprint of 1871 edition published in London by J. Murray.)
Unesco Statistical Yearbook 1983. 1983. Paris, Unesco.
Unesco Statistical Yearbook 1984. 1984. Paris, Unesco.
UNESCO. 1974. *New Trends in the Utilization of Educational Technology for Science Education.* Paris, Unesco. 247 pp.
------. 1977. *New Trends in Biology Teaching.* Vol. IV. Paris, Unesco. 235 pp. (The Teaching of Basic Sciences.)
------. 1978a. Brain, Memory and Learning: Comment. *Impact of Science on Society* (Paris, Unesco), Vol. XXVIII, No. 1, pp. 3–9.
------. 1978b. *Population Education. A Contemporary Concern. International Study of the Conceptualization and Methodology of Population Education.* Paris, Unesco. 120 pp. (Educational Studies and Documents, 28.)
------. 1978c. *Statistics on Radio and Television, 1969–1976.* Paris, Unesco. (Statistical Reports and Studies, 23.)
------. 1979. *Learning and Working.* Paris, Unesco. 349 pp. (*Prospects* Report.)
------. 1980a. *Environmental Education in the Light of the Tbilisi Conference.* Paris, Unesco. 100 pp. (Education on the Move.)
------. 1980b. *Informatics: A Vital Factor in Development; Unesco's Activities in the Field of Informatics and its Applications.* Paris, Unesco. 56 pp.
------. 1981a. *Cultural Development: Some Regional Experiences.* Paris, Unesco. 477 pp.
------. 1981b. *Cultural Needs and Aspirations: A Cross-national Study.* Paris, Unesco. 159 pp. (Cultural Co-operation: Studies and Experiences, 1.)
------. 1981c. *Planning Education for Reducing Inequalities: An IIEP Seminar.* Paris, Unesco. 142 pp.
------. 1981d. *A Systems Approach to Teaching and Learning Procedures. A Guide for Educators.* 2nd rev. ed. Paris, Unesco. 203 pp.
------. 1982a. *Methodologies for Relevant Skill Development in Biology Education.* Paris, Unesco. (Science and Technology Education Series, 2.) (Unesco doc. ED.81/WS/139.)
------. 1982b. *World Problems in the Classroom.* Paris, Unesco. (Educational Studies and Documents, 41.)
------. 1983a. *Maternal and Young Child Nutrition.* Paris, Unesco. (Nutrition Education Document Series, 3.) (Unesco doc. ED.83/WS/3.)
------. 1983b. *The Role of Colleges in Education.* Paris, Unesco. (Nutrition Education Document Series, 2.) (Unesco doc. ED.82/WS/119.)

References

UNESCO. 1983c. *Second Medium-Term Plan (1984–1989)*. Paris, Unesco. (4XC/4 Approved.)
——. 1983d. *Technical and Vocational Education in the World 1970–1980: A Statistical Report*. Paris, Unesco. 89 pp. (Current Surveys and Research in Statistics.) (CSR. E.47.)
——. 1983e. *Interdisciplinarité et sciences humaines*. Vol. 1. Paris, Unesco. 343 pp.
——. 1984a. *Approved Programme and Budget for 1984–1985*. Paris, Unesco. (Unesco doc. 22C/5 Approved.)
——. 1984b. *Glossary of Educational Technology Terms*. Paris/Geneva, Unesco/IBE. 250 pp. (IBEdata.)
——. 1985a. *International French-language Seminar on the Dissemination of Educational Research Findings, Paris 1984*. Paris, Unesco. 133 pp. (Unesco doc. ED-85/WS/17.)
——. 1985b. *Reflections on the Future Development of Education*. Paris, Unesco. 291 pp.
UNESCO GENERAL CONFERENCE. TWENTY-SECOND SESSION (Paris, 1983). 1983. *Introduction to the General Policy Debate*, by Amadou-Mahtar M'Bow, Director-General. Paris, Unesco. 34 pp. (Unesco doc. 22C/INF. 15 prov.).
UNESCO INSTITUTE OF EDUCATION. 1980. Problems of Teaching Moral Values in a Changing Society. *International Review of Education*, Vol. XXVI, No. 2.
——. 1983. The Debate on Education for Peace. Special issue of *International Review of Education*, Vol. 29, No. 3.
UNESCO/UNEP. 1983. Actions of the International Environmental Education Programme 1975–1983. *Connect, Unesco–UNEP Environmental Education Newsletter* (Paris), Vol. VIII, No. 3, pp. 1–2.
UNITED NATIONS. 1980. *Towards the New International Economic Order, Analytical Report on Developments in the Field of International Economic Cooperation since GA 6th Special Session*. New York, United Nations. 132 pp.
——. 1981. *Statistical Yearbook*. New York, United Nations.
——. 1982. *World Population Trends and Policies. 1981. Monitoring Report*. Vol. 1: *Population Trends*. New York, United Nations.
——. 1983. *United Nations Report on the World Social Situation in 1983*. New York, United Nations.
UNITED NATIONS. DEPARTMENT OF INTERNATIONAL ECONOMIC AND SOCIAL AFFAIRS. 1980. *Concise Report on the World Population Situation in 1979*. New York, United Nations. 115 pp.
——. 1985. *United Nations Report on the World Social Situation in 1985*. New York, United Nations. 110 pp.
UNITED NATIONS. GENERAL ASSEMBLY. 1981. *Resolutions and Decisions Adopted by the General Assembly during its Thirty-fifth Session, 16 September–17 December 1980, 15 and 16 January, 2–6 March and 11 May 1981*. New York, United Nations. 320 pp. (A/35/48: General Assembly, Official Records, 35th session, Supplement No. 48.)
UNITED STATES. 1980/81. *The Global 2000 Report to the President. Entering the Twenty-first Century*. Washington, D.C., United States Government Printing Office. 3 vols.
VAIDEANU, G. 1967. *Cultura estetica scolara* [Aesthetic Development in School]. Bucharest, EDP.
——. 1970. Pedagogy and Aesthetics. *Fundamenta paedogogique*, pp. 93–4. Bucharest, EDP.
——. 1971. Restructurer la technologie didactique en fonction des objectifs pédagogiques. *Revista de pedagogia* (Bucharest), No. 12.

References

———. 1974. L'évolution de l'éducation sur la base de l'interdisciplinarité. *Problemi della pedagogia* (Rome), Nos. 4 and 5.
———. 1976. *The Seminar of Socialist Countries on Education For and Through Work; Report.* Paris, Unesco, 1976.
———. 1979. L'école, education morale et les impératifs du monde contemporain. *International Review of Education* (Hamburg, Unesco Institute of Education), Vol. XXV, No. 1, pp. 43–51.
———. 1982. Les structures de l'apprentissage en Roumanie: unité et diversité. *International Review of Education* (Hamburg, Unesco Institute of Education), Vol. 28, No. 2, pp. 209–26. (Special issue on 'Formal, Nonformal and Informal Structures of Learning'.)
VANDEVELDE, L. 1983. *Conceptual and Methodological Considerations Concerning the Notion of a 'Common Core' of Training.* Paris, Unesco. 28 pp. (Unesco doc. ED/HEP/TEP.)
VIELLE, J. P. 1981. The Impact of Research on Educational Change. *Prospects, Quarterly Review of Education* (Paris, Unesco), Vol. XI, No. 3, pp. 313–25.
VIET, J.; VAN SLYPE, G. (eds.). 1984. *Eudised Multilingual Thesaurus for Information Processing in the Field of Education.* Paris, Mouton. (Issued under Council of Europe auspices.)
WAGAR, W. W. 1971. *Building the City of Man; Outlines of a World Civilisation.* New York, Grossman Press. 180 pp.
WARD, B.; DUBOS, R. 1972. *Only One Earth: The Care and Maintenance of a Small Planet.* New York, Norton. 255 pp.
WHISTON, T.; SENKER, P.; MACDONALD, P. 1980. *An Annotated Bibliography on the Relationship between Technological Change and Educational Development.* Paris, Unesco/IIEP. 168 pp.
WINTERBURN, R.; EVANS, L. 1980. *Educational Technology in the Year 2000.* London, Kogan Page/Association for Educational Training and Technology. 351 pp. (Aspects of Educational Technology, 14.)
WORLD BANK. 1980. *Education Sector Policy Paper.* 3rd ed. Washington, D.C. 143 pp.
———. 1982. *World Development Report 1982.*
———. 1983. *World Development Report 1983.* Oxford University Press. 214 pp.
———. 1985. *World Development Report 1984.*
WORLD CONGRESS ON DISARMAMENT EDUCATION (Paris, 1980). 1980. *Report and Final Document.* Paris, Unesco. (Unesco doc. SS.80/CONF.401/37 REV.)
WORLD FUTURE SOCIETY. 1977. *Information Sources for the Study of the Future.* Washington, D.C. 348 pp. (Resources Directory for America's Third Century, 1.)
———. 1979. *The Future, a Guide to Information Sources.* 2nd ed. Washington, D.C. 722 pp.
WHO (WORLD HEALTH ORGANIZATION). 1981. *Global Stretagy for Health for All by the Year 2000.* Geneva, WHO. 90 pp.
YERODIA, A. 1981. *Culture as a Methodological Guarantor of Relevance in the Education Systems.* Paris, Unesco. 15 pp. (Unesco doc. ED.81/WS/126.)

[II] ED.86/D.160/A